LET ME PRAISE YOUR ENDURING MERCY, LORD

PRAYING THE PSALMS FOR AUTHENTIC FORMATION IN DISCIPLESHIP

MICHAEL FONSECA, D.MIN

Copyright © 2020 GOD'S EMBRACE MINISTRIES, INC.
Published by God's Embrace Publishing All Rights Reserved.

Except as permitted by U.S. Copyright Law, no part of this book may be reprinted, reproduced, transmitted, or utilized in any form by electronic, mechanical, or other means, now known or hereafter invented, including photocopying, microfilming, and recording, or in any information storage or retrieval system, without the express written permission from God's Embrace Ministries, Inc.

ISBN 9798653264740 printed and bound by Kindle direct publishing

For more information on this title and other books and resources available through God's Embrace Ministries, Inc., please visit: www.godsembrace.org

GOD'S EMBRACE MINISTRIES, INC.
1601 HIGH HILL ROAD, SCHULENBURG, TX 78956

Phone: (979) 561-8883 Email: info@godsembrace.org

ACKNOWLEDGEMENTS

It is with deep gratitude and appreciation that Cherrie, my wife and I acknowledge the gift of *God's Embrace Ministries,* both as ministry and covenant community of Christian disciples.

We acknowledge as well, the Holy Spirit's transforming power and presence in our midst, as we seek to bring renewal to our beloved Catholic Church, especially at the parish and diocesan level.

We acknowledge with anticipation the participation of future Christian seekers in *God's Embrace Ministries* and pray that they will surrender wholeheartedly to the transforming power of the Holy Spirit in their lives!

In a special way, we wish to acknowledge our deep gratitude to Irma Rerich and Stacy Oeding, our trusted staff at God's Embrace Ministries. They bring a level of devotion and commitment to our ministry that is rarely seen and greatly appreciated. No task is too much or too difficult. Their joyful attitude and servant-hearts are a source of much edification and security. Cherrie and I are deeply grateful and ask the Lord to bestow His choicest blessings upon Irma and Stacy and their families.

We are deeply grateful to Steve and Patty Fase who have been ardent supporters of *God's Embrace Ministries* and have extended their hospitality during our GEM visits to Michigan. Along with them, we are deeply grateful to Chris and Kim Cruickshank who believe very strongly in the ministry and have been facilitators for several years in Michigan. They are ardent supporters as well, and without their gentle persistence, I would have kept delaying the completion of this book on the psalms.

As always, we are deeply grateful to Ralph and Linda Schmidt for the continued support and encouragement to *God's Embrace Ministries.* We ask Our Lord to embrace them and their family with His tender loving kindness.

It is our hope that many will come to support *God's Embrace Ministries* as we seek ardently the renewal of our beloved Catholic Church.

May *Let Me Praise Your Enduring Mercy, Lord,* stir many hearts toward a deeper commitment to our Lord and Savior, Jesus Christ! May our Triune God be praised now and forever!

INTRODUCTORY REMARKS

THE VISION FOR GOD'S EMBRACE:

God's Embrace Ministries is a Non-Profit Ecclesial Corporation established to bring about renewal in the Catholic Church. Our formation programs are based on prayer and spirituality that is Trinitarian in emphasis, and contemplative in approach. The programs rely on a threefold source: familiarity with the Old and New Testaments in the Bible so that the participant's developing spirituality is steeped in God's revelation of Himself through Jesus Christ, and in the Blessed Trinity's glorious plan of salvation for us. Secondly, GEM strengthens the participant's reliance on the rich heritage of Catholic Spirituality, to make sure that the Word of God that they ponder in the Scriptures becomes the Word of God dwelling in their hearts. Thirdly, in all our programs we emphasize familiarity with the Catechism of the Catholic Church which stands, in the words of Saint John Paul II, as "a sure norm for teaching the faith," and an "authentic text." The desired outcome is living within the Trinitarian embrace, completely linked to the divine life of the Blessed Trinity, and to one another in God's covenant family.

It is our hope that you will receive all the necessary help to satisfy your own hunger for God. God's invitation to enter into covenant union with Him is an urgent and enthusiastic one, and Jesus has made this invitation a reality through His death and resurrection: *"Behold, I stand at the door and knock. If anyone hears my voice and opens the door, [then] I will enter his house and dine with him, and he with me. I will give the victor the right to sit with me on my throne, as I myself first won the victory and sit with my Father on his throne"* (Revelation 3: 20-21).

LET ME PRAISE YOUR ENDURING MERCY, LORD:

Let Me Praise your Enduring Mercy, Lord is a reflection on the Book of Psalms, the most well-known and cherished Biblical Book of Prayers among Jews and Christians. Our Lord Himself used the

Psalms, both in prayer, as when He prayed Psalm 22 on the Cross, and in His teachings, as when He opened the Scriptures to the two disciples on their way to Emmaus. The psalms were inspired for prayer, worship, instruction, and prophecy. The Church lays great emphasis on praying the Psalms and requires the clergy to pray the Liturgy of the Hours every day. Through the psalms, the soul learns to commune with God. In our reflection and prayer, we will ponder and pray with 90 of the 150 psalms of the Psalter. We have chosen the New American Bible Revised Edition (NABRE), for our text. Our prayer is that you will come to a deep appreciation of the psalms as a book of prayer and spiritual formation.

THE BENEFITS OF JOURNALING:

Journaling helps you become more familiar with the guidance and direction of the Holy Spirit in your life. Through the Journal you will be training yourself to listen closely to the Holy Spirit, both in your prayer and throughout the day. The questions that you will be responding to daily will be a significant key to this formation. Let us look at the questions:

What is God saying to you?

In prayer we express our sentiments and petitions to God and listen to how He wants us to live our lives. Prayer becomes truly efficacious when we learn the art of listening to God's voice manifesting itself through the various movements generated in our minds, senses, imagination, memory, and hearts. Teaching us this art is the work of the Holy Spirit, and it requires diligent practice. Sometimes the Holy Spirit will reveal to you a deeper appreciation of the teachings of Jesus. Sometimes, in doubt and confusion, you will be strengthened to stay true to the teachings of Jesus. At other times, you will get a deeper insight into yourself, whether it is your sinfulness, or God's great love for you, or God's unwavering compassion and forgiveness upon your repentant heart. There will be times when the Holy Spirit will give you confirmation about the rightness of your actions to help you persevere and fight the good fight. On occasion, you will know the Presence is there, and you can not quite reach, or touch God. It will seem like you are in a fog, reaching out for the Good Shepherd's hand and not finding it, or so it will seem. And you will understand that you are being asked to believe and trust in the constant Presence of Jesus. Then there will be times when you will be swept into the Mystery of the Divine Presence. In those moments your communion with the Divine will be in awed silence.

For what are you grateful? For what are you contrite?
You are answering these questions at the end of the day, after you have made your Examination of Conscience. St. Ignatius of Loyola emphasized the importance of the Examination of Conscience as a great help toward union with God. A significant part of the Examination of Conscience it to recall the blessings and graces that God has bestowed upon us during the day. Responding generously to God's love for us can be considered to be an important dimension of our gratitude to God for His help and grace. We engage in this daily prayer of gratitude by answering the question: For what are you grateful? We depend on God for absolutely everything! Then in the light of God's loving kindness toward us, we examine our own failed response to God's invitation to give ourselves to Him. Examining our conscience is the other significant aspect of this prayer. We enter into union with God through repentance of our sins and God's forgiveness of us. Your answer to the question: For what are you contrite? gives you a deeper appreciation of this very special relationship that God has with you.

What spiritual discipline, including fasting, do you need to focus on tomorrow?
As you proceed on this life-changing journey into God's heart, you will see that there is a special connection between your daily Face to Face with God and your nightly Examination of Conscience. In your Face to Face with God, the Holy Spirit has offered you insights and graces as to how you are to improve your

following of Jesus. During your Nightly Review, you can ponder these movements on a deeper level. Similarly, the Holy Spirit will encourage your progress as well as convict you about your sinfulness and lapses, without ever condemning you. Your answer to this question tells you whether you are taking to heart the Holy Spirit's guidance and direction. This question highlights the importance of taking every means possible to stay on the straight and narrow road into God's heart and fasting can hasten our return to a state of consolation.

What prayer would you compose to express what God has said to you this week?

This question is a follow-up of the questions that you have been answering each day: What is God saying to you? For what are you grateful? For what are you contrite? What spiritual discipline, including fasting, do you need to focus on tomorrow? By forming a prayer to capture what God has been saying to you, you will develop a growing appreciation of how intimately God is involved in your life. You will also begin to see how solicitous and industrious the Holy Spirit is in re-creating you in the image and likeness of Jesus. Your prayer will need to come from your heart. Listen to the promptings of the Holy Spirit in your heart and compose your prayer accordingly.

HOW DO I USE THIS MANUAL?

- **Why are the days of the week numbered rather than named?**

    In some cases, you may be part of a group that meets regularly, or you may be taking this journey on your own. In either case, our intention is to relieve you of any restrictions to scheduling your personal prayer time. We want you to move at your own pace. The "weeks" and "days of prayer" simply give us structure as we attempt to disciple our personal prayer life.

- **Why do we begin each morning session with set prayers of the Act of Faith, Act of Hope, Act of Charity, and the Daily Offering?**

  The Acts of Faith, Hope, and Charity are creedal statements. They express our core beliefs. They also express the intimate relationship between our Trinitarian God and God's covenant family, His Church. A good example of the necessary bond established by God, between Himself and His Church, is the statement in the Act of Faith: I believe these and all the truths which the holy Catholic Church teaches, because in revealing them you cannot deceive nor be deceived.

  The Daily Offering makes clear to us that we are living our daily lives, expressed in our prayers, works, joys and sufferings, within the Eucharistic celebration, in union with the sacrificial Offering of our Lamb, now interceding for us before the throne of God, and surrounded by His communion of saints. Jesus is interceding for us along with His covenant family that offers their prayers in union with the Lamb's intercession (Revelation 5: 8). The Church has always singled out Mary's intercessory role, on our behalf, in the communion of saints. When these set prayers are done daily at the very beginning of each day, they become a solid foundation on which our discipleship is built.

- **Why do we ask for the Holy Spirit's guidance at the beginning of each prayer session, and end with a prayer to the Holy Trinity?**

  Our discipleship can only grow and deepen under the guidance of the Holy Spirit. Jesus has entrusted us to the Holy Spirit's guardianship. Hence it is necessary to begin every prayer with earnest petition to the Holy Spirit. Similarly, at the end of every prayer, it makes sense to address the Holy Trinity in thanksgiving and praise for the Three Persons' constant love and companionship. After all, we are in covenant union with our Triune God.

- **Why do we do a Prayer of Thanksgiving and an Act of Contrition as part of our Night Prayer?**
  The Examination of Conscience is an important tool of formation in discipleship. It is a review of the day, which includes the Prayer of Thanksgiving, an Examination of Conscience, followed by an Act of Contrition. You will be given instructions as to how to go about making the Examination of Conscience in the guidebook. Your answer to the questions, 'For what are you grateful?' and 'For what are you contrite?' and 'What spiritual discipline, including fasting, do you need to focus on tomorrow?' is part of the Examination of Conscience.

- **Is it important to journal on a daily basis or even to journal at all?**
  Saints, like Ignatius of Loyola, Teresa of Avila, Mary Faustina Kowalska, have emphasized the rich benefits that accrue to anyone who journals about their relationship with God. They made journaling a serious practice in their own lives. Their written reflections confirmed and deepened their graces and insights received in prayer. Hence, your spiritual life will surely benefit from journaling.

TABLE OF CONTENTS

INTRODUCTION TO THE PSALMS 11

BOOK ONE: 31
PSALMS 1 TO 41: ABIDING TRUST IN DIRE STRAITS
Week One: Psalms 1, 2, 3, 4, 5, 6 31
Week Two: Psalms 8, 15, 18, 19, 22, 23 54
Week Three: Psalms 25, 26, 27, 28, 29, 30 82
Week Four: Psalms 32, 33, 36, 38, 39, 41 106

BOOK TWO: 132
PSALMS 42 TO 72: CELEBRATION AND PRAISE
Week One: Psalms 42, 44, 45, 46, 47, 48 132
Week Two: Psalms 50, 51, 52, 53, 54, 56 160
Week Three: Psalms 57, 61, 62, 63, 65, 66 186
Week Four: Psalms 67, 68, 69, 70, 71, 72 210

BOOK THREE: 242
PSALMS 73-89: PURIFICATION THROUGH TRIBULATION
Week One: Psalms 73, 74, 76, 78, 79, 80 242
Week Two: Psalms 81, 84, 85, 87, 88, 89 271

BOOK FOUR: 298
PSALMS 90 TO 106: ISRAEL'S BANISHMENT
Week One: Psalms 90, 91, 92, 93, 95, 98 298
Week Two: Psalms 99, 100, 101, 102, 104, 106 322

BOOK FIVE: 346
PSALMS 107 TO 150: LOOKING TOWARD THE MESSIAH
Week One: Psalms 107, 110, 112, 114, 118, 119 346
Week Two: Psalms 120, 122, 127, 130, 132, 136 378
Week Three: Psalms 138, 139, 143, 145, 147, 150 405

INTRODUCTION TO THE PSALMS

THE SIGNIFICANCE OF THE PSALMS:

The Book of Psalms is probably the most well-known and cherished Book of Prayers among Jews and Christians. Our Lord Himself used the Psalms, both in prayer, as when He prayed Psalm 22 on the Cross, and in His teachings, as when He opened the Scriptures to the two disciples on their way to Emmaus: *"These are my words that I spoke to you while I was still with you, that everything written about me in the law of Moses and in the prophets and psalms must be fulfilled"* (Luke 24:44). And the Apostles, in imitation of Our Lord, asked the faithful to make use of the psalms in community worship: *"Be filled with the Spirit, addressing one another [in] psalms and hymns and spiritual songs, singing and playing to the Lord in your hearts, giving thanks always and for everything in the name of our Lord Jesus Christ to God the Father"* (Ephesians 5:19). From then on, the psalms became an important part of the Church's prayer. The Psalter will always continue to be the unique and inexhaustible treasury of devotion for individuals and for the Church. The Church lays great emphasis on praying the Psalms and requires the clergy to pray the Liturgy of the Hours every day. Every four weeks, along with 26 canticles from the Old Testament, and 11 canticles from the New Testament, all the psalms are prayed, except for Psalms 58, 83, and 109, because their content is deemed excessively violent. Through the psalms, the soul learns to commune with God.

The Psalter consists of 150 psalms. 'Psalm' comes from the Greek translation of the Hebrew word *'mizmor,'* meaning 'a melody of praise.' A Psalm is a poem sung to music from a stringed instrument, such as the lyre or harp. King David was famous for playing the lyre. Around 73 psalms were composed by David who established the whole genre of Hebrew psalmody. A few other psalms have been attributed to his authorship. Several of the other psalms were written under his influence as David appointed most of the other named authors of the psalms. According to 1 and 2 Chronicles, David appointed Asaph, Heman, and Ethan as composers and song leaders, and established the Sons of Korah, a clan of Levites, as gatekeepers in the Temple. Asaph, David's choir leader, composed a dozen psalms. The Sons of Korah gave us about a dozen psalms as well. Two of these choir members, Heman and Ethan, wrote a psalm each, Psalms 88 and 89 respectively. Two psalms are of King Solomon, Psalms 72 and 127. And finally, Moses wrote Psalm 90. Many psalms are anonymous, and many of these were written long after David. In Book Five of the Psalter, Psalms 107 to 150, we find psalms that were clearly written up to five or six hundred years after David, after the Israelites returned from the Babylonian exile and rebuilt the Temple under Ezra and Nehemiah. The various psalms were compiled into a collection, perhaps by King David himself around 1000 B.C., and later codified by Ezra the Scribe after the Babylonian Exile. Hence, the psalms were written over several centuries, largely between 1000 and 400 B.C.

The psalms were inspired for prayer, worship, instruction, and prophecy. Many of the psalms are *'laments,'* individual or communal, where an individual or Israel are suffering and crying to God for help. Some of the laments point toward Jesus, the Suffering Servant. There are *'thanksgiving'* psalms, *'todah'* in Hebrew, giving thanks to God for a special deed God performed for the worshiper. Still other psalms praise God for His goodness and greatness, as Psalm 150 does. *'Wisdom'* psalms, on the other hand, give glory to God's law and instruction as a sound guide for living, as in Psalms 1, 19, and 119. *'Royal'* psalms glorify God as king, or praise God for putting the king in place. Related to royal psalms are *'Zion'* psalms that glorify Zion, which is another name for Jerusalem, the royal capital and site of the Temple, for example Psalms 46 to 48, 84, and 132. *'Messianic'* psalms contain prophecies of Jesus. All the royal psalms are messianic, but there are other messianic psalms as well, such as Psalm 22, a lament which Jesus prayed on the Cross. Finally, there are a few psalms that call down curses on enemies. They are called *'imprecatory'* psalms. Psalm 137 is such an example.

THE CONTENTS OF THE BOOK OF PSALMS:

Since the psalms were composed mostly by David and others whom he appointed for temple liturgical worship, their subject matter relates to the history of salvation as it unfolded during the reigns of Saul, of David and his descendants in the Davidic dynasty, and extending beyond the return from the Babylonian exile. The timeline is roughly from 1000 B.C. to about 400 B.C. The historical background to the psalms is found in 1 and 2 Samuel, as well as in 1 and 2 Kings, and 1 and 2 Chronicles. Several psalms were composed long after David's death, before, during, and after the Babylonian exile that occurred from 587 to 537 B.C. The historical and religious details of the chosen people's covenant relationship with God during this period, are provided by the Prophets Amos, Isaiah, Jeremiah, and Ezekiel, as well as by Ezra and Nehemiah who led the exiles back to Judah and had the Temple and Jerusalem rebuilt, and the post- exilic prophets, like Haggai.

In reflecting on their current historical crises and events, the Psalmists looked back on their history as God's covenant people, for answers and reassurance in their present circumstances. In doing so, they marveled at God as the Creator of the Universe who made humans in the divine image and likeness. And He accomplished these wondrous deeds because He wanted to be in covenant with His people, establishing a permanent family bond with them. Several psalms harken to the wondrous deeds of God as Creator. But they especially emphasize the centrality of God in their history as their Redeemer and Protector. He is their God over all other gods, He saved and brought them forth from Egypt through the Exodus, across the treacherous desert on a journey that lasted forty years and ended with their long-awaited arrival in the Promised Land.

It is important to note that David and the Psalmists of 1000-900 B.C. were only familiar with the Pentateuch and the Books of

Joshua and Judges, in their partially written and oral forms. The other books of the Old Testament as we know them, were still in the works. Some psalms see the end of the journey into the Promised Land when King David made his triumphant entry into Jerusalem from Kiriath-jearim of Judah, bringing the Ark of the Covenant to its final dwelling place in the Temple. Many of the psalms, in recalling Israel's past history as God's covenant people, highlight two major aspects of their covenant relationship with God: God's wondrous deeds in creation and for their redemption, along with His enduring mercy and faithfulness offered against the backdrop of their repeated sins of rebellion and idolatry. In a very real sense, the present generation kept replicating the sins and rebellion of their ancestors against God. The psalms express an abiding trust in the loving kindness of God, *hesed* in Hebrew, confident that God would always forgive their sins if they had a repentant heart, and His mercy toward them would be enduring, from everlasting to everlasting.

David and his fellow Psalmists continually point to the intricate balance and causal connection between God as their Creator and Provider, and God as their Protector and Redeemer! The purpose for creating this magnificent universe with humans created in His image and likeness at its center, and providing them with food and nurturance, was so that God could establish a covenant or family bond with them, becoming their God and making them His people. References are made to the various covenants that God made with His people, moving in incremental revelatory steps from the first covenant with Adam and Eve, to Abraham, Moses, and David. Despite God's enduring faithfulness and mercy, Israel failed repeatedly in being faithful and generous covenant partners. They paid lip-service to the Law of Moses and ignored the message of the prophets to repent and return to the Lord. Some of the psalms talk about sacrifices becoming empty rituals that insulted God because they were not accompanied with a repentant heart.

All the covenants, and especially the Davidic Covenant, highlight the fact that there was a pronounced missing piece. Even though the Israelites developed a greater understanding of their covenant relationship with God over several centuries, their covenants served as signs or harbingers, anticipating a new and eternal covenant that God would establish with His people. And this perfect covenant would be established through Jesus, the Incarnate Son of God, with human beings scattered all over the world. Many of the psalms, therefore, are prophetic, messianic, and royal, pointing continually to Jesus who will fulfill the law and the prophets through His ministry as Messiah, culminating in His death by crucifixion and resurrection, and becoming the Sovereign Ruler of the Universe! The New Testament begins with, *"The book of the genealogy of Jesus Christ, the Son of David, the Son of Abraham"* (Matthew 1:1). That opening verse makes Jesus the overarching bridge, connecting the promises and covenants given to Abraham and to his forebears and descendants, Moses among them, all the way to David. In fact, Jesus came to fulfill what was missing in all the previous covenants.

THE COMPOSITION OF THE BOOK OF PSALMS:

The Psalms are divided into five separate books. The First Book runs from Psalms 1 to 41. The first two psalms act as a twofold introduction to the entire Psalter. *Psalm 1: True Happiness in God's Law,* introduces us to the wisdom of God and the lifestyle that is guided by the good counsel of the Holy Spirit. *Psalm 2: A Psalm for a Royal Coronation,* introduces us to the Davidic Covenant and Kingdom that God established with King David and his successors, leading ultimately to Jesus, *"and of his kingdom there will be no end"* (Luke 1: 33). These first two psalms set the template for two significant themes in the Book of Psalms. As was mentioned earlier, the psalms were inspired for prayer, worship, instruction, and prophecy. Many of them are exhortations to help the believer arrive at a deeper covenant union with the Lord. By following the instruction offered in the psalms, the believer can develop a richer life of prayer and worship. And many of the psalms point to a fuller revelation from God, as they are prophetic in nature, announcing the full restoration of God's plan of salvation through His Son Jesus, who will establish the universal kingdom of God and be our Messiah and Lord!

Book One has as its theme, *Abiding Trust in Dire Straits*. Understandably, it has an anxious and sorrowful tone to it, as it has the largest concentration of the psalms of lament. Psalms 3, 4, 5, 7, 9-10, 13, 14, 17, 22, 25, 26, 27, 28, 31, 36, 40, and 41 are individual laments by David. Psalms 6, 32, and 38 are three of the Seven Penitential Psalms that are included in Book One. They too are individual songs of lament. Psalm 35 is an Imprecatory psalm and can be classified as an individual lament. And there is one communal lament, Psalm 12. Of the 30 individual laments and 12 communal laments in the Psalter, Book One carries 22 of them!

All 41 psalms have been composed by David and they relate very personally and intimately to his years with King Saul who was insanely jealous and threatened by David. Saul made him a fugitive for seven long years and sought repeatedly to kill him. They also relate to his later years as king of Israel, when his son Absalom usurped the throne and made his father a fugitive for the second time in his life. Many of these psalms will offer us prophetic echoes pointing to Jesus during His ministry, but especially in His passion, death, and resurrection.

In these 41 psalms, several are very uplifting in their tone and substance. For instance, Psalm 8 tells of the beginning of salvation history when God created man in the divine image and likeness. Psalms 18, 19, 21, 24, 29, 30, 32, and 34, are individual *todah* psalms, or psalms of praise and thanksgiving. They highlight the truth that God is present with us in all our circumstances and provides a silver lining to our darkest moments. In some of these psalms of lament, David praises God even before God has rescued him from a difficult situation, as a sign of his inherent trust and confidence in God's love and faithfulness to him. Even though most of the psalms in Book One focus on life that is being buffeted by dangers and persecution from enemies, what stands out is that it is a book of unquestioning faith in God, and therefore, a school of prayer and spiritual formation. 1 and 2 Samuel can be your spiritual reading as they provide the historical background for many of the psalms. Reading the Books of Genesis, Exodus, and Numbers will enhance your appreciation of the background of many of the psalms.

Book Two consists of Psalms 42 to 72. The Second Book makes a radical shift in mood from Book One. It has as its theme, *Celebration and Praise,* thus striking a more confident tone. Much of the focus is on David's reign as King of Israel, during which period the kingdom experienced prosperity, peace, and expansion. In particular, the worship of God was centralized at the temple in Jerusalem after David made Jerusalem his capital and brought the Ark of the Covenant from Kiriathjearim of Judah to dwell permanently in the temple. Through the psalms, many of which were his own compositions, David enhanced temple worship by developing an orderly and sophisticated liturgy. David also emphasized the *todah* or thanksgiving offering as being superior to the *ola* or burnt offerings of animals. He composed many of his psalms of thanksgiving and praise to celebrate the *todah* sacrifice. Psalm 50 expresses the covenant established between God and David and highlights this shift in emphasis from *ola* to *todah*. Psalm 50 prepares us for the eventual *todah* or Eucharistic sacrifice in Jesus.While there are 3 community laments in Psalms 44, 58, and 60, and 12 individual laments in Psalms 43, 52, 53, 54, 55, 56, 57, 59, 61, 64, 70, and 71, there are many more psalms that resonate with exuberant praise and thanksgiving to God. For the first time, we have psalms composed by the choir leaders David appointed. Psalms 42 to 49 were composed by the Sons of Korah; Psalm 45 is an enthronement psalm and prepares us for the enthronement of Jesus as King of the Universe. Psalm 50 is the work of Asaph. There are psalms that glorify Jerusalem as David's beautiful capital, and prefigure the Church as bride of Christ, and the heavenly Jerusalem. Book Two ends with a glorious description of the reign of Solomon, which anticipates the perfect reign that will be established over the world through Jesus.

Book Three has a different mood than Book Two and includes Psalms 73 to 89. Its theme could be described as *Purification through Tribulation*. The 17 psalms of Book Three plunge us into Israel's lowest depths of ignominy and shame during the 9th Century B.C., when after a glorious period of peace and prosperity under King David, and for some time during King Solomon's reign, she was devastated by national misfortune and calamity. The ten tribes of Israel, restless under Solomon's punishing taxes and resentful of his wasteful habits, rebelled and took Jeroboam as their king, becoming the Northern Kingdom of Israel, and the southern part went with Rehoboam, Solomon's son, and became the Kingdom of Judah. With the break-up of the kingdom came the first destruction of the Temple by Shishak, King of Egypt, during the fifth year of king Rehoboam's reign. Thus, Israel endured colossal disaster and ruin.

The psalms of lament in Book Three, six community laments and five individual laments, point prophetically toward the permanent destruction of the monarchy in 597 B.C. when Zedekiah, the last legitimate son of David to rule Jerusalem, was taken into exile. And the Temple, God's dwelling place among His people and symbol of God's protection, was destroyed in 587 B.C., and the Israelites were subjected to the Babylonian Exile lasting 50 years. Book Three is one long lament, moving from impending fear and helplessness to shame and humiliation, even to the edge of despair, especially in Psalms 88 and 89, the last two of Book Three. Psalm 88 ends without any hope for the future, which is rare for a psalm, and Psalm 89 ends with the king deposed from his throne and dragged into exile, and the kingdom in ruins. Book Three represents the downfall of David's kingdom. Psalm 86, a song of lament, is the only psalm of David in Book Three.

If there is a silver lining to the period after the destruction of the monarchy and Temple between 597 and 587 B.C., and the impending exile into Babylon looming over the kingdom of Judah, it is that God's people were forced to look inward and focus on what really mattered in the larger scheme of affairs. This led to a greater emphasis on covenant songs like Psalms 78, 81, and 89, and songs of Zion or Jerusalem like Psalms 76, 84, 87, thus highlighting the covenant relationship with God. 1 and 2 Kings can be your spiritual reading as they provide the historical background for many of the psalms in Book Three. Prophets like Amos, Isaiah, Jeremiah, and Hosea offer their inspired reflections on this period of Israelite history.

Psalms 90 to 106 comprise Book Four. The psalms focus primarily on the Babylonian exile and the theme of Book Four could be described as *Israel's Banishment*. Book Four is an introspective and meditative reflection on the darkest period of Israel's history. The people are trying to make sense of this colossal calamity that has befallen them with the destruction of the monarchy and the Temple, God's dwelling place, which was supposed to have been impregnable. The monarchy did not turn out to be the panacea their ancestors thought it would be when they coerced Samuel to give them a king. Book Four begins with Psalm 90, the only psalm from Moses, suggesting a return to leadership that was tried, and remained true. They review their history in Psalm 105 that highlights God's faithfulness and enduring mercy, and Psalm 106 that highlights their obduracy and rebellion against God, thus bringing ruin and disaster upon themselves. David is mentioned only twice. Psalms 93 to 99 emphasize the kingship of God over any earthly king and kingdom and recognize that God's reign over them is the only true and proper reign to have. These psalms also point to the kingdom of God that Jesus the Messiah will establish through His death and resurrection. The book ends with Psalm 106, with a prayer for God to bring the people back from exile. Ezekiel as well as Ezra and Nehemiah can be your spiritual reading as they provide the historical background for many of the psalms in Book Four.

The mood changes in Book Five, Psalms 107 to 150. The theme of Book Five is *Looking toward the Messiah* or the 'Son of David' whom David and the Davidic Dynasty prefigured. Psalm 107 begins Book Five by thanking God for bringing His people back from exile. The time of exile is over, and Book Five includes several psalms that were written once the people of Judah had come back to their land and rebuilt their city and Temple in the late 5th Century and 4th Century B.C. Psalm 126 describes the unbelievable joy of returning to Jerusalem and the hard work of restoration that lay before them. At the heart of Book Five is a collection of 'Psalms of Ascents' written for the pilgrimage up to Jerusalem and the rebuilt Temple. They were composed both before and after the exile. The Books of Ezra and Nehemiah are good spiritual reading for Book Five.

The Psalter ends on a high note of praise and thanksgiving to God in Psalm 150 which is an eloquent and passionate cry to all creation to give God the praise due to Him. But one is still left with a question mark. The crown and scepter representing the Davidic Dynasty, very prominent in the psalms of the first three books, are missing. Although the Temple has been rebuilt and is operational in Book Five, no psalm clearly points to the restoration of the Davidic king, because in fact, the earthly Davidic king would not be restored. However, given its prophetic nature, the Psalter still expects it to happen, as there are psalms about the Davidic Covenant even in Book Five: Psalms 110, 132, and 144. These royal messianic psalms anticipate the final and permanent restoration that will take place through the 'Son of David' who will restore the new kingdom of Israel. They anticipate Jesus, 'Son of David' (Messianic Title) and Son of God!

SIGNIFICANT REVELATORY MILESTONES IN THE PSALMS, REVEALING GOD'S TOTAL PLAN OF SALVATION

- **GOD'S CREATION IS AN ESSENTIAL PART OF HIS PLAN OF SALVATION:**
  David and his fellow Psalmists continually point to the intricate balance and causal connection between God as their Creator and Provider, and God as their Protector and Redeemer! The purpose for creating this magnificent universe with humans created in His image and likeness at its center, and providing them with food and nurturance was so that God could establish a covenant or family bond with them, becoming their God and making them His people. References are made to the various covenants that God made with His people, moving in incremental revelatory steps from the first covenant with Adam and Eve, to Abraham, Moses, and David. All the covenants, and especially the Davidic Covenant, highlight the fact that there was a pronounced missing piece. These various covenants remained signs or pre-figurations, anticipating a new and eternal covenant that God would establish with His image and likeness. And this perfect covenant would be established through Jesus, the incarnate Son of God. In fact, Jesus came to fulfill all that was missing in the previous covenants.

- **THE NECESSITY OF RETELLING THE STORY OF CREATION AND SALVATION:**
  As you ponder and pray with the message of the psalms, you will notice that the same revealed truths are being offered repeatedly for reflection and prayer. Why would the psalms need to emphasize the divinely revealed truths repeatedly? The Psalmists were inspired by the Holy Spirit to use their human authorship and life's experiences to express the sublime and inexhaustible truths of God's splendid acts of creation and salvation. Going over or remembering the same sublime and venerable truths is necessary because the revelation of who God is

and what He has done, is fathomless and inexhaustible. There is an absolute necessity to return continually to the source of eternal life, both to quench our thirst and enter more deeply into covenant union with our Triune God. God's truth being inexhaustible, we can never take it all in, however many times we drink from the fountain of eternal life! Hence, in all prayer and worship traditions, both in the Old and New Testaments, the practice of praying the same prayers and engaging in the same sacred actions every day is of paramount importance. We do our vocal prayers every day, and in time we realize that we continue to be overwhelmed by the inexhaustible truths contained in them. The Mass is quintessentially a Prayer of Thanksgiving and Remembrance. Jesus' sacrifice on the Cross was offered once and for all on our behalf as it was the perfect oblation. And we celebrate it daily because it is ever-present in our midst and is inexhaustible.

- **THE MOSAIC COVENANT CONTEXTUALIZED BY THE DAVIDIC COVENANT:**

After Abraham, Moses is the next most significant Patriarch who features very prominently in the Pentateuch. He was Israel's Lawgiver, and God's covenant with His people ratified at Mount Sinai is known as the Mosaic Covenant. Moses is therefore a central figure in the Israelite history of salvation. Moses is mentioned about eight hundred times or so, but almost all those references are found in the Pentateuch. It is easy to conclude that Moses is the most important person of the Old Testament.

In God's Economy of Salvation, it becomes clear that God would contextualize the Mosaic Covenant through His covenant with David and his sons, and bring it to its replacement by the new and eternal covenant through Jesus, David's son and the Son of God. Jesus would become the 'Son of David' (Messianic title) who would fulfill the Law and the Prophets (the Mosaic Covenant) by replacing it with the New and Everlasting Covenant through His death on the cross: *"From his fullness we have all received, grace in place of grace, because while the law was given by Moses, grace and truth came through Jesus Christ"* (John 1: 1617). Moses himself conversed with Jesus about this fulfillment during the Transfiguration: *"And behold, two men were conversing with him, Moses and Elijah, who appeared in glory and spoke of his exodus that he was going to accomplish in Jerusalem"* (Luke 9: 30-31).

Therefore, outside of the Pentateuch, primarily Exodus through Deuteronomy, David dominates the Old Testament. David is first mentioned in the Book of Ruth and more than a thousand times in the rest of the Old Testament. The Book of Psalms is largely by and about David. The Wisdom books are attributed to Solomon, David's son. The historical books are about the rise and demise of the Davidic kingdom. The Prophetic books preach repentance and return to living in covenant with God, and prophesy the return of David's son and heir, Jesus. Through the establishment of the new and eternal covenant through His death and resurrection, Jesus would fulfill the original intent of God's covenant with David! The psalms flow out of the Davidic covenant, and therefore, play a significant role in understanding Jesus who is the 'Son of David'! The necessary link between the Old Covenant (Moses) and the New Covenant (Jesus) is David. The Davidic Covenant is the middle period between Moses and Jesus.

- **THE TODAH CYCLE:**

King David was instrumental in making the *Todah Cycle* a significant religious tradition. The cycle would begin when an Israelite experienced a crisis, either getting into trouble because of their sins, or because of some economic or personal hardship. And such a crisis was endangering their lives. They would then take the next step by taking their burdens to God, crying out for help and promising to make a thanksgiving offering, called the *todah,* when God answered their prayer. Most of the psalms of lament addressed the first step. When God took the second step by bringing them relief and salvation, the devotee would take the third step. They would make a pilgrimage to the Temple to offer the thanksgiving sacrifice or *todah* and have a feast to praise and thank God publicly. Many of the psalms of thanksgiving and praise were composed for the thanksgiving sacrifice. Moses emphasized the burnt offering (*'ola'*) where the entire animal was consumed in fire, but David encouraged the thank offering (*'todah'*), where the animal was sacrificed and eaten in a meal of thanksgiving and praise. We will be well acquainted with the *Todah Cycle,* as we pray with the psalms.

- **MOVING AWAY FROM THE OLA SACRIFICES TOWARD THE TODAH OFFERING:**

    David constantly gave thanks to God for all the things God had done for him, all the dangers he had escaped, and the disasters from which God had protected him. Many of his reflections about his dangers and asking for God's help were situated within the context of the Exodus event, the quintessential experience of salvation and freedom that the Israelites experienced in Egypt. He composed psalms to express his profound gratitude and used them during his celebration of the *todah* sacrifice (Leviticus 7: 11-14). David would offer an animal on God's altar as a sign of thanksgiving, and then hold a feast with the sacrificed animal. He would take the opportunity to witness to God's good deeds in front of the Gathering. David preferred the *todah offering* over the *ola sacrifices.* According to the ancient rabbis, once the Messiah appeared, all sacrifices would disappear except for the thanksgiving offering. With the Messiah's victory over Satan and sin, sin offerings would be unnecessary. Only the thanksgiving offering would continue, as it would be necessary to thank God for salvation. The Eucharist, meaning Thanksgiving, is our *todah* offering.

- **THE PROPHETIC NATURE OF THE PSALMS:**

    The psalms are the inspired product of David and the other Psalmists. The Holy Spirit used human authorship to reveal the intimate stages of God's plan of salvation. The psalms were a significant tool of spiritual formation for the Israelites as well.

They were especially instrumental in calling God's people to repentance and faithful covenant living with God. The psalms also reminded God's covenant people to remember constantly God's great deeds of creation and salvation on their behalf, especially the Exodus event, as the blessings and graces of those deeds were ever present to them in their covenant relationship with God!

An equally significant purpose of the psalms was to foreshadow the coming of the Messiah, the son of David, who would become the Messianic Son of David, and reveal Himself as the Son of God. The psalms keep affirming the fact that they are prophetic and messianic in intent, pointing inexorably to the coming of Jesus and the fulfillment of God's economy of salvation through the new and eternal covenant. The psalms keep telling us what Jesus stated categorically: that He had come to fulfill the law and the prophets. In His conversation with the disciples during His appearance to them in Jerusalem, Jesus included the psalms as well: *"These are my words that I spoke to you while I was still with you, that everything written about me in the law of Moses and in the prophets and psalms must be fulfilled"* (Luke 24: 44). Hence, the psalms are quoted extensively by Jesus and the Apostles, and the early Christian community.

- **PUNISHMENT OF ENEMIES AND FORGIVENESS:**

How does one answer the question that we all grapple with: *Should we seek vengeance on our enemies, those who hate us and/or whom we hate? Is it appropriate to ask God to avenge our enemies?* The answer to these questions has been offered in several psalms. David and the other Psalmists do invoke God's wrath and vengeance on their enemies. They view their enemies as being God's enemies, as they profess the 'way of the wicked,' as contrasted with the 'way of the just' which is the lifestyle of the Psalmist and anyone who seeks to live obediently according to God's word. Consequently, God's enemies are their enemies. God is more powerful than their enemies, and the Psalmist is confident that God will vanquish them and vindicate His people. It is left then to God to deal with them in His justice. In some psalms, however, the psalmist expresses the plea that the wicked will see the error of their ways and reform themselves. Even though Saul and Absalom were his avowed enemies, David did not kill Saul when he had a chance, and pleaded with Joab, his Commander-in-Chief, to spare his son Absalom when he was captured. (2Samuel 18).

Jesus, however, makes forgiveness of enemies a fundamental teaching and an essential dimension of His lifestyle. His death on the cross was the ultimate expression of God's enduring mercy for sinners! Jesus prayed and died for His enemies so that they would become God's children, and share His divine life! Our enemies are God's sons and daughters, in Jesus! Our enemies are Jesus' brothers and sisters! Our enemies are, therefore, our brothers and sisters, too! Jesus, the last royal son of David and Son of God, brings to perfection and completion His ancestor's answer in the psalms regarding the question of forgiveness of enemies. What remains true in Jesus' complete answer is the fact that God has overcome sin, Satan, and death. Hence, God has Satan on a leash, and we can rest secure in God's protection, regardless of our trying circumstances. Psalm 23 highlights this state of safety and union with Jesus, our Good Shepherd: *"Even though I walk through the valley of the shadow of death, I will fear no evil, for you are with me; your rod and your staff comfort me."*

HELPS FOR THE JOURNEY

- **SPIRITUAL READING OF THE PSALMS:**

Over 15 weeks of reflection and prayer with the psalms, you will have pondered 90 psalms, six psalms each week. We trust that you will have enough background and appreciation of the Psalmody to be able to taste and relish the truths of the other 60 psalms that will not be covered in our reflections. We encourage you to ponder these psalms as part of your spiritual reading over 15 weeks: 17 psalms in Book One over four weeks; 6 psalms in Book Two over four weeks; 5 psalms in Book Three over two weeks; 5

psalms in Book Four over two weeks; and 26 psalms over three weeks in Book Five: 7 in Week One, 11 in Week Two, and 8 in Week Three.

- **LECTIO DIVINA OR THE BENEDICTINE METHOD OF PRAYER:**

    Lectio Divina (Divine Reading) is a very ancient method of prayer going back to the early Christian centuries. This practice has been kept alive in the monastic traditions of the Church, especially by the Benedictines. Hence, the alternative name is 'The Benedictine Method of Prayer.' Given that this method originated in monasteries, it was very conducive to the monastic lifestyle which developed into a balanced and natural rhythm of life, with the equally important strands of prayer, study, work, and rest. While Lectio Divina could be classified as discursive prayer, meaning that it uses words, thoughts, images, and gestures, much like human communication, to relate to God, in many ways it could also be classified as contemplative prayer because it leads the disciple into God's Mystery when words become inadequate. This would be especially true of a disciple who has been taught by the Holy Spirit to wait on God in quiet and loving expectation.

    The first step is _Lectio or Reading the Word of God_ which is the passage selected for prayer, and to hear it "with the ear of our hearts," in the words of St. Benedict. It is God reading to us through inspired human authors! It is the Holy Spirit who will teach us how to listen to the Scriptures while we read them. In Lectio Divina, we are obeying this exhortation to listen to the Lord with our hearts. We read slowly, attentively, trustingly, gently listening for a word or phrase that is God's word for us this day. Our attitude must be one of peaceful anticipation and confident hope that we will be mentored by the Holy Spirit.

    The second step is _Meditatio or Repetition._ We ponder this morsel given to us by the Holy Spirit, chewing on it, tasting and relishing it, as well as allowing it to interact with our thoughts, hopes, desires and memories, in short, with our lives. Mary, Mother of Jesus, in the way she "*kept all these things, reflecting on them in her heart*" (Luke 2: 19), is our Scriptural role model, when it comes to doing this second step. It is God's Living Word, in the Person of Jesus Christ, who touches us and transforms our lives. Our ancient Christian brethren saw this step as the equivalent of "chewing the cud," that is, tasting and relishing God's revealed food to us. According to our ancient Christian brethren, the term 'repetition' instead of 'meditation,' highlights the pondering of God's Living Word.

The third step is <u>*Oratio or Prayer.*</u> The disciple now addresses God through the Scriptural message that they have received from reading and listening to the Holy Spirit. Prayer leads to an offering of self, shaped by the living word of God. If the Scripture is short, you can ponder the same word or phrase by repeating the first three steps two or three times. If the passage is long, you can break it up into smaller portions and follow the same procedure for each portion.

The fourth step is <u>*Contemplatio or Contemplation.*</u> In this step, we simply rest in the Presence of God who has used His living word to bring us into His Loving Embrace. In our Christian tradition, this wordless, quiet communing is called contemplation. Lectio Divina has the uncanny knack of unlocking the precious treasures of God's heart in this silentcommunion with Him. It unlocks the treasures of our own hearts as well, making us know ourselves as God does.

- **THE METHOD OF MEDITATION:**

The method of Meditation has been in vogue since the Middle Ages. Saints Ignatius of Loyola and Teresa of Avila used the method themselves and taught it too. Meditation begins with a *Preparatory Prayer*. We ask God to direct all our intentions, desires, and actions, to the praise and service of God. The Preparatory Prayer sets the context of our relationship with God. We are there on God's terms and we declare our earnest commitment to the Lord. In God's Embrace Ministries, our Preparatory Prayer is our Prayer to the Holy Spirit. We then create the environment for our prayer session with two preludes which are preparatory steps as well.

The *First Prelude* is also known as the Composition of place. St. Ignatius suggests that we create an image of the Scriptural scene or the theme on which we will be praying. For instance, to imagine Jesus being born in a cave if we are praying on the birth of Jesus. By situating our prayer within an image or context, our imagination becomes an active player in our prayer, and our chances of being focused and attentive to the Lord increase. If utilized well, imagination can be an effective help to our prayer.

In the *Second Prelude* we ask God for the grace that we seek. St. Ignatius assumes that we spent some time discerning what topic or theme the Holy Spirit was prompting us to take up in our prayer. St. Ignatius never hesitated to ask God for what he believed he needed so that he could be the best possible instrument in God's hands. His only desire was to attain *"the greater praise and service of God, Our Lord."*

The next step moves us into reflecting on the passage. St. Ignatius divided up the subject matter into *three points,* as a way of breaking it down into manageable morsels. We could do it in a way that suits us. In each point, we ponder God's truth as being presented *for us* in the Scripture passage. We spend time reflecting, comparing, contrasting, and deriving lessons for our own life: "Why is Jesus saying this? What is Jesus asking of me? What do I want and need to do for Jesus? This kind of reflection, if done purposefully and with care, will stir our hearts deeply and move us to offer Jesus a response. St. Ignatius was adamant about tasting and relishing the truth in prayer. If one point suffices in this regard, there is no need to go through all three.

St. Ignatius insists that at the end of our prayer we express directly to God the stirrings of our hearts, known as the *Colloquy.* Through our sentiments, the Holy Spirit is beckoning us toward repentance, commitment, and action. Through the colloquy, St. Ignatius wants to make sure that we spend time *in a face-to-face dialogue with God.* As we become familiar with this method, we will speak directly to God through all the points and listen to Him as well, as we reflect on the Word of God. The ideal would be to reflect and converse simultaneously. However, if we have not spent much time conversing directly with God, St. Ignatius suggests that at least we end our prayer with a colloquy.

BOOK ONE – PSALMS 1-41: ABIDING TRUST IN DIRE STRAITS
Psalms 1, 2, 3, 4, 5, and 6

WHAT IS AT THE HEART OF BOOK ONE, WEEK ONE?

Psalms 1 to 41 comprise Book One of the Psalter. The dominant theme in Book One could be described as *'Abiding Trust in Dire Straits.'* All 41 psalms have been composed by David, and through them he gives us a vivid description of his faith and trust in God's help in difficult and dangerous circumstances. Most of the psalms are individual laments. Many of the incidents to which David is referring, occurred when he was in the service of King Saul, and after he was enthroned as the King of Israel. He was a fugitive from Saul for about seven years, 1018 to 1011 B.C. During a year and four months of this period, David lived among the Philistines, archenemies of the Israelites. He sought refuge with the Philistines even though he had slain Goliath, a Philistine giant and their ablest warrior. David's decision to seek refuge among his archenemies tells us how very impossible his life had become under King Saul. During his reign as King of Israel, David became a fugitive from his son, Absalom. All this information can be found in the First and Second Books of Samuel. He is threatened by the fact that his enemies have gathered to surround him and kill him. He is assailed by sickness and ill health as well. And David's soul is in danger too because of his sins.

David offers us a good example of how we are to handle our own hardships and sufferings. He does not give in to despair and hopelessness in his laments, and through thick and thin, maintains his trust in God. Repeatedly, David calls to mind the many times when God rescued him from dire peril and devastation. In this way, he can keep his hope alive under very trying circumstances. Not infrequently, David reiterates his faith in God's saving power, refusing to believe that God will let him down and fail to come to his rescue. When David sins, he comes to God with a repentant heart and asks for forgiveness.

Several psalms of praise and thanksgiving to God have been included in Book One, such as Psalms 8, 18, 19, 24, 29, and 34. They highlight the truth that God is present with us in all our circumstances, and provides a silver lining to our darkest moments. In these psalms, David sometimes praises God even before God has rescued him from a difficult situation, as a sign of his inherent trust and confidence in God's love and faithfulness to him. Even though most of the psalms in Book One focus on life that is being buffeted by dangers and persecution from enemies, what stands out is that it is a book of unquestioning faith in God, and therefore, a school of prayer.

Book I of the Psalter, paints David as the suffering, persecuted king. All through Psalms 3-41, David is persecuted, and many times, because he has been righteous. Therefore, it often foreshadows the suffering and persecution of Jesus, the preeminent Son of David. In fact, during His ministry, and especially during His Passion, Jesus refers to these psalms frequently. The Beatitudes echo some of the sentiments of Book One of the psalms: *"Blessed are those who are persecuted for righteousness' sake"* (Matthew 5: 10). At the Last Supper, Jesus takes up Psalm 41: 10: *"Even my trusted friend, who ate my bread, has raised his heel against me,"* to describe the betrayal by Judas: *"Amen, I say to you, one of you will betray me, one who is eating with me"* (Mark 14: 18). During His Crucifixion, He cries out the first line of Psalm 22: *"My God, my God, why have you abandoned me?"* Just before His death, Jesus quotes Psalm 31: 6: *"Into your hands I commend my spirit."*

On Days One and Two, we will ponder *Psalms 1: True Happiness in God's Law* and *Psalm 2: A Psalm for a Royal Coronation,* which act as the Preface to the Book of Psalms, introducing us to two major themes. Psalm 1 introduces us to the wisdom of God and the lifestyle that is guided by the good counsel of the Holy Spirit. Psalm 2 introduces us to the Davidic Covenant and Kingdom that God established with King David and his successors, leading ultimately to Jesus, *"and of his kingdom there will be no end"* (Luke 1: 33).

On Day Three, we will pray with *Psalm 3: Threatened but Trusting,* entering more deeply into David's faith and trust in God as he fled as a fugitive from his own son, Absalom. In the light of his experience of God's salvation, he exhorts the wicked to *"tremble and sin no more, weep bitterly within your hearts, wail upon your beds, offer fitting sacrifices and trust in the LORD."*

On Day Four, we will ponder *Psalm 4: Trust in God,* which is one of many laments that David prays to God. In the light of his severe trials and tribulations, David has gained much wisdom in his relationship with God. He has developed an abiding trust in the saving power of God because he has experienced wonders at the hands of the Lord. He therefore prays with confidence that God will set him free when he is hemmed in by troubles.

On Day Five, we will pray with *Psalm 5: Prayer for Divine Help,* another one of David's laments. David is contrasting the security of abiding in God's Temple with the insecurity and dangers of keeping company with evildoers. In Jesus, we have become His sanctuary and can always abide in God's Temple!

On Day Six, we will ponder *Psalm 6: Prayer in Distress,* the first of the seven Penitential Psalms. The designation 'Penitential Psalms' became popular in the Seventh Century A.D. and described psalms that were suitable to express repentance. The Seven Penitential Psalms are 6, 32, 38, 51, 102, 130, and 143.

On Day Seven, we will reflect on the salient advice that these psalms have offered us to enhance and strengthen our own following of Jesus and our commitment to His Church.

SPIRITUAL READING FOR BOOK ONE OF THE PSALMS:
1 and 2 Samuel
Psalms 1 to 41
1 and 2 Kings (after you have read 1 and 2 Samuel)
1 and 2 Chronicles (after you have read 1 and 2 Kings)

DAY ONE:
MORNING PRAYER: Acts of Faith, Hope, Charity; Daily Offering

MORNING FACE TO FACE WITH GOD:
Begin with Prayer to the Holy Spirit
*Prayer on Psalm 1: **True Happiness in God's Law***

Psalm 1 introduces us to the wisdom of God and the lifestyle that is guided by the good counsel of the Holy Spirit. Psalm 1 lets us know that the Psalter is a Book of Prayer and an excellent manual for the formation of disciples. The Psalter teaches us how to walk in the way of the Lord. In Scripture, 'the way' is the lifestyle that a person chooses, either the way or law of the Lord, or the way of sinners and the counsel of the wicked. Acts 9: 1-2 described the disciples of the Lord as belonging to the Way: *"Now Saul, ...went to the high priest and asked him for letters to the synagogues in Damascus, that, if he should find any men or women who belonged to the Way, he might bring them back to Jerusalem in chains."*

Psalm 1 offers us a sharp contrast between the way of the Lord and the way of sinners. In the way of the Lord, the disciple lives in obedience to the Holy Spirit and is strengthened by it: *"The law of the LORD is his joy; and on his law he meditates day and night."* In choosing God, the teachings of Jesus become the disciple's priority. The disciple *"does not walk in the counsel of the wicked, nor stand in the way of sinners, nor sit in company with scoffers."* Walking, standing, and sitting, suggest a chosen lifestyle that influences every aspect of a person's life. The wicked are aptly described as *'chaff driven by the wind.'* Their lifestyle is built on sand, as their rejection of God and His ways leads them to ruin!

Our true happiness can only rest in God in whose image and likeness we have been created. There is an umbilical bond between God and us. In being obedient to God's word, our relationship with Him is deepened and we share intimately in God's life. His abundant blessings become an integral part of our lives. The psalm offers us a vivid image of what a life of union with God through Jesus would look like: *"He is like a tree planted near streams of water, that yields its fruit in season; its leaves never wither; whatever he does prospers."* Echoing the same thought, Jesus talks about the wise man who built his house on rock: *"The rain fell, the floods came, and the winds blew and buffeted the house. But it did not collapse; it had been set solidly on rock"* (Matthew 7: 25). And Revelation 22: 2 echoes the image of the tree planted near streams of water of Psalm 1, and brings it to its ultimate perfection: *"On either side of the river grew the tree of life that produces fruit twelve times a year, once each month; the leaves of the trees serve as medicine for the nations."* Psalm 1 invites us to do an inventory of our discipleship: *Are we blowing hot, lukewarm, or cold? And what is the Holy Spirit asking of us?*

Reflect and Pray on Psalm 1, using Lectio Divina or the Method of Meditation. Make sure you converse intimately with the Blessed Trinity:

Prayer on Psalm 1: True Happiness in God's Law

I.

"1 Blessed is the man who does not walk in the counsel of the wicked, nor stand in the way of sinners, nor sit in company with scoffers. 2 Rather, the law of the LORD is his joy; and on his law he meditates day and night. 3 He is like a tree planted near streams of water, that yields its fruit in season; its leaves never wither; whatever he does prospers.

II.

4 But not so are the wicked, not so! They are like chaff driven by the wind. 5 Therefore, the wicked will not arise at the judgment, nor will sinners in the assembly of the just. 6 Because the LORD knows the way of the just, but the way of the wicked leads to ruin."

End with Prayer to the Holy Trinity
NIGHT PRAYER: The Examination of Conscience

DAY TWO:
MORNING PRAYER: Acts of Faith, Hope, Charity; Daily Offering

MORNING FACE TO FACE WITH GOD:
Begin with Prayer to the Holy Spirit
Psalm 2: A Psalm for a Royal Coronation

The focus in Psalm 2 is on the Davidic Covenant and the Davidic Kingdom. In 2Samuel 7, it was revealed to King David through Nathan the prophet that God had established a covenant with him and his sons, thus bringing David into a father-son relationship with Himself. David is God's Anointed One. Only kings and priests were anointed, specifically emphasizing the fact that they had been set apart by God for their sacred office. Consequently, if anybody opposed the anointed one, they were opposing God: *"Kings on earth rise up and princes plot together against the LORD and against his anointed one."*

As part of that covenant with David and his sons, God promised that *"your house and your kingdom are firm forever before me; your throne shall be firmly established forever"* (2Samuel 7: 16). Both David and Solomon ruled over Israel and the surrounding nations as well. Their expansion efforts are found in 2Samuel 10, and 1Kings 4. The surrounding nations chafed under the Israelite kingship and sought to rebel: *"Let us break their shackles and cast off their chains from us!"* Such an action called for a swift reaction from God, consonant with His covenant relationship with the king, His anointed one, and with *'hesed'* or God's everlasting kindness and fidelity: *"The one enthroned in heaven laughs; the Lord derides them ... I myself have installed my king on Zion, my holy mountain."*

The Psalmist highlights the significance of the covenant relationship between God and the king of Israel by proclaiming it as a divine decree. The word 'decree' is synonymous with covenant. Through the Davidic Covenant, God has established a Father-son relationship with David and his sons, the most significant son being Jesus: *"I will proclaim the decree of the LORD, he said to me, "You are my son; today I have begotten you. Ask of me, and I will give you the nations as your inheritance, and, as your possession, the ends of the earth."*

The New Testament highlights the fulfillment of Psalm 2 in Jesus. It is probably the most important psalm referred to in the New Testament. In the two pivotal events of Jesus' life, His

Baptism and Transfiguration, we hear the voice of God the Father referring to Jesus as His Beloved Son (Matthew 3:17 and 17:5). And before His Ascension, Jesus commissioned His disciples to make the ends of the earth His kingdom: *"Go, therefore, and make disciples of all nations, baptizing them in the name of the Father, and of the Son, and of the holy Spirit, teaching them to observe all that I have commanded you. And behold, I am with you till the end of the age"* (Matthew 28:19-20).

Psalm 2 is significant in the preaching of the Apostles. The early Church was faced with a severe persecution. In response, they placed their trust in God and prayed in the spirit of Psalm 2: *"Indeed, they gathered in this city against your holy servant Jesus whom you anointed, Herod and Pontius Pilate, together with the Gentiles and the peoples of Israel ... And now, Lord, take note of their threats, and enable your servants to speak your word with all boldness... As they prayed, the place where they were gathered shook, and they were all filled with the holy Spirit and continued to speak the word of God with boldness"* (Acts 4: 23-31).

In Psalm 2, God promised the son of David, kingship over the whole world. In the New Testament, God fulfilled that promise through Jesus who is the 'Son of David' (a messianic title used by Jesus) and the Son of God. Jesus has established a new Israel, a kingdom not of this world, a kingdom that will have no end. The last words of Psalm 2 capture that sentiment: *"Blessed are all who take refuge in him."*

Reflect and Pray on Psalm 2, using Lectio Divina or the Method of Meditation. Make sure you converse intimately with the Blessed Trinity:

Psalm 2: A Psalm for a Royal Coronation

"1 Why do the nations protest and the peoples conspire in vain? 2 Kings on earth rise up and princes plot together against the LORD and against his anointed one; 3 "Let us break their shackles and cast off their chains from us!" 4 The one enthroned in heaven laughs; the Lord derides them, 5 then he speaks to them in his anger, in his wrath he terrifies them: 6 "I myself have installed my

king on Zion, my holy mountain." 7 I will proclaim the decree of the LORD, he said to me, "You are my son; today I have begotten you. 8 Ask of me, and I will give you the nations as your inheritance, and, as your possession, the ends of the earth. 9 With an iron rod you will shepherd them, like a potter's vessel you will shatter them." 10 And now, kings, give heed; take warning, judges on earth. 11 Serve the LORD with fear; exult with trembling, accept correction lest he become angry and you perish along the way when his anger suddenly blazes up. Blessed are all who take refuge in him!"

End with Prayer to the Holy Trinity
NIGHT PRAYER: The Examination of Conscience

DAY THREE:
MORNING PRAYER: Acts of Faith, Hope, Charity; Daily Offering

MORNING FACE TO FACE WITH GOD:
Begin with Prayer to the Holy Spirit
Psalm 3: Threatened but Trusting

Psalm 3 is David's first psalm of lament and introduces us to a significant dimension of our relationship with God amidst the trials and tribulations of life. King David is in the throes of a critical period of his reign. His son Absalom has revolted against him and installed himself as king instead. The account is found in 2Samuel 15-18. Absalom seemed to lead a successful rebellion against his father. Many of King David's friends and associates abandoned him and joined forces with Absalom, including Ahitophel, his chief councilor whose counsel was *"as though one sought the word of God"* (2Samuel 16: 23). David was forced to flee Jerusalem: *"An informant came to David with the report, "The Israelites have given their hearts to Absalom, and they are following him." At this, David said to all his servants who were with him in Jerusalem: "Get up, let us flee, or none of us will escape from Absalom. Leave at once, or he will quickly overtake us, and then bring disaster upon us, and put the city to the sword"* (2Samuel 15: 13-14). All the twelve tribes of Israel began acknowledging Absalom as their king in place of David.

In this perilous situation, David echoes his sentiments at the beginning of Psalm 3: *"How many are my foes, LORD! How many rise against me! How many say of me, "There is no salvation for him in God."* His enemies were gloating over the fact that David was beyond divine help. They believed that God was unwilling to help David who had committed the sin of adultery with Bathsheba and murder against her husband, Uriah. His enemies believed as well that David had caused the downfall of Saul's kingdom. 2Samuel 16: 8 tells us that Shimei, a Benjaminite, was King David's avowed enemy: *"The LORD has paid you back for all the blood shed from the family of Saul, whom you replaced as king, and the LORD has handed over the kingdom to your son Absalom. And now look at you: you suffer ruin because you are a man of blood."* In Shimei's mind, David was condemned by God! David's predicament could have led him to despair if he were convinced that God had abandoned him.

However, David's faith was impregnable. God was with him and would write straight on his very crooked lines: *"But you, LORD, are a shield around me; my glory, you keep my head high. With my own voice I will call out to the LORD, and he will answer me from his holy mountain."* David never questioned God's faithfulness and love for him. Under attack from a ruthless and cunning enemy, God was his protection, his shield. Even though his own glory (fame, power, prestige) among his people and their loyalty to him had collapsed into suspicion, hostility, and open revolt, David remained trusting in God's glory. In previous perils, God had manifested His glory through His powerful presence and protection. David, therefore, had peace of mind amidst this raging storm: *"You keep my head high."* Despite fleeing from Jerusalem, his Capital, where his LORD dwelled in the Temple, David knows that when he calls out to God, He will answer from His holy mountain or Temple. Though Absalom occupied Jerusalem, David knew that it was the LORD who held that ground and would hear

David's prayer.

A significant consequence of David's rock-like trust in God is that he is not subject to anxiety and fear: *"I lie down and I fall asleep, [and] I will wake up, for the LORD sustains me. I do not fear, then, thousands of people arrayed against me on every side."* It was the LORD's special grace that enabled David to sleep soundly and awaken refreshed while thousands of people were arrayed against him: *"Ahitophel went on to say to Absalom: "Let me choose twelve thousand men and be off in pursuit of David tonight. If I come upon him when he is weary and discouraged, I shall cause him panic, and all the people with him will flee, and I shall strike the king alone"* (2Samuel 17: 1-2). David knew that God was more powerful than all his enemies. He was rewarded miraculously with sound sleep in the jaws of death and awakened with steadfast hope when he could have wondered whether he would live another day.

David ends the Psalm on a high note of confidence and trust: *"Arise, LORD! Save me, my God! For you strike the cheekbone of all my foes; you break the teeth of the wicked."* Given what God had done for David in the past, he is confident that God will provide for all his needs in his present crisis. Not only will God protect David, but more importantly, God will have total victory over his foes. It is befitting that David ends his lament on a note of praise and thanksgiving for God's salvation, and a petition that God's blessings would continue to rain upon His people: *"Salvation is from the LORD! May your blessing be upon your people!"*

Reflect and Pray on Psalm 3, using Lectio Divina or the Method of Meditation. Make sure you converse intimately with the Blessed Trinity:

Psalm 3: Threatened but Trusting

I.

"1 A psalm of David, when he fled from his son Absalom. 2 How many are my foes, LORD! How many rise against me! 3 How many say of me, "There is no salvation for him in God." 4 But you, LORD, are a shield around me; my glory, you keep my head high.

II.

5 With my own voice I will call out to the LORD, and he will answer me from his holy mountain. 6 I lie down and I fall asleep, [and] I will wake up, for the LORD sustains me. 7 I do not fear, then, thousands of people arrayed against me on every side.

III.

8 Arise, LORD! Save me, my God! For you strike the cheekbone of all my foes; you break the teeth of the wicked. 9 Salvation is from the LORD! May your blessing be upon your people!"

End with Prayer to the Holy Trinity
NIGHT PRAYER: The Examination of Conscience

DAY FOUR:
MORNING PRAYER: Acts of Faith, Hope, Charity; Daily Offering

MORNING FACE TO FACE WITH GOD:
Begin with Prayer to the Holy Spirit
Prayer on Psalm 4: Trust in God

Psalm 4 can be better appreciated in the light of David's experience with his son Absalom that formed the context for Psalm 3. David begins this psalm of lament with a prayer of supplication: *"Answer me when I call, my saving God. When troubles hem me in, set me free; take pity on me, hear my prayer."* David has experienced God's protection and salvation in previous tribulations. His knowledge of God's faithfulness in the past gives him the assurance that God will come to his rescue in his present plight.

David is pondering the plight of his enemies, and those who have abandoned the God of the Mosaic Covenant. Though beleaguered by them, he knows that they cannot win because they are fighting against God. God chose David as king, not Absalom. So, when they pursue David, God's anointed one, they are opposing God. The truth is that God will listen to David when he calls on God because he is God's anointed one and has developed an intimate relationship with the LORD! In his prayer, David wonders how long they will remain hard of heart. He invites them to abandon false gods and to repent and return to the LORD: *"How long, O people, will you be hard of heart? Why do you love what is worthless, chase after lies? Know that the LORD works wonders for his faithful one; the LORD hears when I call out to him. Tremble and sin no more; weep bitterly within your hearts, wail upon your beds, offer fitting sacrifices and trust in the LORD."*

The last three verses of the psalm offer us the most food for thought. They point to an important dimension of discipleship: *"Many say, "May we see better times! LORD, show us the light of your face!" But you have given my heart more joy than they have when grain and wine abound. In peace I will lie down and fall asleep, for you alone, LORD, make me secure."* David had God as his security and shield. Consequently, every situation was blessed by the presence and peace of the Lord, even in very trying circumstances. He was able to sleep in peace, as his security in the Lord surpassed every mortal danger that he faced. Psalm 4 invites us to make God our All, as only God can guarantee our immortal security!

Reflect and Pray on Psalm 4, using Lectio Divina or the Method of Meditation. Make sure you converse intimately with the Blessed Trinity:

Prayer on Psalm 4: Trust in God

"1 For the leader; with stringed instruments. A psalm of David.

I.

2 Answer me when I call, my saving God. When troubles hem me in, set me free; take pity on me, hear my prayer.

II.

3 How long, O people, will you be hard of heart? Why do you love what is worthless, chase after lies? 4 Know that the LORD works wonders for his faithful one; the LORD hears when I call out to him. 5 Tremble and sin no more; weep bitterly within your hearts, wail upon your beds, 6 offer fitting sacrifices and trust in the LORD.

III.

7 Many say, "May we see better times! LORD, show us the light of your face!" 8 But you have given my heart more joy than they have when grain and wine abound. 9 In peace I will lie down and fall asleep, for you alone, LORD, make me secure."

End with Prayer to the Holy Trinity
NIGHT PRAYER: The Examination of Conscience

DAY FIVE:
MORNING PRAYER: Acts of Faith, Hope, Charity; Daily Offering

MORNING FACE TO FACE WITH GOD:
Begin with Prayer to the Holy Spirit
Psalm 5: Prayer for Divine Help

When David composed Psalm 5, we do not know what his circumstances were. We do know that he had enemies who threatened him for most of his life. From this and other psalms, we do know that honest and humble contact with God daily was a must for David. His faith and trust in God never faltered, even when he was burdened by his sins: *"Give ear to my words, O LORD, understand my sighing. Attend to the sound of my cry, my king and my God! For to you I will pray, LORD; in the morning you will hear my voice; in the morning I will plead before you and wait."* In viewing the happenings in the world, one could easily think that evil is more powerful than good, and that God has been rendered ineffective by the forces of evil. David keeps echoing the central message of the Bible that God will always be victorious. David's mind and heart were shaped by the wisdom and grace of the Holy Spirit: *"You are not a god who delights in evil, no wicked person finds refuge with you; the arrogant cannot stand before your eyes. You hate all who do evil; you destroy those who speak falsely. A bloody and fraudulent man the LORD abhors."* In Jesus, God's victory over Satan and sin is total: *"The armies of heaven followed him, mounted on white horses and wearing clean white linen. Out of his mouth came a sharp sword to strike the nations ... He has a name written on his cloak and on his thigh, "King of kings and Lord of lords"* (Revelation 20: 14-16). Evil will implode upon itself as it is based on the illusion that humans are greater than God and can replace the Almighty!

The Temple was a significant building for David. David wanted to build an elaborate temple, but God told him that it would be his son Solomon who would build it instead. In David's makeshift Temple, David addressed his supplications to God: *"But I, through the abundance of your mercy, will enter into your house. I will bow down toward your holy sanctuary out of fear of you."* We are God's temple, as Jesus abides in us, along with the Father who abides in Him, and the Holy Spirit who has become our Advocate. As Catholics, we have the great privilege of visiting Jesus present in the Blessed Sacrament of our churches whenever we want.

The heart of David's prayer is asking God to give him the proper guidance as he walks through the valley of darkness with his enemies seeking his destruction: *"LORD, guide me in your justice because of my foes, make straight your way before me. For there is no sincerity in their mouth; their heart is corrupt. Their throat is an open grave, on their tongue are subtle lies. Declare them guilty, God; make them fall by their own devices. Drive them out for their many sins; for they have rebelled against you."* When human wisdom leans on itself and stands up against divine wisdom, it leads to ruin and turmoil.

Psalm 5 ends on a familiar truth to anyone who has made God the Center of their lives. In God, they have an abiding peace and joy. They have the assurance that they are safe in God's hands. They are protected by God and are filled with constant gratitude: *"Then all who trust in you will be glad and forever shout for joy. You will protect them and those will rejoice in you who love your name. For you, LORD, bless the just one; you surround him with favor like a shield."*

Reflect and Pray on Psalm 5, using Lectio Divina or the Method of Meditation. Make sure you converse intimately with the Blessed Trinity:

Psalm 5: Prayer for Divine Help
"1 For the leader; with wind instruments. A psalm of David.

I.
2 Give ear to my words, O LORD, understand my sighing. 3 Attend to the sound of my cry, my king and my God! For to you I will pray, LORD; in the morning you will hear my voice; 4 in the morning I will plead before you and wait.
II.
5 You are not a god who delights in evil, no wicked person finds refuge with you; 6 the arrogant cannot stand before your eyes. You hate all who do evil; 7 you destroy those who speak falsely. A bloody and fraudulent man the LORD abhors.
III.
8 But I, through the abundance of your mercy, will enter into your house. I will bow down toward your holy sanctuary out of fear of you. 9 LORD, guide me in your justice because of my foes, make straight your way before me.
IV.
10 For there is no sincerity in their mouth; their heart is corrupt. Their throat is an open grave, on their tongue are subtle lies. 11 Declare them guilty, God; make them fall by their own devices. Drive them out for their many sins; for they have rebelled against you.
V.
12 Then all who trust in you will be glad and forever shout for joy. You will protect them and those will rejoice in you who love your name. 13 For you, LORD, bless the just one; you surround him with favor like a shield."

End with Prayer to the Holy Trinity
NIGHT PRAYER: The Examination of Conscience

DAY SIX:
MORNING PRAYER: Acts of Faith, Hope, Charity; Daily Offering

MORNING FACE TO FACE WITH GOD:
Begin with Prayer to the Holy Spirit
Psalm 6: Prayer in Distress (First Penitential Psalm)

    Psalm 6 is the first of the Seven Penitential Psalms, the others being Psalms 32, 38, 51, 102. 130, and 143. They were designated as Penitential Psalms from the Seventh Century onwards. The lament is about sin. The Psalmist acknowledges his sin and is focused on repentance or returning to have his relationship with God healed and reinstated. Sin in the Bible is both the sinful act as well as the consequences that sin brings upon the sinner and others who are affected by it.

The Psalmist begins with a profound sense of sinfulness. We do not know what sin David was confessing to God. He felt keenly that God was convicting him. Feeling very burdened and strained in his relationship with God, he was asking God to lighten and shorten the chastisement. In his agony, David experienced weakness of body and uneasiness of soul. These trials drove David to seek God's mercy: *"Do not reprove me in your anger, LORD, nor punish me in your wrath. Have pity on me, LORD, for I am weak; heal me, LORD, for my bones are shuddering. My soul too is shuddering greatly – and you, LORD, how long ...?"* David appeals to God's loving kindness to heal him. God convicts us and will never condemn us. Hebrews 12: 7 tells us that God chastens us as a mark of our adoption, because we are God's sons and daughters: *"Endure your trials as "discipline"; God treats you as sons. For what "son" is there whom his father does not discipline."*

Because of his sin, David felt distant from God and was pleading for a return of intimacy between God and himself. He asks God to be merciful to him while he is still on earth so that he could praise and thank God for His tender mercies. It would be unfortunate if he died before receiving God's mercy, as he would not be able to praise God in Hades: *"Turn back, LORD, rescue my soul; save me because of your mercy. For in death there is no remembrance of you. Who praises you in Sheol?" I am wearied with sighing; all night long I drench my bed with tears; I soak my couch with weeping. My eyes are dimmed with sorrow, worn out because of all my foes."* God's chastising hand was heavy upon David. His life was full of tears and misery. He felt God was angry with him; he lacked a sense of God's presence, and he could not sleep. His short and finite life weighed on David, as in his time, the certainty of after-life was still a vague concept. Certainty of eternal life came around the sixth century B.C.: *"As for me, I know that my vindicator lives, and that he will at last stand forth upon the dust. This will happen when my skin has been stripped off, and from my flesh I will see God: I will see for myself, my own eyes, not another's, will behold him: my inmost soul is consumed with longing"* (Job 19: 25-27).

In the last verses of the psalm, David is moving into a state of consolation. A change of heart is taking place: *"Away from me, all who do evil! The LORD has heard the sound of my weeping. The LORD has heard my plea; the LORD will receive my prayer. My foes will all be disgraced and will shudder greatly; they will turn back in sudden disgrace."* David's relationship with God has been restored and renewed. Repentance always leads to a joyful outcome.

Reflect and Pray on Psalm 6, using Lectio Divina or the Method of Meditation. Make sure you converse intimately with the Blessed Trinity:

Psalm 6: Prayer in Distress

"1 For the leader; with stringed instruments, "upon the eighth." A psalm of David.

I.

2 Do not reprove me in your anger, LORD, nor punish me in your wrath. 3 Have pity on me, LORD, for I am weak; heal me, LORD, for my bones are shuddering. 4 My soul too is shuddering greatly – and you, LORD, how long ...? 5 Turn back, LORD, rescue my soul; save me because of your mercy. 6 For in death there is no remembrance of you. Who praises you in Sheol?"

II.

7 I am wearied with sighing; all night long I drench my bed with tears; I soak my couch with weeping. 8 My eyes are dimmed with sorrow, worn out because of all my foes.

III.

9 Away from me, all who do evil! The LORD has heard the sound of my weeping. 10 The LORD has heard my plea; the LORD will receive my prayer. 11 My foes will all be disgraced and will shudder greatly; they will turn back in sudden disgrace."

End with Prayer to the Holy Trinity
NIGHT PRAYER: The Examination of Conscience

DAY SEVEN:
MORNING PRAYER: Acts of Faith, Hope, Charity; Daily Offering

MORNING FACE TO FACE WITH GOD:
Learning Discipleship from the Psalms
Begin with Prayer to the Holy Spirit

- The Psalter is a book of prayers and an excellent manual for the formation of disciples. Psalm 1 suggests that the Psalter teaches us how to walk in the way of the Lord. In the way of the Lord, the disciple lives in obedience to the Holy Spirit: *"The law of the LORD is his joy; and on his law he meditates day and night."* In choosing God, the teachings of Jesus become the disciple's priority.
- The disciple *"does not walk in the counsel of the wicked, nor stand in the way of sinners, nor sit in company with scoffers."* The wicked are aptly described as *'chaff driven by the wind,'* as their reliance on sin and rejection of God and His ways lead them to ruin!
- Psalm 1 offers us a vivid image of what a life of union with God through Jesus would look like: *"He is like a tree planted near streams of water, that yields its fruit in season; its leaves never wither; whatever he does prospers."* Revelation 22: 2 echoes the image of the tree planted near streams of water in Psalm 1, and brings it to its ultimate perfection: *"On either side of the river grew the tree of life that produces fruit twelve times a year, once each month; the leaves of the trees serve as medicine for the nations."*
- In Psalm 2, God promised the son of David kingship over the whole world. In the New Testament, God fulfills that promise through Jesus who is the Son of David and the Son of God. Jesus has established a new Israel, a kingdom not of this world,

a kingdom that will have no end. The last line of Psalm 2 captures that sentiment: *"Blessed are all who take refuge in him."* Very Good News indeed!

- The last verses of Psalm 4 point to an important dimension of discipleship: *"Many say, "May we see better times! LORD, show us the light of your face!" But you have given my heart more joy than they have when grain and wine abound. In peace I will lie down and fall asleep, for you alone, LORD, make me secure."* David had God as his salvation. Consequently, every situation was blessed by the Lord's presence and peace, even in very trying circumstances. He was able to sleep in peace as his security in the Lord surpassed every danger that he faced.
- Psalm 5 ends on a truth that is familiar to anyone who has made God the Center of their lives. In God, they have an abiding peace and joy. They are protected by God and are filled with constant gratitude: *"Then all who trust in you will be glad and forever shout for joy. You will protect them and those will rejoice in you who love your name. For you, LORD, bless the just one; you surround him with favor like a shield."*
- Psalm 6 is the first of Seven Penitential Psalms. The Psalmist acknowledges his sin and is focused on repentance or returning to have his relationship with God healed and reinstated. David appeals to God's loving kindness to heal him. David's relationship with God has been restored and renewed because repentance always leads to a joyful outcome.

End with Prayer to the Holy Trinity
NIGHT PRAYER: The Examination of Conscience

JOURNAL FOR BOOK ONE, WEEK ONE: ABIDING TRUST IN DIRE STRAITS

DAY ONE: Morning Prayer: Psalm 1: True Happiness in God's Law
What is God saying to You?

Nightly Examination of Conscience:
For what are you grateful?

For what are you contrite?

What spiritual discipline, including fasting, do you need to focus on tomorrow?

DAY TWO: Morning Prayer: Psalm 2: A Psalm for a Royal Coronation
What is God saying to You?

Nightly Examination of Conscience:
For what are you grateful?

For what are you contrite?

What spiritual discipline, including fasting, do you need to focus on tomorrow?

DAY THREE: Morning Prayer: Psalm 3: Threatened but Trusting
What is God saying to You?

Nightly Examination of Conscience:
For what are you grateful?

For what are you contrite?

What spiritual discipline, including fasting, do you need to focus on tomorrow?

DAY FOUR: Morning Prayer: Psalm 4: Trust in God
What is God saying to You?

Nightly Examination of Conscience:
For what are you grateful?

For what are you contrite?

What spiritual discipline, including fasting, do you need to focus on tomorrow?

DAY FIVE: Morning Prayer: Psalm 5: Prayer for Divine Help
What is God saying to You?

Nightly Examination of Conscience:
For what are you grateful?

For what are you contrite?

What spiritual discipline, including fasting, do you need to focus on tomorrow?

DAY SIX: Morning Prayer: Psalm 6: Prayer in Distress
What is God saying to You?

Nightly Examination of Conscience:
For what are you grateful?

For what are you contrite?

What spiritual discipline, including fasting, do you need to focus on tomorrow?

DAY SEVEN: Morning Prayer: Learning Discipleship from the Psalms
What is God saying to You?

Nightly Examination of Conscience:
For what are you grateful?

For what are you contrite?

What spiritual discipline, including fasting, do you need to focus on tomorrow?

What prayer would you compose to express what God has said to you this week?

BOOK ONE – PSALMS 1-41: ABIDING TRUST IN DIRE STRAITS
Psalms 8, 15, 18, 19, 22, and 23

WHAT IS AT THE HEART OF BOOK ONE, WEEK TWO?

During Week Two, we will be praying with some of the psalms of praise and thanksgiving that are included in Book One whose dominant theme could be described as *'Abiding Trust in Dire Straits.'* These psalms of praise and thanksgiving highlight enduring faith and trust in God in very threatening circumstances. God is present with us in all our circumstances and will always provide us with peace and strength to carry our crosses. Praise and thanksgiving to God for His tender mercies and protection provides the silver lining to our darkest moments. We will pray and reflect on three of these psalms of praise and thanksgiving, Psalms 8, 18, and 19. Psalm 15 echoes the longings of the pilgrim's heart to be right with God and to offer Him psalms of praise, like the ones of this week. However, in keeping with the primary theme and tone of Book One, we will also consider Psalm 22 which is the song of lament that Jesus prayed while He hung on the cross. And we will reflect on Psalm 23 which has traces of a lament, but in fact, highlights the Psalmist's indomitable faith and trust in God as His Good Shepherd. Tellingly, all these psalms have great relevance in relationship to Jesus because they veil messianic prophecies made by David.

On Day One, we will ponder *Psalm 8: Divine Majesty and Human Dignity.* We will ponder the immense truth of the Divine Majesty's relationship to humans. God created us in His image and likeness so that He could invite us into a covenant union with Him, thereby establishing a seemingly contradictory truth that the creature can indeed participate in the divine life of the Creator. But most especially, Psalm 8 has relevance in relationship to Jesus as it unveils a messianic prophecy made by David about *"a son of man"* who is little less than a god whom God has given mastery over the universe. Jesus was only a little less than God during His earthly life, as He chose not to cling to His divinity, humbling Himself to becoming obedient even to death on a cross, as Paul tells us in Philippians 2: 8. Jesus called Himself the 'Son of Man' which is a title for the Master of the Universe (Daniel 7: 13-14).

On Day Two, we will reflect prayerfully on *Psalm 15: The Righteous Israelite*. Israelites came from all over the kingdom to worship the LORD in Jerusalem. Entering the house of the LORD called for serious introspection and commitment to a life of righteousness or living according to the Ten Commandments. Pilgrims did a serious inventory to determine whether they were making God their overriding priority.

On Day Three, we will ponder *Psalm 18: A King's Thanksgiving for Victory*. David describes himself as the servant of the LORD. He owes his total allegiance to God, His Master, who has delivered him from all his enemies over many years. The relationship between God and his servant, David, is indeed a covenant relationship.

On Day Four, we will pray with *Psalm 19: God's Glory in the Heavens and in the Law*. David delves into two great books of wisdom to sustain and deepen his love of God. Besides the book of Nature, David had constant recourse to the Law of Moses. There, David has found the perfect formula for covenant living with the living God! Despite every effort to adhere to the statutes of the LORD, David is aware that he could sin inadvertently. He asks God to free him from mortal sin.

On Day Five, we will reflect and pray with *Psalm 22: The Prayer of an Innocent Person*. Jesus prayed Psalm 22 as He hung on the cross in the heaving throes of his life. The whole psalm is a prophecy of the passion, crucifixion, death, and resurrection of Jesus.

On Day Six, we will ponder *Psalm 23: The Lord, Shepherd and Host*. Of all the psalms, most of us would consider Psalm 23 to be our favorite. Along with the Song of Songs, Psalm 23 was the favorite text of the Church Fathers to teach about the sacraments.

On Day Seven, we will ponder the salient advice that these psalms have offered us to enhance and strengthen our own following of Jesus and our commitment to His Church.

SPIRITUAL READING FOR BOOK ONE OF THE PSALMS:
1 and 2 Samuel
Psalms 1 to 41
1 and 2 Kings (after you have read 1 and 2 Samuel)
1 and 2 Chronicles (after you have read 1 and 2 Kings)

DAY ONE:
MORNING PRAYER: Acts of Faith, Hope, Charity; Daily Offering
MORNING FACE TO FACE WITH GOD:
Begin with Prayer to the Holy Spirit

Prayer on Psalm 8: Divine Majesty and Human Dignity

Psalm 8 is the first among the six psalms of praise and thanksgiving that have been included among the 41 psalms of Book One. The redactors of the Book of Psalms were inspired by the Holy Spirit to insert Psalm 8 after four songs of lament, with the first Penitential Psalm being among them. Probably, the lesson to be learned is that when we are intimately connected with God, trusting Him and emphasizing total obedience to His will, all is well. Psalm 8 emphasizes the fact that the Creator of the Universe who created us in His image and likeness will necessarily be our Provider, Protector, and Redeemer who seeks to share His life in a covenant relationship with us! The truths revealed in Psalm 8 are far greater and more efficacious than any of our daily travails and tribulations.

We will ponder the immense truth of the Divine Majesty's relationship to humans. The chasm between our Creator and us is so infinite that the Psalmist gurgles sounds amounting to the prattle of babies and infants: *"O LORD, our Lord, how awesome is your name through all the earth! I will sing of your majesty above the heavens with the mouths of babes and infants."* Humans seem so puny and insignificant compared to the grandeur and majesty of

God's creation that we behold in our immense universe: *"When I see your heavens, the work of your fingers, the moon and stars that you set in place – what is man that you are mindful of him, and a son of man that you care for him?"*

And yet, the Psalmist is equally amazed by the stupendous truth that there is an amazing likeness between the Divine Majesty and His human creatures created in the divine image and likeness. In the presence of this awesome God, human beings would have been a mere dot on the pages of history, were it not for His *hesed* or loving kindness toward us: *"Yet you have made him little less than a god crowned him with glory and honor."* God created us in His image and likeness in order to invite us into a covenant union with Him, thereby establishing a seemingly contradictory truth that the creature can indeed participate in the divine life of the Creator. To make His intentions obvious, God shares His dominion over creatures with humans, asking them to act in His name: *"You have given him rule over the works of your hands, put all things at his feet: All sheep and oxen, even the beasts of the field, the birds of the air, the fish of the sea, and whatever swims the paths of the seas. O LORD, our Lord, how awesome is your name through all the earth!"*

But most especially, Psalm 8 has relevance in relationship to Jesus, as it unveils a messianic prophecy made by David about *"a son of man"* who is little less than a god whom God has given mastery over the universe. Jesus was only a little less than God during His earthly life because, as St. Paul tells us that *"though he was in the form of God, did not regard equality with God something to be grasped. Rather, he emptied himself taking the form of a slave, coming in human likeness"* (Philippians 2: 6- 7). Jesus called Himself the 'Son of Man' which is a Messianic title for the Lord of the Universe: *"When Jesus heard that they had thrown him out, he found him and said, "Do you believe in the Son of Man?" He answered and said, "Who is he, sir, that I may believe in him?" Jesus said to him, "You have seen him and the one speaking with you is he." He said, "I do believe, Lord,"* and he *worshiped him"* (John 9: 35-37).

Daniel the prophet first talked about the Son of Man as the Lord of the Universe: *"As the visions during the night continued, I saw coming with the clouds of heaven One like a son of man. When he reached the Ancient of Days and was presented before him, He received dominion, splendor, and kingship; all nations, peoples and tongues will serve him. His dominion is an everlasting dominion that shall not pass away, his kingship, one that shall not be destroyed"* (Daniel 7: 13-14). Jesus calls Himself the 'Son of Man' sixty-nine times in the gospels. The phrase 'Son of Man' becomes a title for Jesus the Messiah, especially in passages dealing with the Second Coming.

Reflect and Pray on Psalm 8, using Lectio Divina or the Method of Meditation. Make sure you converse intimately with the Blessed Trinity:

Prayer on Psalm 8: Divine Majesty and Human Dignity

"1 For the leader; "upon the gittith." A psalm of David.
2 O LORD, our Lord, how awesome is your name through all the earth! I will sing of your majesty above the heavens 3 with the mouths of babes and infants. You have established a bulwark against your foes, to silence enemy and avenger. 4 When I see your heavens, the work of your fingers, the moon and stars that you set in place – 5 What is man that you are mindful of him, and a son of man that you care for him? 6 Yet you have made him little less than a god, crowned him with glory and honor. 7 You have given him rule over the works of your hands, put all things at his feet: 8 All sheep and oxen, even the beasts of the field, 9 The birds of the air, the fish of the sea, and whatever swims the paths of the seas. 10 O LORD, our Lord, how awesome is your name through all the earth!"

End with Prayer to the Holy Trinity
NIGHT PRAYER: The Examination of Conscience

DAY TWO:
MORNING PRAYER: Acts of Faith, Hope, Charity, Daily Offering

MORNING FACE TO FACE WITH GOD:

Begin with Prayer to the Holy Spirit
Psalm 15: The Righteous Israelite

David had a makeshift temple in Jerusalem. It was a tent made from goat skins which housed the Ark of the Covenant. David called this tent the House of the LORD. And because the temple was erected on Mount Zion in Jerusalem, David believed that this made Jerusalem holy as well. People who loved the LORD came to His house from all the reaches of the kingdom. They were essentially pilgrims who were visiting the LORD during the pilgrimage festivals, to pay Him their respects and offer Him sacrificial offerings of atonement, thanksgiving, and praise.

Psalm 15 addresses the required disposition of the pilgrim coming to visit the LORD in His House. Who was qualified to *"abide in your tent? Who may dwell on your holy mountain?"* These questions were probably asked of the pilgrims by a Levite who welcomed them at the threshold of the tent? Loving service of the neighbor was the requisite answer to these questions. These actions of service of the neighbor, called for a serious commitment to holiness, striving with God's grace to act like a saint in every circumstance of life: *"Whoever walks without blame, doing what is right, speaking truth from the heart... (who) does not slander with his tongue, does no harm to a friend, never defames a neighbor; ... who keeps an oath despite the cost, lends no money at interest, accepts no bribe against the innocent. Whoever acts like this shall never be shaken."* David did indeed make a serious commitment to being in covenant union with the LORD and obeying His commandment to love his neighbor as himself. In our prayer, we can examine our own answer to the two questions and see if they match David's responses.

Reflect and Pray on Psalm 15, using Lectio Divina or the Method of Meditation. Be sure to converse intimately with the Blessed Trinity:
Psalm 15: The Righteous Israelite
"1 A psalm of David.
I.
LORD, who may abide in your tent? Who may dwell on your holy mountain?

II.

2 Whoever walks without blame, doing what is right, speaking truth from the heart; 3 who does not slander with his tongue, does no harm to a friend, never defames a neighbor; 4 who disdains the wicked, but honors those who fear the LORD, who keeps an oath despite the cost, 5 lends no money at interest, accepts no bribe against the innocent.

III.

Whoever acts like this shall never be shaken."

End with Prayer to the Holy Trinity
NIGHT PRAYER: The Examination of Conscience

DAY THREE:
MORNING PRAYER: Acts of Faith, Hope, Charity; Daily Offering

MORNING FACE TO FACE WITH GOD:
Begin with Prayer to the Holy Spirit

Prayer on Psalm 18: A King's Thanksgiving for Victory

Psalm 18 is indeed a long hymn of praise and thanksgiving to God for His numerous blessings, especially for the fact that *"the LORD rescued David from the clutches of all his enemies and from the hand of Saul."* There are only three other psalms that are longer than Psalm 18; they are Psalms 78, 89, and 119. David describes himself as the servant of the LORD. He owes his total allegiance to God, His Master, who has delivered him from all his enemies over many years. Even though Saul was his sworn enemy, David refrained from describing him as an enemy. On one occasion, David could have killed Saul, but instead chose to let him live: *"Abishai whispered to David: "God has delivered your enemy into your hand today. Let me nail him to the ground with one thrust of the spear; ...!" But David said to Abishai, "Do not harm him, for who can lay a hand on the LORD's anointed and remain innocent"* (1Samuel 26: 8-9). David is undeservedly kind to Saul and does not include him among his enemies because he is God's anointed one.

Psalm 18 is virtually the same Psalm that David sang at the end of his life as is recorded in 2Samuel 22: 2-51. David is looking back on his life. Despite all his failings, he had pursued a committed relationship to the LORD, and always remained profoundly grateful for God's numerous blessings and favors, especially for rescuing him from mortal dangers: *"I love you, LORD, my strength, LORD, my rock, my fortress, my deliverer, my God, my rock of refuge, my shield, my saving horn, my stronghold! Praised be the LORD, I exclaim!... The cords of death encompassed me; the torrents of destruction terrified me. The cords of Sheol encircled me; the snares of death lay in wait for me... I cried out to my God, from his temple he heard my voice; my cry to him reached his ears."* Almost breathlessly, David gushes forth with an abundance of superlative qualifiers to describe God's loving kindness and faithfulness to him when the torrents of destruction engulfed him. David describes death as cords suffocating him and snares set to trap him. During your prayer, you will have the opportunity to taste and relish these attributes for God!

David offers a poignant reason as to why God delivered him from mortal dangers: *"he rescued me because he loves me."* God's love for David strengthened his decision to love and serve the LORD who delivered him so spectacularly, time and again: *"I was not disloyal to my God. For his laws were all before me, his decrees I did not cast aside. I was honest toward him; I was on guard against sin, so the LORD rewarded my righteousness, the cleanness of my hands in his sight."* David was a fugitive from Saul for many years, wandering from hiding place to hiding place in fear and trepidation. They were very trying years when he was cut off from his family and felt abandoned and victimized by Saul's insane jealousy. By his own assessment, David remained steadfast and committed to God, and God remained faithful to His promise made at his anointing that he would be crowned the King of Israel: *"Thus I will praise you, LORD, among the nations; I will sing praises to your name. You have given great victories to your king, and shown mercy to his anointed, to David and his posterity forever."*

Reflect and Pray on Psalm 18, using Lectio Divina or the Method of Meditation. Make sure you converse intimately with the Blessed Trinity:

Prayer on Psalm 18: A King's Thanksgiving for Victory
"1 For the leader. Of David, the servant of the LORD, who sang to the LORD the words of this song after the LORD had rescued him from the clutches of all his enemies and from the hand of Saul. 2 He said:

I.

I love you, LORD, my strength, 3 LORD, my rock, my fortress, my deliverer, my God, my rock of refuge, my shield, my saving horn, my stronghold! 4 Praised be the LORD, I exclaim! I have been delivered from my enemies.

II.

5 The cords of death encompassed me; the torrents of destruction terrified me. 6 The cords of Sheol encircled me; the snares of death lay in wait for me. 7 In my distress I called out: LORD! I cried out to my God, from his temple he heard my voice; my cry to him reached his ears. 8 The earth rocked and shook; the foundations of the mountains trembled; they shook as his wrath flared up. 9 Smoke rose from his nostrils, a devouring fire from his mouth; it kindled coals into flame. 10 He parted the heavens and came down, a dark cloud under his feet. 11 Mounted on a cherub he flew, borne along on the wings of the wind. 12 He made darkness his cloak around him; his canopy, water-darkened storm clouds. 13 From the glean before him, his clouds passed, hail and coals of fire. 14 The LORD thundered from heaven; the Most High made his voice resound. 15 He let fly his arrows and scattered them; shot his lightning bolts and dispersed them. 16 Then the bed of the sea appeared; the world's foundations lay bare, at your rebuke, O LORD, at the storming breath of your nostrils. 17 He reached down from on high and seized me; drew me out of the deep waters. 18 He rescued me from my mighty enemy, from foes too powerful for me. 19 They attacked me on my day of distress, but the LORD was my support. 20 He set me free in the open; he rescued me because he loves me.

III.

21 The LORD acknowledged my righteousness, rewarded my clean hands. 22 For I kept the ways of the LORD; I was not disloyal to my God. 23 For his laws were all before me, his decrees I did not cast aside. 24 I was honest toward him; I was on guard against sin, 25 So the LORD rewarded my righteousness, the cleanness of my hands in his sight. 26 Toward the faithful you are faithful; to the honest man you are honest; 27 toward the pure, you are pure; but to the perverse you are devious. 28 For humble people you save; haughty eyes you bring low. 29 For you, LORD, give light to my lamp; my God brightens my darkness. 30 With you I can rush an armed band, with my God to help I can leap a wall. 31 God's way is unerring; the LORD's promise is refined; he is a shield for all who take refuge in him.

IV.

32 Truly, who is God except the LORD? Who but our God is the rock? 33 This God who girded me with might, kept my way unerring, 34 who made my feet like a deer's, and set me on the heights, 35 who trained my hands for war, my arms to string a bow of bronze.

V.

36 You have given me your saving shield; your right hand has upheld me; your favor made me great. 37 You made room for my steps beneath me; my ankles never twisted. 38 I pursued my enemies and overtook them; I did not turn back till I destroyed them. 39 I decimated them; they could not rise; they fell at my feet. 40 You girded me with valor for war, subjugated my opponents beneath me. 41 You made my foes expose their necks to me; those who hated me I silenced. 42 They cried for help, but no one saved them; cried to the LORD but received no answer. 43 I ground them to dust before the wind; I left them like mud in the streets. 44 You rescues me from the strife of peoples; you made me head over nations. A people I had not known served me; 45 as soon as they heard of me they obeyed. Foreigners submitted before me; 46 foreigners cringed; they came cowering from their dungeons.

VI.
47 The LORD lives! Blessed be my rock! Exalted be God, my savior! 48 O God who granted me vengeance, made peoples subject to me, 49 and saved me from my enemies, truly you have elevated me above my opponents, from a man of lawlessness you have rescued me. 50 Thus I will praise you, LORD, among the nations; I will sing praises to your name. 51 You have given great victories to your king, and shown mercy to his anointed, to David and his posterity forever."

End with Prayer to the Holy Trinity
NIGHT PRAYER: The Examination of Conscience
DAY FOUR:
MORNING PRAYER: Acts of Faith, Hope, Charity; Daily Offering

MORNING FACE TO FACE WITH GOD:
Begin with Prayer to the Holy Spirit
Prayer on Psalm 19: God's Glory in the Heavens and in the Law

David was a shepherd who spent many a starry night watching over his flock and beholding the waxing and waning of the moon. In the night sky, he observed the passing of the seasons in the way the galaxies and stars aligned themselves. David was a deeply spiritual man and the heavens spoke to him of the majesty, power, and wisdom of God. In the heavens, David saw the glory or visible manifestation of God's presence: *"The heavens declare the glory of God; the firmament proclaims the works of his hands. Day unto day pours forth speech; night unto night whispers knowledge. There is no speech, no words; their voice is not heard."* Through Nature, God spoke to David in silence, lifting him into the realm of the eternal.

David also spent many break-of-dawn moments when he watched the sun rise over the high Moab Plateau across the Dead Sea in the East. He was awed by the break of day and used his poetic genius to express His unabashed admiration for God as he described his experience: *"He has pitched in them a tent for the sun; it comes forth like a bridegroom from his canopy, and like a hero joyfully runs its course. From one end of the heavens it comes forth; its course runs through to the other; nothing escapes its heat."* David did not need human discourse to converse in awed silence with the Creator and LORD of this immense universe. It was indeed a prayer emerging from the depths of a heart beloved by God.

There were two great books of wisdom that David delved into to sustain and deepen his love of God. Besides the book of Nature, David had constant recourse to the Law of Moses: *"The law of the LORD is perfect, refreshing the soul. The decree of the LORD is trustworthy, giving wisdom to the simple. The precepts of the LORD are right, rejoicing the heart. The command of the LORD is clear, enlightening the eye."* In the law of the LORD, David found the perfect formula for covenant living with the living God! David only had the first five books of the Old Testament known as the Torah or Pentateuch, in written and oral tradition. The Torah and the Book of Joshua preceded him by about two hundred years even though they were codified as we know them during and after the Babylonian Exile. David's attitude toward making the law of the LORD his way of life is akin to the attitude of the devotee who has made a total offering of self to God: *"The fear of the LORD is pure, enduring forever. The statutes of the LORD are true, all of them just; more desirable than gold, than a hoard of purest gold, sweeter also than honey or drippings from the comb. By them your servant is warned; obeying them brings much reward."*

David was aware that he could sin inadvertently. He sought to live in constant repentance and asked God to free him from any mortal sin: *"Who can detect trespasses? Cleanse me from my inadvertent sins. Also from arrogant ones restrain your servant; let them never control me. Then shall I be blameless, innocent of grave sin."*

Reflect and Pray on Psalm 19, using Lectio Divina or the Method of Meditation. Make sure you converse intimately with the Blessed Trinity:

Prayer on Psalm 19: God's Glory in the Heavens and in the Law
"1 For the leader. A psalm of David.

I.
2 The heavens declare the glory of God; the firmament proclaims the works of his hands. 3 Day unto day pours forth speech; night unto night whispers knowledge. 4 There is no speech, no words; their voice is not heard; 5 a report goes forth through all the earth, their messages, to the ends of the world. He has pitched in them a tent for the sun; 6 it comes forth like a bridegroom from his canopy, and like a hero joyfully runs its course. 7 From one end of the heavens it comes forth; its course runs through to the other; nothing escapes its heat.

II.
8 The law of the LORD is perfect, refreshing the soul. The decree of the LORD is trustworthy, giving wisdom to the simple. 9 The precepts of the LORD are right, rejoicing the heart. The command of the LORD is clear, enlightening the eye. 10 The fear of the LORD is pure, enduring forever. The statutes of the LORD are true, all of them just; 11 more desirable than gold, than a hoard of purest gold, sweeter also than honey or drippings from the comb. 12 By them your servant is warned; obeying them brings much reward.

III.
13 Who can detect trespasses? Cleanse me from my inadvertent sins. 14 Also from arrogant ones restrain your servant; let them never control me. Then shall I be blameless, innocent of grave sin. 15 Let the words of my mouth be acceptable, the thoughts of my heart before you, LORD, my rock and my redeemer."

End with Prayer to the Holy Trinity
NIGHT PRAYER: The Examination of Conscience

DAY FIVE:
MORNING PRAYER: Acts of Faith, Hope, Charity; Daily Offering

MORNING FACE TO FACE WITH GOD:
Begin with Prayer to the Holy Spirit

Prayer on Psalm 22: The Prayer of an Innocent Person

Psalm 22 is probably the most gut-wrenching lament in the Psalter, and, as with most psalms of lament, ends in praise of God.

Given the severe trials and life-threatening tribulations that David faced, this psalm does indeed evoke a period of excruciating physical pain and spiritual agony. While David is alluding to his own circumstances, more importantly, he is prophesying what the 'Son of David' (the Messiah) will endure as He establishes the new kingdom of Israel, the Kingdom of God. It is not surprising, then, that Jesus prayed this psalm as He hung on the cross. Jesus was experiencing every verse of this psalm during the agonizing hours of His death. We can assume as well that His mother, Mary, John, the beloved disciple, and Mary Magdalene, were praying Psalm 22 with Jesus.

On the cross, Jesus became our sin so that we might participate in His righteousness as 2Corinthians 5: 21 tells us. On the cross, then, Jesus experienced the worst possible dregs of our sinful rebellion against God. In praying Psalm 22, Jesus was experiencing on our behalf this passage from our rebellious sin to abundant new life in His righteousness. Jesus begins by telling us that He felt abandoned by God: *"My God, my God, why have you abandoned me? Why so far from my call for help, from my cries of anguish? My God, I call by day, but you do not answer, by night, but I have no relief."* When we choose to remain entangled in the snares of sin, we experience alienation from God. In our case, we create this abandonment from God which could lead to everlasting abandonment by God if we do not repent. In His experience of God abandoning Him, Jesus was atoning for our rebelliousness and assuring us that through Him we would receive the grace to never abandon God.

In the next several verses, Jesus teaches us how to deal with our sufferings. Even in our most difficult circumstances, certain unassailable truths should always form the bedrock of our lives so that we are never thrown into despair. Jesus was feeling abandoned by God, feeling like *"a worm, not a man, scorned by men, despised by the people."* And yet in His excruciating agony, He was extolling God's everlasting goodness: *"Yet you are enthroned as the Holy One; you are the glory of Israel. In you our fathers* trusted; they trusted and you rescued them. To you they cried out and they escaped; in you they trusted and were not disappointed." While His experience of abandonment by God was real, Jesus still knew that His Father was with Him in His agony.

Jesus experiences the rage and forces of evil surrounding Him: *"All who see me mock me; they curl their lips and jeer; they shake their heads at me: "He relied on the LORD – let him deliver him; if he loves him, let him rescue him."* Luke 23: 35 speaks to the fulfillment of this verse: *"He saved others, let him save himself if he is the chosen one, the Messiah of God."*

As Jesus prays the next verses of the psalm, He is well aware of His mother standing beneath the cross and united with Him in His excruciating agony of salvation on our behalf: *"For you drew me forth from the womb, made me safe at my mother's breasts. Upon you I was thrust from the womb; since my mother bore me you are my God."* These verses bridge the Annunciation and Birth of Jesus with His Crucifixion and sacrifice on the Cross, and Mary, His mother, has played a significant role in this salvific passage. It brings to the fore Mary's seven sorrows, especially the last four which encompass her Calvary experience: journeying with Jesus to Calvary, standing beneath the cross, taking the dead Jesus into her arms, and burying Him. In order to save us, Jesus had to be drawn forth from a sinless human womb so that He, as Son of God, could be our worthy human representative before God, atoning for our sins.

In the next verses, we can sense palpably the evil bedlam that has broken out on Calvary all around Jesus, as He asks His Father to stay close to help Him: *"Do not stay far from me, for trouble is near, and there is no one to help. Many bulls surround me; fierce bulls of Bashan encircle me. They open their mouths against me, lions that rend and roar... They have pierced my hands and my feet. I can count all my bones."* David wrote Psalm 22 in 1000 B.C., when crucifixion as capital punishment was unknown. Crucifixion is first attested to among the Persians in the third century B.C., who probably adopted it from the Assyrians. It was later employed by the Greeks, especially Alexander the Great, and by the Carthaginians, from whom the Romans adapted the practice as a punishment for slaves and non-citizens. The Romans conquered Palestine in 63 B.C.

The last verses of Psalm 22 allude to the resounding victory over Satan and sin that Jesus accomplished on our behalf through His death on the cross and resurrection. The last verses tell us in no uncertain terms that the Son of God would suffer, die, and rise from the dead. They clearly point toward the resurrection of Jesus: *"All who sleep in the earth will bow low before God; all who have gone down into the dust will kneel in homage. And I will live for the LORD; my descendants will serve you. The generation to come will be told of the Lord, that they may proclaim to a people yet unborn the deliverance you have brought."*

Psalm 22 goes through the complete *todah cycle*. The cycle begins with Jesus being in a severe death-by-crucifixion stranglehold: *"My God, my God, why have you abandoned me?"* Given that Jesus was praying the whole psalm, He is confident that God would answer His prayer and bring about redemption through His ordeal on the cross: *"Yet you are enthroned as the Holy One; you are the glory of Israel. In you our fathers trusted; they trusted and you rescued them..."* God answered Jesus' prayer by raising Him from the dead and this called for a Eucharistic celebration that Jesus instituted at the Last Supper: *"...And I will live for the LORD; ... that they may proclaim to a people yet unborn the deliverance you have brought."* Psalm 22 is the quintessential messianic and Eucharistic psalm!

Reflect and Pray on Psalm 22, using Lectio Divina or the Method of Meditation. Be sure to converse intimately with the Blessed Trinity:

Prayer on Psalm 22: The Prayer of an Innocent Person
"1 For the leader; according to "The deer of the dawn." A psalm of David.

I.
2 My God, my God, why have you abandoned me? Why so far from

my call for help, from my cries of anguish? 3 My God, I call by day, but you do not answer, by night, but I have no relief. 4 Yet you are enthroned as the Holy One; you are the glory of Israel. 5 In you our fathers trusted; they trusted and you rescued them. 6 To you they cried out and they escaped; in you they trusted and were not disappointed. 7 But I am a worm, not a man, scorned by men, despised by the people. 8 All who see me mock me; they curl their lips and jeer; they shake their heads at me: 9 "He relied on the LORD – let him deliver him; if he loves him, let him rescue him." 10 For you drew me forth from the womb, made me safe at my mother's breasts. 11 Upon you I was thrust from the womb; since my mother bore me you are my God. 12 Do not stay far from me, for trouble is near, and there is no one to help.

II.

13 Many bulls surround me; fierce bulls of Bashan encircle me. 14 They open their mouths against me, lions that rend and roar. 15 Like water my life drains away; all my bones are disjointed. My heart has become like wax, it melts away within me. 16 As dry as a potsherd is my throat; my tongue cleaves to my palate; you lay me in the dust of death. 17 Dogs surround me; a pack of evildoers closes in on me. They have pierced my hands and my feet 18 I can count all my bones. They stare at me and gloat; 19 they divide my garments among them; for my clothing they cast lots. 20 But you, LORD, do not stay far off; my strength, come quickly to help me. 21 Deliver my soul from the sword, my life from the grip of the dog. 22 Save me from the lion's mouth, my poor life from the horns of wild bulls.

III.

23 Then I will proclaim your name to my brethren; in the assembly I will praise you: 24 "You who fear the LORD, give praise! All descendants of Jacob, give honor; show reverence, all descendants of Israel! 25 For he has not spurned or disdained the misery of this poor wretch, did not turn away from me, but heard me when I cried out. 26 I will offer praise in the great assembly; my vows I will fulfill before those who fear him. 27 The poor will eat their fill;

those who seek the LORD will offer praise. May your hearts enjoy life forever!"

IV.

28 All the ends of the earth will remember and turn to the LORD; all the families of nations will bow low before him. 29 For kingship belongs to the LORD, the ruler over the nations. 30 All who sleep in the earth will bow low before God; all who have gone down into the dust will kneel in homage. 31 And I will live for the LORD; my descendants will serve you. 32 The generation to come will be told of the Lord, that they may proclaim to a people yet unborn the deliverance you have brought."

End with Prayer to the Holy Trinity
NIGHT PRAYER: The Examination of Conscience

SUGGESTED SPIRITUAL READING FOR DAY 5:

The Suffering Servant Oracles: Isaiah 42: 1-9; 49: 1-7; 50: 1-11; 52: 1353:
1-12.
The Crucifixion Narratives in the Gospels: Matthew 27: 33-56; Mark 15: 22-41; Luke 23: 33-49; John 19: 17-37.

DAY SIX:
MORNING PRAYER: Acts of Faith, Hope, Charity; Daily Offering

MORNING FACE TO FACE WITH GOD:
Begin with Prayer to the Holy Spirit
Prayer on Psalm 23: The Lord, Shepherd and Host

The tone of Psalm 23 would suggest that David composed it in his later years. He offers us a unique window into his deeply committed relationship with God. He speaks with a confident and mellow faith in God that has been honed and strengthened through many trials and tribulations. David seems to be reminiscing about his own life as a shepherd and how God, indeed, has been his Good Shepherd and Host. Amidst the intertwining of his years as a shepherd when he traversed the hills and valleys of the Judaean countryside, with the tempestuous years of warfare and rebellion during his reign as king, God was always there as the Good

Shepherd and Protector.

Psalm 23 falls into two halves where the Psalmist uses different imagery to display God's solicitous guardianship over David. In Section One, the LORD is presented as a Shepherd who is prepared to do whatever it takes to ensure the wellbeing of His sheep. In the light of his own experience as a devoted shepherd, David appreciates God's shepherding of him throughout his life: *"The Lord is my shepherd; there is nothing I lack... even though I walk through the valley of the shadow of death, I will fear no evil, for you are with me; your rod and staff comfort me."* God remains undaunted in His solicitude for His sheep even when they walk through the valley of the shadow of death. The valleys in the Judaean wilderness, with summer temperatures reaching 120 degrees, were death traps. David had first-hand experience of them in his years as a fugitive. Even in the jaws of death, the believer fears no evil as God is there with rod and staff, instruments of protection and guidance.

In Section Two, David presents God as the perfect Host to His guest: *"You set a table before me in front of my enemies; you anoint my head with oil; my cup overflows."* David is using the image of the Passover Meal that God set up for His people in Egypt. They ate their last meal in Egypt, surrounded by ruthless forces. When God is our Host, we can live in peace and contentment even when evil is all around us. The conclusion emphasizes the power and presence of God in the believer's life, resulting in abiding peace and joy: *"Indeed, goodness and mercy will pursue me all the days of my life; I will dwell in the house of the LORD for endless days."*

Jesus makes Psalm 23 a prophetic statement when He speaks of Himself as the Good Shepherd: *"I am the good shepherd, and I know mine and mine know me, just as the Father knows me and I know the Father; and I will lay down my life for my sheep. I have other sheep that do not belong to this fold. This is why the Father loves me, because I lay down my life in order to take it up again"* (John 10: 14-18). Throughout His ministry, there was steady and mounting opposition to Jesus from the Jewish leadership. The Sanhedrin was required to safeguard and promote proper temple worship and religious practices. However, as a body, they were corrupt and self-serving, imposing unjust burdens upon the people for their own selfish purposes. The people did not listen to them because they were *"thieves and robbers"* (John 10: 8).

As opposed to them, Jesus describes Himself as the Good Shepherd of Psalm 23. He contrasts Himself with frauds who masquerade as shepherds: thieves, marauders, strangers, hired hands. For His sheep, Jesus is willing to give His life. He will not hesitate, therefore, to sacrifice Himself on the cross on behalf of His sheep. Such a mission would be ludicrous and impossible if it belonged to anyone other than Jesus. Sheep are supposedly dumb and dependent animals who need a watchful and devoted shepherd if they are to survive and thrive in the wild. We are aptly described as sheep because of the foolishness and danger of sin lurking in our hearts. Through His Holy Spirit, Jesus brings about our transformation so that we will know Him in the same way that the Father knows Him, and He knows the Father. Jesus is talking about an intimate union with us along the lines of Trinitarian union, a Mystery that is beyond our comprehension, and yet stirs our hearts deeply! There are other sheep that need to be brought into the fold. Jesus continues to increase His flock by sending His followers to make disciples of those who choose Him as their Good Shepherd and Lord!

Psalm 23 has been used by the Church Fathers since ancient times to explain the Sacraments of Initiation: Baptism, Confirmation, and Holy Communion. The catechumens memorized the psalm. In the first two centuries, the newly baptized sang Psalm 23 as they processed to receive Holy Communion during the Easter Vigil, knowing that martyrdom might be in store for them. Jesus is the Good Shepherd. Scripture is the pasture that nourishes the heart and gives strength to the soul. It is indeed a place of rest. The still waters are the waters of Baptism that cleanse the soul of sin and regenerate the life of Jesus in the baptized. The sacraments and teachings of Jesus lead us on the straight and narrow path even through the valley of the shadow of death. Consequently, the believer fears no evil. The rod and the staff symbolize the gift of the Holy Spirit.

Robed in white, after the liturgy of the Word, the catechumens received the Holy Spirit in the Sacrament of Confirmation, when their heads were anointed with oil and the sign of the cross was made on their foreheads as a sign of identity and protection. They were then brought to the Supper of the Lamb. At Holy Communion, they participated for the first time in Christ's sacrificial meal. They received the Body, Blood, Soul, and Divinity of Jesus: *"For my flesh is true food, and my blood is true drink"* (John 6: 55). Dwelling in the house of the LORD for endless days is a pilgrimage of conversion, a journey into the heart of God through the visible mediation of the Church, the bride of Christ.

Reflect and Pray on Psalm 23, using Lectio Divina or the Method of Meditation. Make sure you converse intimately with the Blessed Trinity:

Prayer on Psalm 23: The Lord, Shepherd and Host
"1 A psalm of David.

I.

The LORD is my shepherd; there is nothing I lack. 2 In green pastures he makes me lie down; to still waters he leads me; 3 he restores my soul. He guides me along right paths for the sake of his name. 4 Even though I walk through the valley of the shadow of death, I will fear no evil, for you are with me; your rod and your staff comfort me.

II.

5 You set a table before me in front of my enemies; you anoint my head with oil; my cup overflows. 6 Indeed, goodness and mercy will pursue me all the days of my life; I will dwell in the house of the LORD for endless days."

End with Prayer to the Holy Trinity
NIGHT PRAYER: The Examination of Conscience

SUGGESTED SPIRITUAL READING FOR DAY 6:
John 10

DAY SEVEN:
MORNING PRAYER: Acts of Faith, Hope, Charity; Daily Offering

MORNING FACE TO FACE WITH GOD:
Learning Discipleship from the Psalms
Begin with Prayer to the Holy Spirit

- Psalm 8 offers us the opportunity to ponder the immense truth of the Divine Majesty's relationship to humans. The chasm between our Creator and His creatures is so infinite that the Psalmist gurgles sounds amounting to the prattle of babies and infants: *"O LORD, our Lord, how awesome is your name through all the earth! I will sing of your majesty above the heavens with the mouths of babes and infants."*
- Humans seem so puny compared to the grandeur of God's creation: *"When I see your heavens, the work of your fingers, the moon and stars that you set in place – what is man that you are mindful of him, and a son of man that you care for him?"* And yet, the Psalmist is equally amazed by the mind-numbing truth that the Divine Majesty has created us in His own image and likeness.
- Most especially, Psalm 8 has relevance in relationship to Jesus as it unveils a messianic prophecy made by David about *"a son of man"* who is little less than a god whom God has given mastery over the universe. Jesus was only a little less than God during His earthly life because He did not regard equality with God something to be grasped. Jesus called Himself the 'Son of Man' from Daniel 7: 13-14 which is a title for the Lord of the Universe.
- Psalm 15 addresses the required disposition of the pilgrim coming to visit the LORD in His house. Who was qualified to *"abide in your tent? Who may dwell on your holy mountain?"* Loving service of the neighbor was the requisite answer to

- these questions. These actions called for a serious commitment to holiness, striving with God's grace to act like a saint in every circumstance of life.
- Psalm 18 is virtually the same Psalm that David sang at the end of his life as recorded in 2Samuel 22: 2-51. David is looking back on his life. Despite all his failings, he had pursued a committed relationship to the LORD, and always remained profoundly grateful for God's numerous blessings and favors, especially for rescuing him from mortal dangers.
- God's love for David strengthened his decision to love and serve the LORD who delivered him so spectacularly time and time again: *"I was honest toward him; I was on guard against sin, so the LORD rewarded my righteousness, the cleanness of my hands in his sight."*
- Psalm 22 is probably the most gut-wrenching lament in the Psalter. While David is alluding to his own circumstances, more importantly, he is prophesying what the 'Son of David' would endure as He established the new kingdom of Israel, the Kingdom of God. On the cross, Jesus experienced the worst possible dregs of our sinful rebellion against God. In praying Psalm 22, Jesus was experiencing on our behalf this passage from our rebellious sin to abundant new life in His righteousness.
- *"For you drew me forth from the womb, made me safe at my mother's breasts. Upon you I was thrust from the womb; since my mother bore me you are my God."* These verses from Psalm 22 bridge the Annunciation and Birth of Jesus with His Crucifixion and sacrifice on the Cross. Mary, His mother, has played a significant role in this salvific passage. It brings to the fore Mary's seven sorrows, especially the last three which encompass her Calvary experience: standing beneath the cross, taking the dead Jesus into her arms, and burying Him. In order to save us, Jesus had to be drawn forth from a sinless human womb so that He, as Son of God, could be our worthy human representative before God

- The last verses of Psalm 22 allude to the resounding victory over Satan and sin that Jesus accomplished through His death and resurrection. The Son of God would suffer, die, and rise from the dead: *"All who sleep in the earth will bow low before God; all who have gone down into the dust will kneel in homage. And I will live for the LORD; my descendants will serve you. The generation to come will be told of the Lord, that they may proclaim to a people yet unborn the deliverance you have brought."*
- Jesus makes Psalm 23 a prophetic statement when He says He is the Good Shepherd: *"I am the good shepherd, and I know mine and mine know me, just as the Father knows me and I know the Father; and I will lay down my life for my sheep. I have other sheep that do not belong to this fold. This is why the Father loves me, because I lay down my life in order to take it up again"* (John 10: 14-18).
- For His sheep, Jesus will not hesitate to sacrifice Himself on the cross. Sheep need a watchful and devoted shepherd if they are to survive and thrive in the wild. We are aptly described as sheep because of the foolishness and danger of sin lurking in our hearts. Through His Holy Spirit, Jesus brings about our transformation so that we will know Him in the same way that the Father knows Him, and He knows the Father.

End with Prayer to the Holy Trinity
NIGHT PRAYER: The Examination of Conscience

JOURNAL FOR BOOK ONE, WEEK TWO: ABIDING TRUST IN DIRE STRAITS

<u>DAY ONE: Morning Prayer: Psalm 8: Divine Majesty and Human Dignity</u>
What is God saying to You?

<u>Nightly Examination of Conscience:</u>
For what are you grateful?

For what are you contrite?

What spiritual discipline, including fasting, do you need to focus on tomorrow?

<u>DAY TWO: Morning Prayer: Psalm 18: A King's Thanksgiving for Victory</u>
What is God saying to You?

<u>Nightly Examination of Conscience:</u>
For what are you grateful?

For what are you contrite?

What spiritual discipline, including fasting, do you need to focus on tomorrow?

DAY THREE: Morning Prayer: Psalm 19: God's Glory in the Heavens and in the Law
What is God saying to You?

Nightly Examination of Conscience:
For what are you grateful?

For what are you contrite?

What spiritual discipline, including fasting, do you need to focus on tomorrow?

DAY FOUR: Morning Prayer: Psalm 22: The Prayer of an Innocent Person
What is God saying to You?

Nightly Examination of Conscience:
For what are you grateful?

For what are you contrite?

What spiritual discipline, including fasting, do you need to focus on tomorrow?

DAY FIVE: Morning Prayer: Psalm 23: The Lord of Majesty acclaimed as King of the World
What is God saying to You?

Nightly Examination of Conscience:
For what are you grateful?

For what are you contrite?

What spiritual discipline, including fasting, do you need to focus on tomorrow?

DAY SIX: Morning Prayer: Psalm 24: The Glory of God in Procession to Zion
What is God saying to You?

Nightly Examination of Conscience:
For what are you grateful?

For what are you contrite?

What spiritual discipline, including fasting, do you need to focus on tomorrow?

DAY SEVEN: Morning Prayer: Learning Discipleship from the Psalms
What is God saying to You?

Nightly Examination of Conscience:
For what are you grateful?

For what are you contrite?

What spiritual discipline, including fasting, do you need to focus on tomorrow?

What prayer would you compose to express what God has said to you this week?

BOOK ONE – PSALMS 1-41: ABIDING TRUST IN DIRE STRAITS
Psalms 25, 26, 27, 28, 29, and 30

WHAT IS AT THE HEART OF BOOK ONE, WEEK THREE?

Psalms 25 to 30 are the six psalms that we will reflect on in Week Three. They offer us much insight into the blessings that could come to someone whose life has become a lament. They offer much mentoring in our covenant relationship with God. David composed some of them as songs of lament because he was in dire straits. His life was being threatened from his avowed enemies like King Saul, who constantly threatened his life and was pursuing him to the death. Or he was in spiritual crisis because of his sins and human weakness. In those difficult circumstances, he realized that only God could rescue him and bring him security and salvation. From his own experience, he came to see that God would always be his Good Shepherd, God's mercy would always be enduring, and in God he could place his complete trust and hope.

In dealing with suffering and danger, David came to understand that the sacrifice of thanksgiving or communion offering was the proper sacrifice to offer God. He came to see that discipleship evolved through a three-step process that is continually at work in a disciple's life. This process came to be known as the *Todah Cycle*. The cycle would begin when an Israelite experienced a crisis, getting into trouble because of their sins, or because of some economic or personal hardship. Such a crisis was endangering their lives. The next step would be to take their burdens to God, crying out for help and promising to make a thanksgiving offering, called the *todah,* when God answered their prayer. Most of the psalms of lament addressed the first step and moved in trust toward the second step. When God brought them relief and salvation, the devotee would take the third step. They would make a pilgrimage to the Temple to offer the thanksgiving sacrifice or *todah* and have a feast to praise and thank God publicly. Many of the psalms of thanksgiving and praise were composed for the thanksgiving sacrifice.

David preferred the thank offering (*todah*) over the burnt offering (*'ola'*). In the burnt offering, the entire animal was consumed in fire, and in the thank offering the animal was sacrificed and eaten in a meal of thanksgiving and praise. The *Todah Cycle* heralded the ultimate *Todah* or *Thanksgiving* Sacrifice that we celebrate as Eucharist! According to the ancient rabbis, with the coming of the Messiah, only the thanksgiving offering would continue. With the Messiah's victory over Satan and sin, sin offerings would be unnecessary.

We will also reflect on psalms that extol the majesty and kingship of the Lord. God established a covenant with David and his sons and asserted that the Davidic Dynasty would last forever. Even though the Davidic kingship collapsed in 587 B.C. leading to the destruction of the Temple and the Monarchy, God's prophecy remained true. It was fulfilled in Jesus who was both the son of David and the Son of God, through His death and resurrection. David was God's anointed one in his time, prefiguring Jesus, the everlasting Anointed One of God!

On Day One, we will pray with *Psalm 25: Confident Prayer for Forgiveness and Guidance.* It is an acrostic psalm as each verse begins with a successive letter of the Hebrew alphabet. It is a psalm of lament. Psalm 25 teaches us to not stop believing and trusting God, especially when life becomes hard and seems meaningless. When we obey God, we will always experience the Divine Presence with His love and compassion.

On Day Two, we will reflect prayerfully on *Psalm 26: Prayer of Innocence.* Some suggest that the psalm is the prayer of a forgiven sinner who is now living in an intimate, honest, and transparent relationship with God. Hence, without hesitation David is agreeable to asking God to do his inventory. The devoted disciple does a daily examination of conscience, desiring that obedience to God's will and integrity of conscience will flavor each day. This disposition buttresses a closer walk with the Lord.

On Day Three, we will ponder *Psalm 27: Trust in God.* David offers us some salutary advice as to how we are to live as disciples of Jesus. David is encouraging us to seek the LORD always, in every circumstance. In our case, as followers of Jesus, it is to be living temples of the Blessed Trinity. Even in very bleak circumstances, the Psalmist exhorts us to *"Wait for the LORD, take courage; be stouthearted, wait for the LORD!"*

On Day Four, we will pray with *Psalm 28: Petition and Thanksgiving.* The kingdom of Israel is God's inheritance. God will therefore safeguard it jealously. Furthermore, the Psalmist projects God as the Good Shepherd who carries His people on His shoulders! In the first centuries of Christianity, the image of Jesus carrying His sheep on His shoulders was in vogue before the crucifix became the standard Catholic symbol.

On Day Five, we will reflect and pray with *Psalm 29: The Lord of Majesty, acclaimed as King of the World.* David is acclaiming the Majesty and power of God amidst a terrifying storm. He begins the psalm with a grand choral entry of the whole heavenly court, the sons of God or the angels, offering praise and glory to Israel's God whom they serve. Psalm 29 ends with a picture of the calm *after* the storm. There is devastation all around, mystifying and awe-inspiring. But nature then begins its return to being re-created and restored. Gradually, everything seems to be back in order. Amidst devastation and destruction, the believer knows that God is in charge and has their back covered. The LORD is in control, enthroned as King in heaven, blessing the people with peace.

On Day Six, we will ponder *Psalm 30: Thanksgiving for Deliverance.* The Introduction, 'A song for the dedication of the Temple,' tells us that it came to have a specific purpose in liturgical worship. Psalm 30 highlights the significance of the Jerusalem Temple for God's people. The Temple was the living expression of the covenant relationship between God and His people, enshrined in the enduring presence of God in the Holy of

Holies, leading to praise and worship of the LORD through sacrificial offerings and prayers of praise, thanksgiving, and petition, and always having the assurance of God's promises to Israel being inviolable. God's covenant with His people remained steadfast, especially in perilous times.

On Day Seven, we will ponder the salient advice that these psalms have offered us to enhance and strengthen our own following of Jesus and our commitment to His Church.

SPIRITUAL READING FOR BOOK ONE OF THE PSALMS:
1 and 2 Samuel
Psalms 1 to 41
1 and 2 Kings (after you have read 1 and 2 Samuel)
1 and 2 Chronicles (after you have read 1 and 2 Kings)

DAY ONE:
MORNING PRAYER: Acts of Faith, Hope, Charity; Daily Offering

MORNING FACE TO FACE WITH GOD:
Begin with Prayer to the Holy Spirit

Prayer on Psalm 25: Confident Prayer for Forgiveness and Guidance

Psalm 25 is an acrostic psalm as each verse begins with a successive letter of the Hebrew alphabet. Acrostic psalms, in general, offer a series of statements that are only loosely connected. Since Psalm 25 is a lament, we can assume that David composed it when he was in crisis.

In the first division, David asks God for help against his enemies: *"To you, O LORD, I lift up my soul, my God, in you I trust; do not let me be disgraced; do not let my enemies gloat over me."* He is assured that all will be well with him because he has chosen the path of righteousness: *"No one is disgraced who waits for you, but only those who are treacherous without cause."* David knows that all would be well with him if he relied on God and walked in the way of the just. He seeks to be an ardent disciple, wanting to be tutored by God: *"Make known to me your ways, LORD; teach me your paths. Guide me by your fidelity and teach me, for you are God my savior, for you I wait all the day long."*

David also knows he is a sinner, and he receives assurance from the fact that God's mercy is constant and ageless: *"Remember your compassion and your mercy, O LORD, for they are ages old. Remember no more the sins of my youth; remember me according to your mercy, because of your goodness, LORD."* Indeed, the Psalmist's reflections on his relationship with God are loosely connected with one another.

In the second division, David highlights the importance of a disciple always having a spirit of repentance and fear of the Lord. The Lord can only teach those who are contrite of heart and submissive to His ways: *"He guides the humble in righteousness, and teaches the humble his way... The counsel of the LORD belongs to those who fear him; and his covenant instructs them. My eyes are ever upon the LORD, who frees my feet from the snare."* In God's holy presence, we are convicted of our sins without being condemned, as we know we have been forgiven.

In the third division, David continues to pour out his heart to God, sharing his great anxiety and fear while reiterating his trust and hope in God. His answer to all his woes is to wait for God: *"Relieve the troubles of my heart; bring me out of my distress. Look upon my affliction and suffering; take away all my sins... Let integrity and uprightness preserve me; I wait for you, O LORD."* In living with integrity and uprightness, God's protective presence will be made manifest.

In the last verse, David offers a plea to God on behalf of Israel: *"Redeem Israel, O God, from all its distress."* The king and his kingdom were joined at the hip. The endangerment of the one was the endangerment of the other, and vice versa. As God's anointed one, David is asking for God's redemption from all evildoers. Psalm 25 teaches us to not stop believing and trusting God, especially when life becomes hard and seems meaningless. When we obey God, we will always experience the Divine Presence with His encompassing love and compassion. As Jesus said, *"And behold, I am with you always, until the end of the age"* (Matthew 28: 20).

Reflect and Pray on Psalm 25, using Lectio Divina or the Method of Meditation. Make sure you converse intimately with the Blessed Trinity:

Prayer on Psalm 25: Confident Prayer for Forgiveness and Guidance
"1 Of David.

I.

To you, O LORD, I lift up my soul, 2 my God, in you I trust; do not let me be disgraced; do not let my enemies gloat over me. 3 No one is disgraced who waits for you, but only those who are treacherous without cause. 4 Make known to me your ways, LORD; teach me your paths. 5 Guide me by your fidelity and teach me, for you are God my savior, for you I wait all day long. 6 Remember your compassion and your mercy, O LORD, for they are ages old. 7 Remember no more the sins of my youth; remember me according to your mercy, because of your goodness, LORD.

II.

8 Good and upright is the LORD, therefore he shows sinners the way, 9 He guides the humble in righteousness, and teaches the humble his way. 10 All the paths of the LORD are mercy and truth toward those who honor his covenant and decrees. 11 For the sake of your name, LORD, pardon my guilt, though it is great. 12 Who is the one who fears the LORD? God shows him the way he should choose. 13 He will abide in prosperity, and his descendants will inherit the land. 14 The counsel of the LORD belongs to those who fear him; and his covenant instructs them. 15 My eyes are ever upon the LORD, who frees my feet from the snare.

III.

16 Look upon me, have pity on me, for I am alone and afflicted. 17 Relieve the troubles of my heart; bring me out of my distress. 18 Look upon my affliction and suffering; take away all my sins. 19 See how many are my enemies, see how fiercely they hate me. 20 Preserve my soul and rescue me; do not let me be disgraced, for in you I seek refuge. 21 Let integrity and uprightness preserve me; I wait for you, O LORD. 22 Redeem Israel, O God, from all its distress."

End with Prayer to the Holy Trinity
NIGHT PRAYER: The Examination of Conscience

DAY TWO:
MORNING PRAYER: Acts of Faith, Hope, Charity; Daily Offering
MORNING FACE TO FACE WITH GOD:
Begin with Prayer to the Holy Spirit
Prayer on Psalm 26: Prayer of Innocence

    Some suggest that Psalm 26, a song of lament, is the prayer of a forgiven sinner who is now living in an intimate, honest, and transparent relationship with God. Hence, without hesitation David is agreeable to asking God to do his inventory. In the first segment, David professes his integrity before the Lord: *"Judge me, LORD! For I have walked in integrity. In the LORD I trust; I do not falter. Examine me, Lord, and test me; search my heart and mind. Your mercy is before my eyes; I walk guided by your faithfulness."* David has been tutored by the Lord over many years. He has developed a relationship with God that has tested and purified him through many trials. David is at home with God and with himself. When he sinned, he always returned to God in repentance and was made clean and whole once again. It is from this place of wellbeing with God and himself that David is pouring out his heart about his integrity. He lives in integrity because of God's constant mercy toward him. He is guided by God's faithfulness. He is a forgiven sinner whose soul is well with God.

    In the second segment, David introduces evidence to support his claim that he is a man of integrity. His first proof is, *"I hate an evil assembly; with the wicked I do not sit."* He has rejected the path of the wicked. His second piece of evidence is, *"I will wash my hands in innocence so that I may process around your altar, Lord, to hear the sound of thanksgiving, and recount all your wondrous deeds."* The washing of the hands was a liturgical act signifying cleanness of heart. It was performed by Aaron and his sons (Exodus 30: 20-21), and later by the king and priests when they offered sacrifice. During Mass, the priest goes through a similar ablution after the Presentation of the Gifts and before the Preface. David's fourth piece of evidence is, *"Lord, I love the refuge of your house, the site of the dwelling-place of your glory."* In God's presence, we experience radiation therapy. The divine rays of God's Presence and love permeate our beings, transforming us from being sinners to becoming saints. David loved being with God in the Temple!

In the third segment, David makes a plea for God's mercy: *"Do not take me away with sinners, nor my life with the men of blood, in whose hands there is a plot, their right hands full of bribery."* He prays that he will continue to choose the path of the just and shun the way of the wicked:

"But I walk in my integrity; redeem me, be gracious to me!" Psalm 26 concludes with a prayer: *"My foot stands on level ground; in assemblies I will bless the LORD."* This delightful composition reflects the humble yet confident peace that resides within the honest soul who is seriously attempting to walk with their Redeemer. The devoted disciple does a daily examination of conscience, so that obedience to God's will and integrity of conscience will flavor each day.

Reflect and Pray on Psalm 26, using Lectio Divina or the Method of Meditation. Make sure you converse intimately with the Blessed Trinity:

Prayer on Psalm 26: Prayer of Innocence
"1 Of David.

I.

Judge me, LORD! For I have walked in integrity. In the LORD I trust; I do not falter. 2 Examine me, Lord, and test me; search my heart and mind. 3 Your mercy is before my eyes; I walk guided by your faithfulness.

II.

4 I do not sit with worthless men, nor with hypocrites do I mingle. 5 I hate an evil assembly; with the wicked I do not sit. 6 I will wash my hands in innocence so that I may process around your altar, Lord, 7 to hear the sound of thanksgiving, and recount all your wondrous deeds. 8 Lord, I love the refuge of your house, the site of the dwelling-place of your glory.

III.

9 Do not take me away with sinners, nor my life with the men of blood, 10 in whose hands there is a plot, their right hands full of bribery. 11. But I walk in my integrity; redeem me, be gracious to me! 12. My foot stands on level ground; in assemblies I will bless the LORD.

End with Prayer to the Holy Trinity
NIGHT PRAYER: The Examination of Conscience

DAY THREE:
MORNING PRAYER: Acts of Faith, Hope, Charity; Daily Offering

MORNING FACE TO FACE WITH GOD:
Begin with Prayer to the Holy Spirit
Prayer on Psalm 27: Trust in God

David offers us some salutary advice as to how we are to live as disciples of Jesus. In Part A, David is enjoying much consolation and favor with God. His trust and confidence in God are unassailable. He has experienced much strength from God amidst adverse circumstances. One such time of consolation was after he slew Goliath (1Samuel 17): *"The LORD is my light and my salvation; whom should I fear? The LORD is my life's refuge; of whom should I be afraid? When evildoers come at me to devour my flesh, these my enemies and foes themselves stumble and fall. Though an army encamp against me, my heart does not fear; though war be waged against me, even then do I trust."*

Such a state of consolation produces many holy thoughts and desires in David. He desires to be with God all the time, and knows as well that God will be with him in every circumstance of his life: *"One thing I ask of the LORD; this I seek: To dwell in the LORD's house all the days of my life, to gaze on the LORD's beauty, to visit his temple. For God will hide me in his shelter in time of trouble, He will conceal me in the cover of his tent; and set me high upon a rock... I will offer in his tent sacrifices with shouts of joy; I will sing and chant praise to the LORD."*

David wants nothing more than to be with God. Echoing St. Augustine, David's heart is restless unless it rests in God! David longs to visit God in His temple where He was present as

Emmanuel, among His people and with David. As followers of Jesus, we have been made into His temple, an abode where the Blessed Trinity dwells. David is encouraging us to seek the LORD always, in every circumstance. As followers of Jesus, we are to be living temples of the Blessed Trinity.

In Part B, David is instructing us about how we are to behave in time of desolation, when life has become difficult, either the result of our own sinfulness, or the problems that our human relationships bring to us. David advises us to never stop asking the Lord to be with us, even when we feel that He is distant and does not hear our plea: *""Come," says my heart, "seek his face"; your face, LORD, do I seek! Do not hide your face from me; do not repel your servant in anger."* We can hold on to our conviction that God will come to our rescue because He has always been faithful to us in the past and there is no reason why He will not continue to be faithful in the present. Against all odds, we can still have hope in God's love and compassion: *"You are my salvation; do not cast me off; do not forsake me, God my savior! Even if my father and mother forsake me, the LORD will take me in."*

David's faith and trust in God remain undeterred and he is convinced that *"I shall see the LORD's goodness in the land of the living."* 'The land of the living' is an epithet for the Jerusalem Temple where the people experienced God's goodness and love, where David always found rest and security. In his fugitive years, David longed for *'the land of the living.'* Because of his confidence in God's help even when circumstances are very bleak, the Psalmist exhorts to us *"Wait for the LORD, take courage; be stouthearted, wait for the LORD!"*

Reflect and Pray on Psalm 27, using Lectio Divina or the Method of Meditation. Make sure you converse intimately with the Blessed Trinity:

Prayer on Psalm 27: Trust in God
"1 Of David.

A.I.

1 The LORD is my light and my salvation; whom should I fear?

The LORD is my life's refuge; of whom should I be afraid? 2 When evildoers come at me to devour my flesh, these my enemies and foes themselves stumble and fall. 3 Though an army encamp against me, my heart does not fear; though war be waged against me, even then do I trust.

II.

4 One thing I ask of the LORD; this I seek: To dwell in the LORD's house all the days of my life, to gaze on the LORD's beauty, to visit his temple. 5 For God will hide me in his shelter in time of trouble, He will conceal me in the cover of his tent; and set me high upon a rock. 6 Even now my head is held high above my enemies on every side! I will offer in his tent sacrifices with shouts of joy; I will sing and chant praise to the LORD

B. 1.

7 Hear my voice, LORD, when I call; have mercy on me and answer me. 8 "Come," says my heart, "seek his face"; your face, LORD, do I seek! 9 Do not hide your face from me; do not repel your servant in anger. 10 Even if my father and mother forsake me, the LORD will take me in.

II.

11 LORD, show me your way; lead me on a level path because of my enemies. Do not abandon me to the desire of my foes; malicious and lying witnesses have risen against me. 13 I believe I shall see the LORD's goodness in the land of the living. 14 Wait for the LORD, take courage; be stouthearted, wait for the LORD!"

End with Prayer to the Holy Trinity
NIGHT PRAYER: The Examination of Conscience

DAY FOUR:
MORNING PRAYER: Acts of Faith, Hope, Charity; Daily Offering

MORNING FACE TO FACE WITH GOD:
Begin with Prayer to the Holy Spirit

Prayer on Psalm 28: Petition and Thanksgiving

The end of Psalm 28 tells us that the King and the Kingdom of Israel were in danger. When God's anointed one was in danger, the whole kingdom too was in danger, and vice versa: *"LORD, you are a strength for your people, the saving refuge of your anointed. Save your people, bless your inheritance; pasture and carry them forever!"* The Psalmist sees the kingdom of Israel as being God's inheritance. God will therefore safeguard it jealously. Furthermore, the Psalmist projects God as the Good Shepherd of His people who carries them on His shoulder! In the first centuries of Christianity, the image of Jesus carrying His sheep on His shoulders was in vogue before the crucifix became the standard symbol of Catholicism.

Given the difficult straits that the kingdom was in, the Psalmist makes an urgent plea to God: *"Hear the sound of my pleading when I cry to you for help, when I lift up my hands toward your holy place."* The *'holy place'* was the holy of holies where God dwelled in the Ark of the Covenant. When the Jews prayed, they lifted up their hands. Basically, they were lifting themselves up to God in offering and surrender. We do the same in our liturgy and prayer. The Temple was a very holy place for Israel and for David. That is where God spoke to His anointed one. His 73 psalms attest to this significant relationship with God.

David is loath to be cast among the wicked because they do not have God's worldview: *"Do not drag me off with the wicked, with those who do wrong, who speak peace to their neighbors though evil is in their hearts... because they do not understand the LORD's works, the work of his hands."* Psalm One, acting as the Preface to the Psalter, presents the way of following God's law versus choosing the way of the wicked. It makes its presence felt in this psalm.

The whole tone of the psalm changes in the second half. The Lord has answered David's earnest plea. The Lord is a strength both for His people and for His anointed one: *"The LORD is my strength and my shield, in whom my heart trusts. I am helped, so my heart rejoices; with my song I proclaim him."* David was God's anointed one in his time. Centuries later, Jesus, the 'Son of David,' would be God's Anointed One. As the Lord was the 'saving refuge' of David, in the same way, He became the saving refuge of

His Son, Jesus: *"LORD, you are a strength for your people, the saving refuge of your anointed. Save your people, bless your inheritance; pasture and carry them forever!"*

Reflect and Pray on Psalm 28, using Lectio Divina or the Method of Meditation. Make sure you converse intimately with the Blessed Trinity:

Prayer on Psalm 28: Petition and Thanksgiving
"1 Of David.

I.

To you, LORD, I call; my Rock, do not be deaf to me, do not be silent toward me, so that I join those who go down to the pit. 2 Hear the sound of my pleading when I cry to you for help when I lift up my hands toward your holy place. 3 Do not drag me off with the wicked, with those who do wrong, who speak peace to their neighbors through evil is in their hearts. 4 Repay them for their deeds, for the evil that they do. For the work of their hands repay them; give them what they deserve. 5 Because they do not understand the LORD's works, the work of his hands, he will tear them down never to rebuild them.

II.

6 Blessed be the LORD, who has heard the sound of my pleading. 7 The LORD is my strength and my shield, in whom my heart trusts. I am helped, so my heart rejoices; with my song I praise him.

III.

8 LORD, you are a strength for your people, the saving refuge of your anointed. 9 Save your people, bless your inheritance; pasture and carry them forever!"

End with Prayer to the Holy Trinity
NIGHT PRAYER: The Examination of Conscience

DAY FIVE:
MORNING PRAYER: Acts of Faith, Hope, Charity; Daily Offering

MORNING FACE TO FACE WITH GOD:
Begin with Prayer to the Holy Spirit
Psalm 29: The Lord of Majesty Acclaimed as King of the World

David spent many years out in the open, when he was

shepherding his sheep during the day and in the night. He also spent many years in the wilderness as a fugitive, hiding and running away from Saul and his enemies, and later as king, from his own son Absalom. In Psalm 29, he is acclaiming the Majesty and power of God during a terrifying storm. He begins the psalm with a grand choral entry of the whole heavenly court, the sons of God or the angels, offering praise and glory to Israel's God whom they serve: *"Give to the LORD, you sons of God, give to the LORD glory and might; give to the LORD the glory due his name. Bow down before the LORD's holy splendor."*

The psalm follows the typical pattern of a hymn of praise. The Psalmist voices multiple calls to praise God in the manifestation of His might and power in nature, and they are all proclaimed in an emphatic tone. The one praying the psalm is drawn into doing the Psalmist's bidding: *"The voice of the LORD is over the waters; the God of glory thunders, the LORD, over the mighty waters. The voice of the LORD is power, the voice of the LORD is splendor. The voice of the LORD cracks the cedars of Lebanon, makes Lebanon leap like a calf, and Sirion like a young bull. The voice of the LORD strikes with fiery flame; the voice of the LORD shakes the desert; the LORD shakes the desert of Kadesh. The voice of the LORD makes the deer dance and strips the forest bare. All in his Temple say, "Glory!"* Amidst furious divine activity, the Psalmist is stunned into eerie silence, until one hears the word of praise, *"Glory,"* from the Psalmist and congregation gathered in the temple. In Psalm 29, the focus is on the mighty acts of God in His creation. Psalms 105 and 106, for instance, focus on the mighty acts of God in the history of salvation. There is an intimate connection between God as Creator and God as Redeemer. He created us at the center of His majestic universe because He wanted a covenant relationship with us. Hence, His merciful redemption will be everlastingly enduring.

The psalms focus on the divine glory being manifest in creation and the wondrous deeds of salvation. Psalm 29 speaks of God's glory as the external manifestation of His being in creation, as well as His glory as displayed in His Kingly rule: *"The LORD sits enthroned above the flood! The LORD reigns as king forever!"* In other psalms, 'glory' is spoken of as the power and grandeur of God's presence as in Psalm 96, or as God's clothing, as in Psalm 93. On occasion, the heavens are viewed as manifesting God's glory as in Psalm 113.

Psalm 29 ends with a picture of the calm *after* the storm. There is devastation all around, mystifying and awe-inspiring. But nature then begins its return to being re-created and restored. Gradually, everything seems to be back in order. In the throes of devastation and destruction, the believer knows that God is in charge and has their back covered. The LORD is in control, enthroned as King in heaven, blessing the people with peace: *"The LORD reigns as king forever! May the LORD give might to his people; may the LORD bless his people with peace!"*

Reflect and Pray on Psalm 29, using Lectio Divina or the Method of Meditation. Make sure you converse intimately with the Blessed Trinity:

Psalm 29: The Lord of Majesty Acclaimed as King of the World
"1 A psalm of David.

I.

Give to the LORD, you sons of God, give to the LORD glory and might; 2 Give to the LORD the glory due his name. Bow down before the LORD's holy splendor!

II.

3 The voice of the LORD is over the waters; the God of glory thunders, the LORD, over the mighty waters; the God of glory thunders, the LORD, over the mighty waters. 4 The voice of the LORD is power; the voice of the LORD is splendor. 5 The voice of the LORD cracks the cedars; the LORD splinters the cedars of Lebanon, 6 makes Lebanon leap like a calf, and Sirion like a young bull. 7 The voice of the LORD strikes with fiery flame; 8 the voice of the LORD shakes the desert of Kadesh. 9 The voice of the LORD makes the deer dance and strips the forest bare. All in his Temple say, "Glory!"

III.
10 The LORD sits enthroned above the flood! The LORD reigns as king forever! 11 May the LORD give might to his people; may the LORD bless his people with peace!"

End with Prayer to the Holy Trinity
NIGHT PRAYER: The Examination of Conscience

DAY SIX:
MORNING PRAYER: Acts of Faith, Hope, Charity; Daily Offering

MORNING FACE TO FACE WITH GOD:
Begin with Prayer to the Holy Spirit

Prayer on Psalm 30: Thanksgiving for Deliverance

The Introduction to Psalm 30, *'A song for the dedication of the Temple,'* tells us that it came to be given a specific purpose in liturgical worship. The dedication of the First Temple took place under King Solomon, after King David's death (1Kings 8: 63). The dedication of the second Temple took place around 515 B.C., under Ezra and Nehemiah, after the Israelites returned from exile in Babylon (Ezra 6: 16). The second Temple was rededicated during the Maccabean era (1Maccabees 4) in 164 B.C., when Antiochus Epiphanes, a Greek ruler, had desecrated the Temple. Psalm 30 was probably given the important function of being used for the dedication of the Temple by religious leaders other than David. David's personal hardships referred to in the psalm, were similar in nature to the crisis engendered by the desecration and destruction of the Temple.

Psalm 30 highlights the significance of the Jerusalem Temple for God's people. The Temple was the living expression of the covenant relationship between God and His people, enshrined in the enduring presence of God in the Holy of Holies. God's presence among His people led to praise and worship of the LORD through sacrificial offerings and prayers of praise, thanksgiving, and petition. Because of this covenant relationship with God, Israel always had the assurance that God's promises to His people would remain inviolable.

God's covenant with His people remained steadfast especially in perilous times. The Psalmist begins the psalm with praise: *"I praise you, LORD, for you raised me up and did not let my enemies rejoice over me. O LORD, my God, I cried out to you for help and you healed me. LORD, you brought my soul up from Sheol; you let me live, from going down to the pit."* God is worthy of praise and gratitude for raising the Psalmist up, healing him, and restoring his life. The Psalmist then shifts the focus from his own rescue and safety and invites the gathered community in the Temple to praise the LORD: *"Sing praise to the LORD, you faithful; give thanks to his holy memory. For his anger lasts but a moment; his favor a lifetime."* The Psalmist offers some salutary advice for the disciple who wishes to grow in holiness. God will convict us of our sins, and at times the conviction will be excruciating. However, God will never condemn us, as His favor lasts a lifetime! So, we can always give thanks *"to his holy memory."* In the next verse, the Psalmist reminds us that God will never abandon us. If it appears to be that way, it will only be a temporary phase: *"at dusk weeping comes for the night; but at down there is rejoicing."*

In the third segment, the Psalmist asks us to be cautious about complacency and arrogance in the spiritual life. We will easily be led to build on the property of another, attributing to ourselves what essentially belongs to God: *"Complacent, I once said, "I shall never be shaken." LORD, you showed me favor, established for me mountains of virtue. But when you hid your face I was struck with terror. To you, LORD, I cried out; with the Lord I pleaded for mercy."* When God strips us of our complacency and arrogance, our enthusiasm and rejoicing are deflated. Suddenly, our dancing turns into mourning. It is only God who can hear our anguished plea and return us to our state of peace and rest with Him: *"Hear, O LORD, have mercy on me; LORD, be my helper."*

In the fourth and last segment, the Psalmist talks about God answering his prayer by showing him favor, and once again establishing for him *"mountains of virtue."* The Psalmist has been brought back into God's good graces: *"You changed my mourning into dancing; you took off my sackcloth and clothed me with gladness... O LORD, my God, forever will I give you thanks."* David's final burst of praise and thanksgiving has a sober lining to it. The Holy Spirit has taught him a valuable lesson in the spiritual life. He has been chastened and humbled by God's conviction of his arrogance and complacency. In the future, he will hold God as the sole architect of his discipleship. As John the Baptist said, *"He must increase and I must decrease"* (John 3: 30).

Reflect and Pray on Psalm 30, using Lectio Divina or the Method of Meditation. Make sure you converse intimately with the Blessed Trinity:

Prayer on Psalm 30: Thanksgiving for Deliverance
"1 A psalm. A song for the dedication of the Temple. Of David.

I.

2 I praise you, LORD, for you raised me up and did not let my enemies rejoice over me. 3 O LORD, my God, I cried out to you for help and you healed me. 4 LORD, you brought my soul up from Sheol; you let me live, from going down to the pit.

II.

5 Sing praise to the LORD, you faithful; give thanks to his holy memory. 6 For his anger lasts but a moment; his favor a lifetime. At dusk weeping comes for the night; but at dawn there is rejoicing.

III.

7 Complacent, I once said, "I shall never be shaken." 8 LORD, you showed me favor, established for me mountains of virtue. But when you hid your face I was struck with terror. 9 To you, LORD, I cried out; with the Lord I pleaded for mercy; 10 "What gain is there from my lifeblood, from my going down to the grave? Does dust give you thanks or declare your faithfulness? 11 Hear, O LORD, have mercy on me; LORD, be my helper."

IV.

12 You changed my mourning into dancing; you took off my sackcloth and clothed me with gladness. 13 So that my glory may praise you and not be silent. O LORD, my God, forever will I give you thanks."

End with Prayer to the Holy Trinity
NIGHT PRAYER: The Examination of Conscience

DAY SEVEN:
MORNING PRAYER: Acts of Faith, Hope, Charity; Daily Offering

MORNING FACE TO FACE WITH GOD:
<u>Learning Discipleship from the Psalms</u>
Begin with Prayer to the Holy Spirit

- In Psalm 25, David highlights the importance of a disciple always having a spirit of repentance and fear of the Lord. The Lord can only teach those who are contrite of heart and submissive to His ways. In God's holy presence, we are convicted of our sins without being condemned, as we know we have been forgiven.

- Psalm 25 teaches us to not stop believing and trusting God, especially when life becomes hard and seems meaningless. When we obey God, we will always experience the Divine Presence with His love and compassion. As Jesus said, *"And behold, I am with you always, until the end of the age"* (Matthew 28: 20).

- Psalm 26 is the prayer of a forgiven sinner who is now living in an intimate, honest, and transparent relationship with God. Hence, without hesitation David is agreeable to asking God to do his inventory. David has been tutored by the Lord over many years. When he sinned, he always returned to God in repentance and was made clean and whole once again.

- Psalm 26 reflects the humble yet confident peace that resides within the honest soul who is seriously attempting to walk with their Redeemer. The devoted disciple does a daily examination of conscience, so that obedience to God's will and integrity of conscience will flavor each day.

- In Psalm 27, David is encouraging us to seek the LORD always, in every circumstance. In our case, as followers of Jesus it is to be living temples of the Blessed Trinity. Because of his confidence in God's help even when circumstances are very bleak, the Psalmist exhorts us to *"Wait for the LORD, take courage; be stouthearted, wait for the LORD!"*

- In time of desolation, either the result of our own sinfulness or the problems that our human relationships bring to us, David advises us to never stop asking the Lord to be with us, even when we feel that He is distant and does not hear our plea. God will come to our rescue because He has always been faithful to us in the past and there is no reason why He will not continue to be faithful in the present.
- In Psalm 28, the kingdom of Israel is God's inheritance. God will therefore safeguard it jealously. Similarly, Jesus will safeguard the Church as His 'Body,' till the end of time. Furthermore, the Psalmist projects God as the Good Shepherd of His people who carries them on His shoulder! In the first centuries of Christianity, the image of Jesus carrying His sheep on his shoulders was in vogue before the crucifix became the standard symbol of Catholicism.
- In Psalm 29, David is acclaiming the Majesty and power of God during a terrifying storm. There is devastation all around, mystifying, and awe-inspiring. In the throes of devastation and destruction, the believer knows that the LORD is in control, enthroned as King in heaven, blessing His people with peace.
- Psalm 30 highlights the significance of the Jerusalem Temple for God's people. The Temple was the living expression of the covenant relationship between God and His people, enshrined in the enduring presence of God in the Holy of Holies, leading to praise and worship of the LORD through sacrificial offerings and prayers of praise, thanksgiving, and petition, and always having the assurance of God's promises to Israel being inviolable.

End with Prayer to the Holy Trinity
NIGHT PRAYER: The Examination of Conscience

JOURNAL FOR BOOK ONE, WEEK THREE: ABIDING TRUST IN DIRE STRAITS

<u>DAY ONE: Morning Prayer: Psalm 25: Confident Prayer for Forgiveness and Guidance</u>
What is God saying to You?

<u>Nightly Examination of Conscience:</u>
For what are you grateful?

For what are you contrite?

What spiritual discipline, including fasting, do you need to focus on tomorrow?

<u>DAY TWO: Morning Prayer: Psalm 26: Prayer of Innocence</u>
What is God saying to You?

<u>Nightly Examination of Conscience:</u>
For what are you grateful?

For what are you contrite?

What spiritual discipline, including fasting, do you need to focus on tomorrow?

DAY THREE: Morning Prayer: Psalm 27: Trust in God
What is God saying to You?

Nightly Examination of Conscience:
For what are you grateful?

For what are you contrite?

What spiritual discipline, including fasting, do you need to focus on tomorrow?

DAY FOUR: Morning Prayer: Psalm 28: Petition and Thanksgiving
What is God saying to You?

Nightly Examination of Conscience:
For what are you grateful?

For what are you contrite?

What spiritual discipline, including fasting, do you need to focus on tomorrow?

DAY FIVE: Morning Prayer: Psalm 29: The Lord of Majesty, King of the World
What is God saying to You?

Nightly Examination of Conscience:
For what are you grateful?

For what are you contrite?

What spiritual discipline, including fasting, do you need to focus on tomorrow?

DAY SIX: Morning Prayer: Psalm 30: Thanksgiving for Deliverance
What is God saying to You?

Nightly Examination of Conscience:
For what are you grateful?

For what are you contrite?

What spiritual discipline, including fasting, do you need to focus on tomorrow?

DAY SEVEN: Morning Prayer: Learning Discipleship from the Psalms
What is God saying to You?

Nightly Examination of Conscience:
For what are you grateful?

For what are you contrite?

What spiritual discipline, including fasting, do you need to focus on tomorrow?

What prayer would you compose to express what God has said to you this week?

BOOK ONE – PSALMS 1-41:
ABIDING TRUST IN DIRE STRAITS
Psalms 32, 33, 36, 38, 39, and 41

WHAT IS AT THE HEART OF BOOK ONE, WEEK FOUR?

The six psalms of Week Four continue to develop the theme of Book One, *'Abiding Trust in Dire Straits.'* We will ponder Psalms 32, 33, 36, 38, 39, and 41. On Day One, we will pray with *Psalm 32: Remission of Sin*. Psalm 32 is the second of seven Penitential Psalms. Like the others, Psalm 32 is about sin and guilt and confidence in receiving God's mercy because of a repentant heart. Repentance truly leads to forgiveness from God resulting in a heart cleansed of deceit and doubt. True joy is about being forgiven and totally accepted and loved by God.

On Day Two, we will reflect prayerfully on *Psalm 33: Praise of God's Power and Providence*. Psalm 33 is a call to praise God in a liturgical setting. The righteous are directed to rejoice, give thanks, and sing to the Lord for a two-fold reason, to praise the word of the LORD, and give thanks for His works which are trustworthy. Psalm 33 highlights the important message of Book One, where even though one's life can be in dire straits, there is always cause for thanksgiving and praise for God's creation and providence, and for His revealed word to us. Encouraged by David's example, the forgiven sinner will develop a worldview where repentance, indeed, becomes the key that unlocks the rich treasures of God's merciful heart.

On Day Three, we will ponder *Psalm 36: Human Wickedness and Divine Providence*. The psalm contains elements characteristic of a lament or call for help, with a complaint, an expression of praise and trust in God, and a cry for deliverance from the 'wicked.' Psalm 36 raises a question whose answer is begun in the Old Testament and completed in the New Testament. In this psalm and several others, David and other Psalmists invoke God's wrath and vengeance on their enemies. They view their own enemies as being God's enemies as they profess the 'way of the wicked,' as contrasted with the 'way of the just' which is the lifestyle of David and the Psalmists. They are confident that even though their enemies are more powerful than they are, that God is far superior and more powerful and will vanquish them and vindicate His people. It is left then to God to deal with them in His justice.

In the light of the New Testament, the question arises whether there is any element of forgiveness and mercy in the Psalmists toward their enemies. In some psalms, the psalmist's plea is that the wicked will see the error of their ways and reform themselves. Even though Saul and Absalom were his avowed enemies, David did not kill Saul when he had a chance and pleaded with Joab, the Commander-in-Chief, to spare his son Absalom when he was captured in battle. It is Jesus, the last royal son of David, and Son of God, who gives us the complete answer about love and forgiveness of our enemies, through His own teaching and behavior. While He hung on the cross, He asked His Father to *'to forgive them for they know not what they do.'*

On Day Four, we will pray with *Psalm 38: Prayer of an Afflicted Sinner,* a Penitential Psalm. It is a song full of pain and dark with guilt, as David felt the sore effects, both physical and spiritual, of his sin.

On Day Five, we will reflect and pray with *Psalm 39: The Vanity of Life*. This psalm can act as an honest and sober inventory of one's life, leading to a meaningful lifestyle centered on God rather than on a life of frivolity and dissipation because the pleasures of this world have become the obsession of one's life.

On Day Six, we will ponder *Psalm 41: Thanksgiving after Sickness*. Psalm 41 is the last psalm in Book One. The Psalmist's thanksgiving springs from the fact that God is greatly concerned for the poor. God listens to the cry of the poor even though they have sinned, because the petitioner is repentant and trusting of God's loving kindness.

On Day Seven, we will ponder the salient advice that these psalms have offered us to enhance and strengthen our own following of Jesus and our commitment to His Church.

SPIRITUAL READING FOR BOOK ONE OF THE PSALMS:
1 and 2 Samuel
Psalms 1 to 41
1 and 2 Kings (after you have read 1 and 2 Samuel)
1 and 2 Chronicles (after you have read 1 and 2 Kings)

DAY ONE:
MORNING PRAYER: Acts of Faith, Hope, Charity; Daily Offering

MORNING FACE TO FACE WITH GOD:
Begin with Prayer to the Holy Spirit
Prayer on Psalm 32: Remission of Sin

Psalm 32 is the second of seven Penitential Psalms. We have already considered Psalm 6 and will ponder Psalm 38 as well in our prayer this week. Like the other Penitential Psalms, Psalm 32 is about sin and guilt, and confidence in receiving God's mercy because of a repentant heart. In fact, the psalm begins on a note of relief and happiness at being forgiven: *"Blessed is the one whose fault is removed, whose sin is forgiven. Blessed is the man to whom the LORD imputes no guilt, in whose spirit is no deceit."* Repentance truly leads to forgiveness from God resulting in a heart cleansed of deceit and doubt. True joy is about being forgiven and totally accepted and loved by God.

Psalm 32 gives us an insider's look into what takes place when the soul is in turmoil and desolation. There is an inherent resistance to move toward repentance, resulting in a posture that indulges in denial of sin and justification of one's actions. Such a stance causes turmoil and debilitating sickness of soul: *"Because I kept silent, my bones wasted away; I groaned all day long. For day and night your hand was heavy upon me; my strength withered as in dry summer heat."*

The only way out of this suffocating prison is to acknowledge our sins: *"Then I declared my sin to you; my guilt I did not hide. I said, "I confess my transgression to the LORD," and you took away the guilt of my sin."* We have a similar experience in the sacrament of reconciliation. It is truly an experience of reconciliation with God and acceptance of ourselves. The Psalmist follows up on the fruits of repentance, which is forgiveness salved by peace and gratitude. The forgiven sinner becomes an ardent witness and desires that every person have their experience of being repentant and forgiven by God. In sheer gratitude, the Psalmist keeps reiterating his message of salvation through forgiveness of his sins: *"Therefore every loyal person should pray to you in time of distress. Though flood waters threaten, they will never reach him. You are my shelter; you guard me from distress; with joyful shouts of deliverance you surround me."*

As a witness for God, the forgiven have a powerful message. They become mentors to others: *"I will instruct you and show you the way you should walk, give you counsel with my eye upon you. Do not be like a horse or mule, without understanding; with bit and bridle their temper is curbed, else they will not come to you."* They make others see that the way of the wicked leads to destruction, and the way of the righteous to living under the mantle of God's mercy and compassion: *"Many are the sorrows of the wicked one, but mercy surrounds the one who trusts in the LORD. Be glad in the LORD and rejoice, you righteous; exult, all you upright of heart."* The psalm ends on a celebratory note of gratitude and joy similar to the way it began, with gratitude and joy.

Reflect and Pray on Psalm 32, using Lectio Divina or the Method of Meditation. Make sure you converse intimately with the Blessed Trinity:

Prayer on Psalm 32: Remission of Sin
"1 Of David. A maskil.

I.

Blessed is the one whose fault is removed, whose sin is forgiven. 2 Blessed is the man to whom the LORD imputes no guilt, in whose spirit is no deceit.

II.

3 Because I kept silent, my bones wasted away; I groaned all day long. 4 For day and night your hand was heavy upon me; my strength withered as in dry summer heat. 5 Then I declared my sin to you; my guilt I did not hide. I said, "I confess my transgression to the LORD," and you took away the guilt of my sin. 6 Therefore every loyal person should pray to you in time of distress. Though flood waters threaten, they will never reach him. 7 You are my shelter; you guard me from distress; with joyful shouts of deliverance you surround me.

III.

8 I will instruct you and show you the way you should walk, give you counsel with my eye upon you. 9 Do not be like a horse or mule, without understanding; with bit and bridle their temper is curbed, else they will not come to you.

IV.

10 Many are the sorrows of the wicked one, but mercy surrounds the one who trusts in the LORD, 11 Be glad in the LORD and rejoice, you righteous; exult, all you upright of heart."

End with Prayer to the Holy Trinity
NIGHT PRAYER: The Examination of Conscience

DAY TWO:
MORNING PRAYER: Acts of Faith, Hope, Charity; Daily Offering

MORNING FACE TO FACE WITH GOD:
Begin with Prayer to the Holy Spirit
Prayer on Psalm 33: Praise of God's Power and Providence

Psalm 33 is a call to praise God in a liturgical setting. This is the first time in the Psalms that musical instruments are mentioned – the ten stringed lyre and the harp. The harp is mentioned in the heavenly liturgy as well: *"The sound I heard was like that of harpists playing their harps. They were singing [what seemed to be] a new hymn before the throne, before the four living creatures and the elders"* (Revelation 14: 2-3). The congregation in the Temple is described as the righteous ones. They are in the temple because they want to be close to God and live according to the right order of things as ordained by God.

Psalm 33 begins with three exhortations to the congregation, to rejoice, praise, and give thanks: *"Rejoice, you righteous, in the*

LORD; praise from the upright is fitting. Give thanks to the LORD on the harp; on the ten-stringed lute offer praise. Sing to him a new song; skillfully play with joyful chant" This exhortation is offered for a two-fold reason: *"For the LORD's word is upright; all his works are trustworthy."* John gives us the best understanding of the uprightness of God's word: *"In the beginning was the Word, and the Word was with God, and the Word was God. He was in the beginning with God. All things came to be through him, and without him nothing came to be"* (John 1: 1-3).

In verses 4-9, we are told about the power of God's word: *"By the LORD's word the heavens were made; by the breath of his mouth all their host. He gathered the waters of the sea as a mound; he sets the deep into storage vaults."* The stars of the sky were viewed as a vast host or army in Nehemiah and the prophets. The power of God's creative word instills a profound sense of awe and reverence in the beholder: *"Let all the earth fear the LORD; let all who dwell in the world show him reverence. For he spoke, and it came to be, commanded, and it stood in place."*

Verses 10 to 12 allude to the splendor of God's works. His plan of salvation is diametrically opposed to the plan of the nations, signifying their adversarial relationship with God. And God's plans will stand forever: *"The LORD foils the plan of nations, frustrates the designs of peoples. But the plan of the LORD stands forever, the designs of his heart through all generations."* And Israel, and any other nation that lives under God will be blessed: *"Blessed is the nation whose God is the LORD, the people chosen as his inheritance."*

Verses 13 to 15 bring out the solicitude and protection of God toward those whom He loves. Like the Good Shepherd, God is watchful over His sheep, knowing their propensities and weaknesses, and always there to protect and save them: *"From heaven the LORD looks down and observes the children of Adam, from his dwelling place he surveys all who dwell on earth. The One who fashioned together their hearts is the One who knows all their works."*

God as Creator is also God the Redeemer. In verses 18 to 19, the Psalmist emphasizes God's *hesed* or unfailing kindness: *"Behold, the eye of the LORD is upon those who fear him, upon those who count on his mercy, to deliver their soul from death, and to keep them alive through famine."* The Psalmist derives much comfort and assurance from the LORD's everlasting faithfulness to His people and voices their sentiments in trust and gratitude: *"Our soul waits for the LORD, he is our help and shield. For in him our hearts rejoice; in his holy name we trust."*

Unfortunately, there are those among the children of Adam who rely on their own resources and think they can go up against God. The Psalmist tells them bluntly that the best laid plans of mice and men go awry: *"A king is not saved by a great army, nor a warrior delivered by great strength. Useless is the horse for safety; despite its great strength, it cannot be saved."*

Throughout this psalm of praise, God's steadfast love, or *hesed*, is highlighted. God's faithful love for us encapsulates His mercy toward us. God's mercy is highlighted in three strategic verses. In verse 5, we are told that *"The earth is full of the mercy of the LORD."* Verse 18 reminds us that *"the eye of the LORD is upon those who fear him, upon those who count on his mercy."* Finally, the Psalm ends with a petitionary finale where we ask God to be merciful toward us: *"May your mercy, LORD, be upon us; as we put our hope in you."*

Reflect and Pray on Psalm 33, using Lectio Divina or the Method of Meditation. Make sure you converse intimately with the Blessed Trinity:

Prayer on Psalm 33: Praise of God's Power and Providence
I.

"1 Rejoice, you righteous, in the LORD; praise from the upright is fitting. 2 Give thanks to the LORD on the harp; on the ten-stringed lyre offer praise. 3 Sing to him a new song; skillfully play with joyful chant. 4 For the LORD's word is upright; all his works are trustworthy. 5 He loves justice and right. The earth is full of the mercy of the LORD.

II.

6 By the LORD's word the heavens were made; by the breath of his mouth all his host. 7 He gathered the waters of the sea as a mound; he sets the deep into storage vaults.

III.

8 Let all the earth fear the LORD; let all who dwell in the world show him reverence. 9 For he spoke and it came to be, commanded, and it stood in place. 10 The LORD foils the plan of nations, frustrates the designs of peoples. 11 But the plan of the LORD stands forever, the designs of his heart through all generations. 12 Blessed is the nation whose God is the LORD, the people chosen as his inheritance.

IV.

13 From heaven the LORD looks down and observes the children of Adam, 14 From his dwelling place he surveys all who dwell on earth. 15 The one who fashioned together their hearts is the One who knows all their works.

V.

16 A king is not saved by a great army, nor a warrior delivered by great strength. 17 Useless is the horse for safety; despite its great strength, it cannot be saved. 18. Behold, the eye of the LORD is upon those who fear him, upon those who count on his mercy, 19. To deliver their soul from death, and to keep them alive through famine.

VI.

20 Our soul waits for the LORD, he is our help and shield. 21 For in him our hearts rejoice; in his holy name we trust. 22 May your mercy, LORD, be upon us; as we put our hope in you."

End with Prayer to the Holy Trinity
NIGHT PRAYER: The Examination of Conscience

DAY THREE:
MORNING PRAYER: Acts of Faith, Hope, Charity; Daily Offering

MORNING FACE TO FACE WITH GOD:
Begin with Prayer to the Holy Spirit
Prayer on Psalm 36: Human Wickedness and Divine Providence

Psalm 36 contains an apt description of the lifestyle of the wicked, an expression of praise and trust in God's mercy and protection, and a cry for deliverance from the wicked. The Psalmist offers us some keen insight into the inner workings of a deceitful and wicked mind. Such a person has adopted the state of darkness and desolation as a lifestyle. They have become hostile to God and are committed to doing evil and creating chaos. Such persons are under the influence and dominion of Satan: *"Sin directs the heart of the wicked man; his eyes are closed to the fear of God. For he lives with the delusion: his guilt will not be known and hated. Empty and false are the words of his mouth; he has ceased to be wise and do good. On his bed he hatches plots; he sets out on a wicked way; he does not reject evil."* We live amidst people, many of whom are godless. There is no acknowledgement of God and acceptance of Jesus as Lord and Savior. For them, the end justifies the means.

In verses 6 through 10, the Psalmist is offering us salutary advice about how we are to live in the world while not being of it. He is describing the way of the just, the faithful who have accepted to live in God's righteousness. God's mercy, or loving kindness, is all-pervasive and continually being offered to them. In God, they live and move and have their being. As Jesus said, *"And behold, I am with you always, until the end of the age"* (Matthew 28: 20). In Jesus, we are reborn, and through Him will always be able to live the abundant life of the Blessed Trinity, no matter how dire our circumstances might be: *"LORD, your mercy reaches to heaven; your fidelity, to the clouds. Your justice is like the highest mountains; ... human being and beast you sustain, LORD. How precious is your mercy, O God! The children of Adam take refuge in the shadow of your wings... from your delightful stream you give them drink. For with you is the fountain of life, and in your light we see light."* The Psalmist thus provides a sharp contrast between the way of the wicked and the way of the just.

In the last three verses, the Psalmist utters a prayer for help. Such a call for help is an essential dimension of a psalm of lament.

The petitioner is always asking for God's continued help and grace. Being realistic, the Psalmist asks God to continue His protection over them living among wicked people: *"Show mercy on those who know you, your just defense to the upright of heart. Do not let the foot of the proud overtake me, nor the hand of the wicked disturb me."* Interestingly, the introduction to the Psalm describes David as the servant of the LORD. The editors, inspired by the Holy Spirit, came up with such a description of David. We are all called to be servants of the LORD and to one another.

Reflect and Pray on Psalm 36, using Lectio Divina or the Method of Meditation. Make sure you converse intimately with the Blessed Trinity:

Prayer on Psalm 36: Human Wickedness and Divine Providence
"1 For the leader. Of David, the servant of the LORD.
I.
"2 Sin directs the heart of the wicked man; his eyes are closed to the fear of God. 3 For he lives with the delusion: his guilt will not be known and hated. 4 Empty and false are the words of his mouth; he has ceased to be wise and do good. 5 On his bed he hatches plots; he sets out on a wicked way; he does not reject evil.
II.
6 LORD, your mercy reaches to heaven; your fidelity, to the clouds. 7 Your justice is like the highest mountains; your judgments, like the mighty deep; human being and beast you sustain, LORD. 8 How precious is your mercy, O God! The children of Adam take refuge in the shadow of your wings. 9 They feast on the rich food of your house; from you delightful stream you give them drink. 10 For with you is the fountain of life, and in your light we see light. 11 Show mercy on those who know you, your just defense to the upright of heart. 12 Do not let the foot of the proud overtake me, nor the hand of the wicked disturb me. 13 There make the evildoers fall; thrust them down, unable to rise."

End with Prayer to the Holy Trinity
NIGHT PRAYER: The Examination of Conscience

DAY FOUR:
MORNING PRAYER: Acts of Faith, Hope, Charity; Daily Offering

MORNING FACE TO FACE WITH GOD:
Begin with Prayer to the Holy Spirit
Prayer on Psalm 38: Prayer of an Afflicted Sinner

Psalm 38 is the third Penitential Psalm that we are pondering in Book One. The Psalm is titled, 'A psalm of David. For Remembrance.' A similar title has been given to Psalm 70. In asking God to remember him, the Psalmist is laying before the LORD a desperate situation in which he needs divine help. Psalm 38 offers us an excruciating description of David's spiritual malaise and crippling guilt, compounded by intense bodily agony from the debilitating effects of a severe illness. We do not know the specific circumstances that David was dealing with when he composed this psalm. However, the psalm leaves us with no doubt that David was struggling with a major crisis in his life.

In the first segment, David presents the LORD with a very graphic picture of the ravages that sin has caused to his relationship with God and to his body and soul. He is in desperate straits, and as his wont has always been, clings to God's mercy and loving kindness as he seeks forgiveness and redemption: *"LORD, do not punish me in your anger; in your wrath do not chastise me! Your arrows have sunk deep in me; your hand has come down upon me. There is no wholesomeness in my flesh because of your anger; there is no health in my bones because of my sin. My iniquities overwhelm me, a burden too heavy for me."* The Psalmist prays with humble repentance. He is in the throes of melancholy and depression. He knows that he has offended God grievously and takes full responsibility for his sinful actions. However, he does not feel condemned by God as he undergoes the divine purification. He trusts that God will forgive him and restore him to health of body and soul. These verses aptly describe Jesus in His passion. Being without sin, He took upon Himself our sin!

In the second segment, the Psalmist describes his agonizing return to God from the devastation caused by sin. He trusts that in an honest and heartfelt confession of his misery, God will be compassionate toward him: *"Foul and festering are my sores because of my folly. I am stooped and deeply bowed; every day I go about mourning. My loins burn with fever; there is no wholesomeness in my flesh. I am numb and utterly crushed; I wail with anguish of heart."* David has no reluctance in exposing his vulnerability before God. Even in his utter defenselessness, he does not make excuses. It is his own folly that has brought about his downfall. He has made his own bed of thorns and has had to lie in it.

His only recourse is God even as he wastes away: *"My Lord, my deepest yearning is before you; my groaning is not hidden from you. My heart shudders, my strength forsakes me; the very light of my eyes has failed."* His friends have abandoned him. In their eyes he has become a pariah and castaway. The common assumption was that severe illness was the result of one's sins and God's punishment of them: *"Friends and companions shun my disease; my neighbors stand far off."* Under these circumstances, his enemies gloat over his misfortune and seek his destruction even more: *"Those who seek my life lay snares for me; they seek my misfortune, they speak of ruin; they plot treachery every day."*

In the third segment, broken down by sickness and subdued by sorrow over his sin, the Psalmist waits on God, like the deaf, hearing nothing, and like the mute, not opening his mouth: *"But I am like the deaf, hearing nothing, like the mute, I do not open my mouth, I am even like someone who does not hear, who has no answer ready. LORD, it is for you that I wait; O Lord, my God, you respond. For I have said that they gloat over me, exult over me if I stumble."*

In the fourth and last segment, the Psalmist continues his song of lamentation before God. He is on perilous ground and his enemies are growing stronger: *"I am very near to falling; my wounds are with me always. I acknowledge my guilt and grieve over my sin. My enemies live and grow strong, those who hate me grow numerous fraudulently."* In this situation of extreme strife and peril, the Psalmist puts his trust in God by acknowledging his sins: *"I acknowledge my guilt and grieve over my sin."* And his enemies are aware of his trust in God and hate him for it: *"Repaying me evil for good, accusing me for pursuing good."*

As in every song of lament, the Psalmist ends on a note of confident trust in God's help and protection: *"Do not forsake me, O LORD; my God, be not far from me! Come quickly to help me, my Lord and my salvation!"* Jesus prayed the psalms and knew that He who was without sin would become sin and take upon Himself all of David's experiences and ours, of sin and human malice, so that we could become free of sin in Him.

Reflect and Pray on Psalm 38, using Lectio Divina or the Method of Meditation. Make sure you converse intimately with the Blessed Trinity:

Prayer on Psalm 38: Prayer of an Afflicted Sinner
"1 A psalm of David. For remembrance.

I.

2 LORD, do not punish me in your anger; in your wrath do not chastise me! 3 Your arrows have sunk deep in me; your hand has come down upon me. 4 There is no wholesomeness in my flesh because of your anger; there is no health in my bones because of my sin. 5 My iniquities overwhelm me, a burden too heavy for me.

II.

6 Foul and festering are my sores because of my folly. 7 I am stooped and deeply bowed; every day I go about mourning. 8 My loins burn with fever; there is no wholesomeness in my flesh. 9 I am numb and utterly crushed; I wail with anguish of heart. 10 My Lord, my deepest yearning is before you; my groaning is not hidden from you. 11 My heart shudders, my strength forsakes me; the very light of my eyes has failed. 12 Friends and companions shun my disease; my neighbors stand far off. 13 Those who seek my life lay snares for me; they seek my misfortune, they speak of ruin; they plot treachery every day.

III.

14 But I am like the deaf, hearing nothing, like the mute, I do not open my mouth. 15 I am even like someone who does not hear, who has no answer ready. 16 LORD, it is for you that I wait; O Lord, my God, you respond. 17 For I have said that they would gloat over me, exult over me if I stumble.

IV.

18 I am very near to falling; my wounds are with me always. 19 I acknowledge my guilt and grieve over my sin. 20 My enemies live and grow strong, those who hate me grow numerous fraudulently, 21 repaying me evil for good, accusing me for pursuing good. 22 Do not forsake me, O LORD; my God, be not far from me! 23 Come quickly to help me, my Lord and my salvation!"

End with Prayer to the Holy Trinity
NIGHT PRAYER: The Examination of Conscience

DAY FIVE:
MORNING PRAYER: Acts of Faith, Hope, Charity; Daily Offering

MORNING FACE TO FACE WITH GOD:
Begin with Prayer to the Holy Spirit

Psalm 39: The Vanity of Life

Psalm 39 is a song of lament of a mortally sick person who is acutely aware of his own mortality and the evanescent nature of life. All is passing, here today, gone tomorrow. The psalm is a meditation on the fragility of man before God. As with all songs of lament, Psalm 39 ends in a prayer for a peaceful life. It is the song of a deeply reflective person who has experienced the fullness of life in his LORD, and its emptiness without Him. It seems reasonable to assume that David composed it in the later years of his life.

In the first segment, David expresses the dilemma and silent agony experienced by a seasoned disciple. He begins the psalm by asking God to give him the proper discernment not to speak foolishly or sinfully before the wicked, as his words would be misconstrued against him. He was feeling the pressure of speaking his earnest feelings while knowing that he ran the risk of being criticized. He therefore wondered if it were better if he remained silent: *"I said, "I will watch my ways, lest I sin with my tongue; I will keep a muzzle on my mouth." Mute and silent before the wicked, I refrain from good things."* However, his silence brought him sorrow and turmoil and he had to burst out his feelings before God: *"But my sorrow increases; my heart smolders within me. In my sighing a fire blazes up, and I break into speech."*

David breaks his silence in the most appropriate manner, by humble prayer. Rather than pour out his fears and doubts before the wicked and run the risk of being manipulated, he would pour them out to God: *"LORD, let me know my end, the number of my days that I may learn how frail I am. To be sure, you establish the expanse of my days; indeed, my life is as nothing before you. Every man is but a breath."* In prayer, David is strengthened by the wisdom that lies in the truth that life is short and frail. Without God it is meaningless, and with God it is full of purpose. David was a man of many accomplishments. In the light of his relationship with God, however, he came to realize that his life was but a breath. David reveals a paradox in his reflection on the brevity of life: with God, life is eternal; without God, life is a mere breath!

In the third segment, the Psalmist offers us much food for thought. He first comments on the person who goes about their daily lives ignoring the brevity and frailty of life. They are mere shadows, living without substance or meaning. Their lives are empty because they are blind to eternal matters. Wealth is their god and they end up living in the shadows. Such a life is built on sand and will crumble: *"Man goes about as a mere phantom; they hurry about, although in vain; he heaps up stores without knowing for whom."* This message was an important teaching in Jesus' ministry. In the Parable of the Rich Fool, Jesus said: *"You fool, this night your life will be demanded of you; and the things you have prepared, to whom will they belong?' Thus will it be for the one who stores up treasure for himself but is not rich in what matters to God"* (Luke 12: 20-21).

By contrast, David asks to live rightly, in dependence and trust in God, no matter what the circumstances of his life might be. His hope in God becomes the bedrock of his life. God will deliver him from his sin: *"And now, LORD, for what do I wait? You are my only hope. From all my sins deliver me; let me not be the taunt of fools. I am silent and do not open my mouth because you are the one who did this."* He is praying during a time of great weakness and painful correction from God. He remains humble and does not justify his actions. He also prays for relief from his affliction: *"Take your plague away from me; I am ravaged by the touch of your hand. You chastise man with rebukes for sin; like a moth you consume his treasures. Every man is but a breath."*

In keeping with a song of lament, David ends his psalm with a humble prayer for restored favor and renewed strength: *"Listen to my prayer, LORD, hear my cry; do not be deaf to my weeping! For I am with you like a foreigner, a refugee, like my ancestors. Turn your gaze from me that I may smile before I depart to be no more."* David's true home was with God. In his misery, he felt like a foreigner before God, a refugee like his ancestors. However, he knew as well that God would make him smile with relief and peace. David did not have a clear certainty of life after death which came much later in the Old Testament. As Christians, we are wayfarers on earth. Jesus is our Bread of Life that we take with us on the journey. He travels with us in whom He abides. And in heaven, our lives will be engulfed in the Beatific Vision of the Blessed Trinity. Psalm 39 is the perfect reflection for a funeral liturgy and the burial of the dead.

Reflect and Pray on Psalm 39, using Lectio Divina or the Method of Meditation. Make sure you converse intimately with the Blessed Trinity:
Psalm 39: The Vanity of Life
"1 For the leader, for Jeduthun. A psalm of David.
I.
"2 I said, "I will watch my ways, lest I sin with my tongue; I will keep a muzzle on my mouth." 3 Mute and silent before the wicked, I refrain from good things. But my sorrow increases; 4 My heart smolders within me. In my sighing a fire blazes up, and I break into speech:

II.

5 LORD, let me know my end, the number of my days, that I may learn how frail I am. 6 To be sure, you establish the expanse of my days; indeed, my life is as nothing before you. Every man is but a breath.

III.

7 Man goes about as a mere phantom; they hurry about, although in vain; he heaps up stores without knowing for whom. 8 And now, LORD, for what do I wait? You are my only hope. 9 From all my sins deliver me; let me not be the taunt of fools. 10 I am silent and do not open my mouth because you are the one who did this. 11 Take your plague away from me; I am ravaged by the touch of your hand. 12 You chastise man with rebukes for sin; like a moth you consume his treasures. Every man is but a breath. 13 Listen to my prayer, LORD, hear my cry; do not be deaf to my weeping! For I am with you like a foreigner, a refugee, like my ancestors. 14 Turn your gaze from me, that I may smile before I depart to be no more."

End with Prayer to the Holy Trinity
NIGHT PRAYER: The Examination of Conscience

DAY SIX:
MORNING PRAYER: Acts of Faith, Hope, Charity; Daily Offering

MORNING FACE TO FACE WITH GOD:
Begin with Prayer to the Holy Spirit
Prayer on Psalm 41: Thanksgiving after Sickness

Psalm 41 is the last song of Book One. It ends with a doxology that was added to the psalm later, to signify the end of the Book. The last psalm of all the five books ends with a similar doxology. Psalm 41 tells us that David was very ill, though we do not know the circumstances. He also states that his illness was because he had violated God's laws. The circumstances of his acute crisis could very well have been caused by sending Uriah to die after he had committed adultery with Bathsheba, Uriah's wife, so that he could marry her. Their first child lived for seven days (2Samuel 11-12). During his sickness, many of his friends came to visit him,

They turned out to be traitors, acting as concerned friends in his presence and plotting his harm behind his back. They wanted him to die so that they could have a new king in Absalom, David's son. The story is found in 2Samuel 15-18.

David begins by identifying himself with the poor who are always cared for and sheltered by God: *"Blessed the one concerned for the poor; on a day of misfortune, the LORD delivers him. The LORD keeps and preserves him, makes him blessed in the land, and does not betray him to his enemies. The LORD sustains him on his sickbed, you turn down his bedding whenever he is ill."* The poor had no political or economic clout in society and were often taken advantage of by the landed gentry. Their only recourse was to come to God with their backs bent double, trusting that God would come to their rescue. In the Beatitudes, Jesus described the poor who depended on God for everything. In Luke 18: 1-8, Jesus offers us the example of the persistent widow as the embodiment of the poor in the Bible. For the Psalmist, the LORD has become his nurse during his illness, making sure that his bedding is comfortably arranged.

In the second segment, David reflects on his sin being the cause of his illness: *"Even I have said, "LORD, take note of me; heal me, although I have sinned against you."* He is confident that God will forgive him because he has a repentant heart. David bares his heart about the negative impact his sins and sickness have had on his human relationships: *"My enemies say bad things against me: 'When will he die and his name be forgotten?' When someone comes to visit me, he speaks without sincerity. His heart stores up malice; when he leaves, he gossips. All those who hate me whisper together against me; they imagine the worst about me: 'He has had ruin poured over him; that one lying down will never rise again.' Even my trusted friend, who ate my bread, has raised his heel against me."*

Probably, his enemies felt justified in venting their death-wish upon David, because *'he has had ruin poured over him.'* He was being punished by God. The death-wish of his enemies is 'Belial' in Hebrew, which is the name of Satan. David knew that no one could place a death-wish on those who obey God. We do not know who the trusted friend was who ate David's bread and raised his heel against him. Was he referring to Ahitophel the Gilonite, David's counselor who went over to Absalom's side as a conspirator (2 Samuel 15: 12, 31)? John 13: 18 cites this same verse to characterize Judas as a false friend and betrayer of Jesus: *"The one who ate my food has raised his heel against me."*

At the end, the Psalmist beseeches God to bestow His justification upon him by healing him and showing His love and kindness toward him: *"But you, LORD, take note of me to raise me up that I may repay them."* By this I will know you are pleased with me, that my enemy no longer shouts in triumph over me. In my integrity may you support me and let me stand in your presence forever."* David's prayer seeks his healing at the hands of God as justification that his enemies were wrong about him.

The last verse was added to the psalm later to denote the end of Book One: *"Blessed be the LORD, the God of Israel, from all eternity and forever. Amen. Amen."* In Book One, the Psalmist is David himself who makes it clear that God was always with him, in times when he had offended God by his sin, in which case he returned to God's protection and loving kindness through a repentant heart. In other circumstances, when he was the victim of treachery and deceit, he experienced God as his Good Shepherd who comforted him with His rod and staff even though he was walking through the valley of the shadow of death. In all circumstances, therefore, we can give thanks to God and praise Him for His mighty works. Jesus told His disciples and us to not be afraid as He was always going to be with us: *"And behold, I am with you always, until the end of the age"* (Matthew 28: 20).

Reflect and Pray on Psalm 41, using Lectio Divina or the Method of Meditation. Make sure you converse intimately with the Blessed Trinity:

Prayer on Psalm 41: Thanksgiving after Sickness

"1 For the leader. A psalm of David.

I.

"2 Blessed the one concerned for the poor; on a day of misfortune, the LORD delivers him. 3 The LORD keeps and preserves him, makes him blessed in the land, and does not betray him to his enemies. 4 The LORD sustains him on his sickbed, you turn down his bedding whenever he is ill.

II.

5 Even I have said, "Lord, take note of me; heal me, although I have sinned against you. 6 My enemies say bad things against me; 'When will he die and his name be forgotten?' 7 When someone comes to visit me, he speaks without sincerity. His heart stores up malice; when he leaves, he gossips. 8 All those who hate me whisper together against me; they imagine the worst about me; 9 'He has had ruin poured over him; that one lying down will never rise again.' 10 Even my trusted friend, who ate my bread, has raised his heel against me.

III.

11 "But you, LORD, take note of me to raise me up that I may repay them." 12 By this I will know you are pleased with me, that my enemy no longer shouts in triumph over me. 13 In my integrity may you support me and let me stand in your presence forever. 14 Blessed be the LORD, the God of Israel, from all eternity and forever. Amen. Amen."

End with Prayer to the Holy Trinity
NIGHT SESSION: The Examination of Conscience

DAY SEVEN:
MORNING PRAYER: Acts of Faith, Hope, Charity; Daily Offering

MORNING FACE TO FACE WITH GOD:
<u>Learning Discipleship from the Psalms</u>
Begin with Prayer to the Holy Spirit

- *"Then I declared my sin to you; my guilt I did not hide. I said, "I confess my transgression to the LORD," and you took away the guilt of my sin."* Psalm 32 is about sin and guilt and confidence in receiving God's mercy because of a repentant heart. Repentance truly leads to forgiveness from God resulting in a heart cleansed of deceit and doubt. We have true joy when we are forgiven and loved by God.

- *"From heaven the LORD looks down and observes the children of Adam, from his dwelling place he surveys all who dwell on earth. The One who fashioned together their hearts is the One who knows all their works"* (Psalm 33: 13-15). Like the Good Shepherd, God is watchful over His sheep, knowing their propensities and weaknesses, and always there to protect and save them. The believer derives much comfort and assurance from the LORD's faithfulness to His people.

- *"Sin directs the heart of the wicked man; his eyes are closed to the fear of God. For he lives with the delusion: his guilt will not be known and hated. Empty and false are the words of his mouth; he has ceased to be wise and do good. On his bed he hatches plots; he sets out on a wicked way; he does not reject evil"* (Psalm 36: 2-5). The deceitful and wicked mind is committed to doing evil and creating chaos. Such persons are under the influence and dominion of Satan. There is no acknowledgement of God and acceptance of Jesus as Lord and Savior.

- *"How precious is your mercy, O God! The children of Adam take refuge in the shadow of your wings. They feast on the rich food of your house; from your delightful stream you give them drink. For with you is the fountain of life, and in your light we see light"* (Psalm 36: 8- 10). The wicked belong to the kingdom of Satan, the righteous are firmly established in a covenant relationship with the Blessed Trinity.

- *"LORD, do not punish me in your anger; in your wrath do not chastise me! Your arrows have sunk deep in me; your hand has come down upon me. There is no wholesomeness in my flesh because of your anger; there is no health in my bones because of my sin. My iniquities overwhelm me, a burden too heavy for me."* (Psalm 38: 25). In desperate straits, David clings to God's mercy and loving kindness as he seeks forgiveness and redemption. He knows that he has offended God and takes full responsibility for his sinful actions.

- *"LORD, let me know my end, the number of my days that I may learn how frail I am. To be sure, you establish the expanse of my days; indeed, my life is as nothing before you. Every man is but a breath."* (Psalm 39: 5-6). David is strengthened by the wisdom that lies in the truth that life is short and frail. Without God it is meaningless, and with God it is full of purpose. David came to realize that his life was but a breath. In life's brevity lay a paradox: with God, life is eternal, without God, life is a mere breath!

- *"My enemies say bad things against me: 'When will he die and his name be forgotten?' ... All those who hate me whisper together against me; they imagine the worst about me: 'He has had ruin poured over him; that one lying down will never rise again.' Even my trusted friend, who ate my bread, has raised his heel against me."* (Psalm 41: 5-10). David knew that no one could place a death-wish on those who obey God. Was David referring to Ahitophel, David's counselor who went over to Absalom's side as a conspirator? (2Samuel 15: 12, 31). John 13: 18 cites this verse to characterize Judas as the betrayer of Jesus: *"The one who ate my food has raised his heel against me."*

- *"Blessed be the LORD, the God of Israel, from all eternity and forever. Amen. Amen."* This verse is a fitting conclusion to the true significance of Book One: *'Abiding Trust in Dire Straits.'* God was always with David, in times when he had offended God and returned to God's loving kindness through a repentant heart. In other circumstances, when he was the victim of treachery and deceit, he experienced God as his Good Shepherd who comforted him with His rod and staff even though he was walking through the valley of the shadow of death.

End with Prayer to the Holy Trinity
NIGHT PRAYER: The Examination of Conscience

JOURNAL FOR BOOK ONE, WEEK FOUR: ABIDING TRUST IN DIRE STRAITS

<u>DAY ONE:</u> Morning Prayer: Psalm 32: Remission of Sin
What is God saying to You?

<u>Nightly Examination of Conscience:</u>
For what are you grateful?

For what are you contrite?

What spiritual discipline, including fasting, do you need to focus on tomorrow?

<u>DAY TWO:</u> Morning Prayer: Psalm 33: Praise of God's Power and Providence
What is God saying to You?

<u>Nightly Examination of Conscience:</u>
For what are you grateful?

For what are you contrite?

What spiritual discipline, including fasting, do you need to focus on tomorrow?

DAY THREE: Morning Prayer: Psalm 36: Human Wickedness and Divine Providence
What is God saying to You?

Nightly Examination of Conscience:
For what are you grateful?

For what are you contrite?

What spiritual discipline, including fasting, do you need to focus on tomorrow?

DAY FOUR: Morning Prayer: Psalm 38: Prayer of an Afflicted Sinner
What is God saying to You?

Nightly Examination of Conscience:
For what are you grateful?

For what are you contrite?

What spiritual discipline, including fasting, do you need to focus on tomorrow?

DAY FIVE: Morning Prayer: Psalm 39: The Vanity of Life
What is God saying to You?

Nightly Examination of Conscience:
For what are you grateful?

For what are you contrite?

What spiritual discipline, including fasting, do you need to focus on tomorrow?

DAY SIX: Morning Prayer: Psalm 41: Thanksgiving after Sickness
What is God saying to You?

Nightly Examination of Conscience:
For what are you grateful?

For what are you contrite?

What spiritual discipline, including fasting, do you need to focus on tomorrow?

DAY SEVEN: Morning Prayer: Learning Discipleship from the Psalms
What is God saying to You?

Nightly Examination of Conscience:
For what are you grateful?

For what are you contrite?

What spiritual discipline, including fasting, do you need to focus on tomorrow?

What prayer would you compose to express what God has said to you this week?

BOOK TWO – PSALMS 42-72: CELEBRATION AND PRAISE
Psalms 42, 44, 45, 46, 47, and 48

WHAT IS AT THE HEART OF BOOK TWO, WEEK ONE?

Book Two contains 30 psalms and the theme could be described as *'Celebration and Praise.'* There is a sharp contrast with Book One. More than 15 of the 30 psalms resound with praise and thanksgiving to God. Even though there are several psalms of lament in Book Two, they subscribe to the theme of celebration and praise as they always end on a note of confidence, trust, and gratitude. Book Two starts off on a somber note, echoing the mood and tone of Book One. Psalms 42 and 43 are psalms of lament. They are really one psalm in two parts. They are followed by Psalm 44 which is a prayer of supplication to God during a time of national defeat. Soon, however, Book Two turns to celebration and praise, ending on a high note with a description of Solomon's perfect reign.

In Book Two, we will encounter several important themes which are added reasons to praise and thank God. Psalm 45 celebrates the glory of a royal wedding, pointing us in the direction of Jesus the King, and Mary, His Queen Mother. Psalms 46 to 48 celebrate the glory of Zion, both the Temple and the City of Jerusalem. God will always uphold this great city, inseparably connected to David who chose it for his capital and the site of the Temple (2Samuel 5 and 7).

Psalms 50 to 64 offer us an admixture of sentiments; there are liturgical movements that have become established tradition, and there is the continued emphasis on God's unfailing *hesed* or loving kindness. Psalm 50 clearly highlights a moment of transition in the way Israel henceforward approaches worship and sacrificial offerings. Through David's influence, the *Todah* or thanksgiving offering is given greater importance than the *Ola* or burnt offering.

Psalms 51 through 64 are 14 psalms from earlier in David's career, when God saved him from his sins (Psalm 51), from Saul (Psalms 52, 54, 57, 59), from atheists (Psalm 53), from the Philistines (Psalm 56), the Edomites (Psalm 60), and from wicked enemies in general (Psalms 61-64). While they are songs of lament, individual and communal, they keep reminding us that God always comes to the rescue of the ones who walk in His ways and trust Him completely.

Psalms 65 to 68 are songs of praise and thanksgiving, glorifying God for His faithfulness and steadfast love. David bursts into exuberant praise and gratitude to God who is constant in His faithfulness and rich in His mercy. Book Two ends with three prayers for deliverance, Psalms 69 through 71. Psalm 71 highlights God's constant and merciful presence even into old age, stretching from the womb into the final reaches of mortal life. Psalm 72, the last psalm of Book Two, highlights the perfect reign of Solomon. While the psalm has been attributed to Solomon, it captures the proud and grateful sentiments of his father David. The tone of Book Two can, therefore, be aptly described as *'Celebration and Praise.'*

There are several authors in Book Two. A further 18 psalms attributed to David have been included. Psalms 51 through 64 are 14 psalms from earlier in David's career. 11 psalms were composed by the Sons of Korah. The Sons of Korah or the Korahites, a family of Levites, were a group that David appointed to be the Gatekeepers of the Temple (1Chronicles 9: 19). Eventually, they became the temple choir (2Chronicles 20: 19). 8 of these 11 psalms have been included in Book Two, Psalms 42 to 49. Asaph with his family is another composer whose 12 psalms have been included in the Psalter. Book Two has one of the 12 psalms, Psalm 50. Asaph was a choir leader and musician that David appointed (1Chronicles 25: 1-2). Two psalms have been attributed to King Solomon. One of them, Psalm 72, has been included as the last psalm of Book Two.

We find the use of two obscure Hebrew terms that are used as superscriptions for almost half of the 30 psalms: *Maskil*, which could be translated as 'contemplative poem' or 'song.' They are Psalms 42; 44-45; 52-55. The other superscription is *Miktam*, whose meaning is unclear, and could be translated as 'prayer.' They are Psalms 56-60.

On Day One, we will pray with *Psalm 42: Longing for God.* Psalms 42 and 43 are really one psalm in two parts. The advice that the Psalmist gives to himself is to praise God: *"Wait for God, for I shall again praise him, my savior and my God"* (Psalm 42: 6). In this way, the intercessor is steadfastly banishing fear and melancholy during a severe crisis by trusting that God will be their Savior and LORD!

On Day Two, we will reflect prayerfully on *Psalm 44: God's Past Favor and Israel's Present Need.* Psalm 44 is a prayer of supplication to God during a time of national defeat. The writer recounts God's mercies and protection in the past and concludes trustingly that divine help will be granted in this present emergency.

On Day Three, we will ponder *Psalm 45: Song for a Royal Wedding.* Psalm 45 celebrates the glory of a royal wedding, probably from the period of Solomon's youth or early reign. Psalm 45 has Marian imagery and can be classified as one of the Messianic psalms.

On Day Four, we will pray with *Psalm 46: God, the Protector of Zion.* Psalms 46 through 48 are the first real Zion psalms that we have in the Psalter. Zion psalms praise and glorify Jerusalem that became the spiritual heart of Israel and indeed the whole world, where God would work the most important events in the history of salvation.

On Day Five, we will pray with *Psalm 47: The Ruler of All the Nations.* Psalm 47 also emphasizes the truth that God will always uphold Jerusalem inseparably connected to David who chose it for his capital and the site of the Temple (2Samuel 5 and 7). Even after David, Zion or Jerusalem, used synonymously for each other, was the spiritual heart of the nation of Israel.

On Day Six, we will ponder *Psalm 49: Confidence in God Rather than in Riches.* Psalm 49 emphasizes the point made in the previous three psalms that trust in God will lead to salvation, and trust in riches will be one's downfall.

On Day Seven, we will ponder the salient advice that these psalms have offered us to enhance and strengthen our own following of Jesus and our commitment to His Church.

SPIRITUAL READING FOR BOOK TWO OF THE PSALMS:
1 and 2 Samuel
Psalms 42 to 72
1 and 2 Kings (after you have read 1 and 2 Samuel)
1 and 2 Chronicles (after you have read 1 and 2 Kings)

DAY ONE:
MORNING PRAYER: Acts of Faith, Hope, Charity; Daily Offering

MORNING FACE TO FACE WITH GOD:
Begin with Prayer to the Holy Spirit
Prayer on Psalm 42: Longing for God

Psalms 42 and 43 form a single lament of three sections, two of which are found in Psalm 42. The same theme is developed in both psalms which are joined together by the refrain that occurs in all three sections: *"Why are you downcast, my soul, why do you groan within me? Wait for God, for I shall again praise him, my savior and my God"* (Psalm 42: 6, 12; Psalm 43: 5). In all three instances, the Psalmist is steadfastly banishing fear and melancholy during a severe crisis by trusting that God will be His Savior and LORD!

The thirsting deer is an apt symbol for the disciple who longs for the security and strength of the Lord's presence in time of crisis and yet feels far removed from Him: *"As the deer longs for streams of water, so my soul longs for you, O God. My soul thirsts for God, the living God. When can I enter and see the face of God? My tears have been my bread day and night, as they ask me every day, "Where is your God?"* As wayfarers on our journey to God, our permanent abode, amidst the perilous paths of life's valley of tears, only our hope in God can sustain us.

The Psalmist asks us, as disciples of Jesus, to recall those moments of grace and blessing from God, especially during our times of worship in prayer and adoration before the Blessed Sacrament: *"Those times I recall as I pour out my soul, when I would cross over to the shrine of the Mighty One, to the house of God, amid loud cries of thanksgiving, with the multitude keeping festival."* Our sad and uncertain present is best tempered by the remembrance of God's joyful presence and blessings in our past. If God was with us so vividly in the past, then assuredly, He is with us in our present circumstances, because God is faithful to His promises to us.

The Psalmist contrasts the chaotic times of tribulation and crisis with the peaceful and joyful times when we are sheltered in the shadow of God's wings. In his present circumstances, the Psalmist is far from Zion which is God's abode. There in the Temple, God is Emmanuel, and he longs for God's presence. David, however, is a fugitive hiding in the wilderness. Most probably, the remote wilderness is in the northeast of Galilee, where Mount Hermon rises in majestic splendor and is the source of the Jordan River. Mount Mizar is another mountain in the same range. The cascades of the Jordan River are tumultuous, not exactly soul- quenching water. They are like the turbulent floodwaters that devastate everything in sight: *"I remember you from the land of the Jordan and Hermon, from Mount Mizar, deep calls to deep in the roar of your torrents, and all your waves and breakers sweep over me. By day may the LORD send his mercy, and by night may his righteousness be with me! I will pray to the God of my life."* The turbulent waters are a powerful description of the Psalmist's adversaries who challenge his committed relationship to God: *"they say to me every day: "Where is your God?"*

In the throes of his intense struggle, the Psalmist asks why God has forgotten him: *"My soul is downcast within me; therefore I will say to God, my rock: "Why do you forget me? Why must I go about mourning with the enemy oppressing me?" It shatters my bones, when my adversaries reproach me."* In his agony, the Psalmist says that he will wait on God: *"Wait for God, for I shall again praise him, my savior and my God."* In Psalm 43, the Psalmist asks that God's light and fidelity will bring him to the Temple to praise and worship God: *"Send your light and your fidelity, that they may be my guide; let them bring me to your holy mountain, to the place of your dwelling, that I may come to the altar of God, to God, my joy, my delight."* Jesus will indeed quench our thirst as our Source of Living Water.

Reflect and Pray on Psalm 42, using Lectio Divina or the Method of Meditation. Make sure you converse intimately with the Blessed Trinity:

(Keep Psalm 43 before you if you wish to pray with all three Sections)
Prayer on Psalm 42: Longing for God
"1 For the leader. A maskil of the Korahites.

I.

1 As the deer longs for streams of water, so my soul longs for you, O God. 3 My soul thirsts for God, the living God. When can I enter and see the face of God? 4 My tears have been my bread day and night, as they ask me every day, "Where is your God?" 5 Those times I recall as I pour out my soul, when I would cross over to the shrine of the Mighty One, to the house of God, amid loud cries of thanksgiving, with the multitude keeping festival. 6 Why are you downcast, my soul; why do you groan within me? Wait for God, for I shall again praise him, my savior and my God.

II.

7 My soul is downcast within me; therefore I remember you from the land of the Jordan and Hermon, from Mount Mizar, 8 Deep calls to deep in the roar of your torrents, and all your waves ad breakers sweep over me. 9 By day may the LORD send his mercy, and by night may his righteousness be with me! I will pray to the God of my life, 10 I will say to God, my rock: "Why do you forget

me? Why must I go about mourning with the enemy oppressing me?" 11 It shatters my bones, when my adversaries reproach me, when they say to me every day: "Where is your God?" 12 Why are you downcast, my soul, why do you groan within me? Wait for God, for I shall again praise him, my savior and my God."

End with Prayer to the Holy Trinity
NIGHT PRAYER: The Examination of Conscience

DAY TWO:
MORNING PRAYER: Acts of Faith, Hope, Charity; Daily Offering

MORNING FACE TO FACE WITH GOD:
Begin with Prayer to the Holy Spirit
Prayer on Psalm 44: God's Past Favor and Israel's Present Need

Psalms 44 and 60 are similar in nature as they are both communal laments about a serious defeat in war that the Israelites had experienced at the hands of their enemies. The dates and occasions of these two psalms are greatly disputed by biblical scholars, some arguing that this calamity took place during the reign of David, and others, placing the composition of these psalms at a much later date, as during the reign of Jehoram: *"Then the LORD stirred up against Jehoram the animosity of the Philistines and of the Arabians who were neighbors of the Ethiopians. They came up against Judah, breached it, and carried away all the wealth found in the king's house, along with his sons and his wives"* (2Chronicles 21: 16-17). Shortly thereafter, Jehoram had a serious disease of the bowels and died in great pain two years later. Jehoram reigned approximately between 849-842 B.C., some 150 years after David. Another opinion suggests that these psalms were depicting the serious defeat of Josiah as described in 2Chronicles 35: 20-24. Josiah reigned from 641 to 610 B.C., some four hundred years after David. However, a safe argument would be that these psalms were composed during David's reign, as Psalm 44 was composed by the Korahites who were appointed by David to be the Gatekeepers in the Temple, and Psalm 60 was composed by

David himself. They can be viewed as being prophetic, foretelling similar disasters that would befall God's people in later centuries.

Amidst their calamity and misfortune, the Israelites are finding solace and strength in remembering their covenant relationship with the LORD, spanning over several centuries, going all the way back to the Exodus from Egypt. The Mosaic Law required all Israelites to teach their children their history, especially the *hesed* or 'loving kindness' that the LORD had shown them. In the throes of this ignominious defeat, they are reminding themselves that the LORD is the ground of their being: *"O God, we have heard with our own ears; our ancestors have told us the deeds you did in their days, with your own hand in days of old: You rooted out nations to plant them, crushed peoples and expelled them... It was your right hand, your own arm, the light of your face for you favored them."* The conquest of Canaan is the historical fact that is referred to in the psalm. Their remembrance especially highlighted the fact that it was the LORD's doing and not theirs that ensured their protection and prosperity: *"Not in my bow do I trust, nor does my sword bring me victory. ... In God we have boasted all the day long; your name we will praise forever."* They boast of God being their God who is more powerful than all other gods!

Part II describes the heartrending experience of their national debacle. It is a loud and bitter complaint. God has cast them off and put them to shame. They have been defeated and despoiled. They seek God's favor to transform them from being the vanquished to becoming the victors again and to replace their shame with joy and gratitude: *"But now you have rejected and disgraced us; you do not march with our armies... You hand us over like sheep to be slaughtered, scatter us among the nations... You make us the reproach of our neighbors, the mockery and scorn of those around us... All day long my disgrace is before me; shame has covered my face at the sound of those who taunt and revile, at the sight of the enemy and avenger."*

Part III emphasizes an added cause for the people's shock and disbelief in the face of their calamity. The Psalmist insists that they have been faithful as God's covenant people: *"All this has come upon us, though we have not forgotten you, nor been disloyal to your covenant. Our hearts have not turned back, nor have our steps strayed from your path. If we had forgotten the name of our God, stretched out our hands to another god, would not God have discovered this, God who knows the secrets of the heart? For you we are slain all the day long, considered only as sheep to be slaughtered."* Such a description could not have been offered about most of the chapters of Israelite history, though there was always the faithful remnant. During periods of David's reign, such a description might have rung true.

At the end, the Psalmist makes his plea for deliverance from this tragedy: *"Awake! Why do you sleep, O Lord? Rise up! Do not reject us forever! Why do you hide your face; why forget our pain and misery?... Rise up, help us! Redeem us in your mercy."* In the light of their history with God, if in this situation God were to cast off His people, He would be casting them off forever! The Israelites had enough trust to know that God would never abandon them!

Reflect and Pray on Psalm 44, using Lectio Divina or the Method of Meditation. Make sure you converse intimately with the Blessed Trinity:

Prayer on Psalm 44: God's Past Favor and Israel's Present Need
"1For the leader. A maskil of the Korahites.

I.

"2 O God, we have heard with our own ears; our ancestors have told us the deeds you did in their days, with your own hand in days of old: 3 You rooted out nations to plant them, crushed peoples and expelled them. 4 Not with their own swords did they conquer the land, nor did their own arms bring victory; it was your right hand, your own arm, the light of your face for you favored them. 5 You are my king and my God, who bestows victories on Jacob. 6 Through you we batter our foes; through your name we trample our adversaries. 7 Not in my bow do I trust, nor does my sword bring me

victory. 8 You have brought us victory over our enemies, shamed those who hate us. 9 In God we have boasted all the day long; your name we will praise forever.

II.

10 But now you have rejected and disgraced us; you do not march with our armies. 11 You make us retreat before the foe; those who hate us plunder us at will. 12 You hand us over like sheep to be slaughtered, scatter us among the nations. 13 You see your people for nothing; you make no profit from their sale. 14 You make us the reproach of our neighbors, the mockery and scorn of those around us. 15 You make us a byword among the nations; the peoples shake their heads at us. 16 All day long my disgrace is before me; shame has covered my face 17 At the sound of those who taunt and revile, at the sight of the enemy and avenger.

III.

18 All this has come upon us, though we have not forgotten you, nor been disloyal to your covenant. 19 Our hearts have not turned back, nor have our steps strayed from your path. 20 Yet you have left us crushed, desolate in a place of jackals; you have covered us with a shadow of death. 21 If we had forgotten the name of our God, stretched out our hands to another god, 22 would not God have discovered this, God who knows the secrets of the heart? 23 For you we are slain all the day long, considered only as sheep to be slaughtered.

IV.

24 Awake! Why do you sleep, O Lord? Rise up! Do not reject us forever! 25 Why do you hide your face; why forget our pain and misery? 26 For our soul has been humiliated in the dust; our belly is pressed to the earth. 27 Rise up, help us! Redeem us in your mercy."

End with Prayer to the Holy Trinity
NIGHT PRAYER: The Examination of Conscience

DAY THREE:
MORNING PRAYER: Acts of Faith, Hope, Charity; Daily Offering

MORNING FACE TO FACE WITH GOD:
Begin with Prayer to the Holy Spirit
Prayer on Psalm 45: Song for a Royal Wedding

Psalm 45 was a nuptial song composed to honor the Davidic king's wedding to a foreign princess from Tyre. The court minstrel is celebrating the marriage between the anointed one of God and his bride to be: *"My heart is stirred by a noble theme, as I sing my ode to the king. My tongue is the pen of a nimble scribe."* The historical data about this wedding are unclear. The Jewish tradition has interpreted this psalm as a song to the Messiah-King. This psalm has remained in the Hebrew Psalter even though Israel did not have a king during and after the Babylonian exile which ended in 537 B.C. As Christians, we believe that Jesus is the Messiah-King, the rightful Son of David who has fulfilled the prophecies of Psalm 45.

Psalm 45 is a nuptial song which exalts the beauty and devotion of love and faithfulness between the spouses. The bridegroom bears the military insignia who will fight for the cause of truth and justice with meekness: *"You are the most handsome of men; fair speech has graced your lips, for God has blessed you forever. Gird your sword upon your hip, mighty warrior! In splendor and majesty ride on triumphant! In the cause of truth, meekness, and justice may your right hand show your wondrous deeds."* He is clothed in elegant and fragrant robes: *"With myrrh, aloes, and cassia your robes are fragrant."*

For this glorious marital celebration, the palaces shine, and the music resonates with festal joy and celebration: *"From ivory-paneled palaces stringed instruments bring you joy."* The throne rises in the center and the scepter is mentioned as well, both signs of power and royalty: *"Your throne, O God, stands forever; your royal scepter is a scepter for justice."* The name 'God,' was addressed to the king himself as he was anointed by the LORD, and therefore, in some way belonged to the divine realm. This would be the perfect name for Jesus, truly man and truly God!

In Part III, the bride is celebrated as the perfect wife for the Davidic king. Her function as being totally dedicated to her husband is emphasized: *"Listen, my daughter, and understand; pay me careful heed. Forget your people and your father's house, that the king might desire your beauty. He is your lord; honor him, daughter of Tyre. Then the richest of the people will seek your favor with gifts."* Her beauty and splendor are extolled as well, as she is the perfect bride for the perfect king: *"All glorious is the king's daughter as she enters, her raiment threaded with gold; in embroidered apparel she is led to the king. The maids of her train are presented to the king. They are led in with glad and joyous acclaim; they enter the palace of the king."* The Christian tradition has understood the Blessed Mother to be the bride to be. In the kingdom of Israel, the Queen was always the Queen-Mother. In the new Kingdom of Israel that Jesus would establish with His death and resurrection, His mother would become the *Gebirah or Great Lady,* the Queen-Mother of the realm.

In line with the Christological interpretation of Psalm 45, two elements are worthy of note. The beauty of the bridegroom expresses the Father's exquisitely tender gaze upon His Son: *"You are the most handsome of men; fair speech has graced your lips, for God has blessed you forever."* God's tender gaze upon His Son at His baptism and transfiguration comes to mind. Jesus is indeed the Perfect Man in whom our humanity has been brought to its original perfection. In His burial, Jesus was clothed with a burial cloth made fragrant with myrrh, aloes, and cassia, pointing to His resurrection: *"With myrrh, aloes, and cassia your robes are fragrant."* In Jesus, we can ascend to moral perfection in a world that is marred by ugliness and degradation. The second element is justice: *"In splendor and majesty ride on triumphant! In the cause of truth, meekness, and justice may your right hand show your wondrous deeds."* When our lives reflect our covenant union with Jesus, His radiant face will shine through us as the Light of the world.

The psalm concludes with the exaltation of the king's throne which will be an everlasting feature of the kingdom of Israel: *"The throne of your fathers your sons will have; you shall make them princes through all the land. I will make your name renowned through all generations; thus nations shall praise you forever."* The New Testament sees the fulfillment of this prophetic acclamation in Jesus, the Messiah-King of the New Israel: *"But of the Son: "Your throne, O God, stands forever and ever; and a righteous scepter is the scepter of your kingdom. You loved justice and hated wickedness; therefore God, your God, anointed you with the oil of gladness above your companions"* (Hebrews 1: 8-9).

Reflect and Pray on Psalm 45 using Lectio Divina or the Method of Meditation. Make sure you converse intimately with the Blessed Trinity:

Prayer on Psalm 45: Song for a Royal Wedding
"1 For the leader; according to "Lilies." A love song.

I.

2 My heart is stirred by a noble theme, as I sing my ode to the king. My tongue is the pen of a nimble scribe.

II.

3 You are the most handsome of men; fair speech has graced your lips, for God has blessed you forever. 4 Gird your sword upon your hip, mighty warrior! In splendor and majesty ride on triumphant! 5 In the cause of truth, meekness, and justice may your right hand show your wondrous deeds. 6 Your arrows are sharp; peoples will cower at your feet; the king's enemies will lose heart. 7 Your throne, O God, stands forever; your royal scepter is a scepter for justice. 8 You love justice and hate wrongdoing; therefore God, your God has anointed you with the oil of gladness above your fellow kings. 9 With myrrh, aloes, and cassia your robes are fragrant. From ivory-paneled palaces stringed instruments bring you joy. 10 Daughters of kings are your lovely wives; a princess arrayed in Ophir's gold comes to stand at your right hand.

III.

11 Listen, my daughter, and understand; pay me careful heed.

Forget your people and your father's house, 12 that the king might desire your beauty. He is your lord; 13 honor him, daughter of Tyre. Then the richest of the people will seek your favor with gifts. 14 All glorious is the king's daughter as she enters, her raiment threaded with gold; 15 in embroidered apparel she is led to the king. The maids of her train are presented to the king. 16 They are led in with glad and joyous acclaim; they enter the palace of the king.

IV.

The throne of your fathers your sons will have; you shall make them princes through all the land. 18 I will make your name renowned through all generations; thus nations shall praise you forever."

End with Prayer to the Holy Trinity
NIGHT PRAYER: The Examination of Conscience

DAY FOUR:
MORNING PRAYER: Acts of Faith, Hope, Charity; Daily Offering

MORNING FACE TO FACE WITH GOD:
Begin with Prayer to the Holy Spirit

Prayer on Psalm 46: God, the Protector of Zion

Psalm 46 celebrates God's dwelling in Zion or Jerusalem. Jerusalem is the Holy City because God dwells in the Temple as Emmanuel, God among His people. Psalms 48, 76, 84, 87, and 122 are the other psalms that center their prayer and utter trust in God dwelling among His people in the Temple. In Psalm 46, the Psalmist expresses the utmost trust and security in the presence and protection of God who is Emmanuel: *"God is our refuge and our strength, an ever-present help in distress. Thus we do not fear, though earth be shaken and mountains quake to the depths of the sea, though its waters rage and foam and mountains totter at its surging."*

The city will remain impregnable because God dwells in Jerusalem. As God's abode, Jerusalem will withstand the onslaught of nations as it is the stronghold of the God of Jacob:

"Streams of the river gladden the city of God, the holy dwelling of the Most High. God is in its midst; it shall not be shaken; God will help it at break of day. Though nations rage and kingdoms totter, he utters his voice and the earth melts. The LORD of hosts is with us; our stronghold is the God of Jacob." God will be their security in moments of deadly upheavals. Jerusalem will not be shaken.

Psalm 46 highlights two key truths, each revelation concluding with an antiphon affirming the truth. The Psalmist views Jerusalem as having *"streams of the river that gladden the city of God, the holy dwelling of the Most High. God is in our midst; it shall not be shaken; God will help it at break of day."* The streams symbolize the *'spring welling up to eternal life'* (John 4: 14), that embraces Jerusalem because of God's Presence and faithfulness. In the phrase, *'God will help it at break of day,'* St. Ambrose of Milan, a great Latin Father of the Church, sees it as a prophetic allusion to the Resurrection which occurred at the break of dawn.

The second truth invites us to behold a regenerated world because God is the God of our human history: *"Come and see the works of the LORD, who has done fearsome deeds on earth; who stops wars to the ends of the earth, breaks the bow, splinters the spear, and burns the shields with fire."* This truth found its fulfillment in Jesus and has been echoed by the Prophets: *"They shall beat their plowshares and their spears into pruning hooks; one nation shall not raise the sword against another, nor shall they train for war again. House of Jacob, come, let us walk in the light of the LORD!"* (Isaiah 2: 4-5). Christian tradition has praised Christ as our Liberator from evil through His death and resurrection and our Prince of Peace. Our reflections on Jerusalem being a holy city and God creating a regenerated world which will occur through Jesus' death on the cross and resurrection, draw us to *"be still and know that I am God!"* We will realize that God is *"exalted among the nations, exalted on the earth. The LORD of hosts is with us; our stronghold is the God of Jacob."*

Reflect and Pray on Psalm 46, using Lectio Divina or the Method of

Meditation. Make sure you converse intimately with the Blessed Trinity:

Prayer on Psalm 46: God, the Protector of Zion (Read Psalm 48 as well)
"1 For the leader. A song of the Korahites. According to alamoth.
I.
"2 God is our refuge and our strength, an ever-present help in distress. 3 Thus we do not fear, though earth be shaken and mountains quake to the depths of the sea, 4 though its waters rage and foam and mountains totter at its surging.
II.
5 Streams of the river gladden the city of God, the holy dwelling of the Most High. 6 God is in its midst; it shall not be shaken; God will help it at break of day. 7 Though nations rage and kingdoms totter, he utters his voice and the earth melts. 8 The LORD of hosts is with us; our stronghold is the God of Jacob.
III.
9 Come and see the works of the LORD, who has done fearsome deeds on earth; 10 who stops wars to the ends of the earth, breaks the bow, splinters the spear, and burns the shields with fire; 11 "Be still and know that I am God! I am exalted among the nations, exalted on the earth." 12 The LORD of hosts is with us; our stronghold is the God of Jacob."

End with Prayer to the Holy Trinity
NIGHT PRAYER: The Examination of Conscience

DAY FIVE:
MORNING PRAYER: Acts of Faith, Hope and Charity; Daily Offering

MORNING FACE TO FACE WITH GOD:
Begin with Prayer to the Holy Spirit
Psalm 47: The Ruler of All Nations

Psalm 47 is a hymn of joyous praise and celebration of God's marvelous deeds among His people. He is the LORD of Israel and the King of the Universe. The psalm begins with loud and effusive praise of God: *"All you peoples, clap your hands; shout to God with joyful cries."* Along with other psalms of praise like Psalms

93, 96 to 98, this psalm shows that praise of God and thanksgiving to Him for being their Covenant God is at the heart of Israel's prayer and worship. Their God has had dominion over nations and peoples that were hostile to the Israelites. These nations were obstructed from sabotaging God's plan for His people. The people feel compelled to praise the LORD, the Most High who carved the Israelites into a nation and made them His heritage: *"For the LORD, the Most High, is to be feared, the great king over all the earth, who made people subject to us, nations under our feet, who chose our heritage for us, the glory of Jacob, whom he loves."*

The Psalmist asserts a second fundamental truth that God will be worshiped and praised by the Israelites and by all nations. *"Sing praise to God, sing praise; sing praise to our king, sing praise. For God is king over all the earth; sing hymns of praise. God rules over the nations; God sits upon his holy throne. The princes of the peoples assemble with the people of the God of Abraham. For the shields of the earth belong to God, highly exalted."* Abraham was the Patriarch of Israel and the Father of all nations. God's chosen people have been given the task of bringing all peoples to worship the God of Abraham, Isaac, and Jacob. The prophets echo a similar prophecy, as in Isaiah 2: 3: *"Many peoples shall come and say: 'Come, let us go up to the LORD's mountain, to the house of the God of Jacob, that he may instruct us in his ways, and we may walk in his paths."* This amazing gathering of peoples became a reality through Jesus. Jesus is the Head and this universal Gathering of Peoples around Him is His body. This movement toward becoming the Catholic Church of Jesus Christ was orchestrated with the Outpouring of the Holy Spirit.

There is an important allusion to the Ascension of the Risen Lord: *"God has gone up with a shout; the LORD, amid trumpet blasts."* God came down from heaven to rescue His people time and again. He was always their Protector who came to their aid when they were in dire straits. As God returns to His heavenly abode, the Israelites are giving Him a joyous send-off. The New

Testament gives us the full understanding of God's comings and goings among us. Jesus says, *"I came down from heaven not to do my own will but the will of the one who sent me"* (John 6: 38). With Jesus' Ascension, our eyes are fixed on the new Jerusalem where the glory of the divine Lamb of God will be revealed: *"After this I had a vision of a great multitude, which no one could count, from every nation, race, people, and tongue. They stood before the throne and before the Lamb, wearing white robes and holding palm branches in their hands. They cried out in a loud voice: "Salvation comes from our God, who is seated on the throne, and from the Lamb"* (Revelation 7: 9-10).

Reflect and Pray on Psalm 47, using Lectio Divina or the Method of Meditation. Make sure you converse intimately with the Blessed Trinity:

Psalm 47: The Ruler of All Nations
"1 For the leader. A psalm of the Korahites.

I.

"2 All you peoples, clap your hands; shout to God with joyful cries. 3 For the LORD, the Most High, is to be feared, the great king over all the earth, 4 who made people subject to us, nations under our feet, 5 who chose our heritage for us, the glory of Jacob, whom he loves.

II.

6 God has gone up with a shout; the LORD, amid trumpet blasts. 7 Sing praise to God, sing praise; sing praise to our king, sing praise.

III.

8 For God is king over all the earth; sing hymns of praise. 9 God rules over the nations; God sits upon his holy throne. 10 The princes of the peoples assemble with the people of the God of Abraham. For the shields of the earth belong to God, highly exalted."

End with Prayer to the Holy Trinity
NIGHT PRAYER: The Examination of Conscience

DAY SIX:
MORNING PRAYER: Acts of Faith, Hope and Charity; Daily Offering

MORNING FACE TO FACE WITH GOD:
Begin with Prayer to the Holy Spirit
Prayer on Psalm 49: Confidence in God rather than in Riches

Psalm 49 is a 'wisdom' psalm like Psalm 1. As we go through life, we are all confronted with questions that arise from the problem of inequality and injustice, resulting from evil in the human heart. Why is it, in many instances, that those who choose to live justly and honestly do not fare as well as those who have made wealth and worldly honor their god? How do we live with wisdom and serenity amidst the conundrums of life? Such problems spare no one, be they of noble birth or raised in poverty. And over our lives hangs the inevitable certainty of death. Assuredly, we are mortal beings and the smell of death is always upon us. How best then can we live with wisdom and true happiness when the inevitable reality of our lives is death? Amidst the inequities and heartaches of life, the Psalmist is offering us meaningful wisdom: *"Hear this, all you peoples! Give ear, all who inhabit the world, you of lowly birth or high estate, rich and poor together. My mouth shall speak words of wisdom, my heart shall offer insights. I will turn my ear to a riddle, expound my question on a lyre."*

The Psalmist begins by pointing out the illusory nature of wealth and power. Without being centered in God, all is vanity. The transitory nature of wealth has the rich person in its death-like vice. The rich will not be able to take anything with them in death, except their dead bodies. And even though the just person will face evil in life, they can remain undaunted because they have surrendered their lives to God: *"Why should I fear in evil days, with the iniquity of my assailants surrounding me, of those who trust in their wealth and boast of their abundant riches? ... Will he live on forever, then, and never see the Pit of Corruption? ... the fool will perish together with the senseless, and they leave their wealth to others. Their tombs are their homes forever, their dwellings through all generations, ... – they perish."* The rich try to buy off death through their accumulation of wealth. In the end, everyone suffers the same permanent separation from everything that they owned. Humanity's constant temptation is to cling to riches as though they were endowed with an invincible power that could buy off even death. In the next verse, the Psalmist exposes the folly of making mammon their god: *"This is the way of those who trust in themselves, and the end of those who take pleasure in their own mouth. "Like a herd of sheep they will be put into Sheol, and Death will shepherd them."* A sobering thought!

Psalm 49 offers us a sober meditation on death, the unavoidable destination of human existence. Our saints advise us to meditate frequently on death. Untold wealth is not the solution to true happiness. It is better to be poor and one with God! A profound blindness overtakes us when we delude ourselves that true happiness and immortality lie in our accumulation of wealth and power. Jesus has offered us the perfect solution to this vexing conundrum: *"Take care to guard against all greed, for though one may be rich, one's life does not consist of possessions"* (Luke 12: 15). Jesus then recounts the Parable of the Rich Fool, who *"stores up treasure for himself but is not rich in what matters to God"* (Luke 12: 21).

The latter half of the psalm offers us a way out of this inevitable impasse in human existence. It is not wealth and power that hold the key to true happiness and enduring immortality. It is God alone: *"But God will redeem my life, will take me from the hand of Sheol."* 'Taking up' is the same Hebrew word used here that described the ascent of Enoch: *"Enoch walked with God, and he was no longer here, for God took him"* (Genesis 5:24); and of Elijah as well: *"As they walked on still conversing, a fiery chariot and fiery horses came between the two of them, and Elijah went up to heaven in a whirlwind, and Elisha saw it happen"* (2Kings 2: 11- 12). The certainty of immortality or life with God began to emerge and become explicit in the Books of Wisdom around the

Sixth Century B.C. Jesus fulfilled this prophecy in Psalm 49. In His atonement for our sins through His death and resurrection, Jesus ransomed us for God, bought us back for God by becoming our price, and ensured our being taken up in our resurrection.

Reflect and Pray on Psalm 49, using Lectio Divina or the Method of Meditation. Please converse intimately with the Blessed Trinity:

Prayer on Psalm 49: Confidence in God rather than in Riches
"1 For the leader. A psalm of the Korahites.
"2 Hear this, all you peoples! Give ear, all who inhabit the world, 3 you of lowly birth or high estate, rich and poor together. 4 My mouth shall speak words of wisdom, my heart shall offer insights. 5 I will turn my ear to a riddle, expound my question on a lyre.

I.

6 Why should I fear in evil days, with the iniquity of my assailants surrounding me, 7 of those who trust in their wealth and boast of their abundant riches? 8 No man can ransom even a brother, or pay to God his own ransom. 9 The redemption of his soul is costly; and he will pass away forever. 10 Will he live on forever, then, and never see the Pit of Corruption? 11 Indeed, he will see that that wise die, and the fool will perish together with the senseless, and they leave their wealth to others. 12 Their tombs are their homes forever, their dwellings through all generations, "They named countries after themselves" 13 – but man does not abide in splendor. He is like the beasts – they perish.

II.

14 This is the way of those who trust in themselves, and the end of those who take pleasure in their own mouth. 15 Like a herd of sheep they will be put into Sheol, and Death will shepherd them. Straight to the grave they descend, where their form will waste away, Sheol will be their palace. 16 But God will redeem my life, will take me from the hand of Sheol. 17 Do not fear when a man becomes rich, when the wealth of his house grows great. 18 At his death he will not take along anything, his glory will not go down after him. 19 During his life his soul uttered blessings; "They will praise you, for you do well for yourself." 20 But he will join the company of his fathers, never again to see the light. 21 In his prime, man does not understand. He is like the beasts – they perish."

End with Prayer to the Holy Trinity
NIGHT SESSION: The Examination of Conscience

DAY SEVEN:
MORNING PRAYER: Acts of Faith, Hope, Charity; Daily Offering

MORNING FACE TO FACE WITH GOD:
<u>Learning Discipleship from the Psalms</u>
Begin with Prayer to the Holy Spirit

- *"Why are you downcast, my soul, why do you groan within me? Wait for God, for I shall again praise him, my savior and my God"* (Psalm 42: 6, 12; Psalm 43: 5). The Psalmist decides to praise God and steadfastly banish fear and melancholy amidst a severe crisis by trusting that God will be His Savior and LORD!

- *"As the deer longs for streams of water, so my soul longs for you, O God. My soul thirsts for God, the living God. When can I enter and see the face of God? My tears have been my bread day and night, as they ask me every day, "Where is your God?"* (Psalm 42: 2-4). The thirsting deer symbolizes aptly the disciple who longs for the security of the Lord's presence in crisis and yet feels far removed from Him. We are wayfarers on our journey to God, amidst the perilous paths of life's valley of tears. Only our hope in God can sustain us.

- *"Those times I recall as I pour out my soul, when I would cross over to the shrine of the Mighty One, to the house of God, amid loud cries of thanksgiving, with the multitude keeping festival"* (Psalm 42: 5). Our sad and uncertain present is best tempered by the remembrance of God's joyful presence and blessings in our past. If God was with us so vividly in the

past, then assuredly, He will continue to be with us because God is faithful and will always keep His promises to us.
- *"Awake! Why do you sleep, O Lord? Rise up! Do not reject us forever! Why do you hide your face; why forget our pain and misery?... Rise up, help us! Redeem us in your mercy"* (Psalm 44). Given their history with God, if in this situation God were to cast off His people, He would be casting them off *forever!* God's apparent tardiness served a good purpose. The Israelites knew that God would not abandon them!
- *"You are the most handsome of men; fair speech has graced your lips, for God has blessed you forever"* (Psalm 45). We have always viewed Jesus as the Perfect Man in whom our humanity was brought to its original perfection. We can ascend to moral perfection in Jesus in a world that is marred by ugliness and degradation.
- In Psalm 45, the upshot of our reflections on Jerusalem being a holy city and God creating a regenerated world which will occur through Jesus' death on the cross and resurrection, is for us to *"be still and know that I am God!"* Like Mary, we will realize that God is *"exalted among the nations, exalted on the earth. The LORD of hosts is with us; our stronghold is the God of Jacob."*
- *"God has gone up with a shout; the LORD, amid trumpet blasts"* (Psalm 47). The Israelites saw God as coming down from heaven on different occasions to rescue His people, and then returning to *'his holy throne'* in heaven. As God returns to His heavenly abode, the Israelites are giving Him a joyous send-off. With Jesus' Ascension, we gaze on the new Jerusalem where the glory of the Lamb of God will be revealed: *"They cried out in a loud voice: "Salvation comes from our God, who is seated on the throne, and from the Lamb"* (Revelation 7: 9-10).
- *"Will he live on forever, then, and never see the Pit of Corruption? Indeed, he will see that the wise die, and the fool*

will perish together with the senseless, and they leave their wealth to others. Their tombs are their homes forever, ... He is like the beasts – they perish" (Psalm 49). A profound blindness overtakes us when we delude ourselves that true happiness and immortality lie in our accumulation of wealth and power. Jesus has offered us the perfect solution to this vexing conundrum: *"Take care to guard against all greed, for though one may be rich, one's life does not consist of possessions"* (Luke 12: 15).

End with Prayer to the Holy Trinity
NIGHT PRAYER: The Examination of Conscience

JOURNAL FOR BOOK TWO, WEEK ONE: CELEBRATION AND PRAISE

DAY ONE: Morning Prayer: Psalm 42: Longing for God's Presence in the Temple
What is God saying to You?

Nightly Examination of Conscience:
For what are you grateful?

For what are you contrite?

What spiritual discipline, including fasting, do you need to focus on tomorrow?

DAY TWO: Morning Prayer: Psalm 44: God's Past Favor and Israel's Present Need
What is God saying to You

Nightly Examination of Conscience:
For what are you grateful?

For what are you contrite?

What spiritual discipline, including fasting, do you need to focus on tomorrow?

DAY THREE: Morning Prayer: Psalm 45: Song for a Royal Wedding
What is God saying to You?

Nightly Examination of Conscience:
For what are you grateful?

For what are you contrite?

What spiritual discipline, including fasting, do you need to focus on tomorrow?

DAY FOUR: Morning Prayer: Psalm 46: God, the Protector of Zion
What is God saying to You?

Nightly Examination of Conscience:
For what are you grateful?

For what are you contrite?

What spiritual discipline, including fasting, do you need to focus on tomorrow?

DAY FIVE: Morning Prayer: Psalm 47: The Ruler of All Nations
What is God saying to You?

Nightly Examination of Conscience:
For what are you grateful?

For what are you contrite?

What spiritual discipline, including fasting, do you need to focus on tomorrow?

DAY SIX: Morning Prayer: Psalm 49: Confidence in God rather than in Riches
What is God saying to You?

Nightly Examination of Conscience:
For what are you grateful?

For what are you contrite?

What spiritual discipline, including fasting, do you need to focus on tomorrow?

DAY SEVEN: Morning Prayer: Learning Discipleship from the Psalms
What is God saying to You?

Nightly Examination of Conscience:
For what are you grateful?

For what are you contrite?

What spiritual discipline, including fasting, do you need to focus on tomorrow?

What prayer would you compose to express what God has said to you this week?

BOOK TWO – PSALMS 42-72: CELEBRATION AND PRAISE
Psalms 50, 51, 52, 53, 54, and 56

WHAT IS AT THE HEART OF BOOK TWO, WEEK TWO?

As we have noted, the Second Book has as its theme, *Celebration and Praise,* thus striking a more confident tone than in Book One. Much of the focus is on David's reign as King of Israel, during which period the kingdom experienced prosperity, peace, and expansion. In particular, the worship of God was centralized at the temple in Jerusalem after David made Jerusalem his capital and brought the Ark of the Covenant from Kiriath-jearim of Judah to dwell permanently in the temple. Through the psalms, many of which were his own compositions, David enhanced temple worship by developing an orderly and sophisticated liturgy. David also emphasized the *todah* or thanksgiving offering as being superior to the *ola* or burnt offerings of animals. He composed many of his psalms of thanksgiving and praise to celebrate the *todah* sacrifice.

This week, we will be praying with Psalms 50, 51, 52, 53, 54, and 56. On Day One, we will pray with *Psalm 50: The Acceptable Sacrifice.* Psalm 50 clearly highlights this moment of transition in the way Israel henceforward approached worship and sacrificial offering. The *Todah Cycle* came into being in the life and worship of ancient Israel. Through David's influence, the *Todah* or thanksgiving offering was given greater importance than the *Ola* or burnt offering. Moses preferred the burnt offering (*'ola'*) where the entire animal was consumed in fire, but David encouraged the thank offering (*'todah'*), where the animal was sacrificed and eaten in a meal of thanksgiving and praise. Psalm 50 expresses the covenant established between God and David and highlights this shift in emphasis from *ola* to *todah*. Psalm 50 prepares us for the eventual *todah* or Eucharistic sacrificial meal in Jesus. In naming the different types of sacrifice, the psalm asserts the superiority of the thanksgiving offering (*todah*) over the burnt offering (*ola*) and other kinds of offerings.

Psalms 51, 52, 53, 54, and 56 are psalms from earlier in David's career. While they are songs of lament, they keep reminding us that God always comes to the rescue of those who walk in His ways and trust Him completely. On Day Two, we will reflect prayerfully on *Psalm 51: The Miserere: A Prayer of Repentance*. Psalm 51 is a Penitential Psalm and among the most famous psalms in the Psalter. It is prayed every Friday, during Morning Prayer of the Liturgy of the Hours. It is the intense passage that takes place in a repentant sinner, moving from sin to forgiveness, from enslavement to guilt to freedom in grace.

On Day Three, we will ponder *Psalm 52: The Deceitful Tongue*. The Psalmist reflects on the insidious nature of evil and the degradation it causes to the soul. Against overwhelming odds, God protected David. David expresses his sincere gratitude and praise to God for providing him with security and preservation from all the dangers and snares laid against him by Saul and his henchmen.

On Day Four, we will pray with *Psalm 53: A Lament over Widespread Corruption*. It is essentially a repetition of Psalm 14, with a few modifications. Both psalms are titled, 'A Lament over Widespread Corruption.' The theme in both psalms is the salvation of God. Both psalms are David's ponderings, and are intended to give faith and courage to Israel during a national challenge, such as the threat of an invasion or a siege.

On Day Five, we will ponder *Psalm 54: Confident Prayer in Great Peril*. Psalm 54 is like Psalm 52 in that both psalms focus on the persecution and oppression that David experienced as a fugitive from Saul. The superscription of Psalm 54 tells us that the Ziphites came and said to Saul, *"David is hiding among us."* David is confident that God will come to his rescue as He has in the past. His rescue at the hands of God will engender within him an intense desire to offer God a *todah* or thanksgiving sacrifice for rescuing and giving him victory over his enemies.

On Day Six, we will reflect and pray with *Psalm 56: Trust in God.* Psalm 56 continues with the trials and tribulations that David experienced during the seven years or so when he was a fugitive from Saul. Psalm 56 is a prayer that springs from David's endangered heart while he was in the city of Gath. Psalm 56 offers us the same recurring themes of asking God for deliverance from enemies and expressing grateful trust in God.

On Day Seven, we will ponder the salient advice that these psalms have offered us to enhance and strengthen our own following of Jesus and our commitment to His Church.

SPIRITUAL READING FOR BOOK TWO OF THE PSALMS:
1 and 2 Samuel
Psalms 42 to 72
1 and 2 Kings (after you have read 1 and 2 Samuel)
1 and 2 Chronicles (after you have read 1 and 2 Kings)

DAY ONE:
MORNING PRAYER: Acts of Faith, Hope, Charity; Daily Offering

MORNING FACE TO FACE WITH GOD:
Begin with Prayer to the Holy Spirit
Prayer on Psalm 50: The Acceptable Sacrifice
Psalm 50 focuses on the acceptable sacrifice in worship at the Temple. The Psalmist opens with a majestic view of God's glorious appearance among His people: *"The God of gods, the LORD, has spoken and summoned the earth from the rising of the sun to its setting. From Zion, the perfection of beauty, God shines forth. Our God comes and will not be silent! Devouring fire precedes him, it rages strongly around him. ..."Gather my loyal ones to me, those who made a covenant with me by sacrifice."* The imagery takes us back to Mount Sinai where God appeared to His people in a dense cloud, with fire, smoke, loud peals of thunder, and lightning. Mount Sinai prefigured Zion or the Temple, where God dwells among His people. The Holy of Holies is now His throne from where He is addressing His people.

In Part II, God offers a scathing condemnation of Israel's callous approach toward worship and sacrificial offerings. They offered sacrifices and burnt offerings without a contrite and repentant heart. They surmised that they merited God's favor because they 'fed God' by offering Him their animals and grain offerings. Their worship was empty because they did not offer their hearts to God: *"Not for your sacrifices do I rebuke you, your burnt offerings are always before me. ... Were I hungry, I would not tell you, for mine is the world and all that fills it. Do I eat the flesh of bulls or drink the blood of he-goats?* God spells out the degradation of soul that occurs when worship and sacrificial offerings have become perfunctory and self-serving, where God is mocked and trivialized: *"But to the wicked God says: 'Why do you recite my commandments and profess my covenant with your mouth? You hate discipline; you cast my words behind you! ...When you do these things should I be silent? ... I accuse you, I lay out the matter before your eyes."*

Instead, God desires that they offer Him thanksgiving offerings. Humility is embedded in the attitude of thanksgiving. Thanksgiving comes from a contrite and grateful heart. Thanksgiving and repentance or turning toward God go hand in hand. The *Todah Cycle* would commence by an Israelite getting into trouble because of their sins, or some crisis resulting in economic or personal hardship, thereby threatening their existence. They would cry out to God for help and promise to make a thanksgiving offering when God answered their prayer. God would save the person and they would make a pilgrimage to the Temple to offer the *todah* or thanksgiving offering and have a feast to praise and thank God publicly: *"Offer praise as your sacrifice to God; fulfill your vows to the Most High. Then call on me on the day of distress; I will rescue you, and you shall honor me."* Psalm 50 asserts the superiority of the thanksgiving offering *(todah)* over the burnt offering *('olâ')* and other kinds of offerings (refer to Leviticus 1-7). It highlights the *Todah Cycle* in affirming the superiority of the Thanksgiving Offering.

The ancient rabbis believed that after the Messiah came, except for the thanksgiving offering, all other sacrifices would be rendered obsolete, as the Messiah would overcome sin. The thanksgiving sacrifice would always be relevant as it behooves us to thank God continually for our salvation. Jesus has put an end to sin by nailing it on the Cross. Today, our one and only sacrifice is the thanksgiving offering of Jesus' death and resurrection called the Eucharist, meaning Thanksgiving. Psalm 50 makes the point that the sacrifice of thanksgiving, now Eucharist for us, is the best offering of all: *"Those who offer praise as a sacrifice honor me; I will let him whose way is steadfast look upon the salvation of God."*

Reflect and Pray on Psalm 50, using Lectio Divina or the Method of Meditation. Make sure you converse intimately with the Blessed Trinity:

Prayer on Psalm 50: The Acceptable Sacrifice
"1 A psalm of Asaph.

I.

"1 The God of gods, the LORD, has spoken and summoned the earth from the rising of the sun to its setting. 2 From Zion, the perfection of beauty, God shines forth. 3 Our God comes and will not be silent! Devouring fire precedes him, it rages strongly around him. 4 He calls to the heavens and to the earth to judge his people: 5 "Gather my loyal ones to me, those who made a covenant with me by sacrifice." 6 The heavens proclaim his righteousness, for God himself is the judge.

II.

7 "Listen, my people, I will speak; Israel, I will testify against you; God, your God, am I. 8 Not for your sacrifices do I rebuke you, your burnt offerings are always before me. 9 I will not take a bullock from your house, or he-goats from your folds. 10 For every animal of the forest is mine, beasts by the thousands on my mountains. 11 I now every bird in the heights; whatever moves in the wild is mine. 12 Were I hungry, I would not tell you, for mine is the world and all that fills it. 13 Do I eat the flesh of bulls or drink the blood of he-goats? 14 Offer praise as your sacrifice to God; fulfill your vows to the Most High. 15 Then call on my in the day of distress; I will rescue you, and you shall honor me."

III.

16 But to the wicked God says: 'Why do you recite my commandments and profess my covenant with your mouth: 17 You hate discipline; you cast my words behind you! 18 If you see a thief, you run with him; with adulterers you throw in your lot. 19 You give your mouth free rein for evil; you yoke your tongue to deceit. 20 You sit and speak against your brother, slandering your mother's son. 21 When you do these things should I be silent? Do you think that I am like you? I accuse you, I lay out the matter before your eyes.

IV.

22 "Now understand this, you who forget God, lest I start ripping apart and there be no rescuer. 23 Those who offer praise as a sacrifice honor me; I will let him whose way is steadfast look upon the salvation of God."

End with Prayer to the Holy Trinity
NIGHT PRAYER: The Examination of Conscience

DAY TWO:
MORNING PRAYER: Acts of Faith, Hope, Charity; Daily Offering

MORNING FACE TO FACE WITH GOD:
Begin with Prayer to the Holy Spirit

Prayer on Psalm 51: The Miserere: Prayer of Repentance

Psalm 51 is the most famous Penitential Psalm in the Psalter. It is prayed every Friday during Morning Prayer of the Liturgy of the Hours. It is the intense passage that takes place in a repentant sinner, moving from sin to forgiveness, from enslavement to guilt to freedom in grace. This Prayer of Repentance has risen from countless Jews and Christians over the centuries, with the confidence that they are addressing a merciful God who will forgive them and reinstate them in His loving kindness.

The psalm was composed by David who was convicted by Nathan the prophet after he had committed adultery with Bathsheba and had her husband, Uriah, killed in battle: *"Why have you despised the LORD and done what is evil in his sight? You have cut down Uriah the Hittite with the sword; his wife you took as your own, and him you killed with the sword of the Ammonites. Now, therefore, the sword shall never depart from your house, because you have despised me and have taken the wife of Uriah the Hittite to be your wife"* (2Samuel 12: 9-10). David's response is, *"Have mercy on me, God, in accord with your merciful love; in your abundant compassion blot out my transgressions. Thoroughly wash away my guilt; and from my sin cleanse me."*

Psalm 51 outlines two worldviews that are diametrically opposed to each other. Firstly, there is the sinister region of sin in which we have been placed from the beginning of our existence: *"Behold, I was born in guilt, in sin my mother conceived me."* Part I offers us a deep analysis of the nature of sin as the sinner pours out their heart to God. Sin is a distortion, interchanging good for evil and evil for good: *"Ah! Those who call evil good, and good evil, who change darkness to light, and light into darkness, who change bitter to sweet, and sweet into bitter!"* (Isaiah 5: 20). Sin is the creature's open rebellion against their Creator.

Repentance moves the sinner to adopt the other worldview proposed in Part II: *"Turn away your face from my sins; blot out all my iniquities. A clean heart create for me, God; renew within me a steadfast spirit."* The sinner confesses their sin and the saving justice of God is ready to purify and cleanse them of their sin. Besides eliminating sin, the Lord recreates sinful humanity through the life-giving action of the Holy Spirit. He replaces the sinner's heart and mind with the heart and mind of Jesus. Under the guidance of the Holy Spirit, the sinner can move in the direction of becoming a saint, developing and deepening a limpid faith and worship pleasing to God.

Psalm 51 reveals several fundamental spiritual practices that should permeate the daily life of the disciple. The psalm encourages us to develop a lively sense of sin and take responsibility for our sinful actions: *"For I know my transgressions; my sin is always before me. Against you, you alone have I sinned; I have done what is evil in your eyes so that you are just in your word, and without reproach in your judgment."* We are encouraged toward not committing deliberate sin. The psalm reinforces the possibility of conversion. The sinner will always be forgiven, no matter how grave their sins might be, if they come to God with a sincere repentant heart, begging Him not to cast them out of His presence: *"Restore to me the gladness of your salvation; uphold me with a willing spirit. I will teach the wicked your ways, that sinners may return to you."*

Psalm 51 ensures us that God will transform the sinner into a new creature who will receive a contrite spirit, humbled heart, and lips of praise: *"Lord, you will open my lips; and my mouth will proclaim your praise. For you do not desire sacrifice or I would give it; a burnt offering you would not accept. My sacrifice, O God, is a contrite spirit; a contrite, humbled heart, O God, you will not scorn."* Saint Faustina wrote, "Even if our sins were as black as the night, divine mercy is greater than our misery. Only one thing is needed: the sinner has to leave the door to his heart ajar… God can do the rest… Everything begins and ends with His mercy."

Reflect and Pray on Psalm 51, using Lectio Divina or the Method of Meditation. Make sure you converse intimately with the Blessed Trinity:

Prayer on Psalm 51: Miserere: Prayer of Repentance
"1 For the leader. A psalm of David, 2 when Nathan the prophet came to him after he had gone in to Bathsheba.

I.

"3 Have mercy on me, God, in accord with your merciful love; in your abundant compassion blot out my transgressions. 4 Thoroughly wash away my guilt; and from my sin cleanse me. 5 For I know my transgressions; my sin is always before me. 6 Against you, you alone have I sinned; I have done what is evil in

your eyes so that you are just in your word, and without reproach in your judgment. 7 Behold, I was born in guilt, in sin my mother conceived me. 8. Behold, you desire true sincerity; and secretly you teach me wisdom. 9 Cleanse me with hyssop, that I may be pure; wash me, and I will be whiter than snow. 10 You will let me hear gladness and joy; the bones you have crushed will rejoice.

II.
11 Turn away your face from my sins; blot out all my iniquities. 12 A clean heart create for me, God; renew within me a steadfast spirit. 13 Do not drive me from before your face, nor take from me your holy spirit. 14 Restore to me the gladness of your salvation; uphold me with a willing spirit. 15 I will teach the wicked your ways, that sinners may return to you. 16 Rescue me from violent bloodshed, God, my saving God, and my tongue will sing joyfully of your justice. 17 Lord, you will open my lips; and my mouth will proclaim your praise. 18 For you do not desire sacrifice or I would give it; a burnt offering you would not accept. 19 My sacrifice, O God, is a contrite spirit; a contrite, humbled heart, O God, you will not scorn.

III.
20 Treat Zion kindly according to your good will; build up the walls of Jerusalem. 21 Then you will desire the sacrifices of the just, burnt offering and whole offerings; then they will offer up young bulls on your altar."

End with Prayer to the Holy Trinity
NIGHT PRAYER: The Examination of Conscience

DAY THREE:
MORNING PRAYER: Acts of Faith, Hope, Charity; Daily Offering

MORNING FACE TO FACE WITH GOD:
Begin with Prayer to the Holy Spirit

Prayer on Psalm 52: The Deceitful Tongue

    The superscription tells us that David composed Psalm 52 when Doeg reported to Saul that David had entered the house of Ahimelech. The full account is found in 1Samuel 20-22. David was fleeing from King Saul who was determined to kill him. David fled to Ahimelech, the priest at Nob who gave him the showbread of the temple, as well as Goliath's sword which was hidden in the temple. Nob was a priestly town in ancient Israel in the vicinity of Jerusalem. It probably was located close to Bahurim, near the Mount of Olives. It likely belonged to the Tribe of Benjamin which was Saul's tribe. Gibeah was Saul's capital city and was located about 3 miles north of Jerusalem along the watershed ridge at 2754 feet above sea level. Jerusalem was at the border between the tribes of Benjamin and Judah and was made the capital after David moved from Hebron to Jerusalem when he was enthroned the King of Judah and Israel. Doeg the Edomite was present when David and Ahimelech met: *"One of Saul's servants was there that day, detained before the LORD; his name was Doeg the Edomite, the chief of Saul's shepherds"* (1Samuel 21: 8). Doeg was probably fulfilling a ritual obligation. The shepherds were Saul's palace guard. David knew that Doeg would betray him to Saul. Doeg was from Idumea between the Dead Sea and the Gulf of Aqaba. He had hoped to secure special favor with Saul by informing him of those who were in league with his enemy David.

Doeg the Edomite informed Saul of David's meeting with Ahimelech. Ahimelech and his priests were summoned before Saul. Saul asked for their slaughter and the king's servants refused. Doeg was happy to oblige: *"The king therefore commanded Doeg, "You, turn and kill the priests!" So Doeg the Edomite himself turned and killed the priests that day – eighty-five who wore the linen ephod. Saul also put the priestly city of Nob to the sword, including men and women, children and infants, and oxen, donkeys and sheep"* (1Samuel 22: 18-19). Doeg's conduct is the subject of this psalm. Very aptly the psalm is titled 'The Deceitful Tongue.'

Part I refers to the character of the calumniator, Doeg the Edomite, who was devoid of any qualms to murder 85 priests and put the priestly city of Nob to the sword, including men and women, children and infants, and oxen, donkeys and sheep: *"Why do you glory in what is evil, you who are mighty by the mercy of God? All day long you are thinking up intrigues; your tongue is like a sharpened razor, you worker of deceit. You love evil more than good, lying rather than saying what is right. You love all the words that create confusion, you, deceitful tongue."* The Psalmist is describing someone who has sold himself to the devil. Intrigue and deceit have become their modus operandi. The end justifies the means and they will pursue their evil gains at any cost. Doeg loved evil more than good and had no hesitation to destroy the character and happiness of others.

In Part II, David pronounces sentence upon his adversary. More than seeking revenge upon his sworn enemy, David is reiterating an unassailable truth that in the titanic clash between the forces of evil marshaled by Satan against the forces of truth and justice commanded by the LORD, the wicked will suffer an ignominious defeat and the just ones will know that their trust in God was vindicated: *"God too will strike you down forever, he will lay hold of you and pluck you from your tent, uproot you from the land of the living. The righteous will see and they will fear; but they will laugh at him: "Behold the man! He did not take God as his refuge, but he trusted in the abundance of his wealth, and grew powerful through his wickedness."* The righteous will see the proper end that comes to someone who sought their own gain in their wicked purposes, who did not make God their strength.

In Part III, David expresses his sincere gratitude and praise to God for providing him with security and preservation from all the dangers and snares laid against him by Saul and his henchmen. David does not expressly voice his sentiments of sorrow and gratitude for his friendship with Jonathan, Saul's son, who helped him with his escape plans, as well as for Ahimelech and his Levite clan who were murdered for being loyal to him. We can assume that David did express his gratitude to the LORD: *"But I, like an olive tree flourishing in the house of God, I trust in God's mercy forever and ever. I will thank you forever for what you have done. I* will put my hope in your name – for it is good, – in the presence of those devoted to you."

David describes himself as an olive tree. The righteous or those *"flourishing in the house of God,"* have been compared to the olive tree, the date palm, and fruitful vines in the psalms and other books of the Old Testament. The olive tree reminded the people of God's largesse and generosity, as it supplied fruit and oil year after year for centuries. Provided with the appropriate growing conditions, olive trees may live to be as old as 1,500 years, the average lifespan being 500 years. Indeed, David's faith and trust in the LORD was indomitable and enduring.

Reflect and Pray on Psalm 52, using Lectio Divina or the Method of Meditation. Make sure you converse intimately with the Blessed Trinity:

Prayer on Psalm 52: The Deceitful Tongue
"1 For the leader. A maskil of David, 2 when Doeg the Edomite entered and reported to Saul, saying to him: "David has entered the house of Ahimelech."

I.
"3 Why do you glory in what is evil, you who are mighty by the mercy of God? All day long 4 you are thinking up intrigues; your tongue is like a sharpened razor, you worker of deceit. 5 You love evil more than good, lying rather than saying what is right. 6 You love all the words that create confusion, you, deceitful tongue.

II.
7 God too will strike you down forever, he will lay hold of you and pluck you from your tent, uproot you from the land of the living. 8 The righteous will see and they will fear; but they will laugh at him: 9 "Behold the man! He did not take God as his refuge, but he trusted in the abundance of his wealth, and grew powerful through his wickedness."

III.
10 But I, like an olive tree flourishing in the house of God, I trust in God's mercy forever and ever. 11 I will thank you forever for what you have done. I will put my hope in your name – for it is good, –

in the presence of those devoted to you."

End with Prayer to the Holy Trinity
NIGHT PRAYER: The Examination of Conscience

DAY FOUR:
MORNING PRAYER: Acts of Faith, Hope, Charity; Daily Offering

MORNING FACE TO FACE WITH GOD:
Begin with Prayer to the Holy Spirit

Prayer on Psalm 53: A Lament over Widespread Corruption

Psalm 53 is essentially a repetition of Psalm 14, with a few modifications. We did not pray with Psalm 14 in Book One, Week Two. Both psalms are titled, 'A Lament over Widespread Corruption.' The theme in both psalms is the salvation of God. Both psalms end with these words: *"Who will bring forth from Zion the salvation of Israel? When God reverses the captivity of his people, Jacob will rejoice and Israel will be glad."* Both psalms are David's ponderings, intended to give faith and courage to Israel during a national threat of an invasion or a siege.

David begins Psalm 53 with a reflection on the godless who are wicked: *"The fool says in his heart, "There is no God."* David is talking of a person who looks at the overwhelming reality of God's creation and asserts that there is no First Cause for it! In wishing God away in their hearts, fools become their own moral yardstick. Consequently, *"They act corruptly and practice injustice; there is none that does good."* Making oneself the moral yardstick will lead inevitably to iniquity and moral degradation. We are born with the capacity and will to do evil. The path of least resistance in the spiritual life leads to desolation and lukewarmth. Jesus echoes this descent into the darkness of sin with the denial of God: *"For everyone who does wicked things hates the light and does not come toward the light, so that his works might not be exposed"* (John 3: 20).

While human beings might deny God and make themselves the idols of their hearts, God will never forget His image and likeness.

For the wicked who refuse to acknowledge God and repent of their sins, their fate has been sealed. They are headed toward destruction: *"God looks out from the heavens upon the children of Adam, to see if there is a discerning person who is seeking God. All have gone astray; each one is altogether perverse. There is not one who does what is good, not even one. Do they not know better, those who do evil, who feed upon my people as they feed upon bread?"* Those who indulge in wickedness invariably discount the devastation that will be heaped upon them. Their rejection of God results in the destruction of God's image and likeness in which they were created. The Psalmist paints a gruesome picture, indeed: *"They are going to fear his name with great fear, though they had not feared it before. For God will scatter the bones of those encamped against you. They will surely be put to shame, for God has rejected them."*

Those who trust God and walk in His ways are assured of their salvation. God is their refuge, and the instigators of evil and wickedness will never hold sway against them. God will deliver them from their misfortune and captivity, as He did many times in their history. Such trust in God will warrant a celebration of praise and thanksgiving to God: *"Who will bring forth from Zion the salvation of Israel? When God reverses the captivity of his people Jacob will rejoice and Israel will be glad."*

Reflect and Pray on Psalm 53, using Lectio Divina or the Method of Meditation. Make sure you converse intimately with the Blessed Trinity:

Prayer on Psalm 53: A Lament over Widespread Corruption
"1 For the leader; according to Mahalath. A maskil of David.
I.
2 The fool says in his heart, "There is no God." They act corruptly and practice injustice; there is none that does good. 3 God looks out from the heavens upon the children of Adam, to see if there is a discerning person who is seeking God. 4 All have gone astray; each one is altogether perverse. There is not one who does what is good, not even one.

II.

5 Do they not know better, those who do evil, who feed upon my people as they feed upon bread? Have they not called upon God? 6 They are going to fear his name with great fear, though they had not feared it before. For God will scatter the bones of those encamped against you. They will surely be put to shame, for God has rejected them.

III.

7 Who will bring forth from Zion the salvation of Israel? When God reverses the captivity of his people Jacob will rejoice and Israel will be glad."

End with Prayer to the Holy Trinity
NIGHT PRAYER: The Examination of Conscience

DAY FIVE:
MORNING PRAYER: Acts of Faith, Hope, Charity; Daily Offering

MORNING FACE TO FACE WITH GOD:
Begin with Prayer to the Holy Spirit

Prayer on Psalm 54: Confident Prayer in Great Peril

Psalm 54 is akin to Psalm 52, in that both psalms focus on the persecution and oppression that David experienced as a fugitive from Saul. The superscription of Psalm 54 tells us that the Ziphites came and said to Saul, *"David is hiding among us."* The account can be found in 1Samuel 23-24, where we witness the sharp contrast in moral rectitude between Saul and David. In 1Samuel 23 we see how Saul is relentless about having David killed to serve his own selfish interests. In 1Samuel 24, we witness David's behavior toward Saul. He continually sought to do God's bidding even toward his enemy, Saul. He spared his life because he was the LORD's anointed one.

In Part I, David seeks protection and security from his mortal enemy Saul, by earnestly invoking God's name and strength: *"O God, by your name save me. By your strength defend my cause. O God, hear my prayer. Listen to the words of my mouth. Strangers have risen against me; the ruthless seek my life; they do not keep*

God before them." David is confident that God will come to his rescue as He has in the past. In having recourse to God's name, David is invoking God's power and benevolence that were necessary to secure his salvation against the treachery of the Ziphites. The Ziphites were not Israelites. They were strangers to the God of his fathers and were willing to betray him. They were people of violence, described as ruthlessly seeking his life.

In the face of this impending crisis, David has recourse to God. God alone can come to his help and he will not fear even though he walks in the valley of the shadow of death. In His faithfulness, the LORD will deliver David from his frightening peril: *"God is present as my helper; the Lord sustains my life. Turn back the evil upon my foes; in your faithfulness, destroy them."* God's rescue of him will engender an intense desire to offer God a *todah* or thanksgiving sacrifice. It is fitting that he offers God public praise and thanksgiving for rescuing him from every trouble and giving him victory over his enemies: *"Then I will offer you generous sacrifice and give thanks to your name, LORD, for it is good. Because it has rescued me from every trouble, and my eyes look down on my foes."*

Reflect and Pray on Psalm 54, using Lectio Divina or the Method of Meditation. Make sure you converse intimately with the Blessed Trinity:

Psalm 54: Confident Prayer in Great Peril
"1 For the leader. On stringed instruments. A maskil of David, 2 when the Ziphites came and said to Saul, "David is hiding among us."

I.

3. O God, by your name save me. By your strength defend my cause. 4. O God, hear my prayer. Listen to the words of my mouth. 5 Strangers have risen against me; the ruthless seek my life; they do not keep God before them.

II.

6. God is present as my helper; the Lord sustains my life. 7. Turn back the evil upon my foes; in your faithfulness, destroy them. 8.

Then I will offer you generous sacrifice and give thanks to your name, LORD, for it is good. 9. Because it has rescued me from every trouble, and my eyes look down on my foes."

End with Prayer to the Holy Trinity
NIGHT PRAYER: The Examination of Conscience

DAY SIX:
MORNING PRAYER: Acts of Faith, Hope, Charity; Daily Offering

MORNING FACE TO FACE WITH GOD:
Begin with Prayer to the Holy Spirit

Prayer on Psalm 56: Trust in God

Psalm 56 continues with the trials and tribulations that David experienced during the seven years or so when he was a fugitive from Saul. The superscription tells us that this psalm records David's experience with God when the Philistines seized him at Gath. 1Samuel 21: 11-14 tells us that *"that same day David fled from Saul, going to Achish, king of Gath."* Gath was a Philistine city, the hometown of Goliath whom David had slain. Even though David escaped to Gath voluntarily, he was in imminent danger from the outset: *"But the servants of Achish said to him, "Is this not David, the king of the land? Is it not for him that during their dances they sing out, 'Saul has slain his thousands, David his tens of thousands'?" David took note of these remarks and became very much afraid of Achish, king of Gath. So, he feigned insanity in front of them and acted like a madman in their custody, drumming on the doors of the gate and drooling onto his beard"* (1Samuel 21: 11-16). David had literally thrust himself into the jaws of death and his prayer-song springs out of the depths of his danger.

This psalm needs to be pondered along with Psalm 34 which we did not consider in Book One, Week Four. Psalm 34 is a song of thanksgiving to God who delivered David from Achish, king of Gath: *"Finally Achish said to his servants: "You see the man is mad. ... Do I not have enough madmen, that you bring this one to rant in my presence? Should this fellow come into my house?" David left Gath and escaped to the cave of Adullam"* (1Samuel 21:

15-16; 22: 1). Psalm 56 is a prayer that springs from David's endangered heart while he was in the city of Gath.

As in his other songs of lament, Psalm 56 offers us the same recurring themes of asking God for deliverance from enemies and expressing grateful trust in God. We could perhaps wonder why David had so many enemies. David was a type of Christ who, as the Son of David, faced the constant enmity of the world and Satan. David is also a type of the disciple we are being invited to become by Jesus: to carry our cross daily and place all our trust in Jesus. As Jesus informed us in the Parable of the Wheat and Weeds, the Kingdom of God is being established among His enemies, and despite them. Their enmity will continue until the end of time when finally, death will be destroyed: *"Then comes the end, when he hands over the kingdom to his God and Father, when he has destroyed every sovereignty and every authority and power. For he must reign until he has put all his enemies under his feet"* (1Corinthians 15: 24-25).

In Part I and a few verses of Part II, David addresses the acute predicament he faces in Gath: *"Have mercy on me, God, for I am treated harshly; attackers press me all day. My foes treat me harshly all the day; yes, many are my attackers. O Most High, when I am afraid, in you I place my trust. I praise the word of God; I trust in God, I do not fear. What can mere flesh do to me? All the day they foil my plans; their every thought is of evil against me. They hide together in ambush; they watch my every step; they lie in wait for my life. They are evil; watch them, God! Cast the nations down in your anger!"* David offers us a stark scenario that has engulfed him. He is alone and defenseless against the wiles and power of his enemies. Along with the hostility of Achish, king of Gath, David is including the bitter determination of Saul to exterminate him as well: *"All the day they foil my plans; their every thought is of evil against me. They hide together in ambush; they watch my every step; they lie in wait for my life. They are evil."*

Imprisoned in the jaws of death, David has two profound

sentiments that shore up his sagging spirit: he is unafraid because he trusts God who will surely come through for him. And what harm can human beings do to him when God is on his side: *"O Most High, when I am afraid, in you I place my trust. I praise the word of God; I trust in God, I do not fear. What can mere flesh do to me?"* Much later, Jesus, the Son of David will tell us that although *'mere flesh'* can destroy the body, they will never be able to destroy the soul: *"And do not be afraid of those who kill the body but cannot kill the soul; rather, be afraid of the one who can destroy both soul and body in Gehenna"* (Matthew 10: 28).

In the second part of Part II, the Psalmist offers a prayer of deliverance that is brimming with confidence and hope. He can see how God is pushing back the tide against David and re-creating his circumstances: *"My foes turn back when I call on you. This I know: God is on my side. I praise the word of the LORD. In God I trust, I do not fear. What can man do to me?"* David has a constant refrain resonating in his heart which he expresses throughout the psalm: *"In God I trust, I do not fear. What can man do to me?"* All his circumstances engendered paralyzing fear in him. But greater than his fear was his abiding trust in God. St. Paul expressed a similar sentiment: *"If God is for us, who can be against us? He who did not spare his own Son but handed him over for us all, how will he not also give us everything else along with him?* (Romans 8: 31-32).

Psalm 56 ends with a beautiful epilogue: *"I have made vows to you, God; with offerings I will fulfill them, for you have snatched me from death, kept my feet from stumbling, that I may walk before God in the light of the living."* David speaks of his deliverance as if it has already taken place. Either the Psalmist had already been rescued or was sure that he would be rescued. In either case, he recalls his obligation to offer God a *todah* sacrifice of praise and thanksgiving to God.

Reflect and Pray on Psalm 56, using Lectio Divina or the Method of Meditation. Make sure you converse intimately with the Blessed Trinity:

Prayer on Psalm 56: Trust in God in Great Peril
"1 For the director. According to Yonath elem rehoqim. A miktam of David, when the Philistines seized him at Gath.

I.

2 Have mercy on me, God, for I am treated harshly; attackers press me all day. 3. My foes treat me harshly all the day; yes, many are my attackers. O Most High, 4. When I am afraid, in you I place my trust. 5. I praise the word of God; I trust in God, I do not fear. What can mere flesh do to me?

II.

6 All the day they foil my plans; their every thought is of evil against me. 7 They hide together in ambush; they watch my every step; they lie in wait for my life. 8. They are evil; watch them, God! Cast the nations down in your anger! 9. My wanderings you have noted; are my tears not stored in your flask, recorded in your book? 10. My foes turn back when I call on you. This I know: God is on my side. 11. I praise the word of God, I praise the word of the LORD. 12. In God I trust, I do not fear, what can man do to me?

III.

13. I have made vows to you, God; with offerings I will fulfill them, 14. for you have snatched me from death, kept my feet from stumbling, that I may walk before God in the light of the living."

End with Prayer to the Holy Trinity
NIGHT PRAYER: The Examination of Conscience

DAY SEVEN:
MORNING PRAYER: Acts of Faith, Hope, Charity; Daily Offering

MORNING FACE TO FACE WITH GOD:
<u>Learning Discipleship from the Psalms</u>
Begin with Prayer to the Holy Spirit

- "But to the wicked God says: 'Why do you recite my commandments and profess my covenant with your mouth? You hate discipline; you cast my words behind you! ... When you do these things should I be silent? ... I accuse you, I lay out the matter before your eyes" (Psalm 50). Spiritual degradation occurs when worship and sacrificial offerings have become perfunctory and self-serving, where God is trivialized, and, therefore, mocked through lip-service.

- *"Those who offer praise as a sacrifice honor me; I will let him whose way is steadfast look upon the salvation of God."* Psalm 50 makes the point that the sacrifice of thanksgiving, now Eucharist for us, is the best offering of all. Thanksgiving to God is always an acknowledgement of our total dependence on God from which emerges our adoration of Him.
- Psalm 51 outlines two worldviews that are diametrically opposed to each other. Firstly, there is the sinister region of sin in which we have been placed from the beginning of our existence: *"Behold, I was born in guilt, in sin my mother conceived me."* Sin is a distortion, interchanging good for evil and evil for good. Sin is open rebellion against God and His plan for human history.
- Repentance, however, moves the sinner to adopt the other worldview: *"Turn away your face from my sins; blot out all my iniquities. A clean heart create for me, God; renew within me a steadfast spirit."* Besides eliminating sin, the Lord re-creates sinful humanity through the lifegiving action of the Holy Spirit. The Holy Spirit replaces the sinner's heart and mind with the heart and mind of Jesus. The sinner can develop a limpid faith and worship that is pleasing to God.
- *"But I, like an olive tree flourishing in the house of God, I trust in God's mercy forever and ever. I will thank you forever for what you have done. I will put my hope in your name – for it is good, – in the presence of those devoted to you."* In Psalm 52, David describes himself as an olive tree. The olive tree was a symbol of God's largesse and generosity as it supplied fruit and oil year after year for centuries. The average lifespan of an olive tree is 500 years. Indeed, David's faith and trust in the LORD was indomitable and enduring, like the olive tree.
- *"Who will bring forth from Zion the salvation of Israel? When*

God reverses the captivity of his people, Jacob will rejoice and Israel will be glad." Psalm 53 assures us that those who trust God and walk in His ways are assured of their salvation. God was the refuge of His people and would deliver them from their misfortune and captivity as He did many times in their history. Such trust in God would result in a celebration of praise and thanksgiving to God.

- Psalm 56 offers us the same recurring themes of asking God for deliverance from enemies and expressing grateful trust in God. David was a type of Christ who as the Son of David faced the constant enmity of the world and Satan. David is also a type of the disciple we are being invited to become by Jesus: to carry our cross daily and place all our trust in Jesus. The Kingdom of God is being established in the world that is hostile to Jesus. Their enmity will continue until the end of time when finally, death will be destroyed.

End with Prayer to the Holy Trinity
NIGHT PRAYER: The Examination of Conscience

JOURNAL FOR BOOK TWO, WEEK TWO: CELEBRATION AND PRAISE

DAY ONE: Morning Prayer: Psalm 50: The Acceptable Sacrifice
What is God saying to You?

Nightly Examination of Conscience:
For what are you grateful?

For what are you contrite?

What spiritual discipline, including fasting, do you need to focus on tomorrow?

DAY TWO: Morning Prayer: Psalm 51: The Miserere: Prayer of Repentance
What is God saying to You?

Nightly Examination of Conscience:
For what are you grateful?

For what are you contrite?

What spiritual discipline, including fasting, do you need to focus on tomorrow?

DAY THREE: Morning Prayer: Psalm 52: The Deceitful Tongue
What is God saying to You?

Nightly Examination of Conscience:
For what are you grateful?

For what are you contrite?

What spiritual discipline, including fasting, do you need to focus on tomorrow?

DAY FOUR: Morning Prayer: Psalm 53: A Lament over Widespread Corruption
What is God saying to You?

Nightly Examination of Conscience:
For what are you grateful?

For what are you contrite?

What spiritual discipline, including fasting, do you need to focus on tomorrow?

DAY FIVE: Morning Prayer: Psalm 54: A Confident Prayer in Great Peril
What is God saying to You?

Nightly Examination of Conscience:
For what are you grateful?

For what are you contrite?

What spiritual discipline, including fasting, do you need to focus on tomorrow?

DAY SIX: Morning Prayer: Psalm 56: Trust in God
What is God saying to You?

Nightly Examination of Conscience:
For what are you grateful?

For what are you contrite?

What spiritual discipline, including fasting, do you need to focus on tomorrow?

DAY SEVEN: Morning Prayer: Learning Discipleship from the Psalms
What is God saying to You?

Nightly Examination of Conscience:
For what are you grateful?

For what are you contrite?

What spiritual discipline, including fasting, do you need to focus on tomorrow?

What prayer would you compose to express what God has said to you this week?

BOOK TWO – PSALMS 42-72: CELEBRATION AND PRAISE
Psalms 57, 61, 62, 63, 65, and 66

WHAT IS AT THE HEART OF BOOK TWO, WEEK THREE?
In Week Three of Book Two, we will be praying with Psalms 57, 61, 62, 63, 65, and 66. The first four psalms are songs of lament, offering us valuable lessons in spiritual formation. They keep reminding us that God always comes to the rescue of the ones who walk in His ways and trust Him completely. Psalm 62, for instance, emphasizes the importance of developing the spiritual practice of trusting God in all our circumstances. Such a practice needs to be emphasized especially in times of crisis and hardship. Through such a practice, God will truly become our refuge and strength. Psalm 63 celebrates God as needing to become the one and only center of our lives as Christian disciples. Psalms 65 and 66 are songs of praise and thanksgiving. They glorify God for His faithfulness and steadfast love. They resonate with exuberant praise and thanksgiving to God. They assert the tone of Book Two in celebrating and praising God. Psalm 57 has a superscription, *Miktam,'* whose meaning is unclear, and could be translated as 'prayer.'

On Day One, we will pray on *Psalm 57: Confident Prayer for Deliverance.* Psalm 57 was composed when David fled from Saul into a cave. When nothing could save him from his peril, David relied upon God alone: *"Have mercy on me, God, have mercy on me. In you I seek refuge. In the shadow of your wings I seek refuge till harm pass by."* In being bathed in God's loving kindness, David experienced security and protection from God who had become his refuge and strength.

On Day Two, we will reflect prayerfully on *Psalm 61: Prayer of the King in time of Danger.* Psalm 61 was composed by King David during a time of great peril. It was written most probably when he was fleeing from his son Absalom who had crowned himself king of Israel, thereby usurping the throne. David expresses his prayer to God arising from an exile's heart: *"Hear my cry, O God, listen to my prayer! From the ends of the earth I call; my heart grows faint."*

On Day Three, we will ponder *Psalm 62: Trust in God alone.* The psalm distinguishes between two types of trust, one that places all one's bets on God alone, and the other that settles for power and material security through unseemly force and intimidation. Trust in God results in moral behavior and a profound sense of security which is extolled in the psalm

On Day Four, we will pray with *Psalm 63: Ardent Longing for God.* Psalm 63 is one of the most beloved of psalms. David was in the wild desolation of the Dead Sea desert. He was there as a fugitive from Absalom, his son, who had usurped his throne and occupied Jerusalem. The psalm celebrates God as being the One and Only Center of the Psalmist's life. Prayer becomes an intense longing for God, a thirst and a hunger because it involves both the soul and the body

On Day Five, we will ponder *Psalm 65: Thanksgiving for God's Blessings.* Psalm 65 draws the obvious conclusion that there is a connection between creation and redemption. Just as in Spring, the earth revives itself through the action of the Creator, so does man rise from his sin through the action of the Redeemer. As Christians, we can pray the psalm as a hymn to God's redeeming grace in Christ.

On Day Six, we will reflect and pray with *Psalm 66: Praise of God, Israel's Deliverer.* The deliverance that Israel experienced from her enemies is so great that they are unable to offer the volume of praise that the occasion deserves. So, the Psalmist asks the earth to join in. The nation's deliverance impacts the whole world as it speaks to the majesty and power of God's glorious reign over all creation.

On Day Seven, we will ponder the salient advice that these

psalms have offered us to enhance and strengthen our own following of Jesus and our commitment to His Church.

SPIRITUAL READING FOR BOOK TWO OF THE PSALMS:
1 and 2 Samuel
Psalms 42 to 72
1 and 2 Kings (after you have read 1 and 2 Samuel)
1 and 2 Chronicles (after you have read 1 and 2 Kings)

DAY ONE:
MORNING PRAYER: Acts of Faith, Hope, Charity; Daily Offering

MORNING FACE TO FACE WITH GOD:
Begin with Prayer to the Holy Spirit
Prayer on Psalm 57: Confident Prayer for Deliverance

Psalm 57 is another song of lament like Psalm 56 that we saw in the previous week. Both psalms have the same opening words: *"Have mercy on me, God."* The superscription tells us that it was composed when David fled from Saul into a cave. 1Samuel 24 tells us that David hid himself in the strongholds of Engedi, near the desert. Saul was told about David's whereabouts. He took three thousand of his best men and went in search of David. Unwittingly, he let himself into the hands of David: *"When he (Saul) came to the sheepfolds along the way, he found a cave, which he entered to relieve himself. David and his men were occupying the inmost recesses of the cave"* (1Samuel 24: 4). David spared Saul's life as he would not kill God's anointed one: *"You see for yourself today that the LORD just now delivered you into my hand in the cave. I was told to kill you, but I took pity on you instead. I decided, 'I will not raise a hand against my master, for he is the LORD's anointed'"* (1Samuel 24: 11). This is the backdrop of Psalm 57.

In Part I, David expresses his precarious situation as he is in the presence of his mortal enemy, Saul. When nothing can save him from his peril, David relies upon God alone: *"Have mercy on me, God, have mercy on me. In you I seek refuge. In the shadow of your wings I seek refuge till harm pass by."* First and foremost,

David seeks God's mercy or loving kindness. In being bathed in God's loving kindness, he will experience security and protection from God who has become his refuge and strength. He seeks the shadow of God's wings. The protective wings of the cherubim spread over the Ark in the inner chamber of the Temple (1Kings 6: 23-28), symbolizing God's protection of His people. For seven years or so, David has been protected and saved by God from one danger after another. And now, he is facing another crisis, and is asking for God's protection till it passes: *"I call to God Most High, to God who provides for me. May God send help from heaven to save me, shame those who trample upon me. May God send fidelity and mercy."*

Instead of killing Saul, David trusted God's providence and protection, and remained obedient to His wishes. David knew that he would be the next king, as the prophet Samuel had anointed him for that role. He knew, however, that it would be wrong for him to help God by killing King Saul. He trusted God's ways even though he might not have realized why God was allowing him to suffer. In his song-prayer, he expressed his total trust in God. Trust involves seeing God as greater than our problems. David makes that clear in the psalm: *"I must lie down in the midst of lions hungry for human prey. Their teeth are spears and arrows; their tongue, a sharpened sword. Be exalted over the heavens, God; may your glory appear above all the earth."* It seems out of place that David would be exalting God while enumerating his problems. Sometimes it takes intense trials to realize how trustworthy the Lord is! During his fugitive years, in constant mortal danger from Saul, David became a deeply righteous man, totally trusting of God who had become his rock and his strength.

Part II makes it clear that God is glorified as we praise Him in our trials: *"My heart is steadfast, God, my heart is steadfast. I will sing and chant praise."* Praise is a matter of witnessing to others about God's faithfulness and loving kindness: *"Awake, my soul; awake, lyre and harp! I will wake the dawn. I will praise you* among the peoples, Lord; I will chant your praise among the nations." In time of crisis, our natural response is to complain and get angry with God or get depressed. On David's part, praising God was a deliberate choice: *"I will sing and chant praise."* Praising God was a matter of doing what was right regardless of the consequences.

David specifies two aspects of God's goodness: *Hesed,* His loving kindness and His faithfulness. 'Loving Kindness' comes from the Hebrew word related to the stork. The Hebrews were amazed at the loyal love of the stork for its young ones and used the image for God's love. God nurtures us with never-ending love. And God's faithfulness is consistent and trustworthy. In times of trial, David's voice anchors us in God's unremitting love and mercy: *"For your mercy towers to the heavens; your faithfulness reaches to the skies. Exalt yourself over the heavens, God; may your glory appear above all the earth."*

Reflect and Pray on Psalm 57, using Lectio Divina or the Method of Meditation. Make sure you converse intimately with the Blessed Trinity:

Prayer on Psalm 57: Confident Prayer for Deliverance
"1 For the director. Do not destroy. A miktam of David, when he fled from Saul into a cave.

I.

1 Have mercy on me, God, have mercy on me. In you I seek refuge. In the shadow of your wings I seek refuge till harm pass by. 3 I call to God Most High, to God who provides for me. 4 May God send help from heaven to save me, shame those who trample upon me. May God send fidelity and mercy. 5 I must lie down in the midst of lions hungry for human prey. Their teeth are spears and arrows; their tongue, a sharpened sword. 6 Be exalted over the heavens, God; may your glory appear above all the earth.

II.

7 They have set a trap for my feet; my soul is bowed down; they have dug a pit before me. May they fall into it themselves! 8 My heart is steadfast, God, my heart is steadfast. I will sing and chant praise. 9 Awake, my soul; awake, lyre and harp! I will wake the dawn. 10 I will praise you among the peoples, Lord; I will chant your praise among the nations. 11 For your mercy towers to the heavens; your faithfulness reaches to the skies. 12 Exalt yourself over the heavens, God; may your glory appear above all the earth."

End with Prayer to the Holy Trinity
NIGHT PRAYER: The Examination of Conscience

DAY TWO:
MORNING PRAYER: Acts of Faith, Hope, Charity; Daily Offering

MORNING FACE TO FACE WITH GOD:
Begin with Prayer to the Holy Spirit

Prayer on Psalm 61: Prayer of the King in Time of Danger

Psalm 61 was composed most probably when David was fleeing from his son Absalom who had crowned himself king of Israel, thereby usurping the throne. David was forced to leave Jerusalem and flee across the Jordan River to Mahanaim. David expresses his prayer arising from an exile's heart: *"Hear my cry, O God, listen to my prayer! From the ends of the earth I call; my heart grows faint."* He was a fugitive forced to leave his beloved Jerusalem and the Temple. In dire straits, he resorted to prayer. In his forlornness, David makes a heartfelt plea: *"Raise me up, set me on a rock, for you are my refuge, a tower of strength against the foe. Let me dwell in your tent forever, take refuge in the shelter of your wings."* For ancient Israel, the rock was a symbol of God's love and protection, an image of the security, serenity, and protection provided by the Lord. Jesus is our Rock and our Salvation.

We know that David loved Absalom deeply and suffered greatly from his rebellion and subsequent tragic death. Now that he is in exile, his longing for God has increased even more so. He desires to dwell with God forever. David seems to be speaking like a high priest when he talks about dwelling in God's tent forever. There is only one great King and High Priest dwelling in the presence of God forever, our Lord Jesus Christ. Jesus has moved into the Sanctuary not made by human hands and we, His body, have moved in with Him: *"For Christ did not enter into a sanctuary made by hands, a copy of the true one, but heaven itself, that he might now appear before God on our behalf"* (Hebrews 9: 24).

In Part II, David makes an ardent prayer for the King, supposedly for himself: *"For you, God, have heard my vows, you have granted me the heritage of those who revere your name. Add days to the life of the king; may his years be as from generation to generation; may he reign before God forever; send your love and fidelity to preserve him – I will duly sing to your name forever, fulfill my vows day after day."* David knew that Absalom's ambitions would be ripped asunder as he was not anointed by God. Here, David speaks of the heritage that God has granted him. The heritage was that distinctive promise which God made to David through the prophet Nathan, assuring him of the eternal continuation of the 'Throne of David,' and one of his seed sitting upon it: *"Your house and your kingdom are firm forever before me; your throne shall be firmly established forever. In accordance with all these words and this whole vision Nathan spoke to David"* (2Samuel 7: 16-17). Thus, the heritage is nothing less than the promise of Christ Himself, the 'Son of David,' who will establish the new Kingdom of Israel and whose reign will last forever.

Reflect and Pray on Psalm 61, using Lectio Divina or the Method of Meditation. Make sure you converse intimately with the Blessed Trinity:

Prayer on Psalm 61: Prayer of the King in Time of Danger
"1 For the leader; with stringed instruments. Of David.
I.
2 Hear my cry, O God, listen to my prayer! 3 From the ends of the earth I call; my heart grows faint. Raise me up, set me on a rock, 4 for you are my refuge, a tower of strength against the foe. 5 Let me dwell in your tent forever, take refuge in the shelter of your wings.
II.

6 For you, God, have heard my vows, you have granted me the heritage of those who revere your name. 7 Add days to the life of the king; may his years be as from generation to generation; 8 may he reign before God forever; send your love and fidelity to preserve him – 9 I will duly sing to your name forever, fulfill my vows day after day."

End with Prayer to the Holy Trinity
NIGHT PRAYER: The Examination of Conscience

DAY THREE:
MORNING PRAYER: Acts of Faith, Hope, Charity; Daily Offering

MORNING FACE TO FACE WITH GOD:
Begin with Prayer to the Holy Spirit

Prayer on Psalm 62: Trust in God Alone

Psalm 62 is distinctly Davidic, because of the use of his favorite expressions for God: *'my rock,' 'my salvation,' 'my fortress,' 'my strength,' 'my refuge.'* The superscription tells us that Jeduthun was the choir leader. He and his sons are mentioned in 1Chronicles 25: 1, 3: *"David and the leaders of the liturgy set apart for the service the sons of Asaph, Heman, and Jeduthun. ... these sons of Jeduthun: Gedaliah, Zeri, Jeshaiah, Shimei, Hashabiah, and Mattithiah; six, under the direction of their father Jeduthun, who prophesied to the accompaniment of a lyre, to give thanks and praise to the LORD."* It seems impossible to know what the circumstances were for the composition of the psalm. There is an element of lament because the danger or crisis is implied but not described. The dominant theme of the psalm, however, is a note of unswerving trust and assured confidence in God. It is one of the few psalms without a prayer of petition. At the end, the Psalmist exhorts us to anchor our lives in God's strength and mercy and cautions us about making mammon our God.

Psalm 62 begins with an antiphon: *"My soul rests in God alone, from whom comes my salvation. God alone is my rock and salvation, my fortress; I shall never fall."* This same antiphon is repeated several verses later: *"My soul, be at rest in God alone, from whom comes my hope. God alone is my rock and my salvation, my fortress, I shall not fall."* The antiphon sounds like a prayer-aspiration that was on David's lips constantly, and he made it a central pillar in his spiritual life: *'God alone will be my strength and stronghold!'*

The psalm distinguishes between two types of trust, one that places all one's bets on God alone, and the other that settles for power and material security through unseemly force and intimidation. Trust in God results in moral behavior and a profound sense of security which is extolled in the psalm: *"My deliverance and honor are with God, my strong rock; my refuge is with God. Trust God at all times, my people! Pour out your hearts to God our refuge!"* Even though he is the target of hostile conspiracies being hatched by his enemies, he feels confident and without fear: *"One thing God has said; two things I have heard: Strength belongs to God; so too, my Lord, does mercy, for you repay each man according to his deeds."*

Trusting in dishonest and evil ways and opposing God's ways is the other choice that is diametrically opposed to trusting in God alone: *"How long will you set yourself against a man? You shall all be destroyed, like a sagging wall or a tumbled down fence! Even highly placed people plot to overthrow him. They delight in lies; they bless with their mouths, but inwardly they curse."* The righteous person casts a critical eye upon such a worldview knowing that it will lead to disaster. Such a trust searches for security and wellbeing through violence, plunder and empty riches: *"Do not trust in extortion; in plunder put no empty hope. On wealth that increases, do not set your heart."*

The Psalmist describes three false gods that are worshiped by those who *"delight in lies."* They are extortion, plunder, and insatiable lust for wealth. By worshiping at the altar of these false gods, humans sooner or later will come to see that they are doomed: *"Mortals are a mere breath, the sons of man but an illusion; on a balance they rise; together they weigh nothing."*

Outside of God, humans are worthless. If we were more aware of our sinfulness and the burdens our evil inclinations impose upon us, we would seek continually to trust in God alone: *"One thing God has said; two things I have heard: Strength belongs to God; so too, my Lord, does mercy, for you repay each man according to his deeds."*

Living with God and staying on the straight and narrow road is difficult, as it calls for courageous decisions always marked by deep trust in God. In this light, the Fathers of the Church have looked upon the man of prayer in Psalm 62 as the Prefiguration of Christ, who like His Father, assures us of His strength and mercy amidst the vicissitudes of life. Hence, we can always rest in Him: *"Come to me, all you who labor and are burdened, and I will give you rest."* (Matthew 11: 28).

Reflect and Pray on Psalm 62, using Lectio Divina or the Method of Meditation. Make sure you converse intimately with the Blessed Trinity:

Prayer on Psalm 62: Trust in God alone
"1 For the leader; 'al Jeduthun. A psalm of David.

I.

2 My soul rests in God alone, from whom comes my salvation. 3 God alone is my rock and salvation, my fortress; I shall never fall. 4 How long will you set yourself against a man? You shall all be destroyed, like a sagging wall or a tumbled down fence! 5 Even highly placed people plot to overthrow him. They delight in lies; they bless with their mouths, but inwardly they curse.

II.

6 My soul, be at rest in God alone, from whom comes my hope. 7 God alone is my rock and my salvation, my fortress, I shall not fall. 8 My deliverance and honor are with God, my strong rock; my refuge is with God. 9 Trust God at all times, my people! Pour out your hearts to God our refuge!

III.

10 Mortals are a mere breath, the sons of man but an illusion; on a balance they rise; together they weigh nothing. 11 Do not trust in extortion; in plunder put no empty hope. On wealth that increases, do not set your heart. 12 One thing God has said; two things I have heard: Strength belongs to God; 13 so too, my Lord, does mercy, for you repay each man according to his deeds."

End with Prayer to the Holy Trinity
NIGHT PRAYER: The Examination of Conscience

DAY FOUR:
MORNING PRAYER: Acts of Faith, Hope, Charity; Daily Offering

MORNING FACE TO FACE WITH GOD:
Begin with Prayer to the Holy Spirit
Prayer on Psalm 63: Ardent Longing for God

Psalm 63 is one of the most loved psalms that David composed in the wild desolation of the Dead Sea desert. He was there as a fugitive from Absalom, his son, who had usurped his throne and occupied Jerusalem. He missed being with God in the Temple. It speaks of the deep communion that David had with God. The psalm celebrates God as being the One and Only Center of the Psalmist's life. Prayer becomes an intense longing for God, a thirst and a hunger because it involves both the soul and the body: *"O God, you are my God – it is you I seek! For you my body yearns; for you my soul thirsts, in a land parched, lifeless, and without water."*

Thirst is the first distinctive feature in the psalm. Believers long to be filled with God, the source of living water. The prophet Jeremiah offers a scathing comment on those who have succumbed to evil ways: *"Two evils my people have done: they have forsaken me, the source of living waters; they have dug themselves cisterns, broken cisterns that cannot hold water"* (Jeremiah 2: 13). Jesus proclaimed Himself as the source of living water, and therefore as God: *"Jesus stood up and exclaimed, "Let anyone who thirsts come to me and drink. Whoever believes in me, as scripture says: 'Rivers of living water will flow from within him'"* (John 7: 37-38). God is the very bedrock of the Psalmist's existence, and therefore, he has to be with God day and night: *"For you my soul thirsts, in a land parched, lifeless, and without water. I look to you in the sanctuary to see your power and glory. For your love is better than life."*

The Psalmist also sings about his hunger for God: *"My soul shall be sated as with choice food, with joyous lips my mouth shall praise you!"* David is probably referring to the *todah* sacrifice at the Temple when the faithful ate the flesh of the sacrificed animal in a sacred banquet: *"One shall present this offering together with loaves of leavened bread along with the thanksgiving communion sacrifice. ... The meat of the thanksgiving communion sacrifice shall be eaten on the day it is offered; none of it may be kept till the next morning"* (Leviticus 7: 13;15). We are reminded of the Eucharistic banquet that Jesus prepared for us on the last evening of His earthly life: *"Jesus said to them, "Amen, amen, I say to you, unless you eat the flesh of the Son of Man and drink his blood, you do not have life within you"* (John 6: 53). In our sacred banquet on the Body and Blood of Jesus through Holy Communion, the ultimate *todah* offering, we become one with God.

In contrast with the righteous disciple who experiences deep communion with God, the wicked will destroy themselves in their wickedness: *"But those who seek my life will come to ruin; they shall go down to the depths of the netherworld! Those who would hand over my life to the sword shall become the prey of jackals!"* David loved his son and knew that Absalom was wrong in his rebellion against his father as he was going against God's anointed one and would bring disaster upon his head. Twenty thousand of Absalom's forces were slain by the sword in the battle that was fought near Mahanaim (2Samuel 18: 6-8). They became the prey of jackals. In ancient wars, jackals assembled in troops to feast on the slain. David's prophecy in the psalm was indeed fulfilled.

Reflect and Pray on Psalm 63, using Lectio Divina or the Method of Meditation. Make sure you converse intimately with the Blessed Trinity:

Prayer on Psalm 63: Ardent Longing for God
"1 A psalm of David, when he was in the wilderness of Judah.

I.

2 O God, you are my God – it is you I seek! For you my body yearns; for you my soul thirsts, in a land parched, lifeless, and without water. 3 I look to you in the sanctuary to see your power and glory. 4 For your love is better than life; my lips shall ever praise you!

II.

5 I will bless you as long as I live; I will lift up my hands, calling on your name. 6 My soul shall be sated as with choice food, with joyous lips my mouth shall praise you! 7 I think of you upon my bed, I remember you through the watches of the night. 8 You indeed are my savior, and in the shadow of your wings I shout for joy. 9 My soul clings fast to you; your right hand upholds me.

III.

10 But those who seek my life will come to ruin; they shall go down to the depths of the netherworld! 11 Those who would hand over my life to the sword shall become the prey of jackals! 12 But the king shall rejoice in God; all who swear by the Lord shall exult, but the mouths of liars will be shut."

End with Prayer to the Holy Trinity
NIGHT PRAYER: The Examination of Conscience

DAY FIVE:
MORNING PRAYER: Acts of Faith, Hope, Charity; Daily Offering

MORNING FACE TO FACE WITH GOD:
Begin with Prayer to the Holy Spirit

Psalm 65: Thanksgiving for God's Blessings

Psalm 65 is a song of thanksgiving for God's blessings. God is praised for His enduring mercy and loving kindness. Burdened by their sins, the people flock to the Temple to pray for deliverance from evil. In receiving God's forgiveness, the faithful feel accepted by God. They are filled with gratitude for their gift of repentance: *"To you we owe our hymn of praise, O God on Zion; to you our vows must be fulfilled, you who hear our prayers. To you all flesh must come. with its burden of wicked deeds. We are overcome by our sins; only you can pardon them. Blessed the one whom you will choose and bring to dwell in your courts. May we be filled with the good things of your house, your holy temple!"*

Sin is an attack on the order and perfection of the world. Obedience to God restores integrity and harmony to the cosmos: *"You answer us with awesome deeds of justice, ... You are robed in power, you set up the mountains by your might. You still the roaring of the seas, the roaring of their waves, the tumult of the peoples."* The Lord can silence the tumult of the ocean waters. *'The roaring of the seas, the roaring of their waves'* is associated with *'the tumult of the peoples.'* God exhibited His power and love in creating our world and in overcoming evil through the forgiveness of our sins. That is the reason why God's majestic power over nature and victory over evil, instill awe and fear among peoples: *"Distant peoples stand in awe of your marvels; the places of morning and evening you make resound with joy."*

Thirdly, nature becomes an eloquent sign of divine action: *"You visit the earth and water it, make it abundantly fertile. God's stream is filled with water; you supply their grain. Thus do you prepare it: You drench its plowed furrows, and level its ridges. With showers you keep it soft, blessing its young sprouts. You adorn the year with your bounty; your paths drip with fruitful rain. The meadows of the wilderness also drip; the hills are robed with joy. The pastures are clothed with flocks, the valleys blanketed with grain; they cheer and sing for joy."* The Psalmist uses colorful imagery to describe the splendor of the earth: the hills are robed with joy; the pastures are clothed with flocks; the valleys are blanketed with grain. All of creation is giving their Creator, praise and adoration.

Through this paean to God's greatness and goodness, the Psalmist draws the obvious conclusion that there is an intimate connection between creation and redemption. God created the Universe and human beings as His image and likeness at its center because He wanted a covenant relationship with us. Through His

Son Jesus, God has restored Creation and humans, making us His sons and daughters!

Reflect and Pray on Psalm 65, using Lectio Divina or the Method of Meditation. Make sure you converse intimately with the Blessed Trinity:

Psalm 65: Thanksgiving for God's Blessings
"1 For the leader. A psalm of David. A song.

I.

2 To you we owe our hymn of praise, O God on Zion; to you our vows must be fulfilled, 3 you who hear our prayers. To you all flesh must come 4 with its burden of wicked deeds. We are overcome by our sins; only you can pardon them. 5 Blessed the one whom you will choose and bring to dwell in your courts. May we be filled with the good things of your house, your holy temple!

II.

6 You answer us with awesome deeds of justice, O God our savior, the hope of all the ends of the earth and of those far off across the sea. 7 You are robed in power, you set up the mountains by your might. 8 You still the roaring of the seas, the roaring of their waves, the tumult of the peoples. 9 Distant peoples stand in awe of your marvels; the places of morning and evening you make resound with joy. 10 You visit the earth and water it, make it abundantly fertile. God's stream is filled with water; you supply their grain. Thus do you prepare it: 11 You drench its plowed furrows, and level its ridges. With showers you keep it soft, blessing its young sprouts. 12 You adorn the year with your bounty; your paths drip with fruitful rain. 13 The meadows of the wilderness also drip; the hills are robed with joy. 14 The pastures are clothed with flocks, the valleys blanketed with grain; they cheer and sing for joy."

End with Prayer to the Holy Trinity
NIGHT PRAYER: The Examination of Conscience

DAY SIX:
MORNING PRAYER: Acts of Faith, Hope, Charity; Daily Offering

MORNING FACE TO FACE WITH GOD:

Begin with Prayer to the Holy Spirit

Prayer on Psalm 66: Praise of God, Israel's Deliverer

Psalm 66 could be referring to the deliverance of Israel from the army of Sennacherib during the reign of Hezekiah: *"That night the angel of the LORD went forth and struck down one hundred and eighty-five thousand men in the Assyrian camp. Early the next morning, there they were, dead, all those corpses!"* (2Kings 19: 35). Psalm 66 could have been composed by Hezekiah or his scribe, first extolling the deliverance of the nation, and then the personal deliverance of the king. The Psalmist begins his song with a raucous burst of joy and celebration: *"Shout joyfully to God, all the earth; sing of his glorious name; give him glorious praise. Say to God: "How awesome your deeds! Before your great strength your enemies cringe. All the earth falls in worship before you; they sing of you, sing of your name!"* The deliverance from their enemies is so great that the people are unable to offer the volume of praise that the occasion deserves. So, the Psalmist asks the earth to join in with her symphony of myriad sounds. The nation's deliverance impacts the whole world as it speaks to the majesty and power of God's glorious reign over all creation.

The Psalmist offers his people proper perspective by presenting their present deliverance within God's miraculous interventions in their history: *"Come and see the works of God, awesome in deeds before the children of Adam. He changed the sea to dry land; through the river they passed on foot. There we rejoiced in him, who rules by his might forever, his eyes are fixed upon the nations. ... You tested us, O God, tried us as silver tried by fire. You led us into a snare; you bound us at the waist as captives. You let captors set foot on our neck; we went through fire and water; then you led us to freedom."* The destruction of Sennacherib's army is viewed within the context of the Exodus event. The destruction of Sennacherib's army was as remarkable and wonderful as the overwhelming annihilation of Pharaoh's army in the Red Sea. The crossing of the Red Sea is the most noteworthy event, viewed with awe and wonder. Psalms 18, 66, 74, 77, 78, 89, 106, and 136 speak of it.

In the third segment, the Psalmist expresses his gratitude to God for the personal deliverance of the king: *"I will bring burnt offerings to your house; to you I will fulfill my vows, which my lips pronounced and my mouth spoke in my distress. Burnt offerings of fatlings I will offer you and sacrificial smoke of rams; I will sacrifice oxen and goats. Come and hear, all you who fear God, while I recount what has been done for me. ... Had I cherished evil in my heart, the Lord would not have heard. But God did hear and listened to my voice in prayer. Blessed be God, who did not reject my prayer and refuse his mercy."* The Psalmist is offering a *todah* or thanksgiving offering. God answered his prayer because he asked in faith and integrity of heart for the deliverance of the nation and himself. The Israelites knew unquestioningly that God always answered the prayer of the clean of heart, those who have rejected evil. The man born blind stated it well: *"We know that God does not listen to sinners, but if one is devout and does his will, he listens to him"* (John 9: 31). We can pray with faith and integrity because of God's steadfast and unchanging love for us.

Reflect and Pray on Psalm 66, using Lectio Divina or the Method of Meditation. Make sure you converse intimately with the Blessed Trinity:

Prayer on Psalm 66: Praise of God, Israel's Deliverer
"1 For the leader. A song; a psalm.

I.

2 Shout joyfully to God, all the earth; sing of his glorious name; give him glorious praise. 3 Say to God: "How awesome your deeds! Before your great strength your enemies cringe. 4 All the earth falls in worship before you; they sing of you, sing of your name!"

II.

5 Come and see the works of God, awesome in deeds before the children of Adam. 6 He changed the sea to dry land; through the river they passed on foot. There we rejoiced in him, 7 who rules by his might forever, his eyes are fixed upon the nations. Let no rebel rise to challenge! 8 Bless our God, you peoples; loudly sound his praise, 9 who has kept us alive and not allowed our feet to slip. 10 You tested us, O God, tried us as silver tried by fire. 11 You led us into a snare; you bound us at the waist as captives. 12 You let captors set foot on our neck; we went through fire and water; then you led us to freedom.

III.

13 I will bring burnt offerings to your house; to you I will fulfill my vows, 14 which my lips pronounced and my mouth spoke in my distress. 15 Burnt offerings of fatlings I will offer you and sacrificial smoke of rams; I will sacrifice oxen and goats. 16 Come and hear, all you who fear God, while I recount what has been done for me. 17 I called to him with my mouth; praise was upon my tongue. 18 Had I cherished evil in my heart, the Lord would not have heard. 19 But God did hear and listened to my voice in prayer. 20 Blessed be God, who did not reject my prayer and refuse his mercy."

End with Prayer to the Holy Trinity
NIGHT SESSION: The Examination of Conscience

DAY SEVEN:
MORNING PRAYER: Acts of Faith, Hope, Charity; Daily Offering

MORNING FACE TO FACE WITH GOD:
<u>Learning Discipleship from the Psalms</u>
Begin with Prayer to the Holy Spirit

- Psalm 57 tells us that God is glorified as we praise Him in our trials: *"My heart is steadfast, God, my heart is steadfast. I will sing and chant praise."* Praise is witnessing to others of God's faithfulness and loving kindness: *"Awake, my soul; awake, lyre and harp! I will wake the dawn. I will praise you among the peoples, Lord; I will chant your praise among the nations."* For David, praising God was a deliberate choice, a matter of obedience, and the test of obedience is to do what is right regardless of the consequences.

- *"For you, O God have heard my vows, you have granted me the heritage of those who revere your name. Add days to the life of the king; may his years be as from generation to generation; may he reign before God forever"* (Psalm 61: 6-8). David speaks of the heritage that God has granted him, that distinctive promise which God gave to him through the prophet Nathan, assuring him of the eternal continuation of the 'Throne of David' (2Samuel 7: 16-17). The heritage is nothing less than the promise of Christ Himself who will establish the new Kingdom of Israel and whose reign will last forever.
- *"My soul rests in God alone, from whom comes my salvation. God alone is my rock and salvation, my fortress; I shall never fall."* The Fathers of the Church have looked upon the man of prayer in Psalm 62 as the prefiguration of Christ, who like His Father, assured us of being able to rest in Him amidst the vicissitudes of life: *"Come to me, all you who labor and are burdened, and I will give you rest."* (Matthew 11: 28).
- Psalm 63 tells us that in contrast with the righteous disciple's communion with God, the wicked will destroy themselves in their wickedness: *"But those who seek my life will come to ruin; they shall go down to the depths of the netherworld! Those who would hand over my life to the sword shall become the prey of jackals!"* David loved his son and knew that Absalom was wrong in his rebellion against his father as he was going against God's anointed one! Subsequently, his rebellion brought disaster upon his head.
- *"To you all flesh must come with its burden of wicked deeds. We are overcome by our sins; only you can pardon them ... You answer us with awesome deeds of justice, O God our savior, the hope of all the ends of the earth ... You visit the earth and water it, make it abundantly fertile."* Psalm 65 speaks of an intimate connection between creation and redemption. Just as in Spring, the earth revives itself through the action of the Creator, so does man rise from his sin through

the forgiving action of the Savior.
- In Psalm 66, The Psalmist asked for the deliverance of the nation and himself. And God answered his prayer. It was an unquestionable conviction among the Hebrew people that God always answered the prayer of the clean of heart, those who have rejected evil. The man born blind stated it well: *"We know that God does not listen to sinners, but if one is devout and does his will, he listens to him"* (John 9: 31). We can pray with faith and integrity of heart because of God's steadfast love for us.

End with Prayer to the Holy Trinity
NIGHT PRAYER: The Examination of Conscience

JOURNAL FOR BOOK TWO, WEEK THREE: CELEBRATION AND PRAISE

DAY ONE: Morning Prayer: Psalm 57: Confident Prayer for Deliverance
What is God saying to You?

Nightly Examination of Conscience:
For what are you grateful?

For what are you contrite?

What spiritual discipline, including fasting, do you need to focus on tomorrow?

DAY TWO: Morning Prayer: Psalm 61: Prayer of the King in Time of Danger
What is God saying to You?

Nightly Examination of Conscience:
For what are you grateful?

For what are you contrite?

What spiritual discipline, including fasting, do you need to focus on tomorrow?

DAY THREE: Morning Prayer: Psalm 62: Trust in God alone
What is God saying to You?

Nightly Examination of Conscience:
For what are you grateful?

For what are you contrite?

What spiritual discipline, including fasting, do you need to focus on tomorrow?

DAY FOUR: Morning Prayer: Psalm 63: Ardent Longing for God
What is God saying to You?

Nightly Examination of Conscience:
For what are you grateful?

For what are you contrite?

What spiritual discipline, including fasting, do you need to focus on tomorrow?

DAY FIVE: Morning Prayer: Psalm 65: Thanksgiving for God's Blessings
What is God saying to You?

Nightly Examination of Conscience:
For what are you grateful?

For what are you contrite?

What spiritual discipline, including fasting, do you need to focus on tomorrow?

DAY SIX: Morning Prayer: Psalm 66: Praise of God, Israel's Deliverer
What is God saying to You?

Nightly Examination of Conscience:
For what are you grateful?

For what are you contrite?

What spiritual discipline, including fasting, do you need to focus on tomorrow?

DAY SEVEN: Morning Prayer: Learning Discipleship from the Psalms
What is God saying to You?

Nightly Examination of Conscience:
For what are you grateful?

For what are you contrite?

What spiritual discipline, including fasting, do you need to focus on tomorrow?

What prayer would you compose to express what God has said to you this week?

BOOK TWO – PSALMS 42-72:
CELEBRATION AND PRAISE
Psalms 67, 68, 69, 70, 71, and 72

WHAT IS AT THE HEART OF BOOK TWO, WEEK FOUR?

In Week Four, we will pray with the last six psalms of Book Two, Psalms 67, 68, 69, 70, 71, and 72. On Day One, we will pray with *Psalm 67: Harvest Thanks and Petition*. Psalm 67 invites us to witness to the world about God's gracious mercy and blessing upon them. The psalm begins with a request for God's blessing: *"May God be gracious to us and bless us; may his face shine upon us."* Through this same request, God made a promise that if Aaron and his sons invoked His name upon the people, He would indeed bless them. We can believe with certainty that God considers it a powerful blessing and gift that He wishes to offer us.

On Day Two, we will reflect on *Psalm 68: The Exodus and Conquest, Pledge of Future Help*. Psalm 68 reflects on the Exodus, the most memorable event in Israelite history, inviting the believer to have an invincible faith in God who will always be Emmanuel, God with us. David was bringing the Ark of the Covenant to Jerusalem where God would dwell among His people in the Temple on a permanent basis. This triumphal procession was the final stage of the Exodus journey that was bringing the Ark of the Covenant to its final dwelling place in Jerusalem. On Day Three, we will ponder *Psalm 69: A Cry of Anguish in Great Distress*. Psalm 69 is a lament complaining of intense suffering, expressing the Psalmist's agony of soul as well as hope and trust in God in dire circumstances. Except for Psalm 22, this is the most quoted psalm in the New Testament. The gospels, the Acts of the Apostles, and Paul's
Letter to the Romans, have several references to Psalm 69.

On Day Four, we will pray with *Psalm 70: Prayer for Divine Help*. This psalm is the lament of a poor and afflicted person who has no resource except God. He cries out to be saved from his enemies. It is almost identical to Psalm 40: 14-17, which we did not consider in Book One, Week Four. David appealed to God on the grounds that he had no other help or deliverer. He would therefore rely completely on God.

On Day Five, we will reflect and pray with *Psalm 71: Prayer in Time of Old Age.* Psalm 71 is clearly the prayer of an elderly man asking God not to forsake him while he is being threatened by dangers. Judging from the titles and names the Psalmist uses for God, like 'rock of refuge,' 'my stronghold,' and 'rock and fortress,' it becomes clear that his trust in God was rock-solid and divinely inspired. It was a trust that spanned years of countless life-threatening crises.

On Day Six, we will ponder *Psalm 72: Solomon's Perfect Reign.* Some have regarded it as David's psalm about his son, Solomon, and his Greater Son, Jesus the Messiah. Others think that Solomon compiled Book Two and composed this psalm as a fitting conclusion for the collection of mostly David's psalms. The composition seems to highlight David's prayer for his son's reign. He describes the glory that surrounds the perfect reign of a king who is obedient to God's covenant with him. This prayer was answered during the first years of Solomon's reign. He built the Temple and the kingdom of Israel reached its highest point, politically and spiritually (1Kings 4-10).

More than anything else, Psalm 72 is pointing toward the perfect reign of David's descendant, Jesus Christ who was the fulfillment of God's plan of salvation through His death on the cross, replacing the Mosaic Covenant with the New and Eternal Covenant. Unexpectedly, Psalm 72 does not focus upon David or Solomon but on the Messiah – the King of Kings and the Son of David. This image of the king and his realm is so close to the prophecies of Isaiah 11: 1-5 and Isaiah 60-62, that it does qualify as a Messianic psalm.

On Day Seven, we will ponder the salient advice that these

psalms have offered us to enhance and strengthen our own following of Jesus and our commitment to His Church.

SPIRITUAL READING FOR BOOK TWO OF THE PSALMS:
1 and 2 Samuel
Psalms 42 to 72
1 and 2 Kings (after you have read 1 and 2 Samuel)
1 and 2 Chronicles (after you have read 1 and 2 Kings)

DAY ONE:
MORNING PRAYER: Acts of Faith, Hope, Charity; Daily Offering

MORNING FACE TO FACE WITH GOD:
Begin with Prayer to the Holy Spirit
Prayer on Psalm 67: Harvest Thanks and Petition

Psalm 67 could have been composed after the Babylonian exile in the late fifth century B.C., when the people began to live in the Diaspora among foreign nations and in new regions. The psalm begins with a request for God's blessing: *"May God be gracious to us and bless us; may his face shine upon us."* The request is threefold, asking God to be gracious or merciful, to bless us, and to let His face shine upon us. Through Moses, God asked Aaron and his sons to bless the Israelites with this same blessing: *"The LORD bless you and keep you! The LORD let his face shine upon you, and be gracious to you! The LORD look upon you kindly and give you peace!"* (Numbers 6: 24-26). God promised that if Aaron and his sons invoked His name upon the people, He would indeed bless them. God considers it a powerful blessing that He offers us.

We all need God's mercy to set our hearts in the right frame of mind. A repentant heart is forgiven by God, and the relationship with God can then be transparent, honest, and joyful. We can ask and receive God's blessing. God's love for us is boundless which makes it possible for Him to both forgive us our sins and receive us into His embrace! And in His embrace, God shines His face upon us. To know that God looks upon us with great tenderness as His own sons and daughters, is a blessing that will always remain priceless. It creates a delightful security within us.

And God loves us with the same love He has for His Son because of who He is and not because of who we are or what we have done. There is no greater source of peace and joy than this amazing truth that we are loved by God!

The Psalmist asks God for this threefold blessing in order to promote the greater glory of God among the nations: *"So shall your way be known upon the earth, your victory among all the nations. May the peoples praise you, God; may all the peoples praise you!"* God's way will be known through God's active blessing upon His people. When we live miraculous lives because God is active in our lives, the world knows and is curious. The greatest hindrance to evangelization is the failure of the Church to witness in her own life and work to the saving power of God! Our holy and ardent desire would be that all nations experience God's salvation through victory over sin. Since Pentecost, Israel's ancient prayer is being fulfilled more magnificently than they could have imagined!

The Psalmist expresses a fervent prayer of petition for all the nations and peoples: *"May the nations be glad and rejoice; for you judge the peoples with fairness, you guide the nations upon the earth. May the peoples praise you, God; may all your peoples praise you!"* In Jesus, God will break the yoke of the oppressor and introduce the Church into the glorious liberty of the children of God. The Psalmist desires that all peoples praise the Lord. It is a prayer of great vision and daring that could only have been inspired by the Holy Spirit. *'May all the peoples praise you'* is repeated twice, sounding like a refrain. Our walk with God is incomplete until we are praising Him!

The Psalmist offers a bountiful harvest as the answer to the prayer that he has made in the last two verses: *"The earth has yielded its harvest; God, our God, blesses us. May God bless us still; that the ends of the earth may revere him."* The psalm might have been composed during the harvest season. When the earth (humans who are its caretakers) knows God's way, God's salvation, and God's praise, she will yield her increase. When we live as God created us, in His image and likeness, God's natural order for creation and mankind is then honored, and blessing is the result. When we share God's heart and vision for the world, we shall be blessed. The Psalmist therefore presents a glorious cycle: we are blessed, and we use that blessing to pray for and reach a hurting world. In doing so, we are blessed even more, and we continue to use our blessings for the salvation of the world. God promised to bless the nations of the earth through the seed of Abraham, and we know this is fulfilled in Jesus Christ. Christian tradition has interpreted Psalm 67 in a Christological and Marian vein as well. For the Fathers of the Church, *'the earth has yielded its harvest'* is the Virgin Mary who gives birth to Christ the Lord.

Reflect and Pray on Psalm 67, using Lectio Divina or the Method of Meditation. Make sure you converse intimately with the Blessed Trinity:

Prayer on Psalm 67: Harvest Feast and Thanksgiving
"1 For the leader; with stringed instruments. A psalm; a song.

I.

2 May God be gracious to us and bless us; may his face shine upon us. 3 So shall your way be known upon the earth, your victory among all the nations. 4 May the peoples praise you, God; may all the peoples praise you!

II.

5 May the nations be glad and rejoice; for you judge the peoples with fairness, you guide the nations upon the earth. 6 May the peoples praise you, God; may all your peoples praise you!

III.

7 The earth has yielded its harvest; God, our God, blesses us. 8 May God bless us still; that the ends of the earth may revere him."

End with Prayer to the Holy Trinity
NIGHT PRAYER: The Examination of Conscience

DAY TWO:
MORNING PRAYER: Acts of Faith, Hope, Charity; Daily Offering

MORNING FACE TO FACE WITH GOD:

Begin with Prayer to the Holy Spirit
Prayer on Psalm 68: The Exodus and Conquest, Pledge of Future Help
Psalm 68 reflects on the Exodus, the most memorable event in Israelite history, inviting the believer to have an invincible faith in God who will always be Emmanuel. David was bringing the Ark of the Covenant to the Temple in Jerusalem where God would dwell among His people on a permanent basis: *"When it was reported to King David that the LORD blessed the household of Obed-edom and all that he possessed because of the ark of God, David went to bring up the ark of God from the house of Obed-edom into the City of David with joy"* (2Samuel 6: 12). This triumphal procession was the final stage of the journey that began with the Exodus from Egypt. It was bringing the Ark of the Covenant to its final dwelling place for God to abide permanently among His people.

The psalm commemorated God's triumphal entry into Jerusalem, and echoed the words with which the Ark set out on all its journeys in the desert, culminating in its protective presence when the Israelites rested for the night: *"Whenever the ark set out, Moses would say, "Arise, O LORD, may your enemies be scattered, and may those who hate you flee before you." And when it came to rest, he would say, "Bring back, O LORD, the myriads of Israel's troops!"* (Numbers 10: 35-36). The opening verse of Psalm 68 begins in similar fashion: *"May God arise; may his enemies be scattered; may those who hate him flee before him."*

The psalm has nine divisions. Part I emphasizes the truth that the righteous person relies on God's triumph over His enemies and theirs, for their ultimate peace and joy.: *"May God arise; may his enemies be scattered; may those who hate him flee before him. ... Then the just will be glad; they will rejoice before God; they will celebrate with great joy."* The righteous have abandoned the path of the wicked. Consequently, God's enemies have become theirs as well.

In Part II, the Psalmist rejoices in praise of God because He is *"the Father of the fatherless, defender of widows – God in his holy abode. God gives a home to the forsaken, who leads prisoners out to prosperity."* God defended His people in their Exodus from Egypt when they were defenseless and He broke their fetters. He was their refuge and strength, being the pillar of fire during the night and a column of cloud by day during their journey toward the Promised Land (Exodus 13: 21). In the Promised Land and through the king, His anointed one, God continued to be their Redeemer from His dwelling place in the Temple of Jerusalem. It was fitting, therefore, that God's people would praise and thank Him: *"Sing to God, praise his name; exalt the rider of the clouds. Rejoice before him whose name is the LORD."*

Part III continues the prayer of grateful and joyful remembrance of God's wondrous ways on behalf of His people during the Exodus from Egypt. Their procession into Jerusalem is trying to replicate this mighty triumph of God in Israelite history: *"God, when you went forth before your people, when you marched through the desert, the earth quaked, the heavens poured, before God, the One of Sinai, before God, the God of Israel. ... Your inheritance was weak and you repaired it. ... You will establish it in your goodness for the poor, O God."* God's enslaved people over four hundred years were a hapless and beaten lot. The God of Abraham, and Isaac, and Jacob, took His weak inheritance and repaired it beyond compare. In God's Presence, filled with His loving kindness, the poor and disenfranchised have become respected citizens.

Part IV highlights the total collapse of the Egyptian army and chariots at the Red Sea. The immediate consequence is that the Israelites are safe and share in the spoils: *"The Lord announced: "...The kings of the armies are in desperate flight. Every household will share the spoil, though you lie down among the sheepfolds, you shall be covered with silver as the wings of a dove, her feathers bright as fine gold."* Divine intervention will always be present in our lives when our trust in God is enduring and resolute. Then we can *"lie down among the sheepfolds,"* secure in the protection and watchful care of the Good Shepherd.

Part V sets the stage for the triumphal entry into Jerusalem. God's dwelling place on Mount Zion far excels the highest and most magnificent mountains in Israel. Part V describes the Ark's final journey into Jerusalem, as the Psalmist frames its completion in the same way Moses did in Numbers 10: 36: *"And when it came to rest, he would say, "Bring back, O LORD, the myriads of Israel's troops!"* The Psalmist echoes these same words as well: *"You mountain of God, mountain of Bashan, you rugged mountains, why look with envy at the mountain where God has chosen to dwell, where the LORD resides forever? God's chariots were myriad, thousands upon thousands; from Sinai the Lord entered the holy place."* God has journeyed from His holy dwelling place on Mount Sinai where He entered into Covenant with His people, to Mount Zion in Jerusalem where He has made the Temple His permanent abode. Part VI echoes the sentiments of Part V.

Part VII describes the orderly and impressive procession into Jerusalem, *'the holy place.'* The procession consists of a great host of people representing all the tribes of Israel: *"Your procession comes into view, O God, your procession into the holy place, my God and king. The singers go first, the harpists follow; in their midst girls sound the timbrels. In your choirs, bless God; LORD, Israel's fountain. In the lead is Benjamin, few in number; there the princes of Judah, a large throng, the princes of Zebulun, the princes of Napthali, too."* Benjamin was Saul's tribe and was in the lead among the tribes. Saul was Israel's first king and David's avowed enemy. It indeed was a magnanimous gesture on David's part to have honored his predecessor in this psalm.

Part VIII is a prayer of intercession, asking God to continue to exhibit His divine power among His people from His dwelling place in Jerusalem. In this way, the kingdom of David will remain secure and prosperous and the neighboring nations will pay tribute to God: *"Summon again, O God, your power, the divine power you once showed for us. From your temple on behalf of Jerusalem, that kings may bring you tribute   Let bronze be brought from Egypt, Ethiopia hurry its hands to God."* Many centuries later, King Herod would bring tribute to the Temple rebuilt after the Babylonian Exile, and add a magnificent extension to it, also known as the Third Temple. He spent exorbitant sums of money on a single gift of the 'golden doors' of the Temple. The Psalmist also asks God to continue vanquishing Israel's enemies as He did in the past: *"Roar at the wild beasts of the reeds, the herd of mighty bulls, the calves of the peoples; trampling those who lust after silver scatter the peoples that delight in war."* The crocodile was the wild beast of the reeds, referring to Egypt.

Part IX, the final stanza, is a song of praise and thanksgiving. The Psalmist is asking Israel to be in an intimate relationship with God and to constantly be mindful of His loving kindness. The Psalmist also asks the kingdoms of the earth to join in this celebration of God's magnanimous power and loving kindness as manifested in Israel from Jerusalem: *"You kingdoms of the earth, sing to God; chant the praises of the Lord. ... Confess the power of God, whose majesty protects Israel, whose power is in the sky. Awesome is God in his holy place, the God of Israel, who gives power and strength to his people. Blessed be God!"*

Psalm 68 highlights the central place of Jerusalem in God's plan of salvation. Jerusalem is God's permanent dwelling place. For Jesus, Jerusalem was the city of destiny. He had to suffer and die in Jerusalem, thereby completing His Exodus and ours, and become our Permanent Temple, replacing the Temple of Jerusalem which was destroyed in A.D. 70. The Psalmist does offer a fitting finale to this glorious processional psalm, describing the entry of the Ark of the covenant into Jerusalem: *'Blessed be God!'*

Reflect and Pray on Psalm 68, using Lectio Divina or the Method of Meditation. Make sure you converse intimately with the Blessed Trinity:

Prayer on Psalm 68: The Exodus and Conquest, Pledge of Future Help
"1 For the leader. A psalm of David; a song.

I.

2 May God arise; may his enemies be scattered; may those who hate him flee before him. 3 As the smoke is dispersed, disperse them; as wax is melted by fire, so may the wicked perish before God. 4 Then the just will be glad; they will rejoice before God; they will celebrate with great joy.

II.

5 Sing to God, praise his name; exalt the rider of the clouds. Rejoice before him whose name is the LORD. 6 Father of the fatherless, defender of the widows – God in his holy abode, 7 God gives a home to the forsaken, who leads prisoners out to prosperity, while rebels live in the desert.

III.

8 God, when you went forth before your people, when you marched through the desert, 9 the earth quaked, the heavens poured, before God, the One of Sinai, before God, the God of Israel. 10 You poured abundant rains, God, your inheritance was weak, and you repaired it. 11 Your creatures dwelt in it; you will establish it in your goodness for the poor, O God.

IV.

12 The Lord announced: "Those bringing news are a great Army. 13 The kings of the armies are in desperate flight. Every household will share the spoil, 14 though you lie down among the sheepfolds, you shall be covered with silver as the wings of a dove, her feathers bright as gold." 15 When the Almighty routs the kings there, it will be as when snow fell on Zalmon.

V.

16 You mountain of God, mountain of Bashan, 17 you rugged mountains, why look with envy at the mountain where God has chosen to dwell, where the LORD resides forever? 18 God's chariots were myriad, thousands upon thousands; from Sinai the Lord entered the holy place. 19 You went up to its lofty height; you

took captives, received slaves as tribute, even rebels, for the LORD God to dwell.

VI.

20 Blessed be the Lord day by day, God, our salvation, who carries us. 21. Our God is a God who saves; escape from death is the LORD God's. 22 God will crush the heads of his enemies, the hairy scalp of the one who walks in sin. 23 The Lord has said: "Even from Bashan I will fetch them, fetch them even from the depths of the sea. 24 You will wash your feet in your enemy's blood; the tongues of your dogs will lap it up.

VII.

25 Your procession comes into view, O God, your procession into the holy place, my God and king. 26 The singers go first, the harpists follow; in their midst girls sound the timbrels. 27 In your choirs, bless God; LORD, Israel's fountain. 28 In the lead is Benjamin, few in number; there the princes of Judah, a large throng, the princes of Zebulun, the princes of Naphtali, too.

VIII.

29 Summon again, O God, your power, the divine power you once showed for us, 30 from your temple on behalf of Jerusalem, that kings may bring you tribute. 31 Roar at the wild beast of the reeds, the herd of mighty bulls, the calves of the peoples; trampling those who lust after silver scatter the peoples that delight in war. 32 Let bronze be brought from Egypt, Ethiopia hurry its hands to God.

IX.

33 You kingdoms of the earth, sing to God; chant the praises of the Lord, 34 who rides the heights of the ancient heavens, who sends forth his voice as a mighty voice? 35 Confess the power of God, whose majesty protects Israel, whose power is in the sky. 36 Awesome is God in his holy place, the God of Israel, who gives power and strength to his people. Blessed be God!"

End with Prayer to the Holy Trinity
NIGHT PRAYER: The Examination of Conscience

DAY THREE:
MORNING PRAYER: Acts of Faith, Hope, Charity; Daily Offering
MORNING FACE TO FACE WITH GOD:
Begin with Prayer to the Holy Spirit
Prayer on Psalm 69: A Cry of Anguish in Great Distress

Psalm 69 was composed by David according to the superscription. It is a lament complaining of intense suffering, expressing the Psalmist's agony of soul as well as hope and trust in God in his dire circumstances. At the same time, from the depths of his agony rises the hope of salvation. The psalm is divided into six stanzas, plunging us into the depths of distress and hopelessness, tinged with desperate pleas for help and vindication, and ending on a note of confidence that God will come to the rescue of Jerusalem and rebuild the cities of Judah. And the Psalmist will be able to voice his praise and thanksgiving to God.

Using the devastating imagery of a destructive flood, Part I describes the desperate straits of the Psalmist: *"Save me, God, for the waters have reached my neck. I have sunk into the mire of the deep, where there is no foothold. I have gone down into the watery depths; the flood overwhelms me."* God created the world from the waters of chaos, which became a common image for intense distress. The Psalmist is asking God to recreate him by bringing back order and salvation to him. In his desperation, he is beseeching God to the point of exhaustion beyond relief: *"I am weary with crying out; my throat is parched. My eyes fail, from looking for my God."*

Numerous enemies have been accusing David falsely of stealing and are forcing him to make restitution: *"More numerous than the hairs of my head are those who hate me without cause. Those who would destroy me are mighty, my enemies without reason. Must I now restore what I did not steal?"* Undeserved blame and accusation have left a gaping wound in his soul. Though David had no share in the plots hatched against Saul, he was held accountable for them. Like David, Jesus had the mighty Sanhedrin hating Him without cause and bent on destroying Him.

Jesus referred to Psalm 69: 5 as it applied to Him: *"But in order that the word written in their law might be fulfilled, 'They hated me without cause'"* (John 15: 25).

In Part II, David alludes to another cause of his intense distress which is the knowledge and sorrow for his own sins. He is concerned that his actions might have caused scandal and harm to others: *"God, you know my folly; my faults are not hidden from you. Let those who wait in hope for you, LORD of hosts, not be shamed because of me. Let those who seek you, God of Israel, not be disgraced because of me."* As in Psalm 51, David is confessing his lesser *(my folly)* and more grievous sins *(my faults)*. To scandalize those who sought God was a source of much sorrow to David. He was concerned that their faith in God would be severely dented.

David then moves on to another source of intense suffering: *"For it is on your account I bear insult, that disgrace covers my face. I have become an outcast to my kindred, a stranger to my mother's children. Because zeal for your house has consumed me, I am scorned by those who scorn you. When I humbled my spirit with fasting, this led to scorn. When I clothed myself in sackcloth; I became a byword for them. Those who sit in the gate gossip about me; drunkards make me the butt of songs."* David's loyalty to God tarnished his relationships with his brothers. They did not take kindly to his ascetical practices. Paradoxically, Jesus too had to deal with His brothers who rejected and treated Him as a stranger: *"For his brothers did not believe in him"* (John 7: 5). David was also rejected by non-family members because of his zeal for God and the honest efforts he made to live a life of serious repentance. He became a derisive topic of gossip at the city gates among drunkards. A similar and worse treatment of humiliation and derision was meted out to the 'Son of David' by the High Priest, the assembled bystanders, and the unrepentant thief on the cross.

In Part III, David pours out his agonizing heart to God: *"But I will pray to you, LORD, at a favorable time. God, in your abundant kindness, answer me with your sure deliverance."* God will hear his prayer as he is appealing to God *'in your abundant kindness.'* David then presents God with his dire situation and asks God to rescue him from it: *"Rescue me from the mire, and do not let me sink. Rescue me from those who hate me and from the watery depths. ... Answer me, LORD, in your generous love; in your great mercy turn to me. Do not hide your face from your servant; hasten to answer me, for I am in distress. Come and redeem my life; because of my enemies ransom me."*

Finally, David is lifting his heart to God to whom he has pledged his total loyalty and commitment. His enemies have turned against him because he has remained faithful to God: *"You know my reproach, my shame, my disgrace; before you stand all my foes. Insult has broken my heart, and I despair; I looked for compassion, but there was none, for comforters, but found none. Instead they gave me poison for my food; and for my thirst they gave me vinegar."* The verse, *"Instead they gave me poison for my food; and for my thirst they gave me vinegar,"* was fulfilled by Jesus according to Matthew 27: 34, 48, and John 19: 28-29.

In Part IV, David asks God to bring about the ruin of his enemies. Jesus came to fulfill the Law and the Prophets, the psalms included among them. The juxtaposition of David cursing his tormentors, and Jesus praying for His enemies, suggests the chasm that was bridged by Jesus, as He brought about the completion of God's plan of salvation through the establishment of the new and eternal covenant through His death on the cross: *"From his fullness we have all received, grace in place of grace, because while the law was given through Moses, grace and truth came through Jesus Christ"* (John 1: 16-17).

Part V offers us a transition that takes place in David's assessment of his situation. He is feeling more confident and determined to praise God for his rescue: *"That I may praise God's name in song and glorify it with thanksgiving. That will please the LORD more than oxen, more than bulls with horns and hooves."*

David will offer God a *'todah'* offering, an offering of thanksgiving and praise, rather than an animal sacrifice. We have seen in Psalm 50 that the thanksgiving sacrifice *(todah)* was preferable to the animal sacrifice *(ola)*, foreshadowing the Eucharist, a thanksgiving offering. In God's rescue of him, David will then become God's powerful witness, proclaiming God's loving kindness to one and all: *"See, you lowly ones, and be glad; you who seek God, take heart! For the LORD hears the poor, and does not spurn those in bondage."*

Psalm 69 ends on a triumphant note. This psalm began in the dregs of human suffering and soars to the highest praise at the end: *"Let the heaven and the earth praise him, the seas and whatever moves in them! For God will rescue Zion, and rebuild the cities of Judah. They will dwell there and possess it; the descendants of God's servants will inherit it; those who love God's name will dwell in it."* David has moved out of himself and is praying for Jerusalem and the cities of Judah, that they may become holy dwelling places, inhabited by people who are *'the descendants of God's servants,'* and *'love God's name.'* In the Beatitudes, Jesus seems to be referring to Psalm 69 when He says, *"Blessed are the meek, for they will inherit the land"* (Matthew 5:5).

Reflect and Pray on Psalm 69, using Lectio Divina or the Method of Meditation. Make sure you converse intimately with the Blessed Trinity:

Prayer on Psalm 69: A Cry of Anguish in Great Distress
"1 For the leader; according to "Lilies." Of David.

I.

2 Save me, God, for the waters have reached my neck. 3 I have sunk into the mire of the deep, where there is no foothold. I have gone down to the watery depths; the flood overwhelms me. 4 I am weary with crying out; my throat is parched. My eyes fail from looking for my God. 5 More numerous than the hairs of my head are those who hate me without cause. Those who would destroy me are mighty, my enemies without reason, must I now restore what I did not steal?

II.

6 God, you know my folly; my faults are not hidden from you. 7 Let those who wait in hope for you, LORD of hosts, not be shamed because of me. Let those who seek you, God of Israel, not be disgraced because of me. 8 For it is on your account I bear insult, that disgrace covers my face. 9 I have become an outcast to my kindred, a stranger to my mother's children. 10 Because zeal for your house has consumed me, I am scorned by those who scorn you. 11 When I humbled my spirit with fasting, this led only to scorn. 12 When I clothed myself in sackcloth; I became a byword for them. 13. Those who sit in the gate gossip about me; drunkards make me the butt of songs.

III.

14. But I will pray to you, LORD, at a favorable time. God, in your abundant kindness, answer me with your sure deliverance. 15 Rescue me from the mire, and do not let me sink. Rescue me from those who hate me and from the watery depths. 16 Do not let the flood waters overwhelm me, nor the deep swallow me, nor the pit close its mouth over me. 17 Answer me, LORD, in your generous love; in your great mercy turn to me. 18 Do not hide your face from your servant; hasten to answer me, for I am in distress. 19 Come and redeem my life; because of my enemies ransom me. 20 You know my reproach, my shame, my disgrace; before you stand all my foes. 21 Insult has broken my heart, and I despair; I looked for compassion, but there was none, for comforters, but found none. 22 Instead they gave me poison for my food; and for my thirst they gave me vinegar.

IV.

23 May their own table be a snare for them, and their communion offerings a trap. 24 Make their eyes so dim they cannot see; keep their backs ever feeble. 25 Pour out your wrath upon them; let the fury of your anger overtake them. 26 Make their camp desolate, with none to dwell in their tents. 27 For they pursued the one you struck, added to the pain of the one you wounded. 28 Heap

punishment upon their punishment; let them gain from you no vindication. 29 May they be blotted from the book of life; not registered among the just!

V.

30 But here I am miserable and in pain; let your saving help protect me, God, 31 that I may praise God's name in song and glorify it with thanksgiving. 32 That will please the LORD more than oxen, more than bulls with horns and hooves: 33 "See, you lowly ones, and be glad; you who seek God, take heart! 34 For the LORD hears the poor, and does not spurn those in bondage. 35 Let the heaven and the earth praise him, the seas and whatever moves in them!"

VI.

36 For God will rescue Zion, and rebuild the cities of Judah. They will dwell there and possess it; 37 The descendants of God's servants will inherit it; those who love God's name will dwell in it."

End with Prayer to the Holy Trinity
NIGHT PRAYER: The Examination of Conscience
DAY FOUR:
MORNING PRAYER: Acts of Faith, Hope, Charity; Daily Offering

MORNING FACE TO FACE WITH GOD:
Begin with Prayer to the Holy Spirit
Prayer on Psalm 70: Prayer for Divine Help

Psalm 70 describes the plight of an individual who is besieged by life- threatening dangers. In his desperation, he has ardent recourse to God. The psalm begins with an earnest prayer fraught with anxiety about one's safety: *"Graciously rescue me, God! Come quickly to help me, LORD!"* There is a great sense of urgency in David's prayer. Jesus refers to the need for urgency in our prayer in the *Parable of the Persistent Widow* in Luke 18: 1-8. Despite the dishonesty and callousness of the unjust judge, the widow is relentless in her petitioning of him. Jesus concludes with an incisive remark that captures David's frame of mind: *"Will not*

God then secure the rights of his chosen ones who call out to him day and night? Will he be slow to answer them?" (Luke 18: 7).

David asks that his adversaries suffer confusion and shame. It was bad enough that his enemies wanted him dead; they also poured ridicule upon him of the worst kind: *"Let those who seek my life be confused and put to shame. Let those who desire my ruin turn back in disgrace. Let those who say "Aha!" turn back in their shame."* David's prayer seems to capture the conviction that he voiced in Psalm 1: *"The way of the wicked leads to ruin."* Maybe the best thing for people who engage in wrongdoing is for their plans to fail. Hopefully, they will then realize the folly of their wrongdoing and move toward repentance.

In the second half, David calls God's people to praise and glorify Him, even though personally he is in a perilous state: *"But may all who seek you rejoice and be glad in you. Those who long for your help always say, "God be glorified!" I am miserable and poor. God, come to me quickly! You are my help and deliverer. LORD, do not delay!"* David could not have found it possible to invite others to praise and glorify God in his present situation, had he not been strengthened by God's peace and joy. He was secure in the truth that God cared for him. Hence, he could appeal to God to be his helper and deliverer without delay.

The psalm rather cryptically highlights the vast difference between the sentiments couched in the *"Aha!"* of David's scorners, and the trust he exuded in *"God be glorified!"* An unbridgeable chasm lies between darkness and light, highlighting the irreconcilable contrast between the way of the wicked and the way of the just.

Reflect and Pray on Psalm 70, using Lectio Divina or the Method of Meditation. Make sure you converse intimately with the Blessed Trinity:

Prayer on Psalm 70: Prayer for Divine Help
"2. Graciously rescue me, God! Come quickly to help me, LORD! 3. Let those who seek my life be confused and put to shame. Let

those who desire my ruin turn back in disgrace. 4. Let those who say "Aha!" turn back in their shame. 5. But may all who seek you rejoice and be glad in you. Those who long for your help always say, "God be glorified!" 6. I am miserable and poor. God, come to me quickly! You are my help and deliverer. LORD, do not delay!

End with Prayer to the Holy Trinity
NIGHT PRAYER: The Examination of Conscience

DAY FIVE:
MORNING PRAYER: Acts of Faith, Hope, Charity; Daily Offering

MORNING FACE TO FACE WITH GOD:
Begin with Prayer to the Holy Spirit

Prayer on Psalm 71: Prayer in Time of Old Age

Psalm 71 is the prayer of an elderly man asking God to not forsake him while he is being threatened by dangers. The Psalmist offers us a brief introduction to his prayer of petition in the first four verses: *"In you, LORD, I take refuge; let me never be put to shame. In your justice rescue and deliver me; listen to me and save me! Be my rock of refuge, my stronghold to give me safety; for you are my rock and fortress. My God, rescue me from the hand of the wicked, from the clutches of the evil and violent."* Judging from the titles and names the Psalmist uses for God, like 'rock of refuge,' 'my stronghold,' and 'rock and fortress,' it becomes clear that his trust in God was rock-solid and divinely inspired. It was a trust that spanned many years and countless life-threatening crises.

In verses 5-8, the Psalmist reinforces these attributes of God by describing his lifelong trust in the LORD: *"You are my hope, Lord; my trust, GOD, from my youth. On you I have depended since birth; from my mother's womb you are my strength; my hope in you never wavers. I have become a portent to many, but you are my strong refuge! My mouth shall be filled with your praise, shall sing your glory every day."* As a youth, David killed Goliath. From his mother's womb, God already destined him to become the king of Israel when he was anointed by Samuel (1Samuel 16: 13). David became a 'portent' or sign to many. People were amazed at his life, some interpreting his trials as God's protection of him, and others as God's punishment. The Psalmist is a seasoned man of faith. He has practiced his trust in God through daily prayer. And God has been constantly faithful to him. The quality of his discipleship rings true as he is speaking to us near the end of his life, and his listeners know his history. The Psalmist then expresses his lament and petition in verses 9-13: *"Do not cast me aside in my old age; as my strength fails, do not forsake me. For my enemies speak against me; they watch and plot against me. They say, "God has abandoned him. Pursue, and seize him! No one will come to his rescue!" God, be not far from me; my God, hasten to help me. Bring to a shameful end those who attack me; cover with contempt and scorn those who seek my ruin."* The Psalmist is undeterred by the assessment of his detractors, who think that he is a castaway, rejected and abandoned by God. In his trust in God, he knows that God will pass judgment on his enemies and come to his rescue!

In verses 14 through 24, the Psalmist knows that his confidence in God has been vindicated. He moves away from lament into total trust in God and praise and thanksgiving. He will be secure in the shadow of God's wings. He assesses his life as being wondrously meaningful because God was always there for him: *"Whatever bitter afflictions you sent me, you would turn and revive me."* He feels compelled therefore to extol God's justice and righteousness: *"My lips will shout for joy as I sing your praise; my soul, too, which you have redeemed. Yes, my tongue shall recount your justice day by day. For those who sought my ruin have been shamed and disgraced."* In like manner, we need to speak of God's redeeming works of loving kindness in our prayer of praise and thanksgiving, as well as to those around us. Our Lamb that was slain for our redemption is worthy of all praise and blessing.

Psalm 71 may well be named a psalm of trust. We could view it as part of a trilogy of psalms of trust: Psalm 131 providing a picture from the beginning of life, Psalm 23 coming out of the stresses and strains of midlife, and Psalm 71, giving expression to the reflections of a senior citizen.

Reflect and Pray on Psalm 71, using Lectio Divina or the Method of Meditation. Make sure you converse intimately with the Blessed Trinity:

Psalm 71: Prayer in Time of Old Age

I.

"1 In you, LORD, I take refuge; let me never be put to shame. 2 In your justice rescue and deliver me; listen to me and save me! 3 Be my rock of refuge, my stronghold to give me safety; for you are my rock and fortress. 4 My God, rescue me from the hand of the wicked, from the clutches of the evil and violent. 5 You are my hope, Lord; my trust, GOD, from my youth. 6 On you I have depended since birth; from my mother's womb you are my strength; my hope in you never wavers. 7 I have become a portent to many, but you are my strong refuge! 8 My mouth shall be filled with your praise, shall sing your glory every day.

II.

9 Do not cast me aside in my old age; as my strength fails, do not forsake me. 10 For my enemies speak against me; they watch and plot against me. 11 They say, "God has abandoned him. Pursue, and seize him! No one will come to the rescue!" 12 God, be not far from me; my God, hasten to help me. 13 Bring to a shameful end those who attack me; cover with contempt and scorn those who seek my ruin. 14 I will always hope in you and add to all your praise. 15 My mouth shall proclaim your just deeds, day after day your acts of deliverance, though I cannot number them all. 16 I will speak of the mighty works of the Lord; O GOD, I will tell of your singular justice.

III.

17 God, you have taught me from my youth; to this day I proclaim your wondrous deeds. 18 Now that I am old and gray, do not forsake me, God, that I may proclaim your might to all generations yet to come, your power 19 and justice, God, to the highest heaven. You have done great things; O God, who is your equal? 20

Whatever bitter afflictions you sent me, you would turn and revive me. From the watery depths of the earth once more raise me up. 21 Restore my honor; turn and comfort me, 22 that I may praise you with the lyre for your faithfulness, my God, and sing your praise; my soul, too, which you have redeemed. 23. My lips will shout for joy as I sing your praise; my soul, too, which you have redeemed. 24. Yes, my tongue shall recount your justice day by day. For those who sought my ruin have been shamed and disgraced."

End with Prayer to the Holy Trinity
NIGHT PRAYER: The Examination of Conscience

DAY SIX:
MORNING PRAYER: Acts of Faith, Hope, Charity; Daily Offering

MORNING FACE TO FACE WITH GOD:
Begin with Prayer to the Holy Spirit

Prayer on Psalm 72: A Prayer for the King

The superscription tells us that Psalm 72 is a Psalm of Solomon. The last line of the psalm, *'The end of the psalms of David, son of Jesse'* refers to the collection of psalms 42-72 of Book Two, separating Book Two from Book Three. It is possible that Solomon compiled Book Two and composed this psalm as a fitting conclusion for the collection of mostly David's psalms. Unexpectedly, it does not focus on David or Solomon, but on the Messiah – the King of Kings and the Son of David.

Psalm 72 is a royal psalm, very dear to Jewish and Christian tradition, a royal psalm on which the Fathers of the Church meditated and reinterpreted in a Messianic way. The first great movement in the psalm takes place in verses 1 to 11. It opens with an intense, choral entreaty to God to grant the sovereign ruler the gift that is fundamental to good government: justice. The entreaty is directed especially toward dealing with the poor, who are usually oppressed by civil authority: *"O God, give your judgment to the king; your justice to the king's son; that he may govern your people with justice, your oppressed with right judgment, that the mountains may yield their bounty for the people, and the hills great abundance, that he may defend the oppressed among the people, save the children of the poor and crush the oppressor."* In ancient biblical understanding, the king was God's visible representative on earth, whose actions, therefore, had to conform to the just action of His God. Violating the rights of those who have no human protectors, is a crime against God. Often, the Scriptures make a connection between just government and the bountiful produce of the land. A community which lives according to righteousness enjoys internal harmony and prosperity in field and flock.

After this lively entreaty for the gift of justice, the Psalmist begins to lift his vision beyond a desire for his own reign to be blessed, toward the anticipation of the reign of a greater Son of David, Messiah and King. The Psalm's horizon broadens to take in the royal, Messianic kingdom as it evolves through time, measured by the sun and moon, and the seasons, measured by rain and abundance. Hence it is a fruitful and serene kingdom that always supports the values of justice and peace. These are the signs of the Messiah's entry into our history: *"May they fear you with the sun, and before the moon, through all generations. May he be like rain coming down upon the fields, like showers watering the earth, that abundance may flourish in his days, great bounty, till the moon be no more."*

Under David and Solomon, Israel's territory included some neighboring territories as well. However, it was still small, comparatively. By contrast, the Messiah's kingdom will have a universal dimension. It will sweep across the whole map of the world as it was then known, which included Arabs and nomads, the kings of remote States and even enemies, in a universal embrace of which the Psalms and Prophets frequently sing: *"May he rule from sea to sea, from the river to the ends of the earth. May his foes kneel before him, his enemies lick the dust. May all kings bow before him, all nations serve him. For he rescues the poor when they cry out, the oppressed who have no one to help. He shows pity* to the needs and the poor and saves the lives of the poor. From extortion and violence he redeems them, for precious is their blood in his sight. Long may he live, receiving gold from Sheba, prayed for without cease, blessed day by day. May his name be forever; as long as the sun, may his name endure."

King Solomon sang of a king far greater than Solomon ever was. This was prophesied in Nathan's prophecy which referred to David's immediate son and successor in Solomon, and his ultimate Son and Successor in Jesus the Messiah: *"When your days have been completed and you rest with your ancestors, I will raise up your offspring after you, sprung from your loins, and I will establish his kingdom. He it is who shall build a house for my name, and I will establish his kingdom. ... Your house and your kingdom are firm forever before me; your throne shall be firmly established forever"* (2Samuel 7: 12-13; 16). The justice Solomon prayed for and aspired after will be perfectly fulfilled in the Greater King. In Psalm 72: 14, the King is represented as taking upon himself the office of Goel or Kinsman-Redeemer, buying back their freedom from slavery by becoming their price and taking their place: *"From extortion and violence he redeems them, for precious is their blood in his sight."*

Psalm 72: 15 highlights a special function of the subjects toward their Messiah-King: *"Long may he live, receiving gold from Sheba, prayed for without cease, blessed day by day."* Inspired by the Holy Spirit, Solomon wrote things regarding the Messiah-King that were beyond his own understanding. He could not have envisaged the resurrection of Jesus when he prayed: *"Long may he live."* The Greater King would receive gifts and honor and praise (gold of Sheba) and in turn would bestow great blessings on the earth: *"May wheat abound in the land, flourish even on the mountain heights..."*.

The closing doxology, Verses 18-19, marks the end of Book Two and signals the beginning of Book Three: *"Blessed be the LORD God, the God of Israel, who alone does wonderful deeds.*

Blessed be his glorious name forever; may he fill all the earth with his glory. Amen and amen." It highlights the mood of Book Two, reminding us that God is always faithful to His promises, and His loving kindness is everlasting. He is worthy of our praise, thanksgiving and adoration.

Reflect and Pray on Psalm 72, using Lectio Divina or the Method of Meditation. Make sure you converse intimately with the Blessed Trinity:

Prayer on Psalm 72: A Prayer for the King
"1 Of Solomon.

I.

2 O God, give your judgment to the king; your justice to the king's son; that he may govern your people with justice, your oppressed with right judgment, 3 that the mountains may yield their bounty for the people, and the hills great abundance, 4 that he may defend the oppressed among the people, save the children of the poor and crush the oppressor.

II.

5 May they fear you with the sun, and before the moon, through all generations. 6 May he be like rain coming down upon the fields, like showers watering the earth, 7 that abundance may flourish in his days, great bounty, till the moon be no more.

III.

8 May he rule from sea to sea, from the river to the ends of the earth. 9 May his foes kneel before him, his enemies lick the dust. 10 May the kings of Tarshish and the islands bring tribute, the kings of Sheba and Seba offer gifts. 11 May all kings bow before him, all nations serve him. 12 For he rescues the poor when they cry out, the oppressed who have no one to help. 13 He shows pity to the needs and the poor and saves the lives of the poor. 14 From extortion and violence he redeems them, for precious is their blood in his sight.

IV.

15 Long may he live, receiving gold from Sheba, prayed for without cease, blessed day by day. 16 May wheat abound in the land, flourish even on the mountain heights. May his fruit be like that of Lebanon, and flourish in the city like the grasses of the land. 17 May his name be forever; as long as the sun, may his name endure. May the tribes of the earth give blessings with his name; may all the nations regard him as favored. 18 Blessed be the LORD God, the God of Israel, who alone does wonderful deeds. 19 Blessed be his glorious name forever; may he fill all the earth with his glory. Amen and amen." The end of the psalms of David, son of Jesse.

End with Prayer to the Holy Trinity
NIGHT PRAYER: Examination of Conscience

DAY SEVEN:
MORNING PRAYER: Acts of Faith, Hope, Charity; Daily Offering

MORNING FACE TO FACE WITH GOD:
<u>Learning Discipleship from the Psalms</u>
Begin with Prayer to the Holy Spirit

- In Psalm 67, The Psalmist seeks to promote the greater glory of God among the nations: *"So shall your way be known upon the earth, your victory among all the nations. May the peoples praise you, God; may all the peoples praise you!"* God's way will be known through God's active blessing upon His people. When we live miraculous lives because God is active in our lives, the world knows and in curious. When God is silent or dead in our lives, Jesus Christ as well might not have come.
- *"You rugged mountain, mountain of Bashan, you rugged mountains, why look with envy at the mountain where God has chosen to dwell, where the LORD resides forever?"* Psalm 68 highlights the central place of Jerusalem in God's plan of salvation. Jerusalem is God's permanent dwelling place. For Jesus, Jerusalem was the city of destiny. He had to suffer and die in Jerusalem, thereby completing His Exodus and ours, and become our Permanent Temple, replacing the Temple of Jerusalem which was destroyed in A.D. 70.
- Psalm 69 began in the dregs of human suffering and soars to the highest praise at the end: *"Let the heaven and the earth*

praise him, the seas and whatever moves in them! For God will rescue Zion, and rebuild the cities of Judah. ... the descendants of God's servants will inherit it; those who love God's name will dwell in it." David is praying for Jerusalem and the cities of Judah, to become holy dwelling places, inhabited by people who are *'the descendants of God's servants,'* and *'love God's name.'* May the same be said of us.

- *"Let those who desire my ruin turn back in disgrace. Let those who say "Aha!" turn back in their shame. But may all who seek you rejoice and be glad in you, those who long for your help always say, "God be glorified!"* Psalm 70 highlights the vast difference between the sentiments couched in the *"Aha!"* of David's scorners, and the trust he exuded in *"God be glorified!"* An unbridgeable chasm lies between darkness and light, highlighting the irreconcilable contrast between the way of the wicked and the way of the just.

- *"On you I have depended since birth; from my mother's womb you are my strength; my hope in you never wavers. I have become a portent to many, but you are my strong refuge! My mouth shall be filled with your praise, shall sing your glory every day"* According to Psalm 71, David became a 'portent' or sign to many. People were amazed at his life, some interpreting his trials as God's protection of him, and others as God's punishment. His communion with God never wavered even when he walked through the valley of the shadow of death. His discipleship rings true as he is speaking at the end of his life, and his listeners know his history.

- In Psalm 72, King Solomon sang of a king far greater than he ever was. This was prophesied in Nathan's prophecy which referred to David's immediate son and successor in Solomon, and his ultimate Son and Successor in Jesus the Messiah: "When your days have been completed and you rest with your ancestors, I will raise up your offspring after you, sprung from your loins, and I will establish his kingdom. He it is who shall build a house for my name, and I will establish his kingdom. ... Your house and your kingdom are firm forever before me; your throne shall be firmly established forever" (2Samuel 7: 12-13; 16).

End with Prayer to the Holy Trinity
NIGHT PRAYER: The Examination of Conscience

JOURNAL FOR BOOK TWO, WEEK FOUR: CELEBRATION AND PRAISE

DAY ONE: Morning Prayer: Psalm 67: Harvest Thanks and Petition
What is God saying to You?

Nightly Examination of Conscience:
For what are you grateful?

For what are you contrite?

What spiritual discipline, including fasting, do you need to focus on tomorrow?

DAY TWO: Morning Prayer: Psalm 68: The Exodus and Conquest, Pledge of Future Help
What is God saying to You?

Nightly Examination of Conscience:
For what are you grateful?

For what are you contrite?

What spiritual discipline, including fasting, do you need to focus on tomorrow?

DAY THREE: Morning Prayer: Psalm 69: A Cry of Anguish in Great Distress
What is God saying to You?

Nightly Examination of Conscience:
For what are you grateful?

For what are you contrite?

What spiritual discipline, including fasting, do you need to focus on tomorrow?

DAY FOUR: Morning Prayer: Psalm 70: Prayer for Divine Help
What is God saying to You?

Nightly Examination of Conscience:
For what are you grateful?

For what are you contrite?

What spiritual discipline, including fasting, do you need to focus on tomorrow?

DAY FIVE: Morning Prayer: Psalm 71: Prayer in Time of Old Age
What is God saying to You?

Nightly Examination of Conscience:
For what are you grateful?

For what are you contrite?

What spiritual discipline, including fasting, do you need to focus on tomorrow?

DAY SIX: Morning Prayer: Psalm 72: A Prayer for the King
What is God saying to You?

Nightly Examination of Conscience:
For what are you grateful?

For what are you contrite?

What spiritual discipline, including fasting, do you need to focus on tomorrow?

DAY SEVEN: Morning Prayer: Learning Discipleship from the Psalms
What is God saying to You?

Nightly Examination of Conscience:
For what are you grateful?

For what are you contrite?

What spiritual discipline, including fasting, do you need to focus on tomorrow?

What prayer would you compose to express what God has said to you this week?

BOOK THREE – PSALMS 73-89: PURIFICATION THROUGH TRIBULATION
Psalms 73, 74, 76, 78, 79, and 80

WHAT IS AT THE HEART OF BOOK THREE, WEEK ONE?

Book Three has the fewest of David's psalms, just Psalm 86, which very appropriately is a lamentation, befitting the theme of Book Three: *Purification through Tribulation.* The 17 psalms of Book Three plunge us into Israel's lowest depths of ignominy and shame during the 9th Century B.C., when after a glorious period of peace and prosperity under King David and for some time during King Solomon's reign, she was devastated by national misfortune and calamity. The northern part of the kingdom, comprising the ten tribes of Israel, restless under Solomon's punishing taxes and resentful of his wasteful habits, rebelled and took Jeroboam as their king, and the southern part, mostly the tribe of Judah, went with Rehoboam, Solomon's son. The Northern Kingdom rejected the Levites and the Temple. With the break-up of the kingdom, came the first destruction of the First Temple by Shishak, King of Egypt, during the fifth year of King Rehoboam's reign. Thus, Israel endured colossal disaster.

The psalms of lamentation in Book Three point prophetically toward the permanent destruction of the monarchy in 597 B.C. when Zedekiah, the last legitimate son of David to rule Jerusalem, was taken into exile. And the Temple, God's dwelling place among His people and a symbol of God's protection, was destroyed in 587 B.C., and the Israelites were subjected to the Babylonian Exile lasting 50 years. Book Three is indeed one long lament for the most part, moving from impending fear and helplessness to shame and humiliation, even to the edge of despair, especially in Psalms 88 and 89, the last two of Book Three.

The first eleven psalms of Book Three are from Asaph. Asaph was King David's music director. He lived between 1020 and 920

B.C., from David's reign, through Solomon's, to Rehoboam's, Solomon's son, when the kingdom was divided between the Northern Kingdom of Israel and the Kingdom of Judah. He worked as director of music at David's Tent of Meeting and at Solomon's Temple. He was in Jerusalem when God gave David the great promise that he would have a son who would be the Messiah, and reign forever (2Samuel 7: 8-17). He also heard David tell the people and elders of Israel that his son Solomon would build God's temple, and God would make sure that David's house and kingdom would last forever. Asaph witnessed the death of David, the enthronement of Solomon, and the building of the Temple. He witnessed the best years of Israel's history and it was truly a mountain-top experience. He also witnessed its descent into the dregs. He wrote most of his psalms when he was an old man.

After Solomon's dedication of the Temple (2Kings 8), Israel's 'golden age' seemed to come apart at the seams. After a promising start, Solomon turned his back on God and pursued power, wealth, luxury, and human wisdom, as well as the worship of other gods. To finance his profligate lifestyle, the people were oppressed with slavery and taxes. Asaph saw Solomon become a wicked man who entrusted the administration of his Kingdom to other wicked men. Neither Asaph nor his brother Zechariah would keep silent about Solomon's wickedness, and Zechariah was murdered and thus paid the ultimate price. After Solomon's death, Asaph, now an old man, saw David's kingdom torn in two by God's decree. In the fifth year of Rehoboam's reign as King of Judah, the Egyptians, along with Israel's neighbors, captured Jerusalem, burned and stripped the Temple, killed many of the priests, and departed, mocking Israel and Israel's God. Many of Asaph's relatives perished in the massacre as many of them served in the Temple as either musicians or doorkeepers. In the winter of his life, Asaph surveyed the wreckage of his hopes. The Kingdom was destroyed, the Temple was in ruins, and many of his own family had been killed. If there ever was a man who had an excuse for being disillusioned, Asaph was that man. Yet through it all, Asaph finds God's faithfulness to be a strong pillar of hope.

Psalms 84, 85, 87, and 88 have been composed by the Korahites who became great leaders in choral and orchestral music during the reign of King David. In all, 11 psalms are attributed to them. Psalms 84, 85, and 87 strike a note of deep devotion and longing for God. Along with the element of lament, they also express great trust in God as our refuge and strength. Psalm 84, particularly, strikes a happy note. Psalm 88 continues the theme expressed in Book Three: intense purification through many tribulations. Psalm 88 is the darkest of psalms, understood as offering us a spiritual portrait of Jesus during His passion.

Ethan the Ezrahite is the composer of Psalm 89. In 1Kings 4: 32, Ethan the Ezrahite is described as a wise man, yet not as wise as King Solomon. Psalm 89 seems to combine two different psalms, the first half composed during the time of David or Solomon, and the second half composed after the last Davidic king was taken captive in 597 B.C. by the Babylonians.

During Week One, you will pray with six psalms composed by Asaph. You will see how they speak to the events of his life and times. On Day One, you will ponder *Psalm 73: The Trial of the Just*. Psalm 73 reflects Asaph's bitterness at the murder of his brother. It also gives us a much- needed commentary on what was happening in Israel in the years between the dedication of the Temple and the end of Solomon's reign. Psalm 73 also reflects accurately the descent into corruption and evil that led to the destruction of the Temple in 587 B.C. and the Babylonian exile.

On Day Two, you will pray with *Psalm 74: Prayer at the Destruction of the Temple*. Psalm 74 is a good example of prayer that is based on God's loving kindness and enduring mercy. Our prayer will always be the supplication of a sinner who is confident that God will listen to the repentant sinner and come to their help. Our prayer will always be effective when we base our petitions on God's covenant with us. Psalm 74 is applicable to the destruction of the Temple in 587 B.C. as well.

On Day Three, you will ponder *Psalm 76: God defends Jerusalem*. Psalm 76 reflects Asaph's pain during the division of Solomon's kingdom when Rehoboam took Judah and Jeroboam took Ephraim and nine other tribes. He does so by reminding his people that Jerusalem or Zion is God's dwelling place and the glue that holds God's people together.

On Day Four, you will pray with *Psalm 78: A New Beginning in Zion and David*. Psalm 78 is a supplicatory psalm of lament. Speaking on behalf of the exiled survivors, the Psalmist acknowledged their sins against God. Their sins have brought about their utter destruction, politically, economically, socially, and religiously. The final verse of the psalm strikes a note of gratitude and praise of God who has always been their Good Shepherd, pastoring them with loving kindness and faithfulness.

On Day Five, you will ponder *Psalm 79: A Prayer for Jerusalem*. Psalm 79 was composed after Jerusalem was attacked and the Temple desecrated. The first desecration occurred during the original Asaph's lifetime when King Shishak of Egypt plundered Jerusalem in the 9th Century B.C. In many circles, this psalm is seen as being a prophecy about the destructionof the Temple by the Babylonians in 587 B.C., or that Asaph was a name that was passed on and referred to the Temple musicians who composed it after the destruction of the Temple in 587 B.C.

On Day Six, you will pray with *Psalm 80: A Prayer to restore God's Vineyard*. Psalm 80 is a communal lament, a passionate plea to God from the entire people of Israel. The Psalmist addresses God as the Shepherd of Israel who leads Joseph like a flock. With great confidence in God's faithfulness and loving kindness, the people beseech God to restore their fortunes and save them.

On Day Seven, you will ponder the salient advice that these psalms have offered us to enhance our own following of Jesus and our commitment to His Church.

SPIRITUAL READING FOR BOOK THREE OF THE PSALMS:
2Kings
Psalms 73 To 89
Jeremiah: Chapters 25-45
Ezekiel: Chapters 1-24

DAY ONE:
MORNING PRAYER: Acts of Faith, Hope, Charity; Daily Offering

MORNING FACE TO FACE WITH GOD:
Begin with Prayer to the Holy Spirit

Prayer on Psalm 73: The Trial of the Just

Psalm 73 sets the tone for Book Three which depicts Israel's intense purification through much travail and tribulation. Asaph faced a conundrum trying to live as a righteous Israelite during his long life, a difficult problem that besets all disciples: why is it that the wicked seem to prosper, leaving the faithful believers to wonder whether it is worth living righteously? As he struggles to arrive at a solution to this existential dilemma, he begins his probe with a tried and true assertion about God. He was deeply aware of God's faithfulness to His promises. He had witnessed God's loving kindness during the reigns of David and Solomon: *"How good God is to the upright, to those who are pure of heart!"*

However, amidst God's faithfulness, Asaph witnessed the wickedness and evil that occurred during the reign of King Solomon. The king had succumbed to a life of luxury and oppressive power over his people, enslaving them with burdensome taxes and worshiping false gods. Asaph himself struggled with the allure of wanting to be like the wealthy and unscrupulous: *"But, as for me, my feet had almost stumbled; my steps had nearly slipped, because I was envious of the arrogant when I saw the prosperity of the wicked."* He soon realizes that he is being lulled into believing that the rich and powerful have the ideal lifestyle. He has invested far too much time and energy in a slippery delusion that could have led to his spiritual destruction: *"For they suffer no pain; their bodies are healthy and sleek. They are free of the burdens of life; they are not afflicted like others."*

He then comes to his spiritual senses and sees that the wicked and prosperous are indulging in a self-destructive illusion. They appear to be carefree but are in fact enslaved by their destructive passions: *"Thus pride adorns them as a necklace; violence clothes them as a robe. Out of such blindness comes sin; evil thoughts flood their hearts. They scoff and spout their malice; from on high they utter threats. They set their mouths against the heavens, their tongues roam the earth"* In standing up against God, they seem to prosper and do well, and their lifestyle appears attractive, drawing the unwary like a magnet: *"So my people turn to them and drink deeply of their words. They say, "Does God really know?" "Does the Most High have any knowledge? Such, then, are the wicked, always carefree, increasing their wealth."*

As the Psalmist grapples with this difficult problem which seems to tangle him in knots, the solution presents itself when he visited the Lord in His sanctuary: *"Though I tried to understand all this, it was too difficult for me, till I entered the sanctuary of God and came to understand their end."* He receives a double revelation in the Temple: the end of the wicked will come unexpectedly: *"You set them, indeed, on a slippery road; you hurl them down to ruin. How suddenly they are devastated; utterly undone by disaster. They are like a dream after waking, Lord, dismissed like shadows when you arise."* And the second revelation is that God is with him and has been with him all along.

In the last segment, the Psalmist reflects on his relationship with God, making the point that when he has been weak, God has always been his strength. This certainty of God always being with him creates a deep peace and gratitude in him: *"Though my flesh and my heart fail, God is the rock of my heart, my portion forever."* By the same token, those who reject God will perish: *"But those who are far from you perish; you destroy those unfaithful to you."* The Psalmist ends with what has now become his mission: to be near God and to declare His works to one and all: *"As for me, to be near God is my good, to make the Lord GOD* my refuge. I shall declare all your works in the gates of daughter Zion."

Reflect and Pray on Psalm 73, using Lectio Divina or the Method of Meditation. Make sure you converse intimately with the Blessed Trinity:

Prayer on Psalm 73: The Trial of the Just
"1 A psalm of Asaph.
How good God is to the upright, to those who are pure of heart!

I.

2 But as for me, my feet had almost stumbled; my steps had nearly slipped, 3 because I was envious of the arrogant when I saw the prosperity of the wicked. 4 For they suffer no pain; their bodies are healthy and sleek. 5 They are free of the burdens of life; they are not afflicted like others. 6 Thus pride adorns them as a necklace; violence clothes them as a robe. 7 Out of such blindness comes sin; evil thoughts flood their hearts. 8 They scoff and spout their malice; from on high they utter threats. 9 They set their mouths against the heavens, their tongues roam the earth. 10 So my people turn to them and drink deeply of their words. 11 They say, "Does God really know?" "Does the Most High have any knowledge?" 12 Such, then, are the wicked, always carefree, increasing their wealth.

II.

13 Is it in vain that I have kept my heart pure, washed my hands in innocence? 14 For I am afflicted day after day, chastised every morning. 15 Had I thought, "I will speak as they do," I would have betrayed this generation of your children. 16 Though I tried to understand all this, it was too difficult for me, 17 till I entered the sanctuary of God and came to understand their end.

III.

18 You set them, indeed, on a slippery road, you hurl them down to ruin. 19 How suddenly they are devastated; utterly undone by disaster! 20 They are like a dream after waking, Lord, dismissed like shadows when you arise.

IV.

21 Since my heart was embittered and my soul deeply wounded, 22 I was stupid and could not understand; I was like a brute beast in your presence. 23 Yet I am always with you; you take hold of my right hand. 24 With your counsel you guide me, and at the end receive me with honor. 25 Whom else have I in the heavens? None beside you delights me on earth. 26 Though my flesh and my heart fail, God is the rock of my heart, my portion forever. 27 But those who are far from you perish; you destroy those unfaithful to you. 28 As for me, to be near God is my good, to make the Lord GOD my refuge. I shall declare all your works in the gates of daughter Zion.

End with Prayer to the Holy Trinity
NIGHT PRAYER: The Examination of Conscience

DAY TWO:
MORNING PRAYER: Acts of Faith, Hope, Charity; Daily Offering

MORNING FACE TO FACE WITH GOD:
Begin with Prayer to the Holy Spirit

Prayer on Psalm 74: Prayer at the Destruction of the Temple

Asaph lived during the reigns of David, Solomon, and Rehoboam, Solomon's son, who succeeded him as King of Israel first, and then of Judah, when the kingdom was divided. In the fifth year of Rehoboam's reign, Shishak, king of Egypt, attacked Jerusalem. *"He took everything, including the treasures of the house of the LORD and the treasures of the house of the king, even the gold shields Solomon had made"* (1Kings 14: 26). Asaph is referring to this first destruction of the Temple. He wrote this communal lament for the destruction of the Temple as he had witnessed it during the fifth year of king Rehoboam's reign. However, Psalm 74 is applicable for all the tragedies that Israel experienced around the destruction of the Temple. This seems to be the understanding of the Israelites who redacted and finalized the Psalter during the Babylonian Exile and upon their return to Israel. It can also be viewed as a prophecy foretelling the final destruction of the Temple in A.D. 70. Psalm 74 is a good example of how we are to relate to God when we have been brought to our knees.

In Section I, the Psalmist is describing in agonizing detail the destruction of His people and the Temple, God's abode. The humiliation of the one is the humiliation of the other, as the LORD God is in covenant with His people. Their enemies have insulted both the LORD and them by ransacking and pillaging God's holy dwelling place. In these dire straits, the people are lost and confused, vulnerable like sheep, and are beseeching God to *"remember your people, whom you acquired of old, the tribe you redeemed as your own heritage, Mount Zion where you dwell."* They are bereft, without a sense of direction. There is no prophet who could speak to them on God's behalf and assuage their fears and bring them salvation: *"They set your sanctuary on fire, profaned your name's abode by razing it to the ground. They said in their hearts, "We will destroy them all! Burn all the assembly-places of God in the land!" Even so we have seen no signs for us, there is no prophet any more, no one among us who knows for how long."* The Psalmist pleads with God to help his people because with the destruction of the Temple, the LORD's reputation plunged among Israel's neighbors. The nations would have concluded that the LORD God was unable to defend His people: *"How long, O God, will the enemy jeer? Will the enemy revile your name forever? Why draw back your hand, why hold back your right hand within your bosom?"*

In Section II, the communal lamentation shifts to remembering God's powerful acts of Creation when God was victorious over chaos by bringing order and harmony through His glorious act of creation. Similarly, the Psalmist sees how God brought redemption to His people, being victorious over His enemies and theirs. If God did such powerful deeds in the past, why would He not do the same now? *"Yet you, God, are my king from of old, winning victories throughout the earth. You stirred up the sea by your might; you smashed the heads of the dragons on the waters. You crushed the heads of Leviathan, gave him as food for the sharks. ... Yours the day and yours the night too; you set the moon and sun in place. You fixed all the limits of the earth; summer and winter you made. ... Look to your covenant, for the recesses of the land are full of the haunts of violence. Let not the oppressed turn back in shame; may the poor and needy praise your name. Arise, God, defend your cause; remember the constant jeering of the fools."*

Psalm 74 is a good example of prayer that is based on God's faithfulness to His Covenant with His people and His enduring mercy. Our prayer will always be the supplication of a sinner who is confident that God will listen to the repentant sinner and come to their help. Our prayer will always be effective when we base our petitions on God's faithfulness to us.

Reflect and Pray on Psalm74, using Lectio Divina or the Method of Meditation. Make sure you converse intimately with the Blessed Trinity:

Prayer on Psalm 74: Prayer at the Destruction of the Temple
"A maskil of Asaph.

I.

Why, God, have you cast us off forever? Why does your anger burn against the sheep of your pasture? 2 Remember your people, whom you acquired of old, the tribe you redeemed as your own heritage, Mount Zion where you dwell. 3 Direct your steps toward the utter destruction, everything the enemy laid waste in the sanctuary. 4 Your foes roared triumphantly in the place of your assembly; they set up their own tokens of victory. 5 They hacked away like a forester gathering boughs, swinging his ax in a thicket of trees. 6 They smashed all its engraved work, struck it with ax and pick. 7 They set your sanctuary on fire, profaned your name's abode by razing it to the ground. 8 They said in their hearts, "We will destroy them all! Burn all the assembly-places of God in the land!" 9 Even so we have seen no signs for us, there is no prophet any more, no one among us who knows for how long. 10 How long,

O God, will the enemy jeer? Will the enemy revile your name forever? 11 Why draw back your hand, why hold back your right hand within your bosom?

II.

12 Yet you, God, are my king from of old, winning victories throughout the earth. 13 You stirred up the sea by your might; you smashed the heads of the dragons on the waters. 14 You crushed the heads of Leviathan, gave him as food for the sharks. 15 You opened up springs and torrents, brought dry land out of the primeval waters. 16 Yours the day and yours the night too; you set the moon and sun in place. 17 You fixed all the limits of the earth; summer and winter you made. 18 Remember how the enemy has jeered, LORD, how a foolish people has reviled your name. 19 Do not surrender to wild animals those who praise you; do not forget forever the life of your afflicted. 20 Look to your covenant, for the recesses of the land are full of the haunts of violence. 21 Let not the oppressed turn back in shame; may the poor and needy praise your name. 22 Arise, God, defend your cause; remember the constant jeering of the fools. 23 Do not forget the clamor of your foes, the unceasing uproar of your enemies.

End with Prayer to the Holy Trinity
NIGHT PRAYER: Examination of Conscience

DAY THREE:
MORNING PRAYER: Acts of Faith, Hope, Charity; Daily Offering

MORNING FACE TO FACE WITH GOD:
Begin with Prayer to the Holy Spirit

Prayer on Psalm 76: God defends Zion

Psalm 76 was composed by Asaph, after the Kingdom of Israel was divided in two. Jeroboam became the King of Israel, taking Ephraim and nine other tribes with him. Asaph was appalled by one of Jeroboam's first decrees as king. He moved the Center of worship away from Jerusalem for his people: *"If this people go up to offer sacrifices in the house of the LORD in Jerusalem, the hearts of this people will return to their master, Rehoboam, king of*

Judah, and they will kill me and return to Rehoboam, king of Judah" (1Kings 12: 27). Accordingly, he set up two places of worship in his kingdom, in Bethel and Dan: *"The king took counsel, made two calves of gold, and said to the people: "You have been going up to Jerusalem long enough. Here are your gods, O Israel, who brought you up from the land of Egypt." And he put one in Bethel, the other in Dan"* (1Kings 12: 28-29).

The purpose of Psalm 76 then, is to reiterate the importance of Jerusalem as God's dwelling place and the Center of worship. The Psalmist captures the central place that Jerusalem had in the hearts of the Israelites: *"Renowned in Judah is God, whose name is great in Israel. On Salem is God's tent, his shelter on Zion."* Salem, meaning peace, was the ancient name of Jerusalem, and Melchizedek was the king of Salem in Abraham's time. The Psalmist seems to be reminding all the tribes of Israel, of both kingdoms, to honor God who dwells in their midst in Jerusalem, whose name was honored in both Judah and Israel.

Psalm 76 could also be viewed as a prophecy foretelling God's victory over Sennacherib, King of Assyria in 701 B.C. Sennacherib, king of Assyria, captured all the fortified cities of Judah and laid siege of Jerusalem. Amidst threats of destruction, Isaiah reassured King Hezekiah and the people that God would save them from the wrath of King Sennacherib (Isaiah 37: 36-37; and 2Kings 18 and 19). In vivid terms, the psalm describes the annihilation of Sennacherib's army: *"There the flashing arrows were shattered, shield, sword, and weapons of war... Despoiled are the stouthearted; they sank into sleep; the hands of all the men of valor have failed. At your roar, O God of Jacob, chariot and steed lay still... the earth was terrified and reduced to silence, when you arose, O God, for judgment to save the afflicted of the land."*

In spite of the desecration of the Temple at the hands of King Shishak of Egypt, and the decree of King Jeroboam of the northern kingdom to sever ties with the Temple in Jerusalem by erecting altars to golden calves in Bethel and Dan, the Psalmist is extolling the Presence, Power, and loving kindness of the God of Israel or all twelve tribes, who has chosen to be their covenant God and dwell in their midst as Emmanuel in the Temple. The last two verses of the psalm are an exhortation to hold sacred the worship of God in the Temple of Jerusalem. These verses are also the people's grateful response to God for being their saving power against a greatly feared enemy: *"Make and keep vows to the LORD your God. May all around him bring gifts to the one to be feared, who checks the spirit of princes, who is fearful to the kings of earth."*

Reflect and Pray on Psalm 76, using Lectio Divina or the Method of Meditation. Make sure you converse intimately with the Blessed Trinity:

Prayer on Psalm 76: God defends Zion
"1 For the leader; a psalm with stringed instruments. A song of Asaph.

I.

2 Renowned in Judah is God, whose name is great in Israel. 3 On Salem is God's tent, his shelter on Zion. 4 There the flashing arrows were shattered, shield, sword, and weapons of war.

II.

5 Terrible and awesome are you, stronger than the ancient mountains. 6 Despoiled are the stouthearted; they sank into sleep; the hands of all the men of valor have failed. 7 At your roar, O God of Jacob, chariot and steed lay still. 8 You, terrible are you; who can stand before you and your great anger? 9 From the heavens you pronounced sentence; the earth was terrified and reduced to silence, 10 When you arose, O God, for judgment to save the afflicted of the land. 11 Surely the wrath of man will give you thanks; the remnant of your furor will keep your feast.

III.

12 Make and keep vows to the LORD your God. May all around him bring gifts to the one to be feared, 13 Who checks the spirit of princes, who is fearful to the kings of earth.

End with Prayer to the Holy Trinity
NIGHT PRAYER: The Examination of Conscience

DAY FOUR:
MORNING PRAYER: Acts of Faith, Hope, Charity; Daily Offering

MORNING FACE TO FACE WITH GOD:
Begin with Prayer to the Holy Spirit

Prayer on Psalm 78: A New Beginning in Zion and David

Psalm 78 is the longest of the historical psalms. It is a profound contemplation by Asaph on the history of Israel. Given what he has experienced during the reigns of Kings David, Solomon, and Rehoboam, he is making a strong plea that history must not repeat itself, and God's people must stop being unbelieving. He tells his people to listen to him as he narrates their history and how God worked wonders in their midst. Their ancestors were always meant to teach their children about the law God established in Israel, and that this law was to be observed and passed on from generation to generation (Deuteronomy 6: 4-7). As it turned out, their ancestors were rebellious, and their descendants followed in their footsteps: *"a generation whose heart was not constant, and whose spirit was not faithful to God... They did not keep God's covenant; they refused to walk according to his law. They forgot his deeds, the wonders he had shown them."* In his own lifetime, Asaph had witnessed a falling away of the kings and their people from the ways of God!

In Section II, Asaph recalls Israel's history, beginning in Egypt where they were enslaved for 400 years. God brought Israel out of Egypt, through the parting of the waters, and gave the people water in the wilderness: *"He split the sea and led them across, making the waters stand like walls. He led them with a cloud by day, all night with the light of fire. He split rocks in the desert, gave water to drink, abundant as the deeps of the sea."* In spite of God's loving Providence and constant protection, Israel remained stubborn and rebellious: *"But they went on sinning against him, rebelling against the Most High in the desert."* They tested God continually, both defiant and doubting that God could take care of them: *"They spoke against God, and said, "Can God spread a table in the wilderness? True, when he struck the rock, water gushed forth, the wadies flooded. But can he also give bread, or provide meat to his people?"* Their sin was to think that God was powerless to give them what they needed!

In the face of their grumbling and rebellion while they were on their way to Mount Sinai (Exodus 16), God manifested His loving kindness by providing them with food and drink miraculously: *"God rained manna upon them for food; grain from heaven he gave them... He rained meat upon them like dust, winged fowl like the sands of the sea, they fell down in the midst of their camp, all round their dwellings."* At Mount Sinai, a sizeable faction remained unbelieving and ungrateful. They committed idolatry and worshiped the golden calf fashioned by Aaron. The most tragic verse in the whole psalm is, *"In spite of all this they went on sinning."* God decreed that such an unrepentant and ungrateful people would never enter the Promised Land. Over forty years they would perish in the wilderness. Only their progeny who remained in covenant with the LORD God would become God's people in the Promised Land.

The Israelites continued in their sinful ways all through their journey toward the Promised Land: *"But they deceived him with their mouths, lied to him with their tongues. Their hearts were not constant toward him; they were not faithful to his covenant"* (refer to Numbers 11). This rebellious behavior continued into the Promised Land. Despite their sinful and idolatrous ways, God remained faithful: *"But God being compassionate forgave their sin; he did not utterly destroy them. Time and again he turned back his anger, unwilling to unleash all his rage. He remembered that they were flesh, a breath that passes on and does not return."*

The Psalmist continues with Israel's history in the Promised Land. There, they worshiped false gods in high places rather than the LORD God in the Temple. During King Saul's reign, the

Philistines defeated Saul's army and captured the Ark of the Covenant (1Samuel 4). The Psalmist describes this defeat in a very poignant verse: *"He gave up his might into captivity, his glorious ark into the hands of the foe. God delivered his people to the sword; he was enraged against his heritage. Fire consumed their young men; their young women heard no wedding songs. Their priests fell by the sword; their widows made no lamentation."*

During the tumultuous reign of King Saul, God fulfilled His prophecy that He had made long ago through Jacob: *"You, Judah, shall your brothers praise – your hand on the neck of your enemies; the sons of your father shall bow down to you"* (Genesis 49: 8). David of the tribe of Judah would be anointed the King of Israel, and his sons would rule after him. And Jesus would be the ultimate Son of David. Psalm 78 ends on a promising note, extolling the reign of David and looking at the kingdom of Israel as God desired it to be: *"God chose the tribe of Judah, Mount Zion which he loved. He built his shrine like the heavens, like the earth which he founded forever. He chose David his servant, took him from the sheepfolds. From tending ewes God brought him, to shepherd Jacob, his people, Israel, his heritage. He shepherded them with a pure heart; with skilled hands he guided them."* Psalm 78 concludes with recognizing God's goodness and expresses gratitude for the integrity and skillfulness of David's rule.

Reflect and Pray on Psalm 78, using Lectio Divina or the Method of Meditation. Make sure you converse intimately with the Blessed Trinity:

(Pray with Psalm 78 from your Bible)
End with Prayer to the Holy Trinity
NIGHT PRAYER: The Examination of Conscience

DAY FIVE:
MORNING PRAYER: Acts of Faith, Hope, Charity; Daily Offering

MORNING FACE TO FACE WITH GOD:
Begin with Prayer to the Holy Spirit
Prayer on Psalm 79: A Prayer for Jerusalem

Psalm 79 was composed after Jerusalem was attacked and the Temple desecrated. The first desecration occurred during the original Asaph's lifetime when King Shishak of Egypt plundered Jerusalem in the 9th Century B.C. In many circles, this psalm is seen as being a prophecy about the destruction of the Temple by the Babylonians in 587 B.C., or that Asaph was a name that referred to the Temple musicians who composed it after the destruction of the Temple in 587 B.C.

The psalm begins with, *"O God, the nations have invaded your inheritance; they have defiled your holy temple; they have laid Jerusalem in ruins. They have left the corpses of your servants as food for the birds of the sky, the flesh of those devoted to you for the beasts of the earth. They have poured out their blood like water all around Jerusalem, and no one is left to do the burying. We have become the reproach of our neighbors, the scorn and derision of those around us."* Like many ancient armies, the Babylonian army consisted of soldiers of many nations that were conquered by the Babylonians. The Psalmist paints a harrowing picture of the utter devastation that occurred in Jerusalem. Jerusalem always seemed invincible because God was dwelling there. The Temple representing God has been destroyed, and the people have been massacred, with dead and rotting bodies littering the streets. To die unburied was the ultimate humiliation. The people have been brought low in utter disgrace and despair. And along with the destruction of the Temple and the City of David, the monarchy has been destroyed as well. Zedekiah, the last King of Judah, was taken into exile and tortured by the Babylonians in 597 B.C.

In pondering their tragic plight, the Psalmist asks God to have pity on them and come to their rescue by avenging their destruction at the hands of their enemies: *"How long, LORD? Will you be angry forever? Will your jealous anger keep burning like fire? Pour out your wrath on nations that do not recognize you, on kingdoms that do not call on your name, For they have devoured Jacob, laid waste his dwelling place."* However, while asking

God to avenge their humiliating defeat, the communal lament does highlight the sins of the people and their infidelity to the LORD: *"Do not remember against us the iniquities of our forefathers; let your compassion move quickly ahead of us, for we have been brought very low. Help us, God our savior, on account of the glory of your name. Deliver us, pardon our sins for your name's sake."* Speaking on behalf of the exiled survivors, the Psalmist humbled himself before God and acknowledged their sins against God. Their sins have brought about their utter destruction, politically, economically, socially, and religiously.

The last verses of the psalm are an earnest plea to God on behalf of their exiled countrymen in Babylon, especially those who were doomed to die. The exiles were not unlike those in Egypt before the Exodus: *"Let the groaning of the imprisoned come in before you; in accord with the greatness of your arm preserve those doomed to die."* The Psalmist is outraged at the dishonor caused to God by the enemies who denied His existence, mocked the divine power, insulted their worship of God, and destroyed God's house. He asks God to exact justice and vengeance upon His enemies and theirs: *"Why should nations say, "Where is their God?" Before our eyes make known to the nations that you avenge the blood of your servants which has been poured out. ... Turn back sevenfold into the bosom of our neighbors the insult with which they insulted you, Lord."* The final verse of the psalm strikes a note of gratitude and praise of God who has always been their Good Shepherd, pastoring them with loving kindness and faithfulness: *"Then we, your people, the sheep of your pasture, will give thanks to you forever; from generation to generation we will recount your praise."*

Reflect and Pray on Psalm 79, using Lectio Divina or the Method of Meditation. Make sure you converse intimately with the Blessed Trinity:

Prayer on Psalm 79: A Prayer for Jerusalem
"1 A psalm of Asaph.

I.
O God, the nations have invaded your inheritance; they have defiled your holy temple; they have laid Jerusalem in ruins. 2 They have left the corpses of your servants as food for the birds of the sky, the flesh of those devoted to you for the beasts of the earth. 3 They have poured out their blood like water all around Jerusalem, and no one is left to do the burying. 4 We have become the reproach of our neighbors, the scorn and derision of those around us.

II.
5 How long, LORD? Will you be angry forever? Will your jealous anger keep burning like fire? 6 Pour out your wrath on nations that do not recognize you, on kingdoms that do not call on your name, 7 For they have devoured Jacob, laid waste his dwelling place. 8 Do not remember against us the iniquities of our forefathers; let your compassion move quickly ahead of us, for we have been brought very low.

III.
9 Help us, God our savior, on account of the glory of your name. Deliver us, pardon our sins for your name's sake. 10 Why should nations say, "Where is their God?" Before our eyes make known to the nations that you avenge the blood of your servants which has been poured out.

IV.
11 Let the groaning of the imprisoned come in before you; in accord with the greatness of your arm preserve those doomed to die. 12 Turn back sevenfold into the bosom of our neighbors the insult with which they insulted you, Lord. 13 Then we, your people, the sheep of your pasture, will give thanks to you forever; from generation to generation we will recount your praise."

End with Prayer to the Holy Trinity
NIGHT PRAYER: The Examination of Conscience

DAY SIX:
MORNING PRAYER: Acts of Faith, Hope, Charity; Daily Offering

MORNING FACE TO FACE WITH GOD:

Begin with Prayer to the Holy Spirit
Prayer on Psalm 80: Prayer to restore God's Vineyard

Psalm 80 is a communal lament, a passionate plea to God from the entire people of Israel. The Psalmist addresses God as the Shepherd of Israel who leads Joseph like a flock. From His throne in heaven, God watches solicitously over His flock, guiding them and protecting them: *"O Shepherd of Israel, lend an ear, you who guide Joseph like a flock! Seated upon the cherubim, shine forth upon Ephraim, Benjamin, and Manasseh."* With great confidence in God's faithfulness and loving kindness, the people beseech God to restore their fortunes and save them: *"Stir up your power, and come to save us. O God, restore us; light up your face and we shall be saved."*

However, God seems to be absent and indifferent to their plight, leaving their enemies to scoff at their humiliation. God does not seem to be moved at their sorry plight: *"LORD of hosts, how long will you smolder in anger while your people pray? You have fed them the bread of tears, made them drink tears in great measure. You have left us to be fought over by our neighbors; our enemies deride us. O God of hosts, restore us; light up your face and we shall be saved."* The Psalmist repeats the same refrain because he is confident that God will return to be the shepherd and defender of His people: *"O God of hosts, restore us; light up your face and we shall be saved."*

In the second half of the psalm, amidst great tension, the Psalmist expresses deep trust in God by introducing another symbol that is very dear in the Bible: the vineyard. Isaiah tells us that the vineyard represents Israel: *"The vineyard of the LORD of hosts is the house of Israel, the people of Judah, his cherished plant"* (Isaiah 5: 7). Since the vineyard has been planted by the Lord, it represents the grace and love of God. On the other hand, it requires the steady labor of the farmer to produce grapes that yield good wine: personal effort and the fruit of good deeds.

Like Isaiah, the Psalmist at first extols the gift and love of God in His creation of Israel as His vineyard: *"You brought a vine out of Egypt; you drove out nations and planted it. You cleared out what was before it; it took deep root and filled the land. The mountains were covered by its shadow, the cedars of God by its branches. It sent out its boughs as far as the sea, its shoots as far as the river."* The Psalmist recalls the major milestones of Hebrew history: their roots in Egypt, their Exodus from Egypt, their entry into the Promised Land, extending as far as the Mediterranean Sea and the Euphrates River. During Solomon's reign, it extended over the whole of Palestine and reached out to the northern mountains of Lebanon with their great cedars.

The Psalmist then bemoans the serious neglect of the vineyard by God's people. God's solicitude and faithfulness were met by infidelity and idolatry, with the kings of Israel and Judah placing their trust in alliances with pagan kings and nations rather than in the God of Israel. Nebuchadnezzar's army devastated the Promised Land. God allowed the invader to plunder and wreak havoc on Israel: *"Why have you broken down its walls, so that all who pass along the way pluck its fruit? The boar from the forest strips the vine; the beast of the field feeds upon it."*

Bereft and laid low, the Psalmist upholds his confidence and trust in God. The Psalmist's hope is messianic, knowing that their salvation can only come from an outside source, from God: *"May your hand be with the man on your right, with the son of man whom you made strong for yourself. Then we will not withdraw from you; revive us, and we will call on your name. LORD God of hosts, restore us; light up your face and we shall be saved."* Perhaps, the Psalmist's first thought is of the Davidic king, who, with the Lord's help will lead the charge for freedom. But confidence in the coming of a future Messiah is implied. Daniel used the title 'Son of Man' for the future Messiah, a title that Jesus would choose to describe Himself as the Messiah.

The Fathers of the Church saw the vine in the psalm as a

prophetic prefiguration of Christ, the true vine, and of the Church, His branches (John 15: 1). Psalm 80 ends on an optimistic note, returning to the refrain that was already used twice in the psalm: *"LORD God of hosts, restore us; light up your face and we shall be saved."* The psalm is marked by intense suffering as well as an abiding trust in God. God will always be ready to return to His people. That will happen when His people are ready to return to God in fidelity. If we turn away from sin, the Lord will turn toward us.

Reflect and Pray on Psalm 80, using Lectio Divina or the Method of Meditation. Make sure you converse intimately with the Blessed Trinity:

Prayer on Psalm 80: Prayer to restore God's Vineyard
"1 For the leader; according to "Lilies." Eduth. A psalm of Asaph.

I.

2 O Shepherd of Israel, lend an ear, you who guide Joseph like a flock! Seated upon the cherubim, shine forth 3 upon Ephraim, Benjamin, and Manasseh. Stir up your power, and come to save us. 4 O God, restore us; light up your face and we shall be saved.

II.

5 LORD of hosts, how long will you smolder in anger while your people pray? 6 You have fed them the bread of tears, made them drink tears in great measure. 7 You have left us to be fought over by our neighbors; our enemies deride us. 8 O God of hosts, restore us; light up your face and we shall be saved.

III.

9 You brought a vine out of Egypt; you drove out nations and planted it. 10 You cleared out what was before it; it took deep root and filled the land. 11 The mountains were covered by its shadow, the cedars of God by its branches. 12 It sent out its boughs as far as the sea, its shoots as far as the river. 13 Why have you broken down its walls, so that all who pass along the way pluck its fruit? 14 The boar from the forest strips the vine; the beast of the field feeds upon it. 15 Turn back again, God of hosts; look down from heaven and see; visit this vine, 16 the stock your right hand has planted, and the son whom you made strong for yourself. 17 Those

who would burn or cut it down – may they perish at your rebuke. 18 May your hand be with the man on your right, with the son of man whom you made strong for yourself. 19 Then we will not withdraw from you; revive us, and we will call on your name. 20 LORD God of hosts, restore us; light up your face and we shall be saved."

End with Prayer to the Holy Trinity
NIGHT PRAYER: The Examination of Conscience

DAY SEVEN:
MORNING PRAYER: Acts of Faith, Hope, Charity; Daily Offering

MORNING FACE TO FACE WITH GOD:
<u>Learning Discipleship from the Psalms</u>
Begin with Prayer to the Holy Spirit

- *"Is it in vain that I have kept my heart pure, washed my hands in innocence? For I am afflicted day after day, chastised every morning"* Psalm 73 depicts Israel's intense purification through much travail and tribulation. Asaph faced a difficult problem trying to live as a righteous Israelite during his long life: Why is it that the wicked seem to prosper, leaving the faithful believers to wonder whether it is worth living righteously?

- As the Psalmist grapples with this difficult problem, the solution presents itself when he visited the Lord in His sanctuary: *"Though I tried to understand all this, it was too difficult for me, till I entered the sanctuary of God and came to understand their end."* He receives a double revelation: the end of the wicked will come unexpectedly, and God has always been his strength. This certainty of God always being with him creates a deep peace and gratitude in him.

- Psalm 74 is a good example of how we are to relate to God when we have been brought to our knees. The communal lamentation shifts to remembering how God brought redemption to His people, being victorious over His enemies and theirs. If God did such powerful deeds in the past, why

would He not do the same now?
- *"Look to your covenant, for the recesses of the land are full of the haunts of violence. Let not the oppressed turn back in shame; may the poor and needy praise your name."* A repentant sinner is confident that God will listen and come to their help.
- Psalm 76 reiterates the importance of Jerusalem as God's dwelling place and the Center of worship. The Psalmist captures the central place that Jerusalem had in the hearts of the Israelites: *"Renowned in Judah is God, whose name is great in Israel. On Salem is God's tent, his shelter on Zion."* Melchizedek was the king of Salem, meaning peace, the ancient name of Jerusalem, in Abraham's time.
- Psalm 79 was composed after Jerusalem was attacked and the Temple desecrated. The Temple was God's dwelling place and Jerusalem always seemed invincible because God was dwelling there. The monarchy has been destroyed as well, as Zedekiah was taken into exile and tortured by the Babylonians in 597 B.C.
- While pondering their tragic plight and asking God to avenge their humiliating defeat, Psalm 79 does highlight the sins of the people and their infidelity to the LORD. The psalm strikes a note of gratitude and praise of God who has always been their Good Shepherd, pastoring them with loving kindness and faithfulness.
- *"You have fed them the bread of tears, made them drink tears in great measure ... O God of hosts, restore us; light up your face and we shall be saved."* Psalm 80 addresses God as the Shepherd of Israel who leads Joseph like a flock. From His throne in heaven, God watches solicitously over His flock, guiding them and protecting them. With great confidence in God's faithfulness and loving kindness, the people beseech God to restore their fortunes and save them.
- *"You brought a vine out of Egypt; you drove out nations and

planted it ... Visit this vine, the stock your right hand has planted, and the son whom you made strong for yourself" Psalm 80 introduces a very dear symbol in the Bible: the vineyard. The Psalmist at first extols the gift and love of God in His creation of Israel as His vineyard, and then bemoans the serious neglect of the vineyard by God's people.
- Psalm 80 is marked by intense suffering as well as abiding trust in God. God will always be ready to return to His people when His people are ready to return to God in fidelity. If we turn away from sin, the Lord will turn toward us.

End with Prayer to the Holy Trinity
NIGHT PRAYER: The Examination of Conscience

JOURNAL FOR BOOK THREE, WEEK ONE: PURIFICATION THROUGH TRIBULATION

<u>DAY ONE:</u> Morning Prayer: Psalm 73: The Trial of the Just
What is God saying to You?

<u>Nightly Examination of Conscience:</u>
For what are you grateful?

For what are you contrite?

What spiritual discipline, including fasting, do you need to focus on tomorrow?

<u>DAY TWO:</u> Morning Prayer: Psalm 74: Prayer at the Destruction of the Temple
What is God saying to You?

<u>Nightly Examination of Conscience:</u>
For what are you grateful?

For what are you contrite?

What spiritual discipline, including fasting, do you need to focus on tomorrow?

DAY THREE: Morning Prayer: Psalm 76: God defends Zion
What is God saying to You?

Nightly Examination of Conscience:
For what are you grateful?

For what are you contrite?

What spiritual discipline, including fasting, do you need to focus on tomorrow?

DAY FOUR: Morning Prayer: Psalm 78: A New Beginning in Zion and David
What is God saying to You?

Nightly Examination of Conscience:
For what are you grateful?

For what are you contrite?

What spiritual discipline, including fasting, do you need to focus on tomorrow?

DAY FIVE: Morning Prayer: Psalm 79: A Prayer for Jerusalem
What is God saying to You?

Nightly Examination of Conscience:
For what are you grateful?

For what are you contrite?

What spiritual discipline, including fasting, do you need to focus on tomorrow?

DAY SIX: Morning Prayer: Psalm 80: Prayer to restore God's Vineyard
What is God saying to You?

Nightly Examination of Conscience:
For what are you grateful?

For what are you contrite?

What spiritual discipline, including fasting, do you need to focus on tomorrow?

DAY SEVEN: Morning Prayer: Learning Discipleship from the Psalms
What is God saying to You?

Nightly Examination of Conscience:
For what are you grateful?

For what are you contrite?

What spiritual discipline, including fasting, do you need to focus on tomorrow?

What prayer would you compose to express what God has said to you this week?

BOOK THREE – PSALMS 73-89: PURIFICATION THROUGH TRIBULATION
Psalms 81, 84, 85, 87, 88, and 89

WHAT IS AT THE HEART OF BOOK THREE, WEEK TWO?

Last week, we considered the historical events that form the backdrop of the psalms of Book Three. During the fifth year of Rehoboam's reign in the ninth century B.C., Israel entered a very dark period of her history. After a glorious period of peace and prosperity under King David, and for some time during King Solomon's reign, she was devastated by national misfortune and calamity. The ten tribes of Israel, rebelled and took Jeroboam as their king, becoming the Northern Kingdom of Israel, and the southern part went with Rehoboam and became the Kingdom of Judah. With the break-up of the kingdom came the first destruction of the Temple by Shishak, King of Egypt, and Israel endured colossal disaster and ruin. The 17 psalms of Book Three point prophetically toward the permanent destruction of the monarchy in 597 B.C. when Zedekiah, the last legitimate son of David to rule Jerusalem, was taken into exile. The Temple, God's dwelling place among His people and symbol of God's protection, was destroyed in 587 B.C., and the Israelites were subjected to the Babylonian Exile lasting 50 years. Thus, Israel entered an intense period of *Purification through Tribulation*. This led to a greater emphasis on covenant songs and psalms extolling the importance of Zion or Jerusalem.

During Week Two of Book Three, we will consider Psalms 81, 84, 85, 87, 88, and 89. On Day One, you will pray with *Psalm 81: An Admonition to Fidelity*. It is one of the few psalms where God speaks directly to His people. God rebukes His people for their sin of idolatry. Idolatry involves worshiping something or someone else other than God, and therefore contains all other sins within it.

On Day Two, you will ponder *Psalm 84: Prayer of a Pilgrim*

to Jerusalem, an unusually happy psalm, very unlike the tenor of Book III. It was composed by Asaph within the context of the three pilgrimage festivals that were celebrated in Jerusalem every year. The Temple is the perfect home where a pilgrim can experience happiness like nowhere else. The psalm also highlights the consolations and joy the pilgrim experiences in the presence and love of God for them.

On Day Three, you will ponder *Psalm 85: Prayer for Divine Favor.* As a national lament, Psalm 85 does express the people's sentiments during their Babylonian Captivity as well as upon their return to a devastated Jerusalem after 50 years! Time and again in their history, God's people found themselves in dire straits of their own making. The people express their gratitude to God for coming to their aid when they were exiles in Babylon. Thanks to His everlasting kindness, they have returned home to Israel. Their guilt, which was a stumbling block in their relationship with God, has been removed because of God's loving kindness and their willingness to repent.

On Day Four, you will ponder *Psalm 87: Zion, the True Birthplace,* which is a hymn to Zion seen as mother, not just of Israel, but of all humanity. Zion is the mother of all humanity because she is the 'City of God.' She is at the foundation of God's plan of salvation.

On Day Five, you will pray with *Psalm 88: A Despairing Lament,* and on Day Six, with *Psalm 89: A Lament over God's Promise of Old.* Both psalms are generally considered to be the bleakest psalms in the Psalter. Book III ends on the lowest emotional and spiritual point in the Psalter with these last two psalms. Psalm 88 concludes with no hope at all. Psalm 89 starts off enthusiastically in praise of God for the covenant with David, and then tumbles into grief and despair at the last Davidic king being taken into exile and humiliated. The psalm ends with the king being mocked, the Psalmist grief-stricken, and the Davidic kingdom and covenant in tatters.

On Day Seven, you will ponder the salient advice that these psalms have offered us to enhance and strengthen our own following of Jesus and our commitment to His Church.

SPIRITUAL READING FOR BOOK THREE OF THE PSALMS:
2Kings
Psalms 73 To 89
Jeremiah: Chapters 25-45
Ezekiel: Chapters 1-24

DAY ONE:
MORNING PRAYER: Acts of Faith, Hope, Charity; Daily Offering

MORNING FACE TO FACE WITH GOD:
Begin with Prayer to the Holy Spirit

Prayer on Psalm 81: An Admonition to Fidelity

Psalm 81 is one of the few psalms where God speaks directly to His people. The occasion of the psalm is the celebration of a pilgrimage feast when people from all over the kingdom of Israel came to Jerusalem to offer their praise and thanksgiving to God and renew their covenant relationship with Him. In accordance with the Sinai ordinances (Exodus 23: 14-17), Israel was required by God to come together and sing God's praises for His marvelous deeds among them. Psalm 81 reminds the people of this ordinance: *"Sing joyfully to God our strength; raise loud shouts to the God of Jacob! Take up a melody, sound the timbrel, the pleasant lyre with a harp ... For this is a law for Israel, an edict of the God of Jacob, He made it a decree for Joseph when he came out of the land of Egypt."* The Psalmist is envisioning the great assembly of God's people as they came out of Egypt and left their slavery behind. They gathered for that initial deliverance, and it became the basis for their future assemblies and feasts.

In Section II, the congregation moves into the next phase of the liturgical celebration: hearing God speak directly to them: *"I heard a tongue I did not know."* They first gathered with God as slaves being given their freedom and invited into a covenant relationship. God is speaking directly to them about this memorable event of their deliverance: *"I removed his shoulder from the burden; his hands moved away from the basket. In distress you called, and I rescued you; I answered you in secret with thunder; At the waters of Meribah I tested you."* God heard the groaning of Israel chafing under their burden of slavery in Egypt. He brought deliverance to them through wonders (the ten plagues) and leaders like Moses. God reminded them of the ratification of their covenant with Him at Mount Sinai when He spoke to them with thunder. Besides delivering Israel, God tested and trained them, as at Meribah, when He provided water miraculously for a complaining and unbelieving Israel.

God then rebukes His people for their sin of idolatry: *"Listen, my people, I will testify against you. If only you will listen to me. There shall be no foreign god among you; you shall not bow down to an alien god. 'I am the LORD your God, who brought you up from the land of Egypt. Open wide your mouth that I may fill it.'"* Our sins have consequences. The sin of idolatry contains all other sins within it because any kind of sin involves worshiping something or someone else other than God. God directly rebukes us even to this day for following everything that is not Him: *"But my people did not listen to my words; Israel would not submit to me. So I thrust them away to the hardness of their heart; 'Let them walk in their own machinations.'"*

God is faithful to His promises. No matter what our sins might be, sincere repentance will bring us back into God's good graces. We will be secure in the shadow of His wings and He will protect us from our enemies, specifically Satan: *"O that my people would listen to me, that Israel would walk in my ways, in a moment I would humble their foes ... But Israel I will feed with the finest wheat, I will satisfy them with honey from the rock."* There is a deep sorrow in God when we sin and rebel against Him. What more can He do to draw us back to Him? From a Christian perspective, *'the finest wheat'* is a Eucharistic image. The Eucharist is the fine wheat flavored with honey that God feeds to those who will listen to Him and walk in His ways. The psalm ends on a poignant note with God grieving over His people's sins and ingratitude toward Him and yet promising them protection and sustenance.

Reflect and Pray on Psalm 81, using Lectio Divina or the Method of Meditation. Make sure you converse intimately with the Blessed Trinity:

Prayer on Psalm 81: An Admonition to Fidelity
"1 For the leader; "upon the gittith." Of Asaph.

I.

2 Sing joyfully to God our strength; raise loud shouts to the God of Jacob! 3 Take up a melody, sound the timbrel, the pleasant lyre with a harp. 4 Blow the shofar at the new moon, at the full moon, on our solemn feast. 5 For this is a law for Israel, an edict of the God of Jacob, 6 He made it a decree for Joseph when he came out of the land of Egypt.

II.

7 I heard a tongue I did not know: "I removed his shoulder from the burden; his hands moved away from the basket. 8 In distress you called and I rescued you; I answered you in secret with thunder; at the waters of Meribah I tested you: 'Listen, my people, I will testify against you. If only you will listen to me, Israel! 10 There shall be no foreign god among you; you shall not bow down to an alien god. 11 'I am the LORD your God, who brought you up from the land of Egypt. Open wide your mouth that I may fill it.' 12 But my people did not listen to my words; Israel would not submit to me. 13 So I thrust them away to the hardness of their heart; 'Let them walk in their own machinations.' 14 O that my people would listen to me, that Israel would walk in my ways, 15 in a moment I would humble their foes, and turn back my hand against their oppressors. 16 Those who hate the LORD will try flattering him, but their fate is fixed forever. 17 But Israel I will feed with the finest wheat, I will satisfy them with honey from the rock."

End with Prayer to the Holy Trinity
NIGHT PRAYER: The Examination of Conscience

DAY TWO:
MORNING PRAYER: Acts of Faith, Hope, Charity; Daily Offering
MORNING FACE TO FACE WITH GOD:
Begin with Prayer to the Holy Spirit

Prayer on Psalm 84: Prayer of a Pilgrim to Jerusalem

Psalm 84 is an unusually happy psalm, very unlike the tenor of Book III. It was composed within the context of the three pilgrimage festivals that were celebrated in Jerusalem every year. They were called pilgrimage feasts because God expressed a desire for all male Israelites to travel to Jerusalem and have the priest offer the animal sacrifice that was incumbent upon them: *"Three times a year, then, all your males shall appear before the LORD, your God, in the place which he will choose: at the feast of Unleavened Bread, at the feast of Weeks, and at the feast of Booths"* (Deuteronomy 16: 16). The feast of Unleavened Bread celebrated the Exodus of the Israelites from Egypt as well as the beginning of the new planting season after the winter rains, or early Spring. The feast of Weeks was an agricultural celebration, falling exactly seven weeks after Passover, or late Spring (also known as Pentecost). The feast of Booths celebrated the wandering of the Israelites in the desert for 40 years where they had to rely only upon God for food and protection. This feast also celebrates the last harvest festival before the onset of the winter rains in Israel, usually in mid-Autumn. These pilgrimage festivals created an opportunity for the people to reaffirm their communal commitment to their covenant with God, strengthen their identity as a theocratic nation, and reiterate the sanctity of Jerusalem and the central place of the Temple.

Psalm 84 highlights the fact that the Temple is the perfect home where a pilgrim can experience happiness like nowhere else: *"How lovely your dwelling, O LORD of hosts! My soul yearns and pines for the courts of the LORD. My heart and flesh cry out for the living God. ... My home is by your altars, LORD of hosts, my king and my God! Blessed are those who dwell in your house! They never cease to praise you."* Psalm 84 expresses a longing that we all have, to remove ourselves from the distractions of the world and be close to God. The psalm also highlights the consolations and joy the pilgrim experiences in the presence and love of God for them. The Psalmist continues to express his amazement and joy that springs from a close union with God: *"Better one day in your courts than a thousand elsewhere. ... For a sun and shield is the LORD God, bestowing all grace and glory."*

At the end of the psalm, the Psalmist reiterates two truths that disciples know are true: God will not withhold any good thing from those who walk without reproach: *"The LORD withholds no good thing from those who walk without reproach."* Jesus reiterates this truth as well: *"If you remain in me and my words remain in you, ask for whatever you want and it will be done for you"* (John 15: 7). The other truth is that the Holy Spirit creates such a longing and hunger for God in the heart of the disciple, that their lives are suffused with gratitude, praise, and joy: *"O LORD of hosts, blessed is the man who trusts in you!"*

Reflect and Pray on Psalm 84, using Lectio Divina or the Method of Meditation. Make sure you converse intimately with the Blessed Trinity:

Prayer on Psalm 84: Prayer of a Pilgrim to Jerusalem
"1 For the leader; "upon the gittith." A psalm of the Korahites.

I.

2 How lovely your dwelling, O LORD of hosts! 3 My soul yearns and pines for the courts of the LORD. My heart and flesh cry out for the living God. 4 As the sparrow finds a home and the swallow a nest to settle her young, my home is by your altars, LORD of hosts, my king and my God! 5 Blessed are those who dwell in your house! They never cease to praise you.

II.

6 Blessed the man who finds refuge in you, in their hearts are pilgrim roads. 7 As they pass through the Baca valley, they find spring water to drink. The early rain covers it with blessings. 8 They will go from strength to strength and see the God of gods on Zion.

III.

LORD God of hosts, hear my prayer; listen God of Jacob. 10 O God, watch over our shield; look upon the face of your anointed.

IV.

11 Better one day in your courts than a thousand elsewhere. Better the threshold of the house of my God than a home in the tents of the wicked. 12 For a sun and shield is the LORD God, bestowing all grace and glory. The LORD withholds no good thing from those who walk without reproach. 13 O LORD of hosts, blessed the man who trusts in you!

End with Prayer to the Holy Trinity
NIGHT PRAYER: The Examination of Conscience

DAY THREE:
MORNING PRAYER: Acts of Faith, Hope, Charity; Daily Offering

MORNING FACE TO FACE WITH GOD:
Begin with Prayer to the Holy Spirit

Prayer on Psalm 85: Prayer for Divine Favor

Psalm 85 is the Psalmist's ponderings on a national crisis that took place during or after the reign of David. This psalm could represent the exiles in Babylon, or after they returned to Jerusalem. Psalm 85 is a national lament, and for our reflection, we will apply it to the sentiments of the returned exiles to Jerusalem.

The returned exiles had come back to a ruined Jerusalem, a desecrated Temple, and a land in mourning. They did not have a king anymore. And they were surrounded by hostile nations. In such a desolate situation, they began rebuilding the Temple. This was in the 6th Century B.C. The Book of Nehemiah describes the situation accurately: *"The survivors of the captivity there in the province are in great distress and under reproach. The wall of Jerusalem has been breached, its gates gutted by fire. When I heard this report, I began to weep and continued mourning for several days, fasting and praying before the God of heaven"* (Nehemiah 1: 3-4). The sentiments expressed by Nehemiah are akin to the thoughts of the post-exilic prophets, like Haggai:

"Reflect on your experience! You have sown much, but have not been satisfied; you have drunk, but have not become intoxicated; you have clothed yourselves, but have not been warmed; and the hired worker labors for a bag full of holes" (Haggai 1: 5-6).

Time and again in their history, God's people found themselves in dire straits of their own making. And they always knew how to find redemption: *"You once favored, LORD, your land, restored the captives of Jacob. You forgave the guilt of your people, pardoned all their sins. You withdrew all your wrath, turned back from your burning anger."* The people express their gratitude to God for coming to their aid when they were exiles in Babylon. Thanks to His everlasting kindness, they have returned home to Israel. Their guilt, which was a stumbling block in their relationship with God, has been removed because of God's loving kindness and their willingness to repent.

Given that God has always been there for them in the past, protecting them, rescuing them, forgiving and restoring them, the Psalmist is confident that God will do the same in their present circumstances: *"Restore us, God of our salvation; let go of your displeasure with us. Will you be angry for all generations? Certainly you will again restore our life, that your people may rejoice in you. Show us, LORD, your mercy; grant us your salvation."* And in restoring them, God will once again establish true peace and righteousness among them, the result of walking in the ways of the LORD.

The people are aware that a long time ago they lived in obedience to God and they were blessed. Then they rebelled against God and died spiritually, as they were separated from God. Now they are asking to be made spiritually alive once again: *"Near indeed is his salvation for those who fear him; glory will dwell in our land. Love and truth will meet; justice and peace will kiss."* *'Hesed'* is translated by *love*, meaning that God's loving kindness toward us and our repentance toward Him will establish truth in our hearts. Similarly, justice and peace will kiss. While

God's justice would condemn us for our rebelliousness, however, when we are repentant, God's enduring mercy will bring about the right order of things or justice in our lives, leading to true peace. In God's great work of salvation, His righteousness and peace are the best of friends.

The proper attitude of the believer praying for the establishment of God's reign is submission and surrender to God: *"Truth will spring from the earth; justice will look down from heaven. Yes, the LORD will grant his bounty; our land will yield its produce. Justice will march before him, and make a way for his footsteps."* God's reign will always be firmly established in our midst and in our hearts when we find our joy in nothing else but God. Justice or the right order of things will always be in our midst when God is Emmanuel.

Reflect and Pray on Psalm 85, using Lectio Divina or the Method of Meditation. Make sure you converse intimately with the Blessed Trinity:

Prayer on Psalm 85: Prayer for Divine Favor
"1 For the leader. A psalm of the Korahites.

I.

You once favored, LORD, your land, restored the captives of Jacob. 3 You forgave the guilt of your people, pardoned all their sins. 4 You withdrew all your wrath, turned back from your burning anger.

II.

5 Restore us, God of our salvation; let go of your displeasure with us. 6 Will you be angry with us forever, prolong your anger for all generations? 7 Certainly you will again restore our life, that your people may rejoice in you. 8 Show us, LORD, your mercy; grant us your salvation.

III.

9 I will listen for what God, the LORD, has to say; surely he will speak of peace to his people and to his faithful. May they not turn to foolishness! 10 Near indeed is his salvation for those who fear him; glory will dwell in our land. 11 Love and truth will meet;

justice and peace will kiss. 12 Truth will spring from the earth; justice will look down from heaven. 13 Yes, the LORD will grant his bounty; our land will yield its produce. 14 Justice will march before him, and make a way for his footsteps.

End with Prayer to the Holy Trinity
NIGHT PRAYER: The Examination of Conscience

DAY FOUR:
MORNING PRAYER: Acts of Faith, Hope, Charity; Daily Offering

MORNING FACE TO FACE WITH GOD:
Begin with Prayer to the Holy Spirit
Prayer on Psalm 87: Zion the True Birthplace

Psalm 87 was composed by the sons of Korah, who were the doorkeepers of the Temple. Psalm 87 is a hymn to Zion or Jerusalem seen as mother, not just of Israel, but of all humanity. God is not a local deity as the whole earth belongs to the Lord. Yet God has a special regard for Jerusalem which is described as situated *'on holy mountains.'* Jerusalem owes its stability and sanctity to God who has made it His foundation or establishment. Consequently, the city or the mountains of Jerusalem are holy. God resides in Jerusalem because *'the LORD loves the gates of Zion more than any dwelling in Jacob.'* As the dwellings of Jacob in the Promised land were beloved by God more than the dwellings of other nations, so He *'loves the gates of Zion more than any dwelling in Jacob.'* The Psalmist's fervent love for Jerusalem is filled with gratitude and praise of God who has chosen the city as His dwelling place. Zion is the mother of all humanity because she is the 'City of God;' she is at the foundation of God's plan: *"Glorious things are said of you, O city of God!"*

God's special regard for Jerusalem does not take away from the fact that He is Lord and God over all the earth. Still, there is a special way in which Zion can be called the 'city of God,' because out of all the places He could have chosen, God chose Jerusalem to focus His redemptive work for the whole world. Melchizedek, king and priest of God most High, reigned and served in Jerusalem, known as Salem, then. Abraham was willing to offer Isaac on Mount Moriah on which the Temple was built. King David made Jerusalem the kingdom's capital and reigned there for 33 years. The Ark of the Covenant found its permanent residence in the great Temple that Solomon built. The institutions of sacrifice, worship, and priestly service were established in Jerusalem for centuries. Jesus recognized and honored the city and observed the pilgrimage feasts and rituals there. In Jerusalem, Jesus died for our sins, was buried, and rose from the dead. There, the Church was born on the day of Pentecost. From Jerusalem, the Apostles took the Gospel to the four corners of the earth.

After the focus on Jerusalem itself, God spoke of the Gentile nations on every side of Israel, who were their rivals and often enemies. God promised that even among the rivals there would be *'those who know me,'* who would have a meaningful relationship with Him. Rahab is Egypt, so called for its strength and pride. Egypt and Babylon were bitter enemies of Jerusalem, both of whom invaded and destroyed the Temple. Philistia and Tyre, symbolizing godless luxury, were far from knowing God. Ethiopia is mentioned as well. All these nations would come to know God in a saving relationship, bowing before Him, and seeking to know Him better. These Gentile nations and peoples could be regarded as citizens of Jerusalem, the city of God, and be registered among God's people.

This reminds us that even though God made His ancient covenant with Abraham, Isaac, Jacob, and their descendants, He would not exclude the Gentile nations. Anyone from the Gentile world was welcome to honor the God of Israel, surrender to His Lordship, and be reckoned among God's people. This was true of Melchizedek, true of Rahab the prostitute, true of Ruth the Moabite, and true of Naaman the Syrian leper. It is also a prophetic picture of what God would do through Jesus, bringing Gentiles into a true relationship with Him through a new birth. It can be said of the one who is born again through Baptism, that *'this one was born there.'* The Psalmist indicates that in the time of God's future blessing in Jesus, all the nations of the world will come to know and praise the true God.

The Bible clearly speaks of God's special regard toward the land of Israel, and for Jerusalem in particular. Yet the idea of being a citizen of Zion and registered as a native citizen of God's City is also a spiritual concept. The New Testament speaks of a heavenly Zion and our registration there: *"No, you have approached Mount Zion and the city of the living God, the heavenly Jerusalem, and countless angels in festal gathering, and the assembly of the firstborn enrolled in heaven"* (Hebrews 12: 22-23). In Jesus Christ, every believer can have the privilege of registration in Zion, of being a citizen of the heavenly City of God.

The psalm ends with the singers and dancers exclaiming, *"All my springs are in you."* The goodness of God often comes to us like water from a spring. It seems to bubble up from a hidden, secret source. Every good and perfect gift is from God. The people of God acknowledge with gratitude Zion as being their true birthplace, and praise God for it.

Reflect and Pray on Psalm 87, using Lectio Divina or the Method of Meditation. Make sure you converse intimately with the Blessed Trinity:

Prayer on Psalm 87: Zion the True Birthplace
"A psalm of the Korahites. A song.

I.

His foundation is on holy mountains, 2. the LORD loves the gates of Zion more than any dwelling in Jacob. 3. Glorious things are said of you. O city of God!

II.

4. Rahab and Babylon I count among those who know me. See, Philistia and Tyre, with Ethiopia, "This one was born there." 5. And of Zion it will be said: "Each one was born in it." The Most High will establish it; 6. The LORD notes in the register of the peoples: "This one was born there."7. So singers and dancers: "All my springs are in you."

End with Prayer to the Holy Trinity
NIGHT PRAYER: The Examination of Conscience

DAY FIVE:
MORNING PRAYER: Acts of Faith, Hope, Charity; Daily Offering

MORNING FACE TO FACE WITH GOD:
Begin with Prayer to the Holy Spirit

Prayer on Psalm 88: A Despairing Lament

Psalm 88 is often regarded as the saddest psalm in the Psalter. Heman the Ezrahite was the composer who was known for his great wisdom (1Kings 4: 31), his musical ability and temple service (1Chronicles 15: 1719), and his service to the king (1Chronicles 25: 6). This sad and dark song was authored by a wise, talented, accomplished, and blessed man. Heman draws a map of his life's history, putting down markers of all the dark places he has traveled. He mentions his sins, sorrows, hopes, fears, woes, and so on.

The opening line is like a ray of light that shines throughout the dark recesses of the psalm: *'LORD, the God of my salvation.'* Throughout the psalm, the Psalmist clings desperately to God as the only source of his salvation. Throughout the psalm, his faith is true though struggling and forlorn: *"For my soul is filled with troubles; my life draws near to Sheol. I am reckoned with those who go down to the pit; ...Your wrath lies heavy upon me; all your waves crash over me."* The Psalmist was so weak and afflicted that he felt, and others regarded him, as practically dead already. Death seemed to be at his doorstep constantly. The emotional duress and sense of hopelessness are similar in spirit to those of Psalm 22. In the tradition of the Church, these two psalms bring us into the passion of Christ on Good Friday.

From beginning to end, there is no trace of bitterness, no desire for revenge on enemies, no angry reflections on God's seeming indifference. Rather, the references to God reveal a remarkable sense of His grace and goodness despite his own agony: *"But I cry out to you, LORD; in the morning my prayer comes before you.*

Why do you reject my soul, LORD, and hide your face from me?" The Psalmist is desperate for God to bend toward him and answer his prayer. No matter how deep and dark Heman's affliction was, he could still talk to God about it: *"Because of you my acquaintances shun me; you make me loathsome to them; caged in, I cannot escape, my eyes grow dim from trouble. All day I call on you, LORD; I stretch out my hands to you."*

The Psalms do not present a comprehensive theology of life after death. The Psalter expresses the agony and uncertainty at death's doorstep. At rare moments, the Psalms have glimpses of rescue from Sheol. Only in and through Jesus, however, have we received first-hand knowledge of the world beyond: *"He saved us and called us to a holy life ... according to his own design and the grace bestowed on us in Christ Jesus ... who destroyed death and brought life and immortality to light through the gospel"* (2Timothy 1: 9-10).

The psalm ends on a very poignant and sad note: *"Because of you friend and neighbor shun me; my only friend is darkness."* He could have been suffering from a contagious disease which caused his friends to shun him. Unlike other psalms of lament, Psalm 88 does not end on a note of confident trust. If it were a living death he was enduring, in God's hands it would bear much fruit. Heman was a sign pointing to Jesus, our Suffering Servant and Lamb of sacrifice. In Jesus, we can come to accept the message of Psalm 88.

On a recent pilgrimage to the Holy Land, we gathered in the lower levels of the Church of St. Peter in Gallicantu, Jerusalem, the site of Caiaphas, the High Priest's home. The lower levels of the Church contain a guardroom and a prisoner's cell, both hewn out of bedrock. The prisoner's cell offers a sobering insight into where Christ might have spent the night before he was brought to Pilate and crucified. We gathered in this sacred pit and prayed Psalm 88. Every single word of Psalm 88 depicted in accurate detail the dire straits that Jesus was in, recalling in vivid detail the intense agony and suffering Jesus endured in that cell. Psalm 88 brought us into the throes of the Four Suffering Servant Oracles of Isaiah as well.

Reflect and Pray on Psalm 88, using Lectio Divina or the Method of Meditation. Make sure you converse intimately with the Blessed Trinity:

Prayer on Psalm 88: A Despairing Lament
"1 A song; a psalm of the Korahites. For the leader; according to Mahalath. For singing; a maskil of Heman the Ezrahite.

I.

2 LORD, the God of my salvation, I call out by day; at night I cry aloud in your presence. 3 Let my prayer come before you; incline your ear to my cry. 4 For my soul is filled with troubles; my life draws near to Sheol. 5 I am reckoned with those who go down to the pit; I am like a warrior without strength. 6 My couch is among the dead, like the slain who lie in the grave. You remember them no more; they are cut off from your influence. 7 You plunge me into the bottom of the pit, into the darkness of the abyss. 8 Your wrath lies heavy upon me; all your waves crash over me.

II.

9 Because of you my acquaintances shun me; you make me loathsome to them; caged in, I cannot escape; 10 my eyes grow dim from trouble. All day I call on you, LORD, I stretch out my hands to you. 11 Do you work wonders for the dead? Do the shades arise and praise you?

III.

12 Is your mercy proclaimed in the grave, your faithfulness among those who have perished? 13 Are your marvels declared in the darkness, your righteous deeds in the land of oblivion?

IV.

14 But I cry out to you, LORD; in the morning my prayer comes before you. 15 Why do you reject my soul, LORD, and hide your face from me? 16 I have been mortally afflicted since youth; I have borne your terrors and I am made numb. 17 Your wrath has swept over me; your terrors have destroyed me. 18 All day they surge round like a flood; from every side they encircle me. 19 Because of you friend and neighbor shun me; my only friend is darkness."

End with Prayer to the Holy Trinity
NIGHT PRAYER: The Examination of Conscience
DAY SIX:
MORNING PRAYER: Acts of Faith, Hope, Charity; Daily Offering

MORNING FACE TO FACE WITH GOD:
Begin with Prayer to the Holy Spirit
Prayer on Psalm 89: A Lament over God's Promise of Old

More than any other passage of Scripture, Psalm 89 lays out clearly the terms and expectations of the Davidic Covenant. The psalm begins with extolling God's mercy: *"I will sing of your mercy forever, LORD, proclaim your faithfulness through all ages (verse 2)."* Mercy is *hesed* in Hebrew, meaning 'covenant faithfulness.' The whole emphasis of Psalm 89, at least through verse 38, is praising God for His covenant faithfulness, as displayed in the natural world and to David and his descendants.

The Davidic king was adopted as a son of God: *"He shall cry to me, 'You are my father, my God, the Rock of my salvation (verse 27)."* The Father-son relationship between God and David makes sense because a covenant is a family relationship sealed with an oath. Furthermore, the Davidic king was destined to rule over not just Israel but the whole world: *"I myself make him the firstborn, Most High over the kings of the earth (verse 28)."* 'Most High' is a divine title, here extended to David as God's own anointed one. As God rules over the members of the heavenly council (verses 6-8), so David, God's representative, rules over earthly kings.

Psalm 89 compares God's covenant with David to His covenant with nature. As surely as God makes the sun rise and set and the seasons to follow in order, in like manner will He be faithful to David. The psalm switches between praise of God in creation to praise of God for His promises to David's house: *"His dynasty will continue forever, his throne, like the sun before me. Like the moon it will stand eternal, forever firm like the sky! (verses 37-38)."*

The shocking twist in the psalm comes in Verse 39, or Sections

IV to VI. Despite all the assurances of God's faithfulness to David and his descendants in the first 38 verses, suddenly God renounces the covenant and leaves the Davidic dynasty in permanent ruin. Such a total collapse almost certainly reflects the Babylonian exile, when the Davidic kingdom was defeated and Zedekiah, the last king of Judah, was taken into exile to Babylon (587-537 B.C.): *"They slew Zedekiah's sons before his eyes; then they put out his eyes, bound him with fetters, and brought him to Babylon"* (2 Kings 25:7). The Davidic kingdom was never restored politically. It would be restored spiritually by Jesus, the Son of David, thus ensuring God's faithfulness to His covenant with David and his descendants.

Psalm 89 is almost two different psalms: it is hard to reconcile verses 1-38 with verses 39-53. Some have suggested that the first 38 verses come from the time of David or Solomon, and verses 39 through 52 were added to the psalm after the Davidic king was taken to Babylon in 587 B.C. Verse 53 is actually an ending for Book III and is not really part of the psalm itself: *"Blessed be the LORD forever! Amen and amen!"*

From a Christian perspective, Psalm 89 is important because it shows us how significant the Davidic Covenant was to the ancient Israelites. It was as important as the cycles of nature! The Davidic Covenant contextualized and nuanced the Mosaic Covenant. The gospels of Matthew and Luke highlight this significance by beginning their accounts with stories and genealogies that connect Jesus to David (Matthew 1-2 and Luke 1-3). God's promises to David had remained unfulfilled for at least 500 years before Jesus was born, causing much anguish and spiritual angst among Jewish believers. How could God have made these glorious promises to David and then not fulfill them? So, the fact that Jesus came from David's line and became King of the world through His resurrection was huge for Jewish Christian believers because it meant that God had finally kept the promises of the Davidic Covenant. It meant that the painful question at the end of Psalm 89 was answered positively by Jesus: *"Where are your former mercies, Lord, that you swore to David in your faithfulness?"* With Jesus, the Davidic Covenant was no longer a painful memory of disaster and abandonment, but instead, one of triumph. The ancient Kingdom of Israel was transformed into an international, supernatural kingdom that we call the Church, which spread over time and space, earth and heaven, and contains billions of people. Through Jesus, God kept His promises to David in a way beyond anything David and his other sons could have imagined!

Reflect and Pray on Psalm 89, using Lectio Divina or the Method of Meditation. Make sure you converse intimately with the Blessed Trinity:

(Pray with Psalm 89 from your Bible)
End with Prayer to the Holy Trinity
NIGHT PRAYER: Examination of Conscience

DAY SEVEN:
MORNING PRAYER: Acts of Faith, Hope, Charity; Daily Offering

MORNING FACE TO FACE WITH GOD:
Learning Discipleship from the Psalms
Begin with Prayer to the Holy Spirit

- The occasion of Psalm 81 is the celebration of a pilgrimage feast when people from all over the kingdom of Israel came to Jerusalem to offer their praise and thanksgiving to God and renew their covenant relationship with Him. The Psalmist is envisioning the great assembly of God's people as they came out of Egypt and left their slavery behind. They gathered for that initial deliverance, and it became the basis for their future assemblies and feasts.

- They first gathered with God as slaves being given their freedom and invited into a covenant relationship with God. And God is speaking directly to them about this memorable event of their deliverance: *"I removed his shoulder from the burden; his hands moved away from the basket. In distress you called, and I rescued you; I answered you in secret with thunder; At the waters of Meribah I tested you: Listen, my people, I will testify*

against you." (Psalm 81: 79).
- God then rebukes His people for their sin of idolatry: *"There shall be no foreign god among you; you shall not bow down to an alien god. 'I am the LORD your God, who brought you up from the land of Egypt. Open wide your mouth that I may fill it'"* (Psalm 81). God directly rebukes us even to this day for following everything that is not Him: *"But my people did not listen to my words; Israel would not submit to me. So I thrust them away to the hardness of their heart; 'Let them walk in their own machinations.'"* (Psalm 81).
- Psalm 84 is an unusually happy psalm and was composed within the context of the three pilgrimage festivals that were celebrated in Jerusalem every year. These pilgrimage festivals had at their core a community-building experience. They created an opportunity for the people to reaffirm their communal commitment to their covenant with God, strengthen their identity as a theocratic nation, and reiterate the sanctity of Jerusalem and the central place of the Temple in the religious consciousness of the people.
- Psalm 84 highlights the fact that the Temple is the perfect home where a pilgrim can experience happiness like nowhere else: *"How lovely your dwelling, O LORD of hosts! My soul yearns and pines for the courts of the LORD. My heart and flesh cry out for the living God. ... My home is by your altars, LORD of hosts, my king and my God! Blessed are those who dwell in your house! They never cease to praise you."*
- Psalm 85 is a national lament. Time and again in their history, God's people found themselves in dire straits of their own making. And they always knew how to find redemption: *"You once favored, LORD, your land, restored the captives of Jacob. You forgave the guilt of your people, pardoned all their sins. You withdrew all your wrath, turned back from your burning anger."* Thanks to His everlasting kindness, they have returned home to Israel from exile. Their guilt, which was a stumbling

block in their relationship with God, has been removed because of God's loving kindness and their willingness to repent.
- And in restoring them, God will once again establish true peace and righteousness among them. The people are aware that a long time ago they lived in obedience to God and they were blessed. Then they rebelled against God and died spiritually, as they were separated from God. Now they are asking to be made spiritually alive once again: *"Near indeed is his salvation for those who fear him; glory will dwell in our land. Love and truth will meet; justice and peace will kiss."* (Psalm 85: 10-11).
- Psalm 87 is a hymn to Zion or Jerusalem seen as mother, not just of Israel, but of all humanity. God has a special regard for Jerusalem which is described as situated *'on holy mountains.'* Jerusalem owes its stability and sanctity to God who has made it His foundation or establishment. Consequently, the city or the mountains of Jerusalem are holy.
- There is a special way in which Zion can be called the 'city of God' because God chose Jerusalem to focus His redemptive work for the whole world. Melchizedek, king and priest of God most High, reigned and served in Jerusalem, known as Salem, then. Abraham was willing to offer Isaac on Mount Moriah on which the Temple was built. David made Jerusalem the kingdom's capital and reigned there for 33 years. The Ark of the Covenant found its permanent residence in the great Temple that Solomon built. Jesus recognized and honored the city and observed the pilgrimage feasts and rituals there. In Jerusalem, Jesus died for our sins, was buried, and rose from the dead. There the Church was born on the day of Pentecost. From Jerusalem, the Apostles took the Gospel to the four corners of the earth.
- Throughout Psalm 88, the Psalmist's faith is true though struggling and forlorn: *"For my soul is filled with troubles; my life draws near to Sheol. I am reckoned with those who go down to the pit; ...Your wrath lies heavy upon me; all your waves*

crash over me." The Psalmist was so weak and afflicted that he felt, and others regarded him, as practically dead already. Death seemed to be at his doorstep constantly. The emotional duress and sense of hopelessness are similar in spirit to those of Psalm 22. In the tradition of the Church, these two psalms bring us into the passion of Christ on Good Friday.

- In Jesus, we can come to accept the message of Psalm 88. On a recent pilgrimage to the Holy Land, we gathered in the lower levels of the Church of St. Peter in Gallicantu, Jerusalem, the site of Caiaphas, the High Priest's home. The lower levels of the Church contain a guardroom and a prisoner's cell, both hewn out of bedrock. The prisoner's cell offers a sobering insight into where Christ might have spent the night before he was brought to Pilate and crucified. We gathered in this sacred pit and prayed Psalm 88. Every single word of Psalm 88 depicted in accurate detail the dire straits that Jesus was in, recalling in vivid detail the intense agony and suffering Jesus endured in that cell. Psalm 88 brought us into the throes of the Four Suffering Servant Oracles of Isaiah as well.
- Psalm 89 compares God's covenant with David to His covenant with nature. As surely as God makes the sun rise and set and the seasons to follow in order, in like manner will He be faithful to David. The psalm actually switches between praise of God in creation to praise of God for His promises to David's house: *"His dynasty will continue forever, his throne, like the sun before me. Like the moon it will stand eternal, forever firm like the sky!"*
- The shocking twist in the psalm comes in Verse 39, or Sections IV to VI. Suddenly God renounces the covenant and leaves the Davidic dynasty in permanent ruin. Such a total collapse almost certainly reflects the Babylonian exile, when the Davidic kingdom was defeated and Zedekiah, the last king of Judah, was taken into exile to Babylon (587-537 B.C.). The Davidic kingdom was never restored politically. However, it would be

restored spiritually by Jesus, the Son of David.
- From a Christian perspective, Psalm 89 is important because it shows us how significant the Davidic Covenant was to the ancient Israelites. It was as important as the cycles of nature! The gospels of Matthew and Luke highlight this significance by beginning their accounts with stories and genealogies that connect Jesus to David (Matthew 1-2 and Luke 1-3).
- With Jesus, the Davidic Covenant was no longer a painful memory of disaster and abandonment but instead one of triumph. The tiny, ancient Kingdom of Israel was transformed into a supernatural kingdom that we call the Church, which spread over time and space, earth and heaven, and contains billions of people. Through Jesus, God kept His promises to David in a way beyond anything David and his sons could have imagined!

End with Prayer to the Holy Trinity
NIGHT PRAYER: The Examination of Conscience

JOURNAL FOR BOOK THREE, WEEK TWO: ISRAEL'S DESERT EXPERIENCE

DAY ONE: Morning Prayer: Psalm 81: An Admonition to Fidelity
What is God saying to You?

Nightly Examination of Conscience:
For what are you grateful?

For what are you contrite?

What spiritual discipline, including fasting, do you need to focus on tomorrow?

DAY TWO: Morning Prayer: Psalm 84: Prayer of a Pilgrim to Jerusalem
What is God saying to You?

Nightly Examination of Conscience:
For what are you grateful?

For what are you contrite?

What spiritual discipline, including fasting, do you need to focus on tomorrow?

DAY THREE: Morning Prayer: Psalm 85: Prayer for Divine Favor
What is God saying to You?

Nightly Examination of Conscience:
For what are you grateful?

For what are you contrite?

What spiritual discipline, including fasting, do you need to focus on tomorrow?

DAY FOUR: Morning Prayer: Psalm 87: Zion the True Birthplace
What is God saying to You?

Nightly Examination of Conscience:
For what are you grateful?

For what are you contrite?

What spiritual discipline, including fasting, do you need to focus on tomorrow?

DAY FIVE: Morning Prayer: Psalm 88: A Despairing Lament
What is God saying to You?

Nightly Examination of Conscience:
For what are you grateful?

For what are you contrite?

What spiritual discipline, including fasting, do you need to focus on tomorrow?

DAY SIX: Morning Prayer: Psalm 89: A Lament over God's Promise of Old
What is God saying to You?

Nightly Examination of Conscience:
For what are you grateful?

For what are you contrite?

What spiritual discipline, including fasting, do you need to focus on tomorrow?

DAY SEVEN: Morning Prayer: Learning Discipleship from the Psalms
What is God saying to You?

Nightly Examination of Conscience:
For what are you grateful?

For what are you contrite?

What spiritual discipline, including fasting, do you need to focus on tomorrow?

What prayer would you compose to express what God has said to you this week?

BOOK FOUR: PSALMS 90 TO 106: ISRAEL'S BANISHMENT
Psalms 90, 91, 92, 93, 95, and 98

WHAT IS AT THE HEART OF BOOK FOUR, WEEK ONE?

Book Four of the Psalter is short like Book Three. It has only 17 psalms. Book Four is even keeled and sober, offering a soul-searching reflection on the collapse of the Davidic kingdom following the Babylonian exile. After the Babylonian exile which lasted from 587 B.C. to 537 B.C., Israel's monarchy collapsed. They no longer had a king to depend upon in the temporal and spiritual affairs of the kingdom. Who then would provide them with proper leadership and guidance? Book Four offers a spiritual perspective and vision on how to act when life has taken a hard turn toward collapse and ruin.

We have already seen that the second half of Psalm 89 acts as the preface for Book Four. It is not accidental that Book Three ends with the disastrous collapse of David's kingdom in the second half of Psalm 89 and Book Four begins with Psalm 90 which is the only psalm attributed to Moses in the Psalter. Now that David and his sons have disappeared from the limelight, whom do we turn to for advice and guidance?

There was the Mosaic Covenant before the Davidic Covenant. The Davidic Covenant was supposed to have laid its foundation on the commandments and laws laid down by God through Moses. Now that David has disappeared, it is time to return to a past beacon of light that guided the Israelites, namely the Mosaic Covenant. All the references to Moses in the Psalter, save one, have been made in Book Four, in Psalms 99, 103, 105, and 106. Psalm 77: 21 from Book Three is the only exception. Similarly, as if to emphasize the need to go back to the basics, three references are made to Abraham in Book Four, in Psalm 105. Psalm 47: 10 is the only other reference to Abraham in the Psalmody: *"The princes of the peoples assemble with the people of the God of Abraham."*

The people have lost their princes. It makes sense, therefore, to return to their Patriarchs, men of the God of their Fathers. Book Four looks to these earlier covenant mediators for direction and inspiration.

Moses offers us sobering advice in Psalm 90, the first psalm of Book Four, which we will consider on Day One. Moses reiterates the same message that he made repeatedly to his recalcitrant and rebellious people as he led them out of Egypt toward the Promised Land: Life is short and hard and infected with the wickedness and evil of sin. God is aware of our sins. Let us pray that God will have pity on us and forgive our sins. Moses' advice is straightforward and sobering. It is meant to help us get through difficult times as He had to and did.

Book Four ends with two psalms that reflect on the history of Israel. They are two sides of the same coin, one reflecting on the history of Israel from the divine perspective, and the other from the human. Psalm 105 reviews Israel's story and concludes that God was always faithful to Israel. Psalm 106 reviews the same story and concludes that Israel was always unfaithful to God. These two psalms offer us a convincing answer to the question, *'Why did Israel suffer the Babylonian exile?'* The blame lies squarely with God's people who refused to be in covenant with God and thereby chose to suffer the consequences of their separation from Him. Psalm 106 ends with a prayer that suggests that Israel has come to true repentance: *"Save us, LORD, our God; gather us from among the nations that we may give thanks to your holy name and glory in praising you."* So, the main movement in Book Four is from Moses' somber advice to heed the ways of God to a prayer for return from the exile and to live as God's people.

What is the focus of Psalms 91 through 104, the psalms in between? We will reflect on some of them on Days Two through Six. These psalms make it clear that the focus in Israel's religious consciousness has shifted greatly. Israel had best focus on God as being their dwelling place in exile as they have just lost Jerusalem as their dwelling place. Several psalms indicate this change of focus: Psalms 91, 92, 94, and 101. Similarly, it is better to focus on God's kingship, as David's kingship has come to a screeching end. Once again, several psalms indicate this need to change focus: Psalms 93, 94, 95, 96, 97, 99, 102, and 103. In like manner, many psalms point to God's glory as revealed in creation as one can no longer point to Jerusalem and the kingdom of David as evidence of God's glory: Psalms 95, 97, 102, and 104.

Lastly, there is a call for a new song in prayer as the old songs of Zion won't work anymore in a foreign land: *"Sing to the LORD a new song; sing to the LORD, all the earth"* (Psalm 96: 1). Psalm 98: 1, makes the same point: *"Sing a new song to the LORD, for he has done marvelous deeds."* There are other themes that are fitting for a people in exile. Psalms 95, 96, and 97 insist that the Lord is above all other gods, as Israel was living among peoples who worshiped other gods. Several psalms, like 96, 97, and 106 criticize idols because Israel was now living among idolaters. Near the end of Book Four, a couple of psalms express the hope that God will forgive His people and restore Jerusalem. *"You will again show mercy to Zion; now is the time for pity; the appointed time has come,"* says Psalm 102, and Psalm 103 offers the assurance that *"He will not always accuse, and nurses no lasting anger; He has not dealt with us as our sins merit, nor requited us as our wrongs deserve."* There is hope, indeed, that the Lord will restore Zion and her kingdom.

On Day Seven, you will ponder the salient advice that these psalms have offered us to enhance and strengthen our own following of Jesus and our commitment to His Church.

SPIRITUAL READING FOR BOOK FOUR OF THE PSALMS:
Psalms 90 to 106
Book of Isaiah: Chapters 40-55

DAY ONE:
MORNING PRAYER: Acts of Faith, Hope, Charity; Daily Offering

MORNING FACE TO FACE WITH GOD:
Begin with Prayer to the Holy Spirit
Prayer on Psalm 90: God's Eternity and Human Frailty

Psalm 90 is the only psalm from Moses. It is a famous psalm with a poignant message. God is our only true refuge in all the tragedies and uncertainties of human history. Throughout human history, persons and organizations have failed us, even our family members and leaders of the Church. However, God always remains faithful and constant: *"Lord, you have been our refuge through all generations. Before the mountains were born, the earth and the world brought forth, from eternity to eternity you are God."*

Moses reminds us of the ephemeral nature of life, how quickly it passes, here today, gone tomorrow: *"Our life ebbs away under your wrath; our years end like a sigh. Seventy is the sum of our years, or eighty, if we are strong; most of them are toil and sorrow; they pass quickly, and we are gone."* Under such circumstances, our best bet is to use our time well, doing things that benefit eternal life: *"Teach us to count our days aright, that we may gain wisdom of heart."* Moses also reminds us that without God, nothing we do will last. His prayer is that we will do everything with the protection and guidance of God: *"May the favor of the Lord our God be ours. Prosper the work of our hands."*

It is significant that Psalm 90 introduces Book Four. The Davidic Dynasty ended in shambles. The Mosaic Covenant was never meant to be overlooked by the Davidic Dynasty. Rather, it was always meant to remain the bulwark of God's covenant relationship with His people. Psalm 90 is exhorting Israel to return to Moses, the man of God. This ignominious end to the Davidic Covenant also pointed to its subsequent and proper fulfillment many centuries later through Jesus, the 'Son of David.'

Meditating on Psalm 90 periodically is a healthy spiritual exercise as it reminds us of what is lasting and what is fleeting, what is valuable and what is worthless in life. Jesus makes the same point, when He says, *"Do not store up for yourselves treasures on earth, where moth and decay destroy, and thieves break in and steal. But store up treasures in heaven, where neither moth nor decay destroys, nor thieves break in and steal. For where* your treasure is, there also will your heart be" (Matthew 6: 19-21).

Reflect and Pray on Psalm 90, using Lectio Divina or the Method of Meditation. Make sure you converse intimately with the Blessed Trinity:

Prayer on Psalm 90: God's Eternity and Human Frailty
"A prayer of Moses, the man of God.

I.

Lord, you have been my refuge through all generations. 2 Before the mountains were born, the earth and the world brought forth, from eternity to eternity you are God. 3 You turn humanity back into dust, saying, "Return, you children of Adam!" 4 A thousand years in your eyes are merely a day gone by, before a watch passes in the night, 5 you wash them away; they sleep, and in the morning they sprout again like an herb. 6 In the morning it blooms only to pass away; in the evening it is wilted and withered.

II.

Truly we are consumed by your anger, filled with terror by your wrath. 8 You have kept our faults before you, our hidden sins in the light of your face. 9 Our life ebbs away under your wrath; our years end like a sigh. 10 Seventy is the sum of our years, or eighty, if we are strong; most of them are toil and sorrow; they pass quickly, and we are gone. 11 Who comprehends the strength of your anger? Your wrath matches the fear it inspires. 12 Teach us to count our days aright, that we may gain wisdom of heart.

III.

13 Relent, O LORD! How long? Have pity on your servants! 14 Fill us at daybreak with your mercy, that all our days we may sing for joy. 15 Make us glad as many days as you humbled us, for as many years as we have seen trouble. 16 Show your deeds to your servants, your glory to their children. 17 May the favor of the Lord our God be ours. Prosper the work of our hands!"

End with Prayer to the Holy Trinity
NIGHT PRAYER: The Examination of Conscience

DAY TWO:
MORNING PRAYER: Acts of Faith, Hope, Charity; Daily Offering

MORNING FACE TO FACE WITH GOD:
Begin with Prayer to the Holy Spirit
Prayer on Psalm 91: Security under God's Protection

Psalm 91 has been characterized as an 'exorcism' or 'spiritual warfare' psalm. It has its rightful place in Book Four, as God's people were engaged in spiritual warfare during their 50 years of exile in Babylon, dealing with their own sinful ways and with the dangers of idolatry and apostasy in a pagan land. This psalm has been prayed and recited for protection against evil spirits and other dangers looming over us. In one of the copies of the Psalter found among the Dead Sea Scrolls, Psalm 91 has been included among other Jewish prayers for exorcism. Psalm 91 is one of the psalms that is prayed during the solemn rite of exorcism in the Catholic Church.

Psalm 91 is a prayer for protection against the forces of evil: *'the fowler's snare;' 'the destroying plague;' 'the terror of the night;' 'the arrow that flies by day;' 'the pestilence that roams in darkness;' 'the plague that ravages at noon.'* All these dangers are references to the forces of evil in our midst, orchestrated by Satan. In the midst of these dangers, God will be our refuge and strength: *"He will shelter you with his pinions, and under his wings you may take refuge; his faithfulness is a protecting shield (verses 3-4)."* And, *"Because you have the LORD for your refuge and have made the Most High your stronghold, no evil shall befall you, no affliction come near your tent (verses 9- 10)."* God is likened to the eagle, the king of birds, that protects its young ones under its powerful wings.

Another means of protection is the guardianship of His angels: *"For he commands his angels with regard to you, to guard you wherever you go. With their hands they shall support you, lest you strike your foot against a stone (verses 11-12)."* Satan deliberately corrupted this verse to tempt Jesus to perform a foolish stunt: *"If you are the Son of God, throw yourself down. For it is written: 'He* will command his angels concerning you' and 'with their hands they will support you, lest you dash your foot against a stone'" (Matthew 4: 6). Despite Satan's attempt to twist this verse, this is one of the Biblical texts that fortifies our belief in the doctrine of the guardian angels: the teaching that each one of us is entrusted to a particular angel who watches over us: "'Beside each believer stands an angel as protector and shepherd leading him to life (St. Basil).' Already here on earth the Christian life shares by faith in the blessed company of angels and men united in God" (CCC 336).

Reflect and Pray on Psalm 91, using Lectio Divina or the Method of Meditation. Make sure you converse intimately with the Blessed Trinity:

Prayer on Psalm 91: Security under God's Protection

I.

"1 You who dwell in the shelter of the Most High, who abide in the shade of the Almighty, 2 say to the LORD, "My refuge and fortress, my God in whom I trust." 3 He will rescue you from the fowler's snare, from the destroying plague, 4 He will shelter you with his pinions, and under his wings you may take refuge; his faithfulness is a protecting shield. 5 You shall not fear the terror of the night nor the arrow that flies by day, 6 nor the pestilence that roams in darkness, nor the plague that ravages at noon. 7 Though a thousand fall at your side, ten thousand at your right hand, near you it shall not come. 8 You need simply watch; the punishment of the wicked you will see. 9 Because you have the LORD for your refuge and have made the Most High your stronghold, 10 no evil shall befall you, no affliction come near your tent. 11 For he commands his angels with regard to you, to guard you wherever you go. 12 With their hands they shall support you, lest you strike your foot against a stone. You can tread upon the asp and the viper, trample the lion and the dragon.

II.

14 Because he clings to me I will deliver him; because he knows my name I will set him on high. 15 He will call upon me and I will answer; I will be with him in distress; I will deliver him and give

him honor. 16 With length of days I will satisfy him, and fill him with my saving power.

End with Prayer to the Holy Trinity
NIGHT PRAYER: The Examination of Conscience

DAY THREE:
MORNING PRAYER: Acts of Faith, Hope, Charity; Daily Offering

MORNING FACE TO FACE WITH GOD:
Begin with Prayer to the Holy Spirit
Prayer on Psalm 92: A Hymn of Thanksgiving for God's Family
Psalm 92 is titled 'A Sabbath Song.' This psalm sets the tone for the tenor of the Sabbath, which was a day of rest as well as for congregational worship. The Sabbath is a day of thanksgiving for God's family, and Psalm 92 provides such an opportunity. Psalm 92 brings out another dimension of the spiritual life. It is situated in Book Four which is an earnest invitation to turn from worldly pursuits and ambitions that glitter only to disappoint. It is emphasizing the need to make God and His worship the focus of human life. Psalm 92 returns us to the focus on God and His praises and away from pursuits and disordered passions that lead to destruction.

The psalm begins with the unequivocal statement that, *"It is good to give thanks to the LORD, to sing praise to your name, Most High, to proclaim your love at daybreak, your faithfulness in the night, with the ten-stringed harp, with melody upon the lyre. For you make me jubilant, LORD, by your deeds; at the works of your hands I shout for joy."* As creatures, we owe God, our Creator and Lord, our adoration, praise, and thanksgiving. The devout heart knows instinctively that praise of God is 'good,' not only as being acceptable to God but also as being a source of much delight to the worshiper.

Segment II highlights some important truths that we need to implement in our lives if our discipleship is to grow strong. When we spend much time in prayer and contemplation, pondering on the works of God in creation, and for our salvation, we move into a meaningful and committed discipleship through our adoration, praise, and thanksgiving to God: *"How great are your works, LORD! How profound your designs!"* Simultaneously, we come to understand that even though the wicked and sinners seem to thrive, they are destined for destruction as the pursuit of evil results in death. These truths bring assurance and comfort to the committed believer. On the other hand, if someone chooses to be an atheist or agnostic, then they fit the description offered in the psalm: *"A senseless person cannot know this; a fool cannot comprehend. Though the wicked flourish like grass and all sinners thrive, they are destined for eternal destruction; but you, LORD, are forever on high."*

In Segment III, the Psalmist continues to emphasize the blessings that are poured out upon the committed believer. They can withstand any adversity and tribulation because they have the strength and anointing of the Lord: *"You have given me the strength of a wild ox; you have poured rich oil upon me."* They live with an inherent resilience and confidence in daily life because they enjoy a vibrant relationship with the Lord: *"The just shall flourish like the palm tree, shall grow like a cedar of Lebanon. Planted in the house of the LORD, they shall flourish in the courts of our God."* When we meet believers, who are full of grace, patience, courage, zeal, and love, we know that the same life of freedom and joy awaits us. The righteous receive the additional blessing of knowing that their enemies and detractors will come to ruin as evil begets desolation. They, however, will be like the Palm tree and the Cedar of Lebanon: *"The just shall flourish like the palm tree, shall grow like the cedar of Lebanon."* A Palm tree is the image of a godly person who is made to live and thrive where all else perishes, as in the desert. The cedars of Lebanon were known for their size, strength, durability, beauty, and usefulness. They were used by Solomon in the building of the first Temple. The blessings upon the righteous bring about the same attributes.

The Palm Tree and Cedar of Lebanon are an apt image for believers who are firmly planted in God's house, the place of His presence, where they live and flourish. They are in the presence of the Lord, youthfully fresh and bearing fruit even in old age: *"They shall flourish in the courts of our God. They shall bear fruit even in old age, they will stay fresh and green."* And their constant refrain is that *"The LORD is just; my rock, in whom there is no wrong."*

Reflect and Pray on Psalm 92, using Lectio Divina or the Method of Meditation. Make sure you converse intimately with the Blessed Trinity:

Prayer on Psalm 92: A Hymn of Thanksgiving for God's Family
"1 A psalm. A sabbath song.

I.

2 It is good to give thanks to the LORD, to sing praise to your name, Most High, 3 to proclaim your love at daybreak, your faithfulness in the night, 4 with the ten-stringed harp, with melody upon the lyre. 5 For you make me jubilant, LORD, by your deeds; at the works of your hands I shout for joy.

II.

6 How great are your works, LORD! How profound your designs! 7 A senseless person cannot know this; a fool cannot comprehend. 8 Though the wicked flourish like grass and all sinners thrive, they are destined for eternal destruction; 9 but you, LORD, are forever on high. 10 Indeed your enemies, LORD, indeed your enemies shall perish; all sinners shall be scattered.

III.

11 You have given me the strength of a wild ox; you have poured rich oil upon me. 12 My eyes look with glee on my wicked enemies; my ears shall hear what happens to my wicked foes. 13 The just shall flourish like the palm tree, shall grow like a cedar of Lebanon. 14 Planted in the house of the LORD, they shall flourish in the courts of our God. 15 They shall bear fruit even in old age, they will stay fresh and green, 16 to proclaim: "The LORD is just; my rock, in whom there is no wrong."

End with Prayer to the Holy Trinity
NIGHT PRAYER: The Examination of Conscience

DAY FOUR:
MORNING PRAYER: Acts of Faith, Hope, Charity; Daily Offering
MORNING FACE TO FACE WITH GOD:
Begin with Prayer to the Holy Spirit

Prayer on Psalm 93: God is a Mighty King

Psalm 93 is the first of seven 'royal' psalms, Psalms 93-99, as they praise God as King. Psalm 93 describes a theocracy as do the six psalms that follow it. Psalm 93 begins wonderfully with the proclamation of God's rule: *"The LORD is king, robed with majesty; the LORD is robed, girded with might."* This verse lifts the covenant God of Israel over every idol and pretender of sovereignty. In His majesty and might, God has constructed a world that *"will surely stand in place, never to be moved."* Not only is the world established, but so is the throne of God which stands firm from of old: *"Your throne stands firm from of old; you are from everlasting."* This truth is highlighted in Jesus, from the seed of David. Earthly thrones and kingdoms are set up and cast down as was the case with the Davidic throne and kingdom. The throne of God is eternal and unchangeable because the son of David is the Son of God.

Psalm 93 alludes to the fact that there are strong forces that seem to oppose the power and might of God. The forces of nature are emblematic of principalities and powers, invisible and visible, that are alienated from God and have become His enemies: *"The flood has raised up, LORD; the flood has raised up its roar; the flood has raised its pounding waves."* Just as in the act of creation, God brought order into the chaotic forces of nature, similarly, God will always hail supreme over evil and injustice. This is a firm conviction that God's people have come to after the destruction of their monarchy and Temple in Jerusalem. They now derive much strength from claiming God as their King and LORD!

The last verse claims that God's *'decrees are firmly established."* As in other psalms, *'decrees'* is a poetic reference to God's word or revelation. In His revelation, God's truth is beyond all question. Therefore, *"holiness befits your house, LORD, for all the length of days."* God's holiness is connected to all He is and does and adorns His very abode. If we are not holy, how can we adorn the house of God? Psalm 93 is an earnest exhortation to acclaim God as our King, as the Center of our lives, and to participate in His holiness for all the length of our days.

Reflect and Pray on Psalm 93, using Lectio Divina or the Method of Meditation. Make sure you converse intimately with the Blessed Trinity:

Psalm 93: God is a Mighty King
"1 The LORD is king, robed with majesty; the LORD is robed, girded with might. The world will surely stand in place, never to be moved. 2 Your throne stands firm from of old; you are from everlasting. 3 The flood has raised up, LORD; the flood has raised up its roar; the flood has raised its pounding waves. 4 More powerful than the roar of many waters, more powerful than the breakers of the sea, powerful in the heavens is the LORD. 5 Your decrees are firmly established; holiness befits your house, LORD, for all the length of days."

End with Prayer to the Holy Trinity
NIGHT PRAYER: The Examination of Conscience

DAY FIVE:
MORNING PRAYER: Acts of Faith, Hope, Charity; Daily Offering

MORNING FACE TO FACE WITH GOD:
Begin with Prayer to the Holy Spirit
Prayer on Psalm 95: A Call to Praise and Obedience

Psalm 95 is one of the nine common psalms used as the Responsorial Psalm during Ordinary Time of the Liturgical calendar. Psalm 95 is also prayed during the Invitatory of the Liturgy of the Hours. The Invitatory is placed at the beginning of the whole sequence of the day's prayer. Psalms 24, 67, or 100 are used along with Psalm 95 as the Invitatory psalm. Sections I and II of Psalm 95 offer an invitation and exhortation to praise God:
"Come, let us sing joyfully to the LORD; cry out to the rock of our salvation. Let us come before him with a song of praise, joyfully sing out our psalms. For the LORD is the great God, the great king over all gods, whose hand holds the depths of the earth; who owns

the tops of the mountains. The sea and dry land belong to God, who made them, formed them by hand." God's people are exhorted to unite in praising the Lord giving full expression to our joy, and chanting hymns of praise to Him who is our salvation.

The Psalmist assigns five reasons as to why God should be praised by us. The first reason is *"For the LORD is the great God, the great king over all gods."* God is the great King, far higher than all other kings, who are sometimes called gods. The second reason is because God's power is supreme throughout the entire world: *"Whose hand holds the depths of the earth; who owns the tops of the mountains."* The third reason is that our God is Lord not only of the land but of the sea as well: *"The sea and dry land belong to God, who made them, formed them by hand."* It is proper, therefore, that humankind which derives so many benefits from the sea, should thank and praise God who gave it to them. The fourth reason is that the same Lord who created the earth and the sea, created us as His image and likeness: *"Enter, let us bow down in worship; let us kneel before the LORD who made us."* The fifth and last reason is because the Lord both made us and governs us with a special providence as a shepherd would his flock: *"For he is our God, we are the people he shepherds, the sheep in his hands."* 'The sheep in his hands' is an interesting turn of phrase, meaning that either God made us in His image and likeness or because God guides us with His hand. God is directly involved in our lives with His solicitude and love.

Psalm 95 is often used as a Lenten Penance Service because of Segment III. The Psalmist asks his listeners to have a repentant heart and listen to God speaking directly to them: *"Oh, that today you would hear his voice."* Then God reminds His people of the hardness of heart and obduracy of spirit of their ancestors in the desert during their march toward the Promised Land: *"Do not harden your hearts as at Meribah, as on the day of Massah in the desert."* 'Meribah' meaning 'contention,' was the place where the Israelites quarreled with God. And *'massah'* was the place where they put God to the test (Exodus 17: 7; Numbers 20: 13). God alludes to their brazen ingratitude and rebelliousness and expresses His own frustration with them: *"There your ancestors tested me; they tried me though they had seen my works. Forty years I loathed that generation; I said: "This people's heart goes astray; they do not know my ways."* The consequence of the people's rebellion is for God to withhold His mercy as they had made themselves incapable of receiving it through their sinful obduracy: *"Therefore I swore in my anger; "They shall never enter my rest."* 'Rest' refers to the Promised Land as in Deuteronomy 12:9. Hebrews 4:3 uses the same verse to denote the eternal rest of heaven. We are invited to ponder our sins from God's point of view. We can also consider our sins as they impact our loved ones and friends who suffer because of our transgressions.

Reflect and Pray on Psalm 95, using Lectio Divina or the Method of Meditation. Make sure you converse intimately with the Blessed Trinity:

Prayer on Psalm 95: A Call to Praise and Obedience

I.

1 Come, let us sing joyfully to the LORD; cry out to the rock of our salvation. 2 Let us come before him with a song of praise, joyfully sing out our psalms. 3 For the LORD is the great God, the great king over all gods, 4 whose hand holds the depths of the earth; who owns the tops of the mountains. 5 The sea and dry land belong to God, who made them, formed them by hand.

II.

6 Enter, let us bow down in worship; let us kneel before the LORD who made us. 7 For he is our God, we are the people he shepherds, the sheep in his hands.

III.

Oh, that today you would hear his voice: 8 Do not harden your hearts as at Meribah, as on the day of Massah in the desert. 9 There your ancestors tested me; they tried me though they had seen my works. 10 Forty years I loathed that generation; I said: "This people's heart goes astray; they do not know my ways." 11 Therefore I swore in my anger: 'They shall never enter my rest."

End with Prayer to the Holy Trinity
NIGHT PRAYER: The Examination of Conscience

DAY SIX:
MORNING PRAYER: Acts of Faith, Hope, Charity; Daily Offering

MORNING FACE TO FACE WITH GOD:
Begin with Prayer to the Holy Spirit

Prayer on Psalm 98: The Coming of God

Psalm 98 is a royal psalm emphasizing God's kingship over His people. The Persians conquered Babylon during the exile, and King Cyrus sent the Israelites back to their homeland to rebuild their temple. About 40,000 Israelites left with Ezra, while a great number stayed behind. Upon their return from Babylon, the Israelites rebuilt their ruined temple, but had no king anymore to rule over them. For another two hundred years, Persia dominated the Middle East and Egypt, and during all that time, Palestine was a tributary state of Persia. In 332 B.C., Alexander the Great from Macedon, Greece, conquered Persia, and Palestine became a Greek vassal state. Foreign rule continued during the lifetime of Jesus and much after. Understandably, in all their historical and national calamities, they came to see clearly that only God was dependable as their true king.

Several centuries ago, the Israelites had insisted that Samuel, their Prophet and last Judge, give them a monarch, like the other nations. Samuel was deeply aggrieved and brought his case to God. This was God's answer: *"Listen to whatever the people say. You are not the one they are rejecting. They are rejecting me as king. They are acting toward you just as they have acted from the day I brought them up from Egypt to this very day, deserting me to serve other gods. Now listen to them; but at the same time, give them a solemn warning and inform them of the rights of the king who will rule over them"* (1Samuel 8: 7-9). The monarchy was installed through the Davidic Covenant and acted as a prefiguration of the installation of Jesus, the son of David, who would establish the new kingdom of Israel, the Kingdom of God in this world and not of this world. The royal Psalms, 93 to 99 especially, are pointing toward the time of fulfillment that Jesus talks about: *"This is the time of fulfillment. The kingdom of God is at hand. Repent, and believe in the gospel"* (Mark 1: 15). Through their bitter experience of exile and slavery in Babylon through 50 long years, they came to realize that God would never abandon them. The exile was a period of much purification, soul-searching, and return to the LORD their God. Psalm 98 echoes their sentiments of gratitude, praise and exaltation of God. Only God was their reliable king on whom they could depend for everything. And their God sent them home through the good graces of Cyrus, King of Persia.

There are striking parallels between Segment I of Psalm 98: 1-3 and Mary's Magnificat (Luke 1: 46-55), suggesting that our Blessed Mother had the psalm in mind as she composed her own hymn: *"Sing a new song to the LORD, for he has done marvelous deeds. His right hand and holy arm have won the victory. The LORD has made his victory known; has revealed his triumph in the sight of the nations, He has remembered his mercy and faithfulness toward the house of Israel. All the ends of the earth have seen the victory of our God."* Mary rightly saw that the promises of the psalm relating to the kingship of God and the victory over Satan, sin, and death would be achieved by Jesus, the son of her womb and the Son of God: *"Behold, you will conceive in your womb and bear a son, and you shall name him Jesus. He will be great and will be called Son of the Most High, and the Lord God will give him the throne of David his father, and he will rule over the house of Jacob forever, and of his kingdom there will be no end"* (Luke 1: 31-33).

Both Psalm 98 and the Magnificat are *new song*s even though they reflect God's eternal truth extending from the beginning of time and unfolding anew in the present historical circumstances. The song is always new as God's redeeming grace can never grow old, even though the same words announce the good news over and over. For this reason, we engage in repetitions of the same subject matter in prayer, because God's truth and love are inexhaustible. For the same reason, we pray our vocal prayers day after day. They lead us into the fount of everlasting life which is inexhaustible!

Psalm 98 gives God praise and thanksgiving for bringing them out of exile, back to Judea where they have been able to rebuild their Temple and live once again in covenant with the LORD God.

Segment II is organized along the lines of a symphony orchestra accompanying an accomplished choir. This vocal and instrumental ensemble resounds with passionate song accompanied by a glorious interplay of string and brass instruments. The overriding sentiment among the members of the ensemble and the worshipers is a profound sense of jubilation, praise, and thanksgiving: *"Shout with joy to the LORD, all the earth; break into song; sing praise. Sing praise to the LORD with the lyre, with the lyre and melodious song. With trumpets and the sound of the horn shout with joy to the King, the LORD."*

Segment III is a musical ensemble of God's noble and awe-inspiring creation. The sea, and all it contains, the rivers, hills, and mountains, all human beings and animate creatures who dwell on the earth, all are being invited to lend their voices, and roar to the praise of God. The only way all creation can praise their Creator is through the voices and songs of human beings who have been created in God's image and likeness. The Psalmist, beholding in spirit the fulfillment of the advent of Jesus and the establishment of God's kingdom, bids the whole earth to break forth into joyous song for *"the LORD who comes, who comes to govern the earth, to govern the world with justice and the peoples with fairness."*

Reflect and Pray on Psalm 98, using Lectio Divina or the Method of Meditation. Make sure you converse intimately with the Blessed Trinity:

Prayer on Psalm 98: The Coming of God

I.

"1 Sing a new song to the LORD, for he has done marvelous deeds. His right hand and holy arm have won the victory. 2 The LORD has made his victory known; has revealed his triumph in the sight of the nations, 3 he has remembered his mercy and faithfulness toward the house of Israel. All the ends of the earth have seen the victory of our God.

II.

4 Shout with joy to the LORD, all the earth; break into song; sing praise. 5 Sing praise to the LORD with the lyre, with the lyre and melodious song. 6 With trumpets and the sound of the horn shout with joy to the King, the LORD.

III.

7 Let the sea and what fills it resound, the world and those who dwell there. 8 Let the rivers clap their hands, the mountains shout with them for joy, 9 before the LORD who comes, who comes to govern the earth, to govern the world with justice and the peoples with fairness."

End with Prayer to the Holy Trinity
NIGHT PRAYER: The Examination of Conscience

DAY SEVEN:
MORNING PRAYER: Acts of Faith, Hope, Charity; Daily Offering

MORNING FACE TO FACE WITH GOD:
Learning Discipleship from the Psalms
Begin with Prayer to the Holy Spirit

- Psalm 90 reminds us that God is our only true refuge in all the tragedies and uncertainties of human history. Throughout human history, persons and organizations have failed us, even our family members and leaders of the Church. However, God always remains faithful and constant: *"Lord, you have been our refuge through all generations. Before the mountains were born, the earth and the world brought forth, from eternity to eternity you are God."* (verses 1-2).
- Moses reminds us of the ephemeral nature of life, how quickly it passes, here today, gone tomorrow: *"Our life ebbs away under your wrath; our years end like a sigh. Seventy is the sum of our years, or eighty, if we are strong; most of them are toil and sorrow; they pass quickly, and we are gone."* (verses 9-10).
- Our best bet is to use our time well, doing things that benefit eternal life: *"Teach us to count our days aright, that we may gain wisdom of heart."* (verse 12). Moses prays that we do

everything with the protection and guidance of God: *"May the favor of the Lord our God be ours. Prosper the work of our hands."* (verse 17).
- Psalm 91 is a prayer for protection against the forces of evil: *'the fowler's snare;' 'the destroying plague;' 'the terror of the night;' 'the arrow that flies by day;' 'the pestilence that roams in darkness;' 'the plague that ravages at noon.'* In the midst of these dangers, God will be our refuge and strength: *"He will shelter you with his pinions, and under his wings you may take refuge; his faithfulness is a protecting shield"* (verses 3-4). God is likened to the eagle, the king of birds, that protects its young ones under its powerful wings.
- Psalm 92 is a Sabbath Song. The Sabbath is a day of thanksgiving for God's family, and Psalm 92 provides such an opportunity. Psalm 92 brings out another dimension of the spiritual life, the need to make God and His worship the focus of human life. Psalm 92 returns us to the focus on God and His praises and away from destructive pursuits and disordered passions.
- The righteous receive the blessing of knowing that their enemies and detractors will come to ruin as evil begets desolation. They are like the Palm tree and the Cedar of Lebanon: *"The just shall flourish like the palm tree, shall grow like the cedar of Lebanon."* (Psalm 92: 13). A Palm tree is the image of a godly person who is made to live and thrive where all else perishes, as in the desert.
- Psalm 93 alludes to the fact that there are strong forces that seem to oppose the power and might of God. In the act of creation, God brought order and harmony into the chaotic forces of nature. Similarly, God will always hail supreme over evil and injustice. After the destruction of their monarchy and Temple, the people derive much consolation and strength from claiming God as their King and LORD!
- Psalm 95 exhorts us to unite in praising the Lord, giving full expression to our joy, and chanting. One of several reasons is

that the Lord both made us and governs us with a special providence as a shepherd would his flock: *"For he is our God, we are the people he shepherds, the sheep in his hands"* (Psalm 95: 7). *'The sheep in his hands'* could mean that either God made us in His image and likeness or that God guides us with His hand.

- Psalm 98 emphasizes God's kingship over His people. Upon their return from Babylon, the Israelites rebuilt their ruined temple, but had no king anymore to rule over them. Palestine always remained a tributary state to various foreign powers. Foreign rule continued during the lifetime of Jesus and much after. Understandably, they came to see clearly that only God was dependable as their true king.
- Many centuries ago, the Israelites had insisted that Samuel, their Prophet and last Judge, give them a monarch to rule over them, like the other nations. The monarchy was installed through the Davidic Covenant and acted as a prefiguration of the installation of Jesus, the son of David, who would establish the new kingdom of Israel, the Kingdom of God in this world and not of this world.

End with Prayer to the Holy Trinity
NIGHT PRAYER: The Examination of Conscience

JOURNAL FOR BOOK FOUR, WEEK ONE: ISRAEL'S BANISHMENT

DAY ONE: Morning Prayer: Psalm 90: God's Eternity and Human Frailty
What is God saying to You?

Nightly Examination of Conscience:
For what are you grateful?

For what are you contrite?

What spiritual discipline, including fasting, do you need to focus on tomorrow?

DAY TWO: Morning Prayer: Psalm 91: Security under God's Protection
What is God saying to You?

Nightly Examination of Conscience:
For what are you grateful?

For what are you contrite?

What spiritual discipline, including fasting, do you need to focus on tomorrow?

DAY THREE: Morning Prayer: Psalm 92: A Hymn of Thanksgiving for God's Fidelity
What is God saying to You?

Nightly Examination of Conscience:
For what are you grateful?

For what are you contrite?

What spiritual discipline, including fasting, do you need to focus on tomorrow?

DAY FOUR: Morning Prayer: Psalm 93: God is a Mighty King
What is God saying to You?

Nightly Examination of Conscience:
For what are you grateful?

For what are you contrite?

What spiritual discipline, including fasting, do you need to focus on tomorrow?

DAY FIVE: Morning Prayer: Psalm 95: A Call to Praise and Obedience
What is God saying to You?

Nightly Examination of Conscience:
For what are you grateful?

For what are you contrite?

What spiritual discipline, including fasting, do you need to focus on tomorrow?

DAY SIX: Morning Prayer: Psalm 98: The Coming of God
What is God saying to You?

Nightly Examination of Conscience:
For what are you grateful?

For what are you contrite?

What spiritual discipline, including fasting, do you need to focus on tomorrow?

DAY SEVEN: Morning Prayer: Learning Discipleship from the Psalms
What is God saying to You?

Nightly Examination of Conscience:
For what are you grateful?

For what are you contrite?

What spiritual discipline, including fasting, do you need to focus on tomorrow?

What prayer would you compose to express what God has said to you this week?

BOOK FOUR: PSALMS 90 TO 106: ISRAEL'S BANISHMENT
Psalms 99, 100, 101, 103, 104, and 106

WHAT IS AT THE HEART OF BOOK FOUR, WEEK TWO?

In Week Two of Book Four, we will reflect on Psalms 99, 100, 101, 103, 104, and 106. Now that David and his sons have disappeared from the limelight, whom do we turn to for advice and guidance? The Davidic Covenant was supposed to lay its foundation on the commandments and laws laid down by God through Moses. Now that David has disappeared, it is time to return to a past beacon of light that guided the Israelites, namely the Mosaic Covenant. Psalms 99, 103, and 106 refer to Moses. Similarly, as if to emphasize the need to go back to the basics, three references are made to Abraham in Psalm 105. Now that David has disappeared from the limelight, Book Four looks to these earlier covenant mediators for direction and inspiration. Psalms 99, 100, 101, 103, and 104 make it clear that the focus in Israel's religious consciousness has shifted greatly. Israel had best focus on God as being their dwelling place as they have just lost Jerusalem as their dwelling place.

On Day One, we will pray with *Psalm 99: The Holy King,* the last of the royal psalms in Book Four. This psalm continues to highlight the central role of God in the lives of His people. God was always central to their lives from the divine perspective. It was God who chose Israel to be His people. On their behalf, He worked amazing miracles and brought them out of the land of Egypt. At Mount Sinai, God established a covenant with them. He became their God and they became His people. In their history, however, despite God's faithfulness, Israel remained unfaithful and rebellious, finally bringing them to their knees in the Babylonian exile. Psalm 99 suggests that they have altered their perspective on God and their relationship with Him, profoundly. They have become repentant and submissive to God's reign over them.

On Day Two, Psalm 100 will become the focus of our prayer. *Psalm 100: Processional Hymn: A Psalm of Thanksgiving* is officially designated for the sacrifice of thanksgiving or *todah*, highlighting the significance of the *todah* for the psalms in general. David would offer an animal on God's altar as a sign of thanks. After that, he would hold a feast where the animal was eaten, and David gave testimony to God's good deeds in front of all the gathered people. That was David's favorite way to worship, through a *todah sacrifice*. The Eucharist is the ultimate thanksgiving sacrifice in which we thank God for saving us from sin and Satan through the sacrifice of Jesus on the Cross. God's enduring mercy toward us pulls together our worship of Him, along with His creation and the stirring events of salvation history culminating in Jesus.

On Day Three, we will pray with *Psalm 101: Norm of Life for Rulers*. David is thinking about the kind of king he should be after Saul's death and his ascension to the throne. David's vision of the just ruler the king should be was never realized. Psalm 101 offers us a soul-searching reflection on the collapse of the Davidic kingdom following the Babylonian exile. They no longer had a king to depend upon and trust in the temporal and spiritual affairs of the kingdom. Psalm 101 is hearkening God's people to return to God as the true Center of their lives and worship. Psalm 101 is pointing to the perfect reign of Jesus over us.

On Day Four, we will pray with *Psalm 103: Praise of Divine Goodness*. The depth of spiritual maturity displayed would suggest that David composed Psalm 103 in the later years of his life when he had a deeper appreciation of the precious gift of forgiveness from God as he had entered the dregs of sin, as compared to his younger days. His clear sense of the frailty of life indicates his weaker years, as also does the very fullness of his praise and gratitude toward God.

On Day Five, we will reflect on *Psalm 104: Praise of God the Creator*. No other psalm goes into such detail about God as Creator and His intimate connection with nature. It is the most beautiful reflection on God's work of Creation and Providence in the whole Psalter. Psalm 104 continues the theme to *'Bless the LORD, my soul!'* found in Psalm 103. Psalm 104 could be viewed as a poetic reflection on the Genesis account. On Day Six, we will consider *Psalm 106: Israel's Confession of Sin.*

Book Four ends with Psalms 105 and 106, two psalms that reflect on the history of Israel. Psalm 105 reviews Israel's story and concludes that God was always faithful to Israel. Psalm 106 reviews the same story and concludes that Israel was always unfaithful to God. These two psalms offer us a convincing answer to the question, *'Why did Israel suffer the Babylonian exile?'* The blame lies solely with God's people who refused to be in covenant with God and thereby chose to suffer the consequences of their separation from Him. Psalm 106 ends with a prayer that suggests that Israel has come to true repentance: *"Save us, LORD, our God; gather us from among the nations that we may give thanks to your holy name and glory in praising you."*

On Day Seven, you will ponder the salient advice that these psalms have offered us to enhance and strengthen our own following of Jesus and our commitment to His Church.

SPIRITUAL READING FOR BOOK FOUR OF THE PSALMS:
Psalms 90 to 106
Book of Isaiah: Chapters 40-55

DAY ONE:
MORNING PRAYER: Acts of Faith, Hope, Charity; Daily Offering

MORNING FACE TO FACE WITH GOD:
Begin with Prayer to the Holy Spirit
Prayer on Psalm 99: The Holy King

Psalm 99 is the last of the royal psalms in Book Four. Along with the other royal psalms, this psalm continues to highlight the central role of God in the lives of His people. God was always central to their lives from the divine perspective. It was God who chose Israel to be His people. On their behalf, He worked amazing miracles and brought them out of the land of Egypt. At Mount

Sinai, God established a covenant with them. He became their God and they became His people. In their history, however, despite God's faithfulness, Israel remained unfaithful and rebellious, finally bringing them to their knees in the Babylonian exile. Psalm 99 suggests that they have altered their perspective on God and their relationship with Him, profoundly. They have become repentant and submissive to God's reign over them.

Psalm 99 begins with the phrase, *"The LORD is king."* This is the third psalm that begins with acknowledging God as king, the other two being Psalms 93 and 97. Psalm 98 expressed a carefree delight in the magnificent presence of the victorious LORD. Here, we recollect how exalted and holy God is, and how profound is the reverence we owe Him. At the end of all three segments of Psalm 99, there is a resounding emphasis on God's holiness: *Holy is he! Holy is he!* and *Holy is the LORD, our God!* This psalm is, therefore, a triple proclamation of God's holiness, an emphasis that Isaiah made in the 8th century B.C.: *"Holy, holy, holy is the LORD of hosts! All the earth is filled with his glory!"* (Isaiah 6: 3).

In the presence of the sovereign God, it is appropriate for His people and all of creation to tremble in reverent adoration: *"The LORD is king, the peoples tremble; he is enthroned on the cherubim, the earth quakes. Great is the LORD in Zion, exalted above all the peoples. Let them praise your great and awesome name: Holy is he!"* While God is present in heaven and in all the earth, He has a special regard for Zion, the city of Jerusalem. In that city, God is exalted above all the peoples!

God's holiness is greatly emphasized in Psalm 99. At its root, holiness has the idea of being set apart, being other than. Holiness is the very essence of God's being. God was revealed to us as separated from everything unjust, untrue, evil, in all His dealings with humans. His holiness, the immaculate purity of His nature, is the reason why God should be exalted, praised, and worshiped.

The Psalmist lists three notable priests from the history of Israel – Moses, Aaron, and Samuel. They represented God's people. They were the ones *'who called on his name'* (prayed), and *'he answered them.'* To encourage the faithful in the worship of God, the examples of Moses, Aaron, and Samuel are cited, men having similar weaknesses like we do, whose prayers were heard both for themselves and for others. *'Priests'* could be loosely translated as servants or intercessors. Those who call upon the name of the LORD belong to a separate class. Their relationship with God is filled with trust in God's power and love. They know that God is a forgiving God, though He calls us to justice. It is a grace given to anyone for the asking and requires a commitment to making God the center of their lives. God speaks to such disciples in a vivid manner, like *'From the pillar of cloud he spoke to them.'*

At the end of the psalm, the reader is compelled to exalt God, to worship Him, and to recognize God's holiness: *"Exalt the LORD, our God; bow down before his holy mountain; holy is the LORD, our God."* God's holiness is the supreme reason for confidence in Him, and the supreme inspiration to worship Him.

Reflect and Pray on Psalm 99, using Lectio Divina or the Method of Meditation. Make sure you converse intimately with the Blessed Trinity:

Prayer on Psalm 99: The Holy King

I.

"1 The LORD is king, the peoples tremble; he is enthroned on the cherubim, the earth quakes. 2 Great is the LORD in Zion, exalted above all the peoples. 3 Let them praise your great and awesome name: Holy is he!

II.

4 O mighty king, lover of justice, you have established fairness; you have created just rule in Jacob. Jacob. 5 Exalt the LORD, our God; bow down before his footstool; holy is he!

III.

6 Moses and Aaron were his priests, Samuel among those who called on his name; they called on the LORD, and he answered them. 7 From the pillar of cloud he spoke to them; they kept his decrees, the law he had given them. 8 O LORD, our God, you answered them; you were a forgiving God to them, though you punished their offenses. 9 Exalt the LORD, our God; bow down before his holy mountain; holy is the LORD, our God."

End with Prayer to the Holy Trinity
NIGHT PRAYER: The Examination of Conscience

DAY TWO:
MORNING PRAYER: Acts of Faith, Hope, Charity; Daily Offering

MORNING FACE TO FACE WITH GOD:
Begin with Prayer to the Holy Spirit

Prayer on Psalm 100: Processional Hymn: A Psalm of Thanksgiving

Psalm 100 is one of the alternative psalms for the Invitatory that begins the Liturgy of the Hours. Unlike the previous psalms in Book Four, Psalm 100 does not begin with a declaration of God's sovereignty and kingship. Rather it begins by exhorting *'all you lands'* to praise God with a joyful shout. This is a call to the nations, extending far beyond Israel's borders.

Psalm 100 is officially designated for the sacrifice of thanksgiving or *todah,* highlighting the significance of the *todah* for the psalms in general. We have seen in Psalm 50 from Book Two, how the thank offering is better than other offerings, especially the burnt offering where the whole animal was burnt up on the altar and ascended to God in heaven as smoke. In time, people got the wrong idea that they were doing God a favor through the burnt offering. Thus, they were meriting God's favor upon them. Psalm 50 makes the point that the best way to worship God is to bring a thank offering when He saves us. It is God who does favors for us, not the other way around!

Verse 3 captures the intricate and compelling balance of God's creation of us in His image and likeness, along with His providence and saving protection as our Shepherd: *"Know that the LORD is God, he made us, we belong to him, we are his people, the flock he shepherds." 'He made us'* (creation). We are *'the flock he shepherds'* (salvation history). It behooves us, therefore, to worship Him with praise and thanksgiving.

The message of Psalm 100 can be summarized in verses 4 and 5: *"Enter his gates with thanksgiving, his courts with praise. Give*

thanks to him, bless his name; good indeed is the LORD, his mercy endures forever, his faithfulness lasts through every generation."
'Giving thanks' refers to offering the *todah* sacrifice, which for us now would be the Eucharist. *"Good indeed is the LORD'* refers to His goodness shown in creation that displays all the wonderful things that God has made for His praise and glory and for our benefit. *'His mercy endures forever'* means his covenant faithfulness. His commitment to His family bond with God's people is shown in the various covenants of salvation history: Adamic, Noahic, Abrahamic, Mosaic, Davidic, and the New and Everlasting Covenant in Jesus. God's creation and His enduring mercy manifested in the stirring events of salvation history culminating in Jesus, galvanizes us to worship Him with adoration, praise, and thanksgiving.

Reflect and Pray on Psalm 100, using Lectio Divina or the Method of Meditation. Make sure you converse intimately with the Blessed Trinity:

Prayer on Psalm 100: Processional Hymn: A Psalm of Thanksgiving
"1 Shout joyfully to the LORD, all you lands; 2 Serve the LORD with gladness; come before him with joyful song. 3 Know that the LORD is God, he made us, we belong to him, we are his people, the flock he shepherds. 4 Enter his gates with thanksgiving, his courts with praise. Give thanks to him, bless his name; 5 good indeed is the LORD, his mercy endures forever, his faithfulness lasts through every generation."

End with Prayer to the Holy Trinity
NIGHT PRAYER: The Examination of Conscience

DAY THREE:
MORNING PRAYER: Acts of Faith, Hope, Charity; Daily Offering

MORNING FACE TO FACE WITH GOD:
Begin with Prayer to the Holy Spirit
Prayer on Psalm 101: Norm of Life for Rulers
Psalms 101 and 103 are the only two psalms composed by David in Book Four. A likely background is that David had

recently ascended the throne. The abuses and confusions of Saul's last troubled years had to be reformed. The new king felt strongly that he was God's viceroy and was declaring his commitment to making his monarchy a copy of God's just and merciful reign over His people. David was anointed king three times. Samuel anointed David in his youth, as a prophecy of his calling and destiny (1Samuel 16: 13). After Saul's death, David was anointed king over the tribe of Judah at Hebron (2Samuel 2: 4). Seven years later, he was anointed king over all the tribes of Israel (2Samuel 5: 3). Before he ascended the throne over all Israel, David had a lot of time to think about the kind of king he should be.

David begins the psalm by exalting God's mercy and justice. As king, David was concerned with mercy and justice and sang of them as a hymn of praise. Before he could exercise mercy and justice in his kingdom, he had to make God's mercy and justice the guiding principles of his life: *"I sing of mercy and justice; to you, LORD, I sing praise. I study the way of integrity; when will you come to me?"* David's longing for the Lord was connected to his desire to live a wise and holy life. He wanted his reign to be marked with integrity and godliness: *"I act with integrity of heart within my household. I do not allow into my presence anything base. I hate wrongdoing; I will have no part of it. May the devious heart keep far from me; the wicked I will not acknowledge."* Mercy and justice would influence David's administration as he had observed and pondered them in the actions and dispensations of God's providence over His people. Acting like God would impel him to reject wrongdoing and anything wicked. He would avoid the wicked and devious of heart.

In his rulings and judgments over his people, David would make sure to silence the slanderers, and rebuke the haughty eyes and arrogant hearts: *"Whoever slanders a neighbor in secret I will reduce to silence. Haughty eyes and arrogant hearts I cannot endure."* Advancing themselves by calumniating others is the common evil of courts and kingdoms. David understood the principle enunciated in 1John 1: 6-7 and was committed to acting upon it as the king of Israel: *"If we say, "We have fellowship with him," while we continue to walk in darkness, we lie and do not act in truth. But if we walk in the light as he is in the light, then we have fellowship with one another, and the blood of his Son Jesus cleanses us from all sin."* David's righteous life had to be real in his conduct within his own house before it could be exercised in the courts of his kingdom. This was a standard that David only imperfectly lived, much to his own harm.

In Segment II, David outlines the vision that he would follow in his reign over his people. He would *"look to the faithful of the land to sit at my side. Whoever follows the way of integrity is the one to enter my service."* It is a wise leader who seeks out such people and then puts authority into their hands. On the other hand, he would reject anyone *"who practices deceit."* And, *"no one who speaks falsely can last in my presence. Morning after morning, I clear all the wicked from the land, to rid the city of the LORD of all doers of evil."* The godly king affirms that his loyalty is to his Covenant God and not to the ways of the world.

Psalm 101 is included in Book Four of the Psalter which offers us a soul-searching reflection on the collapse of the Davidic kingdom following the Babylonian exile. They no longer had a king to depend upon in the temporal and spiritual affairs of the kingdom. Book Four highlights the spiritual perspective and vision that David offers in Psalm 101. When God is the Center of our lives and in our responsibilities over others, God's blessings will be bestowed upon us in abundance. When God is abandoned as King over His people, chaos and disaster ensue. Psalm 101 is hearkening God's people to return to God as the true Center of their lives and worship. Psalm 101 is pointing to the perfect reign of Jesus over us.

Reflect and Pray on Psalm 101, using Lectio Divina or the Method of Meditation. Make sure you converse intimately with the Blessed Trinity:

Prayer on Psalm 101: Norm of Life for Rulers
"1 A psalm of David.

I.

"I sing of mercy and justice; to you, LORD, I sing praise. 2 I study

the way of integrity; when will you come to me? I act with integrity of heart within my household. 3 I do not allow into my presence anything base. I hate wrongdoing; I will have no part of it. 4 May the devious heart keep far from me; the wicked I will not acknowledge. 5 Whoever slanders a neighbor in secret I will reduce to silence. Haughty eyes and arrogant hearts I cannot endure.

II.

6 I will look to the faithful of the land to sit at my side. Whoever follows the way of integrity is the one to enter my service. 7 No one who practices deceit can remain within my house. No one who speaks falsely can last in my presence. 8 Morning after morning I clear all the wicked from the land, to rid the city of the LORD of all doers of evil."

End with Prayer to the Holy Trinity
NIGHT PRAYER: The Examination of Conscience

DAY FOUR:
MORNING PRAYER: Acts of Faith, Hope, Charity; Daily Offering

MORNING FACE TO FACE WITH GOD:
Begin with Prayer to the Holy Spirit

Prayer on Psalm 103: Praise of Divine Goodness

Psalm 103 is another psalm attributed to David and included in Book Four. The depth of spiritual maturity behind the composition would suggest that David was composing his song from a rare vantage point. He knew intimately the grace and deliverance of God many times in his life. While it could have been written at many different times of his life, a more convincing argument would be that he wrote it in the later years of his life. Then he had a deeper appreciation of God's forgiveness of his grievous sins causing much scandal. His sense of the frailty of life indicates his weaker years, as also does the fullness of his praise and gratitude toward God. It is one of the most perfect songs of praise to be found in the Bible.

David begins his song to God by asking his soul to bless the

LORD and to bless Him with all his being: *"Bless the LORD, my soul; all my being, bless his holy name!"* David gives us several reasons as to why we must praise and reverence God with all our hearts, minds, and souls: *"Bless the LORD, my soul ... who pardons all your sins, and heals all your ills, who redeems your life from the pit, and crowns you with mercy and compassion, who fills your days with good things, so your youth is renewed like the eagle's."* 'Pardon of sins' is at the top of David's list of benefits. In his mind, the most important thing was to have sins forgiven. Another great benefit is God's care of our bodies. God brings healing to us in this life through both natural, medical, and miraculous ways. The phrase, *'who redeems your life from the pit,'* suggests the redemption of life by a *Goel,* a kinsman-redeemer (Leviticus 25: 47-49). Jesus became our kinsman-redeemer, partaking of our flesh and blood so that He could have the obligation/right to redeem our souls from death, the pit of destruction, by atoning for our sins through His death on the cross!

In Segment II, David extols God's righteous deeds and justice. Through God's righteous deeds, we are crowned with His mercy and compassion. His mercy, manifested in His unbreakable bond with us through the new and everlasting covenant in Jesus, is always going to be enduring. God's compassion is His profound commitment to walking in our shoes, in the misery and messiness of our lives, and passaging us into His divine love and Trinitarian life. Consequently, our days are filled with true satisfaction from good things. This satisfaction originating from God, becomes a source of strength and energy, evoking the image of our youth being renewed like the eagle's, the very picture of buoyant, tireless fortitude and power.

David proclaims God as being *'merciful and gracious.'* God shows His greatness by doing *"righteous deeds, ... justice to all the oppressed."* It is important that we magnify the Lord for His goodness to others. This segment further emphasizes the manifestation of God's greatness through His self-revelation: *"He made known his ways to Moses, to the Israelites his deeds."*

Segment II also offers a sharp contrast between God's generosity and goodness and man's rebellious sinfulness: *"He will not always accuse, and nurses no lasting anger; He has not dealt with us as our sins merit, nor requited us as our wrongs deserve."* David knew the slow anger and abounding mercy of God personally. He knew that his sins and the sins of his people deserved much greater condemnation than they had received. God chose to deal with our sins in His Son who atoned for them through His death on the cross, rather than condemn us and separate us from Him permanently.

Segment III describes God's mercy in very moving and familial terms. Our hearts cannot but be moved deeply by God's love for us: *"For as the heavens tower over the earth, so his mercy towers over those who fear him. As far as the east is from the west, so far has he removed our sins from us. As a father has compassion on his children, so the LORD has compassion on those who fear him."* David cites an interesting reason that spurs God's mercy toward us: *"For he knows how we are formed, remembers that we are dust. As for man, his days are like the grass; he blossoms like a flower in the field. A wind sweeps over it and it is gone; its place knows it no more."* Man's mortality and weakness is buttressed by the hope and confidence we can have in the assurance of God's mercy toward us: *"But the LORD's mercy is from age to age, toward those who fear him. His salvation is for the children's children of those who keep his covenant, and remember to carry out his precepts."*

David began the psalm by telling his own soul to bless the Lord, but he knew that the praise and honor to God should extend all the way to the angels and the creatures of this world: *"Bless the LORD, all you his angels, mighty in strength, acting at his behest, obedient to his command... Bless the LORD, all his creatures, everywhere in his domain. Bless the LORD, my soul!"* It behooves all of creation, visible and invisible, earthly and heavenly, to praise and honor God, because God is our Creator. He is holy, and will be from everlasting to everlasting, long after we are gone: *"The*

LORD has set his throne in heaven; his dominion extends over all."
Fittingly, David ends the psalm as he began it: *"Bless the LORD, my soul!"*

Reflect and Pray on Psalm 103, using Lectio Divina or the Method of Meditation. Make sure you converse intimately with the Blessed Trinity:

Prayer on Psalm 103: Praise of Divine Goodness
"1 Of David.

I.

Bless the LORD, my soul; all my being, bless his holy name! 2 Bless the LORD, my soul; and do not forget all his gifts, 3 who pardons all your sins, and heals all your ills, 4 who redeems your life from the pit, and crowns you with mercy and compassion, 5 who fills your days with good things, so your youth is renewed like the eagle's.

II.

6. The LORD does righteous deeds, brings justice to all the oppressed. 7 He made known his ways to Moses, to the Israelites his deeds. 8 Merciful and gracious is the LORD, slow to anger, abounding in mercy. 9 He will not always accuse, and nurses no lasting anger; 10 He has not dealt with us as our sins merit, nor requited us as our wrongs deserve.

III.

11 For as the heavens tower over the earth, so his mercy towers over those who fear him. 12 As far as the east is from the west, so far has he removed our sins from us. 13 As a father has compassion on his children, so the LORD has compassion on those who fear him. 14 For he knows how we are formed, remembers that we are dust. 15 As for man, his days are like the grass; he blossoms like a flower in the field. 16 A wind sweeps over it and it is gone; its place knows it no more. 17 But the LORD's mercy is from age to age, toward those who fear him. His salvation is for the children's children of those who keep his covenant, and remember to carry out his precepts.

IV.

The LORD has set his throne in heaven; his dominion extends over all. 20 Bless the LORD, all you his angels, mighty in strength, acting at his behest, obedient to his command. 21 Bless the LORD, all you his hosts, his ministers who carry out his will. 22 Bless the LORD, all his creatures, everywhere in his domain. Bless the LORD, my soul!"

End with Prayer to the Holy Trinity
NIGHT PRAYER: The Examination of Conscience

DAY FIVE:
MORNING PRAYER: Acts of Faith, Hope, Charity; Daily Offering

MORNING FACE TO FACE WITH GOD:
Begin with Prayer to the Holy Spirit

Prayer on Psalm 104: Praise of God the Creator

Psalm 104 is unique in the Psalter because no other psalm goes into such detail about God as Creator and His intimate connection with all of nature. It is the most beautiful reflection on God's work of Creation and Providence in the whole Psalter. The doctrine of Creation concerns God's making of the world from nothing (ex nihilo); the doctrine of Providence concerns God's care of what He has made. This psalm is the background for Jesus' teaching in the Sermon on the Mount: *"Look at the birds of the air: they neither sow nor reap nor gather into barns, and yet your heavenly Father feeds them. Are you not of more value than they?"* (Matthew 6: 26). In His preaching, Jesus highlighted God's loving kindness in His creation and providence as expressed in Psalm 104: God cares for all creation, and especially for those who abide in Him.

Psalm 104 continues the theme to *'Bless the LORD, my soul!'* found in Psalm 103. Psalm 104 begins and ends with the same refrain. This phrase is a call to worship God from our inmost being. The invisible God has made Himself visible through His creation. This is the deepest meaning of creation, that the Universe is the garment of God! The psalm is modeled rather closely on God's act of Creation in Genesis 1, taking the various stages of creation as starting points for praise. Psalm 104 could be viewed as a poetic reflection on the Genesis account.

Just as the Creation account begins with describing the creation of light, so the Psalmist first mentions light in his song: *"You are clothed with majesty and splendor, robed in light as with a cloak."* We can understand the idea of light as a garment by considering the appearance of Jesus at His Transfiguration: *"His face shone like the sun and his clothes became while as light"* (Matthew 17: 2). As the Psalmist waxes eloquent in his effusive praise of God's supreme might in Creation, he highlights the glory of God in His creation of light, angels, earth, and waters: the power of God evident at the flood and its aftermath; the glory of God in living things, plants, and animals; the glory of God in the sun and moon, in the wonder of the sea and all its creatures; in creation's dependence on God who keeps everything in order. Psalm 104 gives voice to the many voices of nature and sings sweetly both of creation and God's providence. The Psalm ends with blessing the God of all creation.

Psalm 104 is used by the Church at the beginning and end of the Easter season to reflect on God who creates through the Holy Spirit. At the beginning of Easter, Psalm 104 is the first Responsorial Psalm after the reading of the Creation story (Genesis 1: 1-2: 4) at the Easter Vigil. At the end of the Easter season, Psalm 104 is the Responsorial Psalm for the Vigil of Pentecost and the Mass of Pentecost during the day, when we conclude the season by celebrating the Outpouring of God's "Creator Spirit." Psalm 104: 30 is the most famous verse: *"Send forth your spirit, they are created and you renew the face of the earth."* This response has been incorporated into the 'Veni Sancte Spiritus' Prayer.

Reflect and Pray on Psalm 104, using Lectio Divina or the Method of Meditation. Make sure you converse intimately with the Blessed Trinity:

(Pray with Psalm 104 from your Bible)
End with Prayer to the Holy Trinity
NIGHT PRAYER: The Examination of Conscience

DAY SIX:
MORNING PRAYER: Acts of Faith, Hope, Charity; Daily Offering

MORNING FACE TO FACE WITH GOD:

Begin with Prayer to the Holy Spirit
Prayer on Psalm 106: Israel's Confession of Sin

Psalm 105 ended with *'Hallelujah'* as it offered praise and worship of God for His many gifts and blessings to Israel. Psalm 106 begins with *'Hallelujah,'* as it sings the praises of God's great mercy to an often rebellious and ungrateful Israel. In Psalm 106, Israel's calamitous history is written with the view of showing human sin and God's forgiveness. It could be viewed as a national confession.

Psalm 106 exemplifies the steps a penitent would take in receiving the sacrament of reconciliation. The penitent has made a concerted effort to be honest and transparent. They have done their inventory and arrived at true repentance of their sinful past. The first verse sets the tone for the whole psalm: *"Hallelujah! Give thanks to the LORD, who is good, whose mercy endures forever."* The thought of God's unspeakable goodness, most appropriately, precedes the psalmist's confession. The sinner moves toward repentance in remembering God's unconditional love and acceptance of them. Their repentance deepens their sorrow for sin at the realization that they scorned God's patient goodness and enduring mercy toward them. The rest of this long psalm describes God's great mercy or loyal covenant love to a disobedient Israel. For all its exposure of man's ingratitude, this is a psalm of praise, for it is God's longsuffering loving kindness that emerges as the real theme.

Building on a foundation of praise and gratitude, the Psalmist opens the door to ask God for help: *"Remember me, LORD, as you favor your people; come to me with your saving help, that I may see the prosperity of your chosen ones, rejoice in the joy of your people, and glory with your heritage."* This psalm mainly focuses on the repeated failures of Israel throughout her history and identifies this present generation with the Israel of old: *"We have sinned like our ancestors; we have done wrong and are guilty."*

In Segment I, the Psalmist offers a sharp contrast between the brazen ingratitude and evil intent of the people, and God's unfailing love and mercy toward them. This is a remarkably humble and straightforward confession of sin. It draws out the dark record of national sin in order to lead to national repentance. The detailed description of Israel's sin is honest and unsparing because the hope of restoration is strong. Such restoration leads to covenant restoration with God and praise of Him: *"Then they believed his words and sang his praise."*

Segments II through VIII expose the fickle and self-serving attitude and obnoxious behavior of the Israelites throughout their history, beginning during the forty years of their wanderings in the desert and long after they had entered the Promised Land. Over many centuries, their repentance and return to the ways of the LORD did not last long. In subsequent chapters of their history, Israel moved from faith and celebration of God's works to ingratitude and disobedience. Psalm 106 acts as a poetic summary of the journey of the Israelites to the Promised Land, highlighting troubling events in the Books of Exodus and Numbers. The Psalmist is generous toward Aaron, calling him *'the holy one of the LORD,'* even though he sinned grievously in the golden calf incident (Exodus 32). Despite serious flaws and mortal sins against God, Aaron remained Israel's priest, suggesting that he had repented of his sins and was serving faithfully as the high priest.

The golden calf sin of idolatry and immorality was a sin of ingratitude. God who did wondrous deeds in bringing them out of Egypt was ignored in their praise of the golden calf. Moses pleaded with the Lord, asking Him to turn away His wrath. God answered the prayer of Moses and Israel was spared (Exodus 32: 11-13). It is a reminder to us to plead with the Lord for this guilty world, especially for His backsliding people. Moses is presented as God's worthy representative, a true leader of his people, who was prepared to die on their behalf, in their stead.

Although the people were unfaithful to God, He nevertheless was faithful to them, which is why a psalm dealing with the sins of God's people can end on a positive note. Psalm 106 seems to have been composed when the mercies of God toward the Israelites in their Babylonian captivity were just beginning to be appreciated. The Psalmist predicted that God's people would respond gratefully, breaking the previous pattern of ingratitude. They would not forget, but triumph in His praise: *"Save us, LORD, our God; gather us from among the nations that we may give thanks to your holy name and glory in praising you."* Verse 48 concludes the psalm, providing a fitting crown to a psalm whose theme has been God's steadfastness in the face of man's fickleness and perversity, and a doxology to conclude Book Four of the Psalter: *"Blessed be the LORD, the God of Israel, from everlasting to everlasting! Let all the people say, Amen! Hallelujah!"*

Reflect and Pray on Psalm 106, using Lectio Divina or the Method of Meditation. Make sure you converse intimately with the Blessed Trinity:

(Pray with Psalm 106 from your Bible)
End with Prayer to the Holy Trinity
NIGHT PRAYER: The Examination of Conscience

DAY SEVEN:
MORNING PRAYER: Acts of Faith, Hope, Charity; Daily Offering

MORNING FACE TO FACE WITH GOD:
<u>Learning Discipleship from the Psalms</u>
Begin with Prayer to the Holy Spirit

- Psalm 99 highlights the central role of God in the lives of His people. God was always central to their lives from the divine perspective. It was God who chose Israel to be His people. On their behalf, He worked amazing miracles and brought them out of the land of Egypt. At Mount Sinai, God entered into a covenant with them. He became their God and they, His people.

- Despite God's faithfulness, Israel remained unfaithful and rebellious, bringing them to their knees in the Babylonian exile. Psalm 99 suggests that they have altered their perspective on God and their relationship with Him, profoundly. They have become repentant and submissive to God's reign over them.

- Psalm 99 offers a resounding emphasis on God's holiness: *Holy is he! Holy is he!* and *Holy is the LORD, our God!* This psalm is, therefore, a triple proclamation of God's holiness, an emphasis that Isaiah made in the 8th century B.C.: *"Holy, holy, holy is the LORD of hosts! All the earth is filled with his glory!"* (Isaiah 6: 3).
- Psalm 100 bears the title, *'A Psalm of Thanksgiving.'* David offered his thanksgiving through a sacrifice of thanksgiving (Leviticus 7: 1114). During the meal where the animal was eaten, David gave testimony to God's good deeds in front of all the gathered people. That was his favorite way to worship God, through a *todah sacrifice* The Eucharist is the ultimate thanksgiving sacrifice in which we thank God for saving us from through the sacrifice of Jesus on the Cross.
- Psalm 101 offers us a soul-searching reflection on the collapse of the Davidic kingdom following the Babylonian exile. When God is abandoned as King over His people, chaos and disaster ensue. Psalm 101 is hearkening God's people to return to God as the true Center of their lives and worship. Psalm 101 is pointing to the perfect reign of Jesus over us.
- In Psalm 103 David had a deeper appreciation of God's forgiveness for his grievous sins. His clear sense of the frailty of life indicates his later years, as also does the very fullness of his praise and gratitude toward God. It is one of the most perfect songs of praise in the Bible.
- Through God's righteous deeds, we are crowned with God's mercy and compassion. God's compassion is His profound commitment to walking in our shoes, in the misery and messiness of our lives, and passaging us into His divine love and Trinitarian life. Consequently, our days are filled with true satisfaction.
- Psalm 103 describes God's mercy in very moving and familial terms. Our hearts cannot but be moved deeply by God's love for us: *"For as the heavens tower over the earth, so his mercy*

towers over those who fear him. As far as the east is from the west, so far has he removed our sins from us. As a father has compassion on his children, so the LORD has compassion on those who fear him."

- David cites an interesting reason that spurs God's mercy toward us: *"For he knows how we are formed, remembers that we are dust. As for man, his days are like the grass; he blossoms like a flower in the field. A wind sweeps over it and it is gone; its place knows it no more."* Man's mortality and weakness is buttressed by the hope and confidence we can have in the assurance of God's mercy toward us.
- Psalm 104 goes into detail about God as Creator and His intimate connection with all of nature. It is the most beautiful reflection on God's work of Creation and Providence in the whole Psalter. The doctrine of Creation concerns God's making of the world from nothing (ex nihilo); the doctrine of Providence concerns God's care of what He has made.
- Psalm 106 exemplifies the steps a penitent would take in receiving the sacrament of reconciliation. The penitent has made a concerted effort to be honest and transparent. They have arrived at true repentance of their sinful past. The thought of God's unspeakable goodness, most appropriately, precedes the psalmist's confession. Their repentance deepens their sorrow for sin at the realization that they scorned God's patient goodness and enduring mercy toward them.

End with Prayer to the Holy Trinity
NIGHT PRAYER: The Examination of Conscience

JOURNAL FOR BOOK FOUR, WEEK TWO: ISRAEL'S BANISHMENT

DAY ONE: Morning Prayer: Psalm 99: The Holy King
What is God saying to You?

Nightly Examination of Conscience:
For what are you grateful?

For what are you contrite?

What spiritual discipline, including fasting, do you need to focus on tomorrow?

DAY TWO: Morning Prayer: Psalm 100: Processional Hymn
What is God saying to You?

Nightly Examination of Conscience:
For what are you grateful?

For what are you contrite?

What spiritual discipline, including fasting, do you need to focus on tomorrow?

DAY THREE: Morning Prayer: Psalm 101: Norm of Life for Rulers
What is God saying to You?

Nightly Examination of Conscience:
For what are you grateful?

For what are you contrite?

What spiritual discipline, including fasting, do you need to focus on tomorrow?

DAY FOUR: Morning Prayer: Psalm 102: Prayer in Time of Distress
What is God saying to You?

Nightly Examination of Conscience:
For what are you grateful?

For what are you contrite?

What spiritual discipline, including fasting, do you need to focus on tomorrow?

DAY FIVE: Morning Prayer: Psalm 104: Praise of God the Creator
What is God saying to You?

Nightly Examination of Conscience:
For what are you grateful?

For what are you contrite?

What spiritual discipline, including fasting, do you need to focus on tomorrow?

DAY SIX: Morning Prayer: Psalm 106: Israel's Confession of Sin
What is God saying to You?

Nightly Examination of Conscience:
For what are you grateful?

For what are you contrite?

What spiritual discipline, including fasting, do you need to focus on tomorrow?

DAY SEVEN: Morning Prayer: Learning Discipleship from the Psalms
What is God saying to You?

Nightly Examination of Conscience:
For what are you grateful?

For what are you contrite?

What spiritual discipline, including fasting, do you need to focus on tomorrow?

What prayer would you compose to express what God has said to you this week?

BOOK FIVE: PSALMS 107 TO 150: LOOKING TOWARD THE MESSIAH
Psalms 107, 110, 112, 114, 118, and 119

WHAT IS AT THE HEART OF BOOK FIVE, WEEK ONE?

Book Five is the longest book in the Psalter. It has an upbeat tone, with the psalms giving God the central place that He deserves in the lives of the people. The Israelites have returned from exile with a purified understanding of what it means to be in covenant with God. The Old Testament as we know it, started to get finalized in its present form during the Babylonian exile, and continued after the return to the Promised Land. Many of the psalms overflow with praise and gratitude to God for His *hesed* or loving kindness and faithfulness, despite Israel's infidelities. Paradoxically, within the context of their loss of the Davidic Monarchy, some psalms speak of the Messiah-king, clearly prefiguring Jesus.

The shift to the upbeat tone of Book Five already begins at the end of Book Four, in Psalm 106, an intentional segué into Book Five. Psalm 106: 47 concludes with a prayer for God to bring the exile to an end: *"Save us, LORD, our God; gather us from among the nations that we may give thanks to your holy name and glory in praising you."* By contrast, Psalm 107: 1- 3 begins Book Five by thanking God for bringing the people back from exile: *"Give thanks to the LORD for he is good, his mercy endures forever!" Let that be the prayer of the LORD's redeemed, those redeemed from the hand of the foe. Those gathered from foreign lands, from east and west, from north and south."* This opening statement from the first psalm starts off the theme of Book Five, praising God for restoring His people from exile, and continuing with this theme to the very end.

Biblical scholars have surmised that there had to have been at least two earlier endings to the Psalter that were changed, when for good reason, more psalms were added. The first conclusion occurred at Psalm 119, the second at Psalm 136, and finally, the Psalter was brought to a definitive end with Psalm 150. Let us begin by looking at what seemed like premature endings to the Psalter. Psalm 107, as we have seen, is clearly the answer to the prayer of Psalm 106. Therefore, it was intentionally placed at the front of Book Five. Psalms 108 and 109 are two of David's lament psalms, leading up to the triumphant royal Psalm 110, which praises the Davidic king as *'a priest forever'* (Psalm 110: 4). This is the first time the Davidic king has been mentioned in a psalm since Psalm 89, the end of Book Three, which echoed the demise of the Davidic dynasty. Despite having no king anymore, the king is making an appearance here again. After a couple of *todah* psalms in Psalms 111 and 112, we then have the Passover Collection: Psalms 113-118. Jews call these six *todah* psalms, the Egyptian Hallel, because of their intimate connection with the Exodus. These six psalms of praise and thanksgiving are recited each year during the annual observance of Passover, one of the holiest celebrations in the Jewish calendar. At the end of this collection of Passover psalms, we have Psalm 119, the longest psalm in the Psalter. Beginning with each successive letter of the Hebrew alphabet, Psalm 119 praises God's law from *aleph* to *tav*. Psalm 119 forms a pair with Psalm 1, which also praises God's law, although much more briefly. Therefore, it seems that the Psalter began with Psalm 1 at the beginning, and Psalm 119 ended the Psalter on the theme of meditating on God's law. Psalm 119 is an epic poem and a great way to wrap things up. It seems logical to assume that there was a time when the Psalter ended with Psalm 119.

But there were other psalms that were sung, from before and after the Babylonian exile, that were not included in the Book of Psalms! After the exile, people would sing songs as they went on pilgrimage to the rebuilt Temple in Jerusalem. Consequently, a whole set of sacred songs grew up around the pilgrimage festivals and other pilgrimages to the Temple from Israelites living outside the walls of Jerusalem. These are the 'Psalms of Ascent,' so called because Jerusalem is situated on top of the mountain range that runs through Israel, from north to south. You almost always had to ascend to Jerusalem. Gradually, these Psalms of Ascent, #120-134, came to be included in the Psalter. After them, two litanies of praise, Psalms 135 and 136, were included to end the Psalter on a resounding note of thanksgiving. Once upon a time, therefore, the Book of Psalms ended with Psalm 136.

There were still some psalms of David that were not included in the Psalter, Psalms 137 to 145, and five other psalms, each beginning with 'Hallelujah!' (Praise the LORD!). Most probably, these fourteen psalms were added to the Psalter after the exile. The five 'Hallelujah' psalms became the concluding psalms of the Psalter. These five psalms are bursting with song and dance, their choruses are polyphonic, all resonating to a crescendo, and acting as a befitting ending to the Psalter.

There are some ups and downs in Book Five. There are laments, for instance, that remind us of Book One, such as Psalms 108, 137, 143, and others. But they are outnumbered by the lengthy and ecstatic praises found in most of the psalms of Book Five. The Psalms of Ascent, # 120-134, are placed in the center of Book Five for a specific purpose. They emphasize the dominant mood of Book Five: joy and celebration at the fact that the people are going up to the Temple, God's restored Sanctuary to worship. As Psalm 122: 1 says, *"I rejoiced when they said to me, 'Let us go to the House of the LORD!"*

The Psalter ends on a high note, but one is still left with a question mark. The crown and scepter, prominent in the psalms of the first three books, are missing. Although the Temple has been rebuilt and is operational in Book Five, no psalm clearly points to the restoration of the Davidic king, because in fact the Davidic king would not be restored. Since the Babylonian exile, Palestine was successively occupied by foreign rulers. After the Assyrians came the Persians, and after them, the Greeks, and later, the Romans who occupied Palestine in 63 B.C. The Psalter expects the restoration to happen, as there are still psalms about the Davidic

Covenant in Book Five: Psalms 110, 132, and 144. These messianic psalms anticipate the son of David who will restore the new kingdom of Israel. They anticipate Jesus, Son of David and Son of God!

SPIRITUAL READING FOR BOOK FIVE OF THE PSALMS:
Psalms 107 to 150
Books of Ezra and Nehemiah Isaiah: Chapters 56-66
Ezekiel: Chapters 33-48

DAY ONE:
MORNING PRAYER: Acts of Faith, Hope, Charity; Daily Offering

MORNING FACE TO FACE WITH GOD:
Begin with Prayer to the Holy Spirit
Prayer on Psalm 107: God the Savior of Those in Distress

Psalm 107: 1-3 is the answer to the prayer offered to God in Psalm 106: 47: *"Give thanks to the LORD for he is good, his mercy endures forever!" Let that be the prayer of the LORD's redeemed, those redeemed from the hand of the foe, those gathered from foreign lands, from east and west, from north and south."* Psalm 107 is full of praise and thanksgiving to God for bringing the Israelites home from exile. They can now rebuild the Temple, God's abode among them, even though they no longer will have a king to rule over them. The psalm gives thanks to God because He is good! God is especially good because *'His mercy endures forever!'* This phrase extolling God's mercy is used more than 30 times in the psalms. It is the people's appreciative declaration of the great loving kindness or covenant love of God, a forgiving and merciful love that endures forever, from everlasting to everlasting. God's mercy has descended upon them through all the blessings that they have experienced in their return from Babylon. And God's mercy will be celebrated throughout the course of the psalm.

Through His mercy, God's people have been redeemed. In Leviticus 25: 47-49, Moses' law anticipated the advent of the *goel* or kinsman-redeemer. If any person was either sold as a slave, or carried away as a captive, then his kinsman, who was nearest to him in blood, had the right and obligation to redeem him by paying the price or by taking his place. Psalm 107 was anticipating Jesus who became our kinsman-redeemer by buying us back for His Father with the price that He paid on the cross! Indeed, God's mercy has endured forever through Jesus' sacrifice on the cross! In the present context, through God's enduring mercy, *"those redeemed from the hand of the foe, those gathered from foreign lands,"* were able to return home. This would have been a fitting statement in the mouths of Daniel, Ezra, or Nehemiah, who as exiles themselves, had occasion to thank God for gathering a remnant of God's people from the lands of captivity and bringing them back to the Promised Land.

This remarkable psalm uses four wonderful images to praise God's deliverance of His people, reaching far back into their history prior to the Babylonian exile. The Psalmist presents the first image in Segment I: *"Some had lost their way in a barren desert; found no path toward a city to live in. They were hungry and thirsty; their life was ebbing away. In their distress they cried to the LORD, who rescued them in their peril, guided them by a direct path so they reached a city to live in."* These verses harken to the wanderings of the Israelites in the desert after they left Egypt and were headed for the Promised Land. The Psalmist encourages the people to thank the LORD for His mercy, *"for he filled the hungry with good things."* In her Magnificat, our Blessed Mother quoted this verse in Luke 1: 53, showing that she loved the psalms.

In the second image presented in Segment II, God rescued those who *"lived in darkness and gloom, imprisoned in misery and chains. Because they rebelled against God's word, and scorned the counsel of the Most High, He humbled their hearts through hardship; they stumbled with no one to help. In their distress they cried to the LORD, who saved them in their peril."* God's people experienced slavery and exile on three different occasions: for 400 years in Egypt before God sent them Moses to lead them out into the desert and bring them to the Promised Land; the Assyrian Exile that took place in the 8th Century B.C.; and the Babylonian Exile from 587 to 537 B.C. The Psalmist is emphasizing the importance of reflecting on human history from God's perspective. God has created the universe and humans in it. It is He who orders and guides nature and human history. Some were punished because *'they rebelled against God.'* God humbled their hearts through hardship, as during the enslavement of the Hebrews in Egypt and in the exiles. And God came to their rescue when they repented and sought His assistance: *"Now indeed the outcry of the Israelites has reached me, and I have seen how the Egyptians are oppressing them. Now, go! I am sending you to Pharaoh to bring my people, the Israelites, out of Egypt"* (Exodus 3: 9-10).

In Segment III, the Psalmist presents an image that has echoes of the hardships and wickedness of their ancestors as they journeyed toward the Promised Land: *"Some fell sick from their wicked ways, afflicted because of their sins. They loathed all manner of food; they were at the gates of death. In their distress they cried to the LORD, who saved them in their peril."* Their troubles were self-inflicted. The phrases, *'they loathed all manner of food,'* and *'were at the gates of death,'* call to mind in our times, the scourge of drug-addiction, as well as our perennial urge to sabotage the best in us and be destroyed. The death of the soul can be averted when in our distress we cry to the Lord!

Segment IV is possibly the most relevant section of Psalm 107 for us. It is beloved of mariners due to its reference to ships and the sea: *"He commanded and roused a storm wind; it tossed the waves on high. They rose up to the heavens, sank to the depths; their hearts trembled at the danger. They reeled, staggered like drunkards; their skill was of no avail. In their distress they cried to the LORD, who brought them out of their peril."* Segment IV foreshadows the calming of the storm at sea in Mark 4: 37-39: *"A violent squall came up and waves were breaking over the boat, so that it was already filling up. Jesus was in the stern, asleep on a cushion. They woke him and said to him, "Teacher, do you not care that we are perishing?" He woke up, rebuked the wind, and said to the sea. "Quiet! Be still!"*

Segment V is a sober reflection on the sovereign power of God over all creation and human history: *"God changed rivers into desert, springs of water into thirsty ground, fruitful land into a salty waste, because of the wickedness of its people. He changed the desert into pools of water, arid land into springs of water, and settled the hungry there; they built a city to live in... God blessed them, and they increased greatly, and their livestock did not decrease."* God's authority is limitless. He can reverse the condition of anything and anybody, and therefore, the way of life of everybody. The Psalmist relied upon God not only for the gathering of God's people from their captivity, but for His blessing and transformation of the land when they returned to it. God's righteous ones will rest secure in their trust of God's judgments in all their circumstances.

Finally, there are two refrains that are echoed in every segment of the psalm: *"Such wondrous deeds for the children of Adam"* reminds us of our first parents and our creation: *"God created mankind in his image; in the image of God he created them; male and female he created them"* (Genesis 1: 27). The other refrain is, *"Let them thank the LORD for his mercy."* God accomplishes His wonderful works of mercy and deliverance, although His chosen people have proven to be faithless repeatedly. The concluding verse leaves us with serious food for thought: *"Whoever is wise will take note of these things, and ponder the merciful deeds of the LORD."*

Reflect and Pray on Psalm 107, using Lectio Divina or the Method of Meditation. Make sure you converse intimately with the Blessed Trinity:

(Pray with Psalm 107) from your Bible)
End with Prayer to the Holy Trinity
NIGHT PRAYER: The Examination of Conscience

DAY TWO:
MORNING PRAYER: Acts of Faith, Hope, Charity; Daily Offering
MORNING FACE TO FACE WITH GOD:

Begin with Prayer to the Holy Spirit
Prayer on Psalm 110: God appoints the King both King and Priest

Although Psalm 110 is included in Book Five, it harkens back to the time of David, not the time after the exile. This is the first time the Davidic king has been mentioned in a psalm since Psalm 89, at the end of Book Three which echoed the demise of the Davidic dynasty. Despite having no king anymore, the king is making an appearance here again. Clearly, the psalm is a prophecy of Jesus, son of David, who will be the Messiah- King and Priest. Psalm 110 is the most quoted and influential psalm in the New Testament. There are about 27 direct quotations or indirect allusions to Psalm 110 in the New Testament, and several of them have been made by Jesus Himself. In particular, the Letter to the Hebrews makes frequent reference to Psalm 110.

The opening verse sets the tone for the psalm which highlights the Messiah as both King and Priest: *"The LORD says to my lord: "Sit at my right hand, while I make your enemies your footstool."* David prophetically revealed the words of the LORD (God the Father) to the Messiah, David's lord, who would be Jesus. This meaning is especially clear by the way this verse is quoted and interpreted in the New Testament. This opening verse is one of the most quoted in the New Testament. Jesus quoted this verse, recognizing that the Messiah was greater than David himself: *"As Jesus was teaching in the temple area he said, "How do the scribes claim that the Messiah is the son of David? David himself, inspired by the holy Spirit, said: 'The Lord said to my lord, "Sit at my right hand until I place your enemies under your feet.'" David himself calls him 'lord'; so how is he his son?"* (Mark 12: 35-37). Peter quoted it after Pentecost, as David's prophecy about the divinity of Jesus and His Ascension: *"For David did not go up into heaven, but he himself said: 'The Lord said to my Lord, "Sit at my right hand until I make your enemies your footstool.'" Therefore let the whole house of Israel know for certain that God made him both Lord and Messiah, this Jesus whom you crucified"* (Acts 2: 34-36). Paul referred to it in emphasizing the rule and dominion of Jesus the Messiah: *"For he must reign until he has put all his enemies under his feet"* (1Corinthians 15: 25). The Letter to the Hebrews uses it to emphasize the superiority of Jesus over any angel: *"But to which of the angels has he ever said: "Sit at my right hand until I made your enemies your footstool"?* And later in the letter, the author explains the rule and dominion of Jesus the Messiah: *"But this one offered one sacrifice for sins, and took his seat forever at the right hand of God; now he waits until his enemies are made his footstool"* (Hebrews 10: 12-13).

The psalm then talks about the very intimate relationship between 'the Lord and His lord.' In Peter's quote, *'The Lord said to my Lord'* (Acts 2: 34), the uppercase for the second 'Lord' clearly refers to Jesus. Psalm 110 describes the relationship between Father and Son as follows: *"In holy splendor before the daystar, like dew I begot you."* Jesus the Messiah has received His power from His Father and is now seated at the right hand of the Father, sharing in His dominion over all enemies. Their relationship is a covenant relationship from all eternity. *'Like dew I begot you,'* would mean literally, 'From the womb of the dawn, I begot you.' The prose version would be that God has a father-son relationship with Jesus who has been His Son from all eternity. The one begotten, shares the same nature as the one begetting, in this instance, the divine nature. They have dwelled *'in holy splendor before the daystar,'* or creation of the world. This divine Sonship comes with a priestly role: *"You are a priest forever in the manner of Melchizedek."* Melchizedek was the ancient priest-king of Jerusalem (called 'Salem' in Genesis 14: 18) who blessed Abraham. When David became king of Jerusalem in 2Samuel 5, he became the heir of Melchizedek's role and titles. David, too, became a priest, as we see him leading worship and wearing priestly clothing in 2Samuel 6, even though he did not belong to the tribe of Levi from which the priests came. This role was passed on to his sons who were also priests (2Samuel 8: 18). The Letter to the Hebrews explains how it is that Jesus, Son of David, is God's High Priest even though he does not come from the line of Aaron of the tribe of Levi: *"It is clear that our Lord arose from Judah, and in regard to that tribe Moses said nothing about priests. It is even more obvious if another priest is raised up after the likeness of Melchizedek, who has become so, not by a law expressed in a commandment concerning physical descent but by the power of a life that cannot be destroyed. For it is testified: "You are a priest forever according to the order of Melchizedek"* (Hebrews 7: 14-17).

This testament or oath that Jesus is a priest forever according to the order of Melchizedek was so important that the Letter to the Hebrews refers to it five times! This was The Father's declaration as to who His Son would be, not a claim that Jesus made for Himself. Jesus serves now and forever as a living, active High Priest, interceding before His Father in heaven for us. The priesthood according to the order of Melchizedek replaced the priestly order of Aaron.

The last verse of Psalm 110 remains puzzling: *"Who drinks from the brook by the wayside and thus holds high his head."* The brook possibly refers to the Gihon Spring, the only freshwater source in Jerusalem. According to tradition, when the king returned from his victories in battle, he would announce officially his return by drinking from the spring. The Gihon Spring was a significant place in Israel's history. Solomon was anointed king over Israel by Zadok the priest and Nathan the prophet at the Gihon Spring (1Kings 1: 33, 38, 35). Psalm 46: 5 describes its importance for Jerusalem: *"Streams of the river gladden the city of God, the holy dwelling of the Most High,"* It also became a symbol of the river of life flowing from God's Temple.

Reflect and Pray on Psalm 110, using Lectio Divina or the Method of Meditation. Make sure you converse intimately with the Blessed Trinity:

Prayer on Psalm 110: God appoints the King both King and Priest
"1 A psalm of David.
The LORD says to my lord: "Sit at my right hand, while I make your enemies your footstool." 2 The scepter of your might: the

LORD *extends your strong scepter from Zion. Have dominion over your enemies! 3 Yours is princely power from the day of your birth. In holy splendor before the daystar, like dew I begot you. 4 The* LORD *has sworn and will not waver: "You are a priest forever in the manner of Melchizedek." 5 At your right hand is the Lord, who crushes kings on the day of his wrath, 6 who judges nations, heaps up corpses, crushes heads across the wide earth, 7 who drinks from the brook by the wayside and thus hold high his head."*

End with Prayer to the Holy Trinity
NIGHT PRAYER: The Examination of Conscience

DAY THREE:
MORNING PRAYER: Acts of Faith, Hope, Charity; Daily Offering

MORNING FACE TO FACE WITH GOD:
Begin with Prayer to the Holy Spirit
Prayer on Psalm 112: The Blessings of the Just

Psalms 111 and 112 are both psalms of thanksgiving *(todah)*. Both hymns are acrostics, meaning that each verse begins with a successive letter of the Hebrew alphabet. They each have 22 lines to correspond with the twenty-two letters of the Hebrew alphabet. They are the same length, fall into identical stanzas, and even have similar phrases that occur at the same places. You might want to consider doing them together for your reflection and prayer.

Psalm 111 focuses on praise and thanksgiving to God for His presence and revelation in Israel's history. His deeds among His people reveal God in His power, mercy, and faithfulness. A fitting nugget to glean from this rich treasure trove is in the last verse: *"The fear of the* LORD *is the beginning of wisdom; prudent are all who practice it. His praise endures forever."* Psalm 112 focuses on God's numerous blessings that have been received by those who choose to remain close to God by obedience to the commandments. Psalm 112 describes the life of the righteous person and its logic resembles Psalms 1 and 111.

Like other psalms in Book Five, Psalm 112 begins with *'Hallelujah!'* The Psalmist was praising God personally and asking the congregation to do the same for all the blessings heaped upon the righteous person. The emphasis throughout the psalm is on the loving kindness of God. Hence, all honor and glory for His grace that has been manifested in the children of God, needs to be given to Him! The first blessing that manifests itself in the righteous person is the fear of the Lord: *"Blessed the man who fears the LORD, who greatly delights in his commands."* The Psalmist explains the blessedness of the one who does fear the Lord: *"(he) greatly delights in his commands."*

Psalm 112 lists a number of blessings that are bestowed on those who fear the Lord: *"A generation of the upright will be blessed. Wealth and riches shall be in his house; his righteousness shall endure forever."* The best way to live purposefully is by making God the Center of their lives and commending their children to His guardianship, rather than to focus on accumulating gold and silver to ensure a flourishing posterity. The Psalmist believes that their life of obedience and honoring God will lead to a sense of security and wellbeing in life. During the Second Temple period after the Babylonian exile, a person's righteousness meant that they were generous in almsgiving: *"As water quenches a flaming fire, so almsgiving atones for sins"* (Sirach 3: 30).

The blessed man's good works and right standing with God are lasting. They will not fade in this world or the world to come: *"Light shines through the darkness for the upright; gracious, compassionate, and righteous. It is good for the man gracious in lending, who conducts his affairs with justice. For he shall never be shaken; the righteous shall be remembered forever."* The beneficence of the righteous person gets emphasized again later in the psalm: *"Lavishly he gives to the poor; his righteousness shall endure forever; his horn shall be exalted forever."*

The Psalmist highlights an unsuspected blessing that comes to the upright of heart. Because they have chosen to be obedient to the commands of God and generous in almsgiving, they accumulate enemies. The pursuit of holiness brings with it the blessings of honor, children, and riches, but also the reality of adversities: *"He shall not fear an ill report; his heart is steadfast, trusting the LORD. His heart is tranquil, without fear, till at last he looks down on his foes."* Evil tidings are all around us and come to us every day. They may come to us from our family, from our health, from business, from the unfaithful, from the culture around us, and from politics. Yet, the one who loves God will not fear an ill report as his heart is steadfast. God will always be greater than any set of earthly circumstances: *"The one who is in you is greater than the one who is in the world"* (1John 4: 4). By contrast, the wicked person *"wastes away."* Their desires are frustrated because they see the blessings that come to those who fear the Lord: *"The wicked sees and is angry; gnashes his teeth and wastes away; the desire of the wicked come to nothing."*

The psalm highlights the character traits of the upright person: *'fears the Lord,' 'greatly delights in his commands,' 'wealth and riches shall be in his house,' 'is gracious, compassionate, and righteous,' 'gracious in lending, who conducts his affairs with justice,' 'shall not fear an ill report,' 'his heart is tranquil, without fear,' 'lavishly he gives to the poor,' 'the desire of the wicked come to nothing.'*

Reflect and Pray on Psalm 112, using Lectio Divina or the Method of Meditation. Make sure you converse intimately with the Blessed Trinity:

Prayer on Psalm 112: The Blessings of the Just
"1 Hallelujah! Blessed the man who fears the LORD, who greatly delights in his commands. 2 His descendants shall be mighty in the land, a generation of the upright will be blessed. 3 Wealth and riches shall be in his house; his righteousness shall endure forever. 4 Light shines through the darkness for the upright; gracious, compassionate, and righteous. 5 It is good for the man gracious in lending, who conducts his affairs with justice. 6 For he shall never be shaken; the righteous shall be remembered forever. 7 He shall not fear an ill report; his heart is steadfast, trusting the LORD. 8 His heart is tranquil, without fear, till at last he looks down on his foes. 9 Lavishly he gives to the poor; his righteousness shall endure

forever; his horn shall be exalted in honor. 10 The wicked sees and is angry; gnashes his teeth and wastes away; the desire of the wicked come to nothing."

End with Prayer to the Holy Trinity
NIGHT PRAYER: The Examination of Conscience

DAY FOUR:
MORNING PRAYER: Acts of Faith, Hope, Charity; Daily Offering

MORNING FACE TO FACE WITH GOD:
Begin with Prayer to the Holy Spirit
Prayer on Psalm 114: The Lord's Wonders at the Exodus

Psalm 114 is second in the set of psalms, 113-118, known as the Egyptian Hallel, which were sung during the Passover Meal. The Egyptian Hallel highlights the Exodus event, and all six psalms of praise should be pondered as celebrating one single event, the deliverance of the Israelites from Egypt: *"When Israel came forth from Egypt, the house of Jacob from an alien people, Judah became God's sanctuary, Israel, God's domain."* Israel's deliverance from Egypt was the central act of redemption under the Mosaic Covenant. This event was to be constantly remembered and celebrated, and Psalm 114 joins in the celebration of the Exodus through the Passover Meal. As Christians, we remember and celebrate our redemption through the death and resurrection of Jesus at Mass, the Passover Meal of the New and Eternal Covenant. At Jesus' command, His death on the cross is celebrated in an un-bloody manner in the Eucharist, and we receive the Body, Blood, Soul, and Divinity of the Lamb of God in Holy Communion.

The first two verses offer a sharp contrast in the status of God's people before and after the Exodus. Even though Israel lived for 400 years in Egypt, they were always made to feel like aliens; they did not belong. In fact, the Israelites knew that they would always live among an alien people as an alien people, unless God brought them redemption. Through the Exodus from Egypt, the Israelites finally came to realize their true status in the world: *"Judah became God's sanctuary, Israel, God's domain."* Judah was the leading tribe of Israel (Genesis 49: 10). Judah represented the whole nation and became God's sanctuary, the dwelling place of God in the Temple of Jerusalem. Judah was the chief of all the tribes, not only in number and power, but also in dignity. David was of the tribe of Judah, and Jerusalem, near the territory of Judah, was his capital. Jesus was the son of David and from the tribe of Judah. Judah and Israel are names for the one people that came out of Egypt at the Exodus. They are declared to be both, *'God's sanctuary,'* and *'God's domain.'*

As in other places, the Psalmist personified nature and described it as responding to God either in fear or reverence: *"The sea saw and fled; the Jordan turned back. The mountains skipped like rams; the hills, like lambs."* The parting of the waters at the Red Sea and the Jordan River, the beginning and end of Israel's journey to the Promised Land, offer us a comprehensive description of God's act of salvation through the Exodus. God began a wonderful deed in Egypt and made sure to bring it to a glorious ending in the Promised Land. The Red Sea fled, and the Jordan River turned back because the Lord was there.

The Exodus event is thought of in its completeness, from the escape from Egypt to the entrance into the Promised Land. Both the Red Sea and the Jordan River, obstacles in their path, are overcome by the presence and power of God. During those forty intervening years, God continued to work marvelous deeds. The mountains skipping like rams probably refers to the strong earthquakes and similar phenomena that happened at Mount Sinai (Exodus 19: 16-20), when God manifested His presence there. The mountains and hills did their dance to celebrate God's deliverance of His people and express their joy and reverence.

The last verse continues to sing of God's marvelous deeds during the forty years in the desert as well as ask the earth to join in the praise and adoration of God: *"Tremble, earth, before the Lord, before the God of Jacob, who turned the rock into pools of water, flint into a flowing spring."* Jesus sang the Hallel psalms, #113-118, during the Last Supper, on the night he was betrayed and arrested (Matthew 26: 30 and Mark 14: 26). He was about to bring the first Exodus to its conclusion in His forthcoming exodus in Jerusalem about which Moses and Elijah were conversing with Him during the Transfiguration (Luke 9: 30-31).

Reflect and Pray on Psalm 114, using Lectio Divina or the Method of Meditation. Make sure you converse intimately with the Blessed Trinity:

Prayer on Psalm 114: The Lord's Wonders at the Exodus
"1 When Israel came forth from Egypt, the house of Jacob from an alien people, 2 Judah became God's sanctuary, Israel, God's domain. 3 The sea saw and fled; the Jordan turned back. 4 The mountains skipped like rams; the hills, like lambs. 5 Why was it, sea, that you fled? Jordan, that you turned back? 6 Mountains, that you skipped like rams? You hills, like lambs? 7 Tremble, earth, before the Lord, before the God of Jacob, 8 Who turned the rock into pools of water, flint into a flowing spring."

End with Prayer to the Holy Trinity
NIGHT PRAYER: The Examination of Conscience

DAY FIVE:
MORNING PRAYER: Acts of Faith, Hope, Charity; Daily Offering

MORNING FACE TO FACE WITH GOD:
Begin with Prayer to the Holy Spirit

Prayer on Psalm 118: Hymn of Thanksgiving

Psalm 118 does not name an author in its title, but Ezra 3: 10-11 suggests that Psalm 118 was sung at the founding of the Second Temple after the return from the Babylonian exile, and they attributed it to David: *"While the builders were laying the foundation of the LORD's temple, the priests in the vestments were stationed with trumpets and the Levites, sons of Asaph, with cymbals to praise the LORD in the manner laid down by David, king of Israel. They alternated in songs of praise and thanksgiving to the LORD, "for he is good, for his love for Israel endures forever."* The psalm partakes of David's spirit; its style is grand and noble. More importantly, it is Jesus' psalm, prophesied many centuries ago, which He sang, along with the other Hallel psalms, in the Upper Room during the Passover Meal.

Psalm 118 is a *todah* or thanksgiving psalm that concludes the Egyptian Hallel, the set of 6 psalms that were chanted at the Passover Meal. Originally, this psalm was composed and sung by David at a thanksgiving sacrifice for deliverance from his enemies and success in war. Later, it became part of the Passover service, and Jesus and His Apostles would have recited this psalm at the Last Supper. Psalms 113- 118 are the 'hymn' mentioned in the gospels (Matthew 26: 30) that Jesus and the Apostles sang before leaving the Upper Room for the Garden of Gethsemane.

Psalm 118 opens with an emphatic call to thank God for His goodness and mercy: *"Give thanks to the LORD, for he is good, his mercy endures forever."* The psalm begins and ends with this declaration. God's *hesed,* His loyal covenant bond with His people which is an unbreakable family bond, will never be taken away from His people. This declaration, *'For His mercy endures forever,'* has a liturgical ring to it, and has been used some 34 times in the psalms to praise and thank God for His everlasting loving kindness toward His people. As Jesus sang this amazing refrain, *'For His mercy endures forever,'* He did it with complete knowledge that the endurance of God's mercy would be tested to the utmost during His agony, crucifixion, and death.

The Psalmist invited the people of Israel, the priests of the house of Aaron, and even Gentiles who honored God, to join in praising the enduring mercy of God: *"Let Israel say: his mercy endures forever. Let the house of Aaron say, his mercy endured forever. Let those who fear the LORD say, his mercy endures forever."* Assuming that this psalm was written by David, the priests had special reason for gratitude on his ascent to the throne, for Saul had slaughtered many of the priests and at various times interfered with their sacred office (1Samuel 22: 11-19).

The never-ending mercy of God was shown in times and situations of great crisis: *"In danger I called on the LORD; the LORD answered me and set me free. The LORD is with me; I am not afraid; what can mortals do against me? The LORD is with me as my helper; I shall look in triumph on my foes. Better to take refuge in the LORD than to put one's trust in mortals. Better to take refuge in the LORD than to put one's trust in princes."* David uttered these words after experiencing God's unfailing protection of him. The Israelites pronounced these words during the Passover Meal with the heartfelt realization that God had brought them out of slavery in Egypt to the Promised Land flowing with milk and honey. And Jesus sang these words confidently, calling on His Father in His distress. He knew that His disciples would forsake Him, and He would go to the cross alone and abandoned. Yet he knew, as he uttered Psalm 22 on the cross, that the Father's loving kindness would always be with Him. Amidst great calamity and distress, the LORD works marvelous deeds. Some of the lines are remarkably prophetic as they apply to Jesus: *"I shall not die but live and declare the deeds of the LORD (verse 17)."* Or, *"I thank you for you answered me; you have been my savior (verse 21)."* Or, *"The stone which the builders rejected has become the cornerstone (verse 22)."* Psalm 118 became a prophecy of the Resurrection. Jesus died on the cross for our salvation, and His resurrection was evidence of His divinity! Liturgically, therefore, Psalm 118 plays a dual role. It is both the psalm sung during Holy Week as well as *the* Easter psalm. It is the Responsorial Psalm at all the Easter Masses and frequently through the Easter season.

    The prophecies offered in Psalm 118 can only make sense when applied to Jesus. He is the one who did not die but lived. He died on the cross and rose from the dead! *"The gates of righteousness"* were opened for Jesus when He ascended to the Father, entering the heavenly Temple and seated at the Father's right hand. Jesus personally identified Himself as *"the stone the builders rejected,'* which has become *"the cornerstone"* in Matthew 21: 42: *"Jesus said to them, "Did you never read in the scriptures: 'The stone that the builders rejected has become the cornerstone; by the Lord has this been done, and it is wonderful in our eyes'?* St. Peter was fond of bringing up this verse in his preaching. He mentioned it on two occasions, in Acts 4: 11: *"He is 'the stone rejected by you, the builders, which has become the cornerstone,'* and 1Peter 2: 7: *"Therefore, its value is for you who have faith, but for those without faith: "The stone which the builders rejected has become the cornerstone."* And St. Paul tells us that Jesus is the cornerstone of the Church, a temple built of living stones made up of us: *"You are fellow citizens with the holy ones and members of the household of God, built upon the foundation of the apostles and prophets, with Christ Jesus himself as the capstone"* (Ephesians 2: 19-22). Psalm 118 began with exuberant and heartfelt praise and thanksgiving, and it ends with the same refrain: *"Give thanks to the LORD, for he is good, his mercy endures forever."*

    Reflect and Pray on Psalm 118, using Lectio Divina or the Method of Meditation. Make sure you converse intimately with the Blessed Trinity:

(Pray with Psalm 118 from your Bible)
End with Prayer to the Holy Trinity
NIGHT PRAYER: The Examination of Conscience

DAY SIX:
MORNING PRAYER: Acts of Faith, Hope, Charity; Daily Offering

MORNING FACE TO FACE WITH GOD:
Begin with Prayer to the Holy Spirit
Prayer on Psalm 119: A Prayer to God, the Lawgiver

    Psalm 119 is the longest chapter in the Bible and is an impressive display of poetic prowess. Psalm 119 is arranged in an acrostic pattern. There are 22 letters in the Hebrew alphabet, and this psalm contains 22 units of 8 verses each. Each of the 22 units is given a letter of the Hebrew alphabet, and each line in that unit begins with that letter. So, verses 1-8 all begin with *Aleph* (Hebrew A), verses 9-16 all begin with *Beth* (Hebrew B), and so on, all the way down to *Taw* (Hebrew T), the twenty-second and last letter of the Hebrew alphabet. Therefore, Psalm 119 has eight times twenty-two, or 176 verses!

    The whole theme of Psalm 119 is praise of God's law. This wonderful psalm, from its great length, helps us to wonder at the immensity of Scripture. There are eight basic words used to describe God's written revelation to us in Scripture. These eight basic words are found in almost every one of the twenty-two units, anywhere from 19 to 25 times. They are Law, Word, Judgments, Promise, Commandments, Statutes, Ordinances, Testimonies, Precepts. The Psalmist wants to praise God in every way, from *Aleph* to *Taw*, and he is quite creative. Psalm 119 is remarkable for how often it refers to God's written revelation, His word. It is referred to in almost every verse. The theme of the glory of Scripture is diligently explored in this psalm, but always in connection with God Himself.

Aleph, or the first unit, describes the blessedness of those who walk in God's word and have an intense longing to keep doing so: *"Blessed those whose way is blameless, who walk by the law of the LORD. Blessed those who keep his testimonies, who seek him with all their hearts."*

Beth, or the second unit, highlights purity of life and meditation on God's word. *Beth* means 'a house.' Some have suggested that this section tells us how to make our heart a home for the word of God: *"In my heart I treasure your promise, that I may not sin against you. Blessed are you, O LORD; teach me your statutes."*

Gimel, or the third unit, focuses on the word of God amidst the trials of life: *I am a sojourner in the land; do not hide your commandments from me. ... Free me from disgrace and contempt, for I keep your testimonies."* When we try to follow God's commandments, the world is going to treat us as aliens. The disciple of Jesus will always feel like a sojourner, passing through, to his/her true home, heaven!

Daleth, or the fourth unit, is the prayer of a person who feels dead: *"My soul clings to the dust; give me life in accord with your word. ... My soul is depressed; lift me up according to your word."* The Psalmist was in crisis. Whatever the crisis, it was deep-seated and unbearable. It cleaved his soul. Dust is the place of death, the place of mourning, and the place of humiliation. And yet, the Psalmist has trust and hope in God's mercy and steadfastness: *"I will run the way of your commandments, for you will broaden my heart."*

He, or the fifth unit, makes a plea asking God to bring about a spirit of true guidance in life: *"Direct my heart toward your testimonies and away from gain. Avert my eyes from what is worthless; by your way give me life."* The general desire expressed in this unit is for guidance, so that understanding and doing the will of God becomes the disciple's lifestyle. Without this understanding, the disciple will not be able to follow the desires of their transformed heart.

Waw, or the sixth unit, focuses on asking God for His mercy so that the Psalmist will be protected by God's word and will speak it boldly to others without fear and anxiety: *Let your mercy come to me, LORD, salvation in accord with your promise. Let me answer my taunters with a word, for I trust in your word. ... I will speak openly of your testimonies without fear even before kings."*

Zayin, or the seventh unit, highlights the power of God's word to comfort and strengthen the disciple: *This is my comfort in affliction, your promise that gives me life. Though the arrogant utterly scorn me, I do not turn from your law... Your statutes become my songs wherever I make my home."* When the Psalmist recalled how God's word had brought him life in the past, he then found comfort in his present affliction.

Heth, or the eighth unit, highlights the transformed heart of the Psalmist who cannot live without God anymore. Everything he does and says is focused on God being the Center of his life: *"My portion is the LORD; ... I am prompt, I do not hesitate in observing your commandments. Though the snares of the wicked surround me, your law I do not forget. At midnight I rise to praise you because of your righteous judgments."*

Teth, or the ninth unit, is a prayer of gratitude and praise that God has used his afflictions and lapses to teach him repentance and true discipleship: *"Before I was afflicted I went astray, but now I hold to your promise ... It was good for me to be afflicted, in order to learn your statutes. The law of your mouth is more precious to me than heaps of silver and gold."*

Yodh, or the tenth unit, highlights the complete confidence that the Psalmist has in God as His Creator and His word. Having God at the center of his life has become his lifestyle. Consequently, he is not averse to letting God know how people are attracted to the changes that they see in him. Indeed, he has become and wants to continue being a powerful witness to the LORD: *"Your hands made me and fashioned me; ... Those who fear you rejoice to see me, because I hope in your word... Show me compassion that I may live, for your law is my delight.... Let those who fear you turn to me, those who acknowledge your testimonies."*

Kaph, or the eleventh unit, highlights the dire straits of the Psalmist. He is sorely afflicted, yet has confidence that he will be revived by God's word: *"I am like a wineskin shriveled by smoke, but I have not forgotten your statutes... They have almost put an end to me on earth, but I do not forsake your precepts. In your mercy give me life, to observe the testimonies of your mouth."*

Lamedh, or the twelfth unit, reflects on the unchanging and enduring word of God because it is from heaven. God's word will always prevail and be a source of strength for the disciple: *"Your word, LORD, stands forever; it is firm as the heavens. Through all generations your truth endures; fixed to stand firm like the earth ... Had your law not been my delight, I would have perished in my affliction."*

Mem, or the thirteenth unit, highlights the sweetness of God's word and the need to love it with all one's heart. It is a song of praise, a pure outpouring of the heart: *"How I love your law, Lord! I study it all day long. ... I have more insight than all my teachers, because I ponder your testimonies. I have more understanding than my elders because I keep your precepts. ... How sweet to my tongue is your promise, sweeter than honey to my mouth!"*

Nun, or the fourteenth unit, emphasizes the Psalmist's unreserved commitment to God's word. Obedience to God's word has become his lifestyle. Notwithstanding the perils and adversities of life, God's precepts are the lamp that guides his feet: *"Your word is a lamp for my feet, a light for my path ... Accept my freely offered praise; LORD, teach me your judgments. My life is always at risk, but I do not forget your law ... My heart is set on fulfilling your statutes; they are my reward forever."*

Samekh, or the fifteenth unit, draws a clear distinction between the way of the righteous and the way of the wicked. They are bitter enemies. The righteous are God's chosen ones; the wicked have rejected God and chosen to be His enemy: *"You are my refuge and shield; in your word I hope. Depart from me, you wicked, that I may keep the commandments of my God ... You reject all who stray from your statutes, for vain is their deceit. Like dross you regard all the wicked on earth; therefore I love your testimonies."*

Ayin, or the sixteenth unit, seeks protection from the Lord against oppressors and the proud. It is not a claim to sinless perfection. Rather, he knew that his life was dedicated to God, and theirs was not: *"I have fulfilled your righteous judgment; do not abandon me to my oppressors. Guarantee your servant's welfare; do not let the arrogant oppress me... I am your servant; give me discernment that I may know your testimonies."*

Pe, or the seventeenth unit, highlight the passionate love that the disciple has developed for God's revelation because their life has been transformed. Simultaneously, they mourn at the fact that God's law is not respected and followed by many around them: *"Wonderful are your testimonies; therefore I keep them... Let your face shine upon your servant; teach me your statutes. My eyes shed streams of tears because your law is not observed."*

Sadhe, or the eighteenth unit, emphasizes the purity and truth of God's word. The written word of God reflects both His righteous character and His faithfulness: *"You are righteous, LORD, and just are your judgments. You have given your testimonies in righteousness and in surpassing faithfulness. ... I rise before dawn and cry out; I put my hope in your words. My eyes greet the night watches as I meditate on your promise... Long have I know from your testimonies that you have established them forever."*

Resh, or the twentieth unit, continues to emphasize the need to be faithful to God's word in times of affliction and hardship. For some, affliction drives them away from God and His word. The psalmist looked for help and salvation outside of himself, in God: *"Look at my affliction and rescue me, for I have not forgotten your law ...Salvation is far from sinners because they do not cherish your statutes, ...Though my persecutors and foes are many, I do not turn from your testimonies ...Your every word is enduring; all your righteous judgments are forever."*

Shin, or the twenty-first unit, expresses the Psalmist's awe of God's word. There is a quiet appreciation and an obedient waiting on God: *"Seven times a day I praise you because your judgments are righteous. Lovers of your law have much peace; for them there is no stumbling block ... I observe your testimonies; I love them very much."*

Taw, or the twenty-second unit, is nearing the end of the psalm. The Psalmist has intensified his entreaties; his petitions exude an intimacy and utmost trust in God. Like Isaiah, he is deeply aware of God's holiness and providence, and his own sinfulness in God's presence: *"May my tongue sing of your promise, for all your commandments are righteous. Keep your hand ready to help me, for I have chosen your precepts. ... I have wandered like a lost sheep; seek out your servant, for I do not forget your commandments."*

Psalm 119 reminds us that the Law of God – whether summarized in the Ten Commandments, the Double Commandment of Love, or the Sermon on the Mount – is a path to liberty and to life.

Reflect and Pray on Psalm 119, using Lectio Divina or the Method of Meditation. Make sure you converse intimately with the Blessed Trinity:

(Pray with Psalm 119 from your Bible)End with Prayer to the Holy Trinity
NIGHT PRAYER: Examination of Conscience

DAY SEVEN:
MORNING PRAYER: Acts of Faith, Hope, Charity; Daily Offering

MORNING FACE TO FACE WITH GOD:
Learning Discipleship from the Psalms

Begin with Prayer to the Holy Spirit
- Psalm 107 is full of praise and thanksgiving to God for bringing the Israelites home from exile. They can now rebuild the Temple, God's abode among them, even though they no longer will have a king to rule over them. God is especially good because *'His mercy endures forever!'* It is the people's appreciative declaration of the great loving kindness or covenant love of God, a forgiving and merciful love that endures forever, from everlasting to everlasting.
- Psalm 107 was anticipating Jesus who became our kinsman-redeemer by buying us back for His Father with the price that He paid on the cross! Indeed, God's mercy has endured forever through Jesus' sacrifice on the cross! In the present context, through God's enduring mercy, *"those redeemed from the hand of the foe, those gathered from foreign lands,"* were able to return home.
- Psalm 110 harkens back to the time of David, not the time after the exile. Despite having no king anymore, the king is making an appearance here again. Clearly, the psalm is a prophecy of Jesus, son of David, who will be the Messiah-King and Priest. Psalm 110 is the most quoted and influential psalm in the New Testament. Several quotes have been made by Jesus Himself.
- The opening verse of Psalm 110 sets the tone which highlights the Messiah as both King and Priest: *"The LORD says to my lord: "Sit at my right hand, while I make your enemies your footstool."* David prophetically revealed the words of the LORD (God the Father) to the

  Messiah, David's lord, who would be Jesus. This meaning is especially clear by the way this verse is quoted and interpreted in the New Testament.
- Jesus quoted this verse, recognizing that the Messiah was greater than David himself: *"As Jesus was teaching in the temple area he said, "How do the scribes claim that the Messiah is the son of David? David himself, inspired by the holy Spirit, said; 'The Lord said to my lord, "Sit at my right*

hand until I place your enemies under your feet.'" David himself calls him 'lord'; so how is he his son?" (Mark 12: 35-37).
- Peter quoted it after Pentecost, as David's prophecy about the divinity of Jesus and His Ascension: *"For David did not go up into heaven, but he himself said: 'The Lord said to my Lord, "Sit at my right hand until I make your enemies your footstool."' Therefore let the whole house of Israel know for certain that God made him both Lord and Messiah, this Jesus whom you crucified"* (Acts 2: 34-36). In Peter's quote, *'The Lord said to my Lord'* (Acts 2: 34), the uppercase for the second 'Lord' clearly refers to Jesus.
- This divine Sonship comes with a priestly role: *"You are a priest forever in the manner of Melchizedek."* Melchizedek was the ancient priest-king of Jerusalem (called just 'Salem' in Genesis 14: 18) who blessed Abraham. When David became king of Jerusalem in 2Samuel 5, he became the heir of Melchizedek's role and titles. David, too, became a priest, as we see him leading worship and wearing priestly clothing in 2Samuel 6, even though he did not belong to the tribe of Levi from which the priests came. This role was passed on to his sons who were also priests (2Samuel 8: 18).
- The Letter to the Hebrews explains how it is that Jesus, Son of David, is God's High Priest even though he does not come from the line of Aaron and Levi: *"It is clear that our Lord arose from Judah, and in regard to that tribe Moses said nothing about priests. It is even more obvious if another priest is raised up after the likeness of Melchizedek, who has become so, not by a law expressed in a commandment concerning physical descent but by the power of a life that cannot be destroyed. For it is testified: "You are a priest forever according to the order of Melchizedek"* (Hebrews 7: 14-17).
- This testament or oath that Jesus is a priest forever according to the order of Melchizedek was so important that the Letter to the Hebrews refers to it five times! This was The Father's declaration as to who His Son would be, not a claim that Jesus

made for Himself. Jesus serves now and forever as a living, active High Priest, interceding before His Father in heaven for them. The priesthood according to the order of Melchizedek replaced the priestly order of Aaron. Psalm 111 focuses on praise and thanksgiving to God for His presence and revelation in Israel's history. His deeds among His people reveal God in His power, mercy, and faithfulness. A fitting nugget to glean from this rich treasure trove is in the last verse: *"The fear of the LORD is the beginning of wisdom; prudent are all who practice it. His praise endures forever."*

- Psalm 114 is second in the set of psalms, 113-118, known as the Egyptian Hallel, which were sung during the Passover Meal. The Egyptian Hallel highlights the Exodus event, and all six psalms of praise should be pondered as celebrating one single event, the deliverance of the Israelites from Egypt: *"When Israel came forth from Egypt, the house of Jacob from an alien people, Judah became God's sanctuary, Israel, God's domain."* This event was to be constantly remembered and celebrated, and Psalm 114 joins in the celebration of the Exodus through the Passover Meal.

- Jesus sang the Hallel psalms, #113-118, during the Last Supper, on the night he was betrayed and arrested (Matthew 26: 30 and Mark 14: 26). He was about to bring the first Exodus to its conclusion, through His exodus in Jerusalem about which Moses and Elijah were conversing with Him during the Transfiguration (Luke 9: 30-31).

- Psalm 118 is a *todah* or thanksgiving psalm that concludes the Egyptian Hallel, the set of 6 psalms that were chanted at the Passover Meal. Originally, this psalm was composed and sung by David at a thanksgiving sacrifice for deliverance from his enemies and success in war. Later, it became part of the Passover service, and Jesus and His Apostles would have recited this psalm at the Last Supper. Psalms 113-118 are the 'hymn' mentioned in the gospels (Matthew 26: 30) that Jesus and the Apostles sang before leaving the Upper Room for the Garden of Gethsemane.

- Psalm 118 opens and ends with an emphatic call to thank God for His goodness and mercy: *"Give thanks to the LORD, for he is good, his mercy endures forever."* God's *hesed,* His loyal covenant bond with His people which is an unbreakable family bond, will never be broken or taken away from His people. This declaration, *'For His mercy endures forever,'* has been used some 34 times in the psalms to praise and thank God for His everlasting loving kindness toward His people. As Jesus sang this amazing refrain, *'For His mercy endures forever,'* He did it with complete knowledge that the endurance of God's mercy would be tested to the utmost in Him during His agony, crucifixion, and death.
- The never-ending mercy of God was shown in times and situations of great crisis: *"In danger I called on the LORD; the LORD answered me and set me free. The LORD is with me; I am not afraid; what can mortals do against me? The LORD is with me as my helper; I shall look in triumph on my foes. Better to take refuge in the LORD than to put one's trust in mortals. Better to take refuge in the LORD than to put one's trust in princes."* Jesus sang these words confidently, calling on His Father in His distress. He knew that His disciples would forsake Him, and He would go to the cross alone and abandoned. Yet he knew, as He uttered Psalm 22 on the cross, that the Father's loving kindness would always be with Him.
- Psalm 119 is the longest chapter in the Bible. The whole theme of Psalm 119 is praise of God's law. There are eight basic words used to describe God's written revelation to us in Scripture. They are Law, Word, Judgments, Promise, Commandments, Statutes, Ordinances, Testimonies, Precepts. Psalm 119 reminds us that the Law of God – whether summarized in the Ten Commandments, the Double Commandment of Love, or the Sermon on the Mount – is a path to liberty and to life.

End with Prayer to the Holy Trinity
NIGHT PRAYER: Examination of Conscience

JOURNAL FOR BOOK FIVE, WEEK ONE: LOOKING TOWARD THE MESSIAH

DAY ONE: Morning Prayer: Psalm 107: God the Savior of Those in Distress
What is God saying to You?

Nightly Examination of Conscience:
For what are you grateful?

For what are you contrite?

What spiritual discipline, including fasting, do you need to focus on tomorrow?

DAY TWO: Morning Prayer: Psalm 110: God appoint the King both King and Priest
What is God saying to You?

Nightly Examination of Conscience:
For what are you grateful?

For what are you contrite?

What spiritual discipline, including fasting, do you need to focus on tomorrow?

DAY THREE: Morning Prayer: Psalm 112: The Blessings of the Just
What is God saying to You?

Nightly Examination of Conscience:
For what are you grateful?

For what are you contrite?

What spiritual discipline, including fasting, do you need to focus on tomorrow?

DAY FOUR: Morning Prayer: Psalm 114: The Lord's Wonders at the Exodus
What is God saying to You?

Nightly Examination of Conscience:
For what are you grateful?

For what are you contrite?

What spiritual discipline, including fasting, do you need to focus on tomorrow?

DAY FIVE: Morning Prayer: Psalm 118: Hymn of Thanksgiving
What is God saying to You?

Nightly Examination of Conscience:
For what are you grateful?

For what are you contrite?

What spiritual discipline, including fasting, do you need to focus on tomorrow?

DAY SIX: Morning Prayer: Psalm 119: A Prayer to God, the Lawgiver
What is God saying to You?

Nightly Examination of Conscience:
For what are you grateful?

For what are you contrite?

What spiritual discipline, including fasting, do you need to focus on tomorrow?

DAY SEVEN: Morning Prayer: Learning Discipleship from the Psalms
What is God saying to You?

Nightly Examination of Conscience:
For what are you grateful?

For what are you contrite?

What spiritual discipline, including fasting, do you need to focus on tomorrow?

What prayer would you compose to express what God has said to you this week?

BOOK FIVE: PSALMS 107 TO 150: LOOKING TOWARD THE MESSIAH
Psalms 120, 122, 127,130, 132, and 136

WHAT IS AT THE HEART OF BOOK FIVE, WEEK TWO?

During Week Two of Book Five, we will pray with Psalms 120, 122, 127, 130, 132, and 136. It was the tradition among the Israelites to sing psalms as they went on pilgrimage to the Temple in Jerusalem, before and after the exile. Consequently, a whole set of sacred songs grew up around the pilgrimage festivals and other pilgrimages to the Temple. They are called 'Psalms of Ascent,' because Jerusalem is situated on top of the mountain range that runs through Israel, from north to south. You almost always had to ascend to Jerusalem. 1Chronicles 13: 6 uses this term 'ascent' or 'bringing up,' to describe the bringing up of the Ark of the Covenant to Jerusalem: *"David and all Israel went up to Baalah, that is, to Kiriath-jearim, of Judah, to bring up from there the ark of God, which was known by the name "LORD enthroned upon the cherubim."* Gradually, these Psalms of Ascent, #120-134, came to be included in the Psalter. After them, two litanies of praise, Psalms 135 and 136, were included, to end the Psalter on a resounding note of thanksgiving. Once upon a time, therefore, the Book of Psalms ended with Psalm 136. During this week, we will reflect on five psalms of ascent, and on Psalm 136 which is a litany of praise and thanksgiving.

As stated earlier, pilgrims from before and after the Babylonian exile, sang these psalms as they approached Jerusalem and the Temple to celebrate the pilgrimage festivals. After the exile, there was added reason to go on pilgrimage to Jerusalem, as the Temple was rebuilt. These songs of longing for God, hope in His loving kindness, and the immediate proximity to the Temple, expressed the sentiments of the pilgrims as they went up to worship their covenant God! We know that the Holy Family, and Jesus during His ministry, went up annually to Jerusalem and the Temple to worship and celebrate the pilgrimage festivals. They too sang these songs of ascent as they approached Jerusalem and the Temple.

Psalm 120: Prayer of a Returned Exile, is a song of thanksgiving for God's rescue, along with fervent prayer for further protection from lying attackers. The people of God often found themselves in distressing circumstances. They knew, however, that they always had a refuge in God in their distress; they could do as the Psalmist did when he cried to the LORD. They could share the singer's testimony, *'the LORD answered me.'* As the pilgrim's journey to Jerusalem began, he was mindful of the weariness endured living apart from the supportive community of God's people. The Psalmist *needed* this trip to Jerusalem at festival time to be in the larger community of the people of God. The psalm begins with a prayer for deliverance and ends with an aching need for peace, or rest in God. It sets forth the discordance between a man and his environment, which urges the soul that feels it to seek a better home. Hence, it is a true pilgrim psalm. Our hearts are restless unless they rest in Thee, O Lord.

We will reflect on *Psalm 122: A Pilgrim's Prayer for Jerusalem,* on Day Two. Psalm 122 is one of the four Songs of Ascent that are specifically attributed to King David. It is possible that David wrote this psalm for the pilgrimage festivals celebrated at the makeshift temple that was regarded as the house of the LORD where David set up the tabernacle and where the Ark of the Covenant and the altar of sacrifice were. It seems more likely that David wrote this psalm in anticipation of the pilgrims who would come to the house of the LORD built by Solomon. The primary purpose of the feasts of Israel was for the people of God to come together and give Him thanks. Their appreciation for what He had done gave them faith for what He would do in the future. The gladness of the pilgrim toward God's city was primarily because the house of the LORD was established there.

On Day Three, we will reflect on *Psalm 127: The Need of God's Blessing.* This is one of Solomon's psalms of ascents, where he displays the wisdom given to him by God concerning matters of the 'house' or family life. The Psalmist is highlighting the central role that God should have in family life. Every circumstance of life should be ordered toward the preservation and well-being of the family. Such security can only be brought about by God. Solomon knew little of this blessing from God. Like much of Solomon's wisdom, the lessons of this psalm were lost on him because he turned away from God. His house became reckless, his kingdom ended in ruin, and his marriages, a denial of God (1Kings 11: 1ff). On Day Four, we will reflect on *Psalm 130: Prayer for Pardon and Mercy,* which begins with a personal testimony of God's rescue from the depths of guilt. From there, the author ascends step by step to a place where he can give confidence to others in their trust in God. Psalm 130 is counted among the seven Penitential Psalms because it is marked by an awareness of sin and a powerful assurance of forgiveness. It is also a pilgrim psalm, or song of ascents, as it bears all the sentiments of a pilgrim's heart.

Psalm 132: The Covenant between David and God, will be our topic for prayer on Day Five. Psalm 132 can be pondered as a covenant ritual between David and God. They are renewing their covenant promises to each other, sealing the unbreakable family bond between them. For the returned Israelites from the Babylonian exile, a meaningful pondering on the past events in the history of Israel would have been helpful. Psalm 132 was sung by the pilgrims going to the Temple in Jerusalem during the pilgrimage festivals. They remembered David's generous heart and commitment to God and used it as their own inspiration. God promised that He would not forsake the sons of David (2Samuel 7: 14-16). While every king of David's line was God's anointed, this prophecy was especially fulfilled in the ultimate Anointed One, Jesus the Messiah.

On Day Six, we will pray with *Psalm 136: Hymn of Thanksgiving for God's Everlasting Mercy.* It is called the Great Hallel for the way it proclaims God's goodness regarding His people and encourages them to praise Him for His merciful and steadfast love. The Psalmist made sure that this sentiment would reverberate through all its verses, from the beginning, through the middle, to the very end: *"Praise the God of heaven, for his mercy endures forever."* The psalm goes over the great events of salvation history – creation, exodus, conquest, settlement, and return from exile – the dramatic moments when God shaped His people Israel. Through it all, God has been faithful to His covenant. Psalm 136 tells us that God is good to all creatures and that He keeps His promises. No psalm emphasizes this central theme more than Psalm 136, where it is repeated 26 times!

On Day Seven, you will ponder the salient advice that these psalms have offered us to enhance and strengthen our own following of Jesus and our commitment to His Church.

SPIRITUAL READING FOR BOOK FIVE OF THE PSALMS:
Psalms 107 to 150
Books of Ezra and Nehemiah Isaiah: Chapters 56-66
Ezekiel: Chapters 33-48

DAY ONE:
MORNING PRAYER: Acts of Faith, Hope, Charity; Daily Offering
MORNING FACE TO FACE WITH GOD:
Begin with Prayer to the Holy Spirit
Prayer on Psalm 120: Prayer of a Returned Exile

Psalm 120 is the first of the 15 songs of Ascents. Probably the best explanation for calling them 'songs of ascents' is because they were sung by the Israelites as they made their way to Jerusalem and the Temple at the three appointed pilgrimage festivals: Passover, Pentecost, and Tabernacles. They are called 'Psalms of Ascents,' because Jerusalem is situated on top of the mountain range that runs through Israel, from north to south. You almost always had to ascend to Jerusalem. 1Chronicles 13: 6 uses this term 'ascent' or 'bringing up,' to describe the bringing up of the Ark of the Covenant to Jerusalem: *"David and all Israel went up to Baalah, that is, to Kiriath-jearim, of Judah, to bring up from there the ark of God, which was known by the name "LORD enthroned upon the cherubim."*

Pilgrims, from before and after the Babylonian exile, sang these psalms as they approached Jerusalem and the Temple to celebrate the pilgrimage festivals. After the exile, there was added reason to go on pilgrimage to Jerusalem, as the Temple was rebuilt. These songs of longing for God, hope in His loving kindness, and the immediate proximity to the Temple, expressed the sentiments of the pilgrims as they went up to worship their covenant God! We know that the Holy Family, and later Jesus during His ministry, went up annually to Jerusalem and the Temple to worship and celebrate the pilgrimage festivals. They too sang these songs of ascents as they approached Jerusalem and the Temple.

Psalm 120 is a song of thanksgiving for God's rescue, along with fervent prayer for further protection from lying attackers: *"The LORD answered me when I called in my distress: LORD, deliver my soul from lying lips, from a treacherous tongue."* The people of God often found themselves in distressing circumstances. They knew, however, that they always had a refuge in God in their distress; they could do as the Psalmist did when he cried to the LORD. They could share the singer's testimony, *'the LORD answered me.'* The distress had to do over 'lying lips' and treacherous tongues. Evil words were spoken against the Psalmist. There was some comfort in this cry to the LORD, knowing that the evil that was spoken against him was not true. We all need deliverance from lies, both the lies that are told *about us,* and the lies that are said *to us.* We can stay uncontaminated by lies told *about us* if we strive to live blamelessly in the ways of the Lord. Lies told *to us* could be about God, about family and friends, about events taking place in the world and the Church; lies about the purpose of life, one's identity, etc. From *these* lies, *'deliver my soul'*, O LORD.

The Psalmist then shifted from his prayer to God, to address the *false tongue* of those who caused him distress. He warned those lying lips of their destiny, of *'what he will inflict on you, O treacherous tongue, and what more besides?'* A treacherous tongue is likened to a sharp razor (Psalm 52: 4), to a sharp sword

(Psalm 57: 5), to sharp arrows (Proverbs 20: 18). The 'treacherous tongue' of the Psalmist's enemies would soon know 'a warrior's arrows.' The warrior's arrows of judgment *'sharpened with coals of brush wood.'* would come against them. The term, *'Coals of brushwood',* suggests that the arrows have been made with the intense heat of brushwood (the Juniper or broom plant) which retains its heat for a long time: The insolent liar will be destroyed with far more potent shafts: *"In all circumstances, hold faith as a shield, to quench all [the] flaming arrows of the evil one. And take the helmet of salvation and the sword of the Spirit, which is the word of God"* (Ephesians 6: 16).

Meshech was a distant place, far from the land of Israel (Ezekiel 27: 13, 32: 26, 39: 1). Kedar was a place associated with the nomadic tribes in the lands surrounding Israel (1Chronicles 1: 29, Isaiah 21: 16-17, Jeremiah 49: 28). They were located so far apart geographically that they can only be taken here as a general term for the heathen. They are examples of warlike tribes, among whom the singers of Psalm 120 had no true home. The Psalmist ached that he lived among the ungodly, distant from Israel and its people. He longed for God's shalom, peace.

As the pilgrim's journey to Jerusalem began, he was mindful of the weariness endured living apart from the supportive community of God's people. The Psalmist *needed* this trip to Jerusalem at festival time to be in the larger community of the people of God. The psalm began with a prayer for deliverance and ends with an aching need for peace, or rest in God. It sets forth the discordance between a man and his environment, which urges the soul that feels it to seek a better home. Hence, it is a true pilgrim psalm. Our hearts are restless unless they rest in Thee, O Lord.

Reflect and Pray on Psalm 120, using Lectio Divina or the Method of Meditation. Make sure you converse intimately with the Blessed Trinity:

Prayer on Psalm 120: Prayer of a Returned Exile
"1 A song of ascents. The LORD answered me when I called in my distress: 2 LORD, deliver my soul from lying lips, from a

treacherous tongue. 3 What will he inflict on you, O treacherous tongue, and what more besides? 4 A warrior's arrows sharpened with coals of brush wood! 5 Alas, I am a foreigner in Meshech, I live among the tents of Kedar! 6 Too long do I live among those who hate peace. 7 When I speak of peace, they are for war."

End with Prayer to the Holy Trinity
NIGHT PRAYER: The Examination of Conscience

DAY TWO:
MORNING PRAYER: Acts of Faith, Hope, Charity; Daily Offering

MORNING FACE TO FACE WITH GOD:
Begin with Prayer to the Holy Spirit
Prayer on Psalm 122: A Pilgrim's Prayer for Jerusalem

Psalm 122 is one of the four Songs of Ascents that are specifically attributed to King David. He wrote it for what Jerusalem was in his day, and for what it would become under his son who would build the Temple, and his successors after Solomon. As far as Psalm 122 is concerned, he seems to have written it for those who were ascending to Jerusalem as pilgrims from the far corners of the kingdom. This psalm seemed suitable for singing when the people had entered the gates of the city, and their feet were within the city. It is reasonable to suppose that David wrote this psalm both to express joy in his new Capital city, and to encourage loyalty toward it as the focal point of the nation's political life and religious worship.

During David's day there was a makeshift temple, a tent made of goatskins. But he knew one would be built, having extensively planned and prepared for it (1Chronicles 22: 2-16). It seems likely that David wrote this psalm in anticipation of the pilgrims who would come to the house of the LORD built by Solomon. They came to Jerusalem because that was where David set up the tabernacle and where the ark of the covenant and the altar of sacrifice were. Later, Solomon built the Temple in Jerusalem that David had prepared for and planned. It is wonderful to think of David's extensive preparation for the people of Israel to come to the temple, especially for the required feasts three times a year.

David had conquered the city of Jerusalem, taking it from the Jebusites who held it as a Canaanite stronghold. David built the city in his own day, and rejoiced in declaring, *'Jerusalem, built as a city.'* Jerusalem was formerly Jebus, a place where the Jebusites committed their abominations like child sacrifice to Moloch. But now, it is devoted to God's service and has become the City of God! Jerusalem was located on the crest of Mount Zion and Mount Moriah, bounded on two sides by steep descents to the Kidron and Tyropaeon valleys, and thus, no more than half a mile in breadth. It had a dramatic setting for one approaching it from a distance, and its tight structure would have impressed any observer. David conquered Jerusalem and established it as the capital of both the political and religious life of Israel because it did not previously belong to a specific tribe, being under Canaanite occupation. It then belonged to all the tribes of the LORD who could come together as one to the house of the LORD. The primary purpose of the feasts of Israel was for the people of God to come together and give Him thanks. Their appreciation for what He had done gave them faith for what He would do in the future.

Jerusalem was to be a city of *justice,* where good was honored and evil corrected. The thrones were for dispensing judgment and may have been visible at the gates of the city. David's house was established to reign over Israel. David's lineage reigned in Jerusalem and will forever reign in the Messiah, the Son of David. Jesus talks about His disciples occupying the thrones of justice in the new Israel, His Church: *"Amen, I say to you that you who have followed me, in the new age, when the Son of Man is seated on his throne of glory, will yourselves sit on twelve thrones, judging the twelve tribes of Israel"* (Matthew 19: 28).

David exhorted pilgrims coming to the holy City to pray for the peace of the city. Jerusalem's name itself marks it as the city of peace (Hebrews 7: 2); in reality it has known much war and conflict, which continues to this day. It is good to pray for the often-elusive peace of Jerusalem. David prayed for blessings for those who loved and prayed for Jerusalem, but the blessing was not only for the individual but for the community of those who cared for the peace of Jerusalem, those who said, *"Peace be with you."* The gladness of the pilgrim toward God's city was not primarily political in nature. It was because the LORD'S house was established there.

David's motive for the prosperity of Jerusalem was twofold: love of God who had fixed the abode of His glory there, and his love of the people of God, his fellow tribal kinsfolk whose happiness was involved in that of their city. The most important reason to love and care for Jerusalem was because it contained the house of the LORD.

Reflect and Pray on Psalm 122, using Lectio Divina or the Method of Meditation. Make sure you converse intimately with the Blessed Trinity:

Prayer on Psalm 122: A Pilgrim's Prayer for Jerusalem
"1. A song of Ascents. Of David.

I.

I rejoiced when they said to me, "Let us go to the house of the LORD." 2 And now our feet are standing within your gates, Jerusalem. 3 Jerusalem built as a city, walled round about. 4 There the tribes go up, the tribes of the LORD, as it was decreed for Israel, to give thanks to the name of the LORD. 5 There are thrones of justice, the thrones of the house of David.

II.

6 For the peace of Jerusalem pray: "May those who love you prosper! 7 May peace be within your ramparts, prosperity within your towers." 8 For the sake of my brothers and friends I say, "Peace be with you." 9 For the sake of the house of the LORD, our God, I pray for your good."

End with Prayer to the Holy Trinity
NIGHT PRAYER: The Examination of Conscience

DAY THREE:
MORNING PRAYER: Acts of Faith, Hope, Charity; Daily Offering

MORNING FACE TO FACE WITH GOD:

Begin with Prayer to the Holy Spirit
Prayer on Psalm 127: The Need of God's Blessing
   Psalm 127 is titled, *'A song of ascents. Of Solomon.'* This is one of Solomon's psalms where he displays the wisdom given to him by God concerning matters of the 'house' or family life. Most probably, it was composed during the early years of his reign when Solomon listened and received his wisdom from God Himself! The Psalmist is highlighting the central role that God should have in family life. Every circumstance of life should be ordered toward the preservation and well-being of the family. such security and well-being can only be brought about by God: *"Unless the LORD build the house, they labor in vain who build. Unless the LORD guard the city, in vain does the guard keep watch. It is vain for you to rise early and put off your rest at night, to eat bread earned by hard toil – all this God gives to his beloved in sleep."* Solomon understood that the work of man had its place. However, it was of little importance in the larger scheme of things, without the work and blessing of God. Without God's blessing, *'they labor in vain who build it.'*

   Solomon himself knew what it was like to both build his own house, as well as the house of God, and to guard the city. In his wisdom, Solomon understood that though God welcomed and even commanded human effort, His work and blessing were more important. Hard work for the purpose of providing daily food and clothing for oneself and the family is ennobled by trusting the Lord in one's work and doing it for His praise and glory.

   In Segment II, Solomon extols the special blessing of children to a family or house: *"Certainly sons are a gift from the LORD, the fruit of the womb, a reward. Like arrows in the hand of a warrior are the sons born in one's youth. Blessed is the man who has filled his quiver with them. He will never be shamed for he will destroy his foes at the gate."* Children are God's special gift that characterize a family. Then as now, the family is the basic unit and most important priority of society. Children are to be raised *'like arrows in the hand of a warrior.'* They must be carefully shaped and formed, guided with skill and strength, given much care or they will not fly straight. They must be given direction as they will not find direction on their own. They are an extension of the warrior's strength and skill. They have potential for much good or evil.

Solomon describes children as *'the fruit of the womb.'* Sadly, though Solomon had 700 wives and 300 concubines (1Kings 11: 3), we know of only one of his descendants, Rehoboam, who succeeded him as king (1Kings 12). Solomon knew little of this blessing from God. Like much of Solomon's wisdom, the lessons of this psalm were lost on him because he turned away from God: *"The LORD became angry with Solomon, because his heart turned away from the LORD, the God of Israel, who had appeared to him twice and commanded him not to do this very thing, not to follow other gods. But he did not observe what the LORD commanded"* (1Kings 11: 9-10). His house became reckless, his kingdom was in ruin, and his marriages, a moral denial of God (1Kings 11: 1ff).

Reflect and Pray on Psalm 127, using Lectio Divina or the Method of Meditation. Make sure you converse intimately with the Blessed Trinity:

Prayer on Psalm 127: The Need of God's Blessing
"1 A song of ascents. Of Solomon.

I.

Unless the LORD build the house, they labor in vain who build. Unless the LORD guard the city, in vain does the guard keep watch. 2 It is vain for you to rise early and put off your rest at night, to eat bread earned by hard toil – all this God gives to his beloved in sleep.

II.

3 Certainly sons are a gift from the LORD, the fruit of the womb, a reward. 4 Like arrows in the hand of a warrior are the sons born in one's youth. 5 Blessed is the man who has filled his quiver with them. He will never be shamed for he will destroy his foes at the gate."

End with Prayer to the Holy Trinity
NIGHT PRAYER: The Examination of Conscience

DAY FOUR:
MORNING PRAYER: Acts of Faith, Hope, Charity; Daily Offering
MORNING FACE TO FACE WITH GOD:
Begin with Prayer to the Holy Spirit
Prayer on Psalm 130: Prayer for Pardon and Mercy

 Psalm 130 begins with a personal testimony of God's rescue from the depths of guilt. From there, the author ascends step by step to a place where he can give confidence to others in their trust in God. Psalm 130 is counted among the seven penitential psalms because it is marked by an awareness of sin and a powerful assurance of forgiveness. It is also a pilgrim psalm, or song of ascents, as it bears all the sentiments of a pilgrim's heart.

 The psalm begins with an urgent plea for forgiveness: *"Out of the depths I call to you, LORD; Lord hear my cry! May your ears be attentive to my cry for mercy. If you, LORD, keep account of sins, Lord, who can stand? But with you is forgiveness and so you are revered."* In other psalms, too, there have been cries from the depths: from the watery depths of the earth as in Psalm 71: 20; from the depths of Sheol as in Psalm 86:13. Once again, from a place of deep and overwhelming danger, the Psalmist cries out to the LORD God. The depth that the Psalmist cried from was the depth of the awareness and guilt of sin. Many have been spiritually drowned in these depths. In asking God to help, the Psalmist also understood that he had no confident reason to ask or be heard by God apart from His great forgiveness. Without this divine graciousness toward us, no one can stand before God! While it is true that the LORD marks all iniquity in His children because He is Justice, He does not do so in order to condemn them. Or else, *'who can stand?'* *'To stand'* is a judicial phrase. The Psalmist notes that the sinner's verdict is absolution or justification rather than condemnation or the guilty verdict. Fear and doubt and misgiving may question but cannot revoke it: *"But with you is forgiveness and so you are revered."*

 Having made his cry from the depths to God, the Psalmist then is determined to wait upon God for his rescue: *"I wait for the*

LORD, my soul waits and I hope for his word. My soul looks for the Lord more than sentinels for daybreak."* The Psalmist could wait upon the LORD because his waiting was filled with hope upon God's promises. The vivid image that he uses of the sentinel, tells us how intense his waiting on God was. The watchman does not doubt that morning will come, but only wonders when. The Psalmist waited with certain expectation that God's forgiveness would come to him even though he did not know when.

In this psalm, we hear of the pearl of great price, our redemption: *"Let Israel hope in the LORD, for with the LORD is mercy, with him is plenteous redemption, and he will redeem Israel from all its sins."* Had the Psalmist not been cast into the depths, he never would have found the pearl of great price. One of the great purposes of God's great forgiveness is to build a sense of gratitude and reverence in those He forgives. Those who have been forgiven are softened and humbled and overwhelmed by God's mercy. They determine never again to sin against such a great and loving kindness. When they do sin, they hurry back to God for deliverance. What the Psalmist has learned from his personal life, he wishes to offer to the whole nation. When God's people humbly look to Him, there is mercy and plenteous redemption. This is the confident conclusion to the psalm, demonstrating trust that God will indeed bring redemption and rescue to both individual and nation overwhelmed in the depths of their sin. The Psalmist is liberated from 'the depths of his own soul,' and can hold out hopes that are far from being tentative.

Reflect and Pray on Psalm 130, using Lectio Divina or the Method of Meditation. Make sure you converse intimately with the Blessed Trinity:

Prayer on Psalm 130: Prayer for Pardon and Mercy
"1 A song of ascents.

I.

Out of the depths I call to you, LORD; 2 Lord hear my cry! May your ears be attentive to my cry for mercy. 3 If you, LORD, keep account of sins, Lord, who can stand? 4 But with you is forgiveness and so you are revered.

II.
5 I wait for the LORD, my soul waits and I hope for his word. 6 My soul looks for the Lord more than sentinels for daybreak, 7 Let Israel hope in the LORD, for with the LORD is mercy, with him is plenteous redemption, 8 And he will redeem Israel from all its sins."

End with Prayer to the Holy Trinity
NIGHT PRAYER: The Examination of Conscience

DAY FIVE:
MORNING PRAYER: Acts of Faith, Hope, Charity; Daily Offering

MORNING FACE TO FACE WITH GOD:
Begin with Prayer to the Holy Spirit
Prayer on Psalm 132: The Covenant between David and God

Psalm 132 is aptly described as *'The Covenant Between David and God.'* Psalm 132 can be pondered as a covenant ritual between David and God. They are renewing their covenant promises to each other, sealing the unbreakable family bond between them. Some references in the psalm go back to the reign of David and Solomon. For the returned Israelites from the Babylonian exile, a meaningful pondering on the past events in the history of Israel would have been helpful.

In the first Segment, the Psalmist is calling on God to remember David and all his afflictions: *"Remember, O LORD, for David all his hardships."* Even though David was Israel's greatest king, he had to endure a remarkable number of hardships. He was placed in many life and death struggles; he was accused of treason and treachery; he lived many years as a fugitive; he faced many enemies in battle; he was openly criticized and despised by his wife; he suffered because of his own sin and scandal; he endured great conflict and problems among his own children; he suffered a coup staged by his son, Absalom, followed by a civil war; he was openly despised and criticized by some of his subjects. God was being asked to remember David's hardships because He was David's covenant God!

The afflictions of David always suggest the afflictions of Jesus, the son of David. For our comfort as Christians, the Father remembered the far greater 'hardships' of His Son, sustained for our sake, when through much tribulation, Jesus accomplished our redemption and entered into His glory. God does indeed remember all our afflictions endured for His greater praise and service.

Within the context of remembering David's afflictions, the Psalmist asks the LORD to remember a specific oath David made to Him. The oath itself is not recorded in 2Samuel 7, but the intent was clearly there. David was absolutely dedicated to building God a temple, a dwelling place: *"he swore an oath to the LORD, vowed to the Mighty One of Jacob; "I will not enter the house where I live, nor lie on the couch where I sleep; I will give my eyes no sleep, my eyelids no rest, till I find a place for the LORD, a dwelling for the Mighty One of Jacob."* David's dedication to this project was so complete that he vowed to refuse himself many comforts of life until the job was finished. After David built himself a fine palace, he felt guilty that a mere tent represented God's dwelling place. David asked Nathan the prophet for permission to build the temple, and Nathan first agreed. Soon afterward, God told Nathan that David was not to build Him a temple, but his son would (2Samuel 7).

David did not build the temple, but he did find the Ark of the covenant and bring it to Jerusalem from Kiriath-jearim or Baala of Judah (2Samuel 6): *"We have heard of it in Ephrathah; we have found it in the fields of Jaar. Let us enter his dwelling; let us worship at his footstool."* Arise, LORD, come to your resting place, you and your mighty ark. Your priests will be clothed with justice; your devout will shout for joy." For the sake of David your servant, do not reject your anointed."* The location of the Ark seems to have been forgotten during the reign of Saul when it was left at Kiriath-jearim by the Bethshemites (1Samuel, chapters 4-7). Ephrathah was the homeland of David, and Jaar was Kiriath-jearim. Psalms 24 and 68 also refer to the arrival of the Ark in

Jerusalem from Kiriath-jearim.

Psalm 132 was sung by the pilgrims going to the Temple in Jerusalem during the pilgrimage festivals. They remembered David's generous heart and commitment to God and used it as their own inspiration: *"Let us enter his dwelling; let us worship at his footstool." Arise, LORD, come to your resting place, you and your mighty ark. Your priests will be clothed with justice; your devout will shout for joy." For the sake of David your servant, do not reject your anointed."* The pilgrims remembered the words of Moses in the wilderness, who called out to resume the journey with the Ark toward the Promised Land: *"Arise, O LORD, may your enemies be scattered, and may those who hate you flee before you"* (Numbers 10: 35). When the pilgrims sang of the goodness and glory of God's temple, they also remembered the important function of God's priests. It was fitting for them to pray that *"your priests will be clothed with justice; your devout will shout for joy."* Segment I concludes with a similar plea for David that was made at the beginning: *"For the sake of David your servant, do not reject your anointed."*

Segment II sheds light on God's commitment to David in their covenant. It is a fitting response to the Psalmist's plea not to reject David, His anointed: *"The LORD swore an oath to David in truth, he will never turn back on it: "Your own offspring I will set upon your throne. If your sons observe my covenant, and my decrees I shall teach them, their sons, in turn, shall sit forever on your throne." Yes, the LORD has chosen Zion, desired it for a dwelling: "This is my resting place forever; here I will dwell, for I desire it. ... There I will make a horn sprout for David; I will set a lamp for my anointed. His foes I will clothe with shame, but on him his crown shall shine."* God promised that He would not forsake the sons of David (2Samuel 7: 14-16). While every king of David's line was God's anointed, this prophecy was especially fulfilled in the ultimate Anointed One, Jesus the Messiah. Once the Ark of the Covenant came to Jerusalem, there was to be no more traveling for the Tabernacle. The Temple, the Tabernacle, the Ark, and the Altar would never rest in another place than Jerusalem. Psalm 132 is alluded to twice in the New Testament. Stephen alludes to Psalm 132: 5 in Acts 7: 46, and Peter alludes to Psalm 132: 11 in Acts 2: 30.

Reflect and Pray on Psalm 132, using Lectio Divina or the Method of Meditation. Make sure you converse intimately with the Blessed Trinity

Prayer on Psalm 132: The Covenant between David and God
"1 A song of ascents.

I.

Remember, O LORD, for David, all his hardships; 2 how he swore an oath to the LORD, vowed to the Mighty One of Jacob; 3 "I will not enter the house where I live, nor lie on the couch where I sleep; 4 I will give my eyes no sleep, my eyelids no rest, 5 till I find a place for the LORD, a dwelling for the Mighty One of Jacob." 6 "We have heard of it in Ephrathah; we have found it in the fields of Jaar. 7 Let us enter his dwelling; let us worship at his footstool." 8 Arise, LORD, come to your resting place, you and your mighty ark. 9 Your priests will be clothed with justice; your devout will shout for joy." 10 For the sake of David your servant, do not reject your anointed.

II.

11 The LORD swore an oath to David in truth, he will never turn back on it: "Your own offspring I will set upon your throne. 12 If your sons observe my covenant, and my decrees I shall teach them, their sons, in turn, shall sit forever on your throne." 13 Yes, the LORD has chosen Zion, desired it for a dwelling: 14 "This is my resting place forever; here I will dwell, for I desire it. 15 I will bless Zion with provisions; its poor I will fill with bread. 16 I will clothe its priests with salvation; its devout shall shout for joy. 17 There I will make a horn sprout for David; I will set a lamp for my anointed. 18 His foes I will clothe with shame, but on him his crown shall shine."

End with Prayer to the Holy Trinity
NIGHT PRAYER: The Examination of Conscience

DAY SIX:
MORNING PRAYER: Acts of Faith, Hope, Charity; Daily Offering
MORNING FACE TO FACE WITH GOD:
Begin with Prayer to the Holy Spirit
Prayer on Psalm 136: Hymn of Thanksgiving for God's Everlasting Mercy

Psalm 136 is known as the 'Great Hallel,' and one could argue that it is the best psalm of praise and thanksgiving in the Psalter. It is called the 'Great Hallel' for the way it rehearses God's goodness regarding His people and encourages them to praise Him for His merciful and steadfast love. At one point in time, Psalm 136 was probably the final psalm in the Psalter, judging from its exquisite crescendo of praise and worship of God. The phrase, *'for his mercy endures forever,'* has a liturgical cadence to it, the assembled people of Israel singing this phrase in response to the direction of the Levites leading the singing and worship in the Temple. Each one of its verses repeats this refrain, twenty-six times! By contrast, Psalm 118 of the 'Egyptian Hallel' sung during the Passover Meal, affirmed this phrase *only* five times!

The LORD is given praise (and thanks) for many blessings. In Segment I, the Psalmist highlights the quintessential divine characteristic: *"Praise the LORD, for he is good; for his mercy endures forever; Praise the God of gods; for his mercy endures forever; Praise the Lord of lords; for his mercy endures forever."* God is good, beyond all others because He is divine. God is the God of gods and the Lord of lords! God's goodness is fundamental to all He does. *'Mercy'* is the translation of the special Hebrew word *'hesed,'* which may be understood as God's loving kindness. His loving kindness is His goodness which makes Him everlastingly committed to His covenant love for us. God's mercy is the superlative expression of His goodness!

Segment II offers God praise and thanksgiving for His glorious and wondrous acts of creation: *"Who alone has gone great wonders, ...Who skillfully made the heavens, ...Who spread the earth upon the waters, ... Who made the great lights, ...the sun to rule the day, ...the moon and stars to rule the night."* All these wondrous acts of creation, once again, are expressions of God's goodness. The work of God as Creator is described with elements from the first four days of creation (Genesis 1: 1-19). Each of these acts of creation is an expression of God's enduring mercy toward His people. God created the universe because He wanted to have a covenant relationship with us in which His mercy and forgiveness would be from everlasting to everlasting.

Psalm 135 mentioned the deliverance of the Israelites from Egypt and the striking of the firstborn. In Segment III of Psalm 136, the Psalmist continues the same theme. God is praised as the One who rescued Israel from their slavery and degradation in Egypt: *"Who struck down the firstborn of Egypt, ... and led Israel from their midst, --- with mighty hand and outstretched arm, ... who split in two the Red Sea, ...who led the people through the desert."* It was an astonishing miracle of God to support so many hundreds of thousands of people in a wilderness totally deprived of all the necessities for life, and that for forty years! All these acts of might and loving kindness on behalf of His people are expressions of God's never-ending mercy! God's creation signaled the divine intention to enter into a covenant relationship with His image and likeness. The Exodus demonstrates God's commitment to His covenant union with us!

Segment IV repeats the theme of God's victory over kings and rulers referred to in Psalm 135. All these mighty acts of God were demonstrations of His enduring mercy for His people: *"Who struck down great kings, ... slew powerful kings, ...Sihon, king of the Amorites, ...Og, king of Basha, ...and made their lands a heritage,... a heritage for Israel, his servant."* These mighty works of God were witnessed in the Promised Land after the Israelites crossed the Jordan River.

Segment V makes a skillful transition from God's great wonders of the past to His faithful and constant help in the present times: *"The Lord remembered us in our low estate, ... freed us from our foes ...and gives bread to all flesh."* It is good for us to look to the past for evidence that God's mercy endures forever, but even better for us to see the evidence in our own day. Our Blessed Mother echoes the sentiments of Segment V in her Magnificat.

The last verse affirms the sentiment of praise and thanksgiving to God for His enduring mercy. The Psalmist began the psalm with this sentiment and made sure that it would reverberate through all its verses, from the beginning, through the middle, to the very end: *"Praise the God of heaven, for his mercy endures forever."* The psalm goes over the great events of salvation history – creation, exodus, conquest, settlement, and return from exile – the dramatic moments when God shaped His people Israel. Through it all, God has been faithful to His covenant. Psalm 136 tells us that God is good to all creatures and that He keeps His promises. No psalm emphasizes this central theme more than Psalm 136, where it is repeated 26 times!

Reflect and Pray on Psalm 136, using Lectio Divina or the Method of Meditation. Make sure you converse intimately with the Blessed Trinity:

Prayer on Psalm 136: Hymn of Thanksgiving for God's Everlasting Mercy

I.

1 Praise the LORD, for he is good; for his mercy endures forever; 2 praise the God of gods; for his mercy endures forever; 3 praise the Lord of lords; for his mercy endures forever.

II.

4 Who alone has done great wonders, for his mercy endures forever; 5 who skillfully made the heavens, for his mercy endures forever; 6 who spread the earth upon the waters, for his mercy endures forever; 7 who made the great lights, for his mercy endures forever; 8 the sun to rule the day, for his mercy endures forever; 9 the moon and stars to rule the night, for his mercy endures forever;

III.

10 who struck down the firstborn of Egypt, for his mercy endures forever; 11 and led Israel from their midst, for his mercy endures forever; 12 with mighty hand and outstretched arm, for his mercy endures forever; 13 who split in two the Red Sea, for his mercy endures forever; 14 and led Israel through its midst, for his mercy endures forever; 15 but swept Pharaoh and his army into the Red Sea, for his mercy endures forever; 16 who lead the people through the desert, for his mercy endures forever;

IV.

17 who struck down great kings, for his mercy endures forever; 18 slew powerful kings, for his mercy endures forever; 19 Sihon, king of the Amorites, for his mercy endures forever; 20 Og, king of Bashan, for his mercy endures forever; 21 and made their lands a heritage, for his mercy endures forever; 22 a heritage for Israel, his servant, for his mercy endures forever.

V.

23 The Lord remembered us in our low estate, for his mercy endures forever; 24 freed us from our foes, for his mercy endures forever; 25 and gives bread to all flesh, for his mercy endures forever.

VI.

26 Praise the God of heaven, for his mercy endures forever."

End with Prayer to the Holy Trinity
NIGHT PRAYER: The Examination of Conscience

DAY SEVEN:
MORNING PRAYER: Acts of Faith, Hope, Charity; Daily Offering

MORNING FACE TO FACE WITH GOD:
<u>Learning Discipleship from the Psalms</u>
Begin with Prayer to the Holy Spirit

- Psalm 120 is a song of thanksgiving for God's rescue along with fervent prayer for further protection from lying attackers: *"The LORD answered me when I called in my distress: LORD, deliver my soul from lying lips, from a treacherous tongue."* The people of God often found themselves in distressing circumstances. They knew, however, that they always had a refuge in God in their distress; they could do as the Psalmist did when he cried to the LORD. They could share the singer's testimony, *'the LORD answered me.'*
- Evil words were spoken against the Psalmist. There was some comfort in this cry to the LORD, knowing that the evil that was

spoken against him was not true. We all need deliverance from lies, both the lies that are told *about us,* and the lies that are said *to us.* We can stay uncontaminated by lies told *about us* if we strive to live blamelessly in the ways of the Lord. Lies told *to us* could be about God, about family and friends, about events taking place in the world and the Church. From *these* lies, *'deliver my soul'*, O LORD.

- Psalm 127 is titled, *'A song of ascents. Of Solomon.'* This is one of Solomon's psalms where he displays the wisdom given to him by God concerning matters of the 'house' or family life. Solomon himself knew what it was like to both build his own house, as well as the house of God, and to guard the city. In his wisdom, Solomon understood that though God welcomed and even commanded human effort, doing His work and receiving His blessing were more important.
- Then as now, the family is the basic unit and most important priority of society. Children are to be raised *'like arrows in the hand of a warrior.'* They must be carefully shaped and formed, guided with skill and strength, given much care or they will not fly straight. They must be aimed and given direction as they will not find direction on their own. They are an extension of the warrior's strength and skill. The fruit does not fall far from the tree. They have potential for much good or evil.
- In Psalm 130, we hear of the pearl of great price, our redemption: *"Let Israel hope in the LORD, for with the LORD is mercy, with him is plenteous redemption, and he will redeem Israel from all its sins."* Had the Psalmist not been cast into the depths, he never would have found the pearl of great price. One of the great purposes of God's great forgiveness is to build a sense of gratitude and reverence in those He forgives. Those who have been forgiven are softened and humbled and overwhelmed by God's mercy.
- Psalm 132 is aptly described as *'The Covenant Between David and God.'* Psalm 132 was sung by the pilgrims going to the Temple in Jerusalem during the pilgrimage festivals. They

remembered David's generous heart and commitment to God and used it as their own inspiration: *"Let us enter his dwelling; let us worship at his footstool." Arise, LORD, come to your resting place, you and your mighty ark. Your priests will be clothed with justice; your devout will shout for joy."*
- Psalm 132 sheds light on God's commitment to David in their covenant as well. It is a fitting response to the Psalmist's plea not to reject David, His anointed: *"The LORD swore an oath to David in truth, he will never turn back on it: "Your own offspring I will set upon your throne. If your sons observe my covenant, and my decrees I shall teach them, their sons, in turn, shall sit forever on your throne."* While every king of David's line was God's anointed, this prophecy was especially fulfilled in the ultimate Anointed One, Jesus the Messiah.
- In the Jewish tradition, Psalm 136 is known as the 'Great Hallel.' It is called the Great Hallel for the way it rehearses God's goodness in regard to His people and encourages them to praise Him for His merciful and steadfast love. Each verse of Psalm 136 repeats the phrase, *'for his mercy endures forever,'* 26 times in all!
- Psalm 136 reverberates from the beginning, through the middle, to the very end with the phrase, *"Praise the God of heaven, for his mercy endures forever."* The psalm goes over the great events of salvation history – creation, exodus, conquest, settlement, and return from exile – the dramatic moments when God shaped His people Israel. Through it all, God has been faithful to His covenant.

End with Prayer to the Holy Trinity
NIGHT PRAYER: The Examination of Conscience

JOURNAL FOR BOOK FIVE, WEEK TWO: LOOKING TOWARD THE MESSIAH

<u>DAY ONE:</u> Morning Prayer: Psalm 120: Prayer of a Returned Exile
What is God saying to You?

<u>Nightly Examination of Conscience:</u>
For what are you grateful?

For what are you contrite?

What spiritual discipline, including fasting, do you need to focus on tomorrow?

<u>DAY TWO:</u> Morning Prayer: Psalm 122: A Pilgrim's Prayer for Jerusalem
What is God saying to You?

<u>Nightly Examination of Conscience:</u>
For what are you grateful?

For what are you contrite?

What spiritual discipline, including fasting, do you need to focus on tomorrow?

DAY THREE: Morning Prayer: Psalm 127: The Need of God's Blessing
What is God saying to You?

Nightly Examination of Conscience:
For what are you grateful?

For what are you contrite?

What spiritual discipline, including fasting, do you need to focus on tomorrow?

DAY FOUR: Morning Prayer: Psalm 130: Prayer for Pardon and Mercy
What is God saying to You?

Nightly Examination of Conscience:
For what are you grateful?

For what are you contrite?

What spiritual discipline, including fasting, do you need to focus on tomorrow?

DAY FIVE: Morning Prayer: Psalm 132: The Covenant between David & God
What is God saying to You?

Nightly Examination of Conscience:
For what are you grateful?

For what are you contrite?

What spiritual discipline, including fasting, do you need to focus on tomorrow?

DAY SIX: Morning Prayer: Psalm 136: Hymn of Thanksgiving for God's Everlasting Mercy
What is God saying to You?

Nightly Examination of Conscience:
For what are you grateful?

For what are you contrite?

What spiritual discipline, including fasting, do you need to focus on tomorrow?

DAY SEVEN: Morning Prayer: Learning Discipleship from the Psalms
What is God saying to You?

Nightly Examination of Conscience:
For what are you grateful?

For what are you contrite?

What spiritual discipline, including fasting, do you need to focus on tomorrow?

What prayer would you compose to express what God has said to you this week?

BOOK FIVE: PSALMS 107 TO 150: LOOKING TOWARD THE MESSIAH
Psalms 138, 139, 143, 145, 147, and 150

WHAT IS AT THE HEART OF BOOK FIVE, WEEK THREE?

As we have seen, Book Five has an upbeat tone, with the psalms giving God the central place that He deserves in the lives of the people. The Israelites have returned from exile with a purified understanding of what it means to be in covenant with God. The Old Testament as we know it, started to get finalized in its present form during the Babylonian exile, and continued after the return to the Promised Land. Many of the psalms overflow with praise and gratitude to God for His *hesed* or loving kindness and faithfulness, despite Israel's infidelities. Paradoxically, within the context of their loss of the Davidic Monarchy, some psalms speak of the Messiah-king, clearly prefiguring Jesus.

There were still some psalms of David that were not included in the Psalter, Psalms 137 to 145, and five other psalms, each beginning with 'Hallelujah!' (Praise the LORD!). Most probably, these fourteen psalms were added to the Psalter after the exile. During the week, we will ponder three psalms from David, Psalms 138, 139, and 143. The five 'Hallelujah' psalms became the concluding psalms of the Psalter. These five psalms are bursting with song and dance, they are exhilarating in their music, their choruses are polyphonic, all resonating to a crescendo, and acting as a befitting ending to the Psalter. We will ponder three of them, Psalms 145, 147, and 150. The dominant mood in these psalms is 'Joy and Celebration and looking toward the Messiah.'

On Day One, we will ponder *Psalm 138: Hymn of a Grateful Heart*. Psalms 137 and 138 need to be pondered together as they are placed in juxtaposition to each other to offer a sharp contrast between circumstances that reject God's presence and influence, and those that welcome Him into their midst. Psalm 137 is about the Israelites in the Babylonian exile. They are filled with sorrow at the loss of the monarchy and Temple in Jerusalem. At the same time, they are filled with hope that God will come to their rescue and return them to Israel. Psalm 138 introduces us to circumstances when it is appropriate to witness boldly to the works and blessings of the LORD! There is a fine blend of humility and reverence before the Lord, and boldness to witness to the Lord's great works. The object of David's praise is God's enduring mercy and faithfulness. At the end of the psalm, David makes a simple and heartfelt plea to the LORD: *"Never forsake the work of your hands!"* God's creating hands brought us into being as His image and likeness; Jesus' nail-pierced hands redeemed us on the Cross; Jesus' glorified hands will hold us fast and never let go of us!

On Day Two, we will reflect on *Psalm 139: The All-Knowing and Ever-Present God.* This psalm is a meditative masterpiece on God's omnipresence and omniscience! God is everywhere, in every part of the universe, and knows everything that is going on, even the most intimate depths of our souls! The Psalmist's thoughts and sentiments are sublime, delicate, sensitively nuanced, clearly emerging from a soul that is immersed in the beauty and grandeur of God. In the psalm, David reflects on the very personal and intimate relationship that God has with him and anyone who would choose to be in an intimate relationship with God. It is not just that God knows everything. He knows me! It is not just that God is everywhere. He is everywhere with me! It is not just that God created everything. He created everything with me in mind!

The Psalmist especially focuses on the wonder of our creation as God's image and likeness in our mothers' wombs. God's solicitude and concern for life begins at conception. Psalm 139 demonstrates that God undoubtedly sees another person in the mother's womb who is not the mother! The workings of the human body are stunning in their design and formation. Indeed, we are wonderfully made!

David uses a powerful image to illustrate God's ever-present solicitude for us: God's designs on our behalf are more in number than the sands on the seashore and in the deserts! These designs of

God are permeated with enduring mercy, unconditional forgiveness, salvation and transformation leading to re-creation in Jesus, just to name a few of God's thoughts!

The psalm ends with a humble prayer to a great and gracious God. David knew that the God of perfect knowledge and constant presence was also a God of love who could be trusted to search him and to know him at the deepest levels. David wanted God to probe and know his thoughts. And he asked God to lead him *"along an ancient path,"* the way to everlasting life.

On Day Three, we will reflect on *Psalm 143: A Prayer in Distress*. Psalm 143 is a song of lament and is also numbered among the Seven Penitential Psalms which are songs of confession and humility before God. David knew he must cry out to God for help or else he would be lost. David appealed to God's faithfulness and righteousness. If God were to deal with him based only on His righteousness, it could mean judgment and damnation for him. So, he asked God to deal with him according to His mercy. David asked God to deal with his enemies, but before that, he asked God to deal with him. If his own covenant relationship with God were uninspired and undirected, it would pose a greater danger than any enemy.

On Day Four, we will pray with *Psalm 145: The Greatness and Goodness of God*. Psalm 145 is the last psalm attributed to David and is indeed a monumental psalm of praise, a fit summary of all that David had learned about being in covenant with God. David is firmly resolved to praise God and his praise is full-throated and wholehearted! In the psalm, David highlights the importance of passing on the praise of God from one generation to another. Our covenant God is the God of our history, from one generation to the other, till the end of time. Psalm 145 reaches its climax in the Eucharistic celebration. Through the Eucharist, we have remembered to praise God the Father, through His Son, in the power of the Holy Spirit, from one generation to the next, and will continue to do so till the end of time! David ends the psalm on the same note he began it: *"All flesh will bless his holy name forever and ever."* Psalm 145 is the last will and testament of David. In it, he praises God and invites others to do the same. Indeed, it is a good way of living as a disciple of Jesus!

On Day Five, we will pray with *Psalm 147: God's Word Restores Jerusalem.* Psalm 147 is the second of the last five psalms of the Psalter that are known as the Hallelujah psalms, as they begin and end with 'Hallelujah' or 'Praise the Lord!' Probably, Psalm 147 was composed after the return of the exiles from Babylon and upon the rebuilding of the Temple. In restoring Jerusalem and the Temple, God has brought healing to the brokenhearted by binding up their wounds. There were many reasons for Israel to grieve their broken hearts, some reasons of their own making, and others that were foisted upon them by their Babylonian masters! God's providence for humanity and all of nature, and the remarkable power of His word should move us to praise Him all the more. Fittingly, the psalm ends with Hallelujah!

On Day Six, we will reflect on *Psalm 150: Final Doxology.* Psalm 150 is an eloquent, passionate cry to all creation to give God the praise due to Him. The command 'Praise' (Hebrew: *Hallelu*) is given *twelve times* in the six verses of this psalm. The number twelve, symbolizes the twelve tribes of Israel, suggesting a complete act of praise from the whole nation. The psalm offers unlimited praise to God who is unlimited in His greatness. Psalm 150 ends with, *"Let everything that has breath give praise to the LORD! Hallelujah!"* It is a remarkably fitting conclusion to this psalm and the entire Book of Psalms. This last psalm of the Psalter begins and ends with *'Hallelujah,'* as the previous four 'Hallelujah' psalms. God is praised, and His people are exhorted to praise Him.

On Day Seven, you will ponder the salient advice that these psalms have offered us to enhance and strengthen our own following of Jesus and our commitment to His Church.

SPIRITUAL READING FOR BOOK FIVE OF THE PSALMS:
Psalms 107 to 150 Books of Ezra Nehemiah Isaiah: Chapters 56-66 Ezekiel: Chapters 33-48

DAY ONE:
MORNING PRAYER: Acts of Faith, Hope, Charity; Daily Offering
MORNING FACE TO FACE WITH GOD:
Begin with Prayer to the Holy Spirit
Prayer on Psalm 138: Hymn of a Grateful Heart

Psalms 137 and 138 need to be pondered together as they are placed in juxtaposition to each other to offer a sharp contrast between those who reject God's presence and influence, and those that welcome Him into their midst. Psalm 137 is about the Israelites in the Babylonian exile. They are filled with sorrow at the loss of the monarchy and Temple in Jerusalem. At the same time, they are filled with hope that God will come to their rescue and return them to Israel. Meanwhile, their captors and tormentors are taunting them to sing psalms of Zion, implying that their God was powerless to protect them: *"Our tormentors, for joy: "Sing for us a song of Zion!" But how could we sing a song of the LORD in a foreign land?"* The exiles see the need to be silent before their revilers as they would be casting pearls before swine.

Psalm 138, on the other hand, is the first of eight psalms from David that are included in the last section of Book Five. Psalm 138 introduces us to circumstances when it is appropriate to witness boldly to the works and blessings of the LORD! There is a fine blend of humility and reverence before the Lord, and boldness to witness to the Lord's great works.

The Psalmist has experienced salvation from his enemies and understands that his rescue has to do with God's loving kindness. And the returned exiles from Babylon can resonate with his sentiments: *"I thank you, Lord, with all my heart; in the presence of the angels to you I sing. I bow low toward your holy temple; I praise your name for your mercy and faithfulness. For you have exalted over all your name and your promise. On the day I cried out, you answered; you strengthened my spirit."* David pours out his whole heart in his act of adoration and praise of God! Even when David was not at the temple, he recognized it as God's appointed place for worship and sacrifice. And he is offering his praise before the angels, God's heavenly host! The object of David's praise is God's enduring mercy and faithfulness.

The Psalmist offers four reasons for praising and thanking God and makes one petition: *"All the kings of earth will praise you, LORD, when they hear the words of your mouth. They will sing of the ways of the LORD: "How great is the glory of the LORD!" The LORD is on high, but cares for the lowly and knows the proud from afar."* As king of Israel, David was convinced that all the kings of the earth would praise God because they would hear the words of God's mouth emanating through those who witness to *'the ways of the LORD.'* The kings would proclaim the glory of the LORD! David's second reason for praise is that even though the LORD is on high, He stoops down to care for the lowly. The humble and afflicted attract God's notice particularly! And God distances Himself from the proud and haughty who have chosen to keep Him out of their lives! James 4: 6 says, *"God resists the proud, but gives grace to the humble."*

As David considered God's greatness and His kindness to the humble, it gave him confidence that God would revive him in his present circumstances: *"Though I walk in the midst of dangers, you guard my life when my enemies rage. You stretch out your hand; your right hand saves me."* We have echoes of Psalm 23 here. David knew that God had a plan for him, and this God of greatness and goodness would make sure to bring that plan to completion! David is expressing his confidence and trust in a spirit of thanksgiving and praise.

The fourth reason for praise and thanksgiving is because, *"The LORD is with me to the end. LORD, your mercy endures forever."* The Israelites understood that God would always be faithful to His covenant with them, that His mercy would always be there, never failing, always enduring, from everlasting to everlasting! David had the utmost trust that the Lord would be with him and His mercy would endure forever!

At the end of the psalm, David makes a simple and heartfelt plea to the LORD: *"Never forsake the work of your hands!"* God's creating hands brought us into being as His image and likeness; Jesus' nail-pierced hands redeemed us on the Cross; Jesus' glorified hands will hold us fast and never let go of us!

Reflect and Pray on Psalm 138, using Lectio Divina or the Method of Meditation. Make sure you converse intimately with the Blessed Trinity:

Prayer on Psalm 138: Hymn of a Grateful Heart
"1 Of David.

I.

I thank you, Lord, with all my heart; in the presence of the angels to you I sing. 2 I bow low toward your holy temple; I praise your name for your mercy and faithfulness. For you have exalted over all your name and your promise. 3 On the day I cried out, you answered; you strengthened my spirit.

II.

4 All the kings of earth will praise you, LORD, when they hear the words of your mouth. 5 They will sing of the ways of the LORD: "How great is the glory of the LORD!" 6 The LORD is on high, but cares for the lowly and knows the proud from afar. 7 Though I walk in the midst of dangers, you guard my life when my enemies rage. You stretch out your hand; your right hand saves me. 8 The LORD is with me to the end. LORD, your mercy endures forever. Never forsake the work of your hands!"

End with Prayer to the Holy Trinity
NIGHT PRAYER: The Examination of Conscience

DAY TWO:
MORNING PRAYER: Acts of Faith, Hope, Charity; Daily Offering

MORNING FACE TO FACE WITH GOD:
Begin with Prayer to the Holy Spirit

Prayer on Psalm 139: The All-Knowing and Ever-Present God

Psalm 139 would easily rank among the most cherished psalms in the Psalter! This psalm is a meditative masterpiece on God's omnipresence and omniscience! God is everywhere, in every part of the universe, and knows everything that is going on, even the most intimate depths of our souls! The Psalmist's thoughts and sentiments are sublime, delicate, sensitively nuanced, clearly emerging from a soul that is immersed in the beauty and grandeur of God.

In Segment I, David reflects on the very personal and intimate relationship that God has with him and anyone who would choose to be in an intimate relationship with God: *"LORD, you have probed me, you know me: you know when I sit and stand; ... you sift through my travels and my rest; with all my ways you are familiar. ... Behind and before you encircle me and rest your hand upon me. Such knowledge is too wonderful for me, far too lofty for me to reach. ... If I take the wings of dawn and dwell beyond the sea, even there your hand guides me, your right hand holds me fast. ... Darkness is not dark for you, and night shines as the day. Darkness and light are but one."* God created everything with me in mind! When we are confident in the love and care of God our Father, His constant knowledge of us is a comfort rather than an anxiety. These verses are vivid and concrete. God's knowledge of us is personal and dynamic! David was humbled and comforted by the fact that God knew him better than he knew himself. The divine presence turns night into day and makes all things manifest before Him! There is no hiding from God.

In Segment II, the Psalmist focuses on the wonder of our creation as God's image and likeness in our mothers' wombs: *"You formed my inmost being; you knit me in my mother's womb. I praise you, because I am wonderfully made; wonderful are your works! My very self you know. My bones are not hidden from you, when I was being made in secret, fashioned in the depths of the earth. ... my days were shaped, before one came to be."* God's solicitude and concern for life begins at conception. Psalm 139 demonstrates that God undoubtedly sees another person in the mother's womb who is not the mother! The workings of the human body are stunning in their design and formation. Indeed, we are wonderfully made! In Segment III, the Psalmist is overcome with a sense of awe: *"How precious to me are your designs, O God; how vast the sum of them! Were I to count them, they would outnumber the sands; when I complete them, still you are with me."* David was filled with amazement and adoration at considering how God knew and cared for him. It is moving and very grounding to know that God would think of us all the time! David used a powerful image to illustrate God's ever-present solicitude for us: God's designs on our behalf are more in number than the sands on the seashore and in the deserts! And they will be permeated with enduring mercy, leading to our re-creation in Jesus, just to name a few of God's designs! David abruptly shifted from a spirit of wonder and adoration, to intense prayer against wicked and bloodthirsty men who were the enemies of God: *"Do I not hate, O LORD, those who hate you? Those who rise against you, do I not loathe? With fierce hatred I hate them, enemies I count as my own."* David's adoration and commitment to his covenant with God filled him with fervent zeal for God's honor. Like God, a good person hates the sins of the person rather than the person themselves; not how God made them, but what they made of themselves.

The psalm ends with a humble prayer to a great and gracious God: *"Probe me, God, know my heart; try me, know my thoughts. See if there is a wicked path in me; lead me along an ancient path."* David knew that the God of perfect knowledge and constant presence was also a God of love and could be trusted to search him and to know him at the deepest levels. David wanted God to probe and know his thoughts. And he asked God to lead him *"along an ancient path,"* the way to everlasting life.

Reflect and Pray on Psalm 139, using Lectio Divina or the Method of Meditation. Make sure you converse intimately with the Blessed Trinity:

Prayer on Psalm 139: The All-Knowing and Ever-Present God
"1 For the leader. A psalm of David.

I.

LORD, you have probed me, you know me: 2 you know when I sit and stand; you understand my thoughts from afar. 3 You sift through my travels and my rest; with all my ways you are familiar. 4 Even before a word is on my tongue, LORD, you know it all. 5 Behind and before you encircle me and rest your hand upon me. 6 Such knowledge is too wonderful for me, far too lofty for me to reach. 7 Where can I go from your spirit? From your presence, where can I flee? 8 If I ascend to the heavens, you are there; if I lie down in Sheol, there you are. 9 If I take the wings of dawn and dwell beyond the sea, 10 even there your hand guides me, your right hand holds me fast. 11 If I say, "Surely darkness shall hide me, and night shall be my light" – 12 Darkness is not dark for you, and night shines as the day. Darkness and light are but one.

II.

13 You formed my inmost being; you knit me in my mother's womb. 14 I praise you, because I am wonderfully made; wonderful are your works! My very self you know. 15 My bones are not hidden from you, when I was being made in secret, fashioned in the depths of the earth. 16 Your eyes saw me unformed; in your book all are written down; my days were shaped, before one came to be.

III.

17 How precious to me are your designs, O God; how vast the sum of them! 18 Were I to count them, they would outnumber the sands; when I complete them, still you are with me. 19 When you would destroy the wicked, O God, the bloodthirsty depart from me! 20 Your foes who conspire a plot against you are exalted in vain.

IV.

21 Do I not hate, LORD, those who hate you? Those who rise against you, do I not loathe? 22 With fierce hatred I hate them, enemies I count as my own. 23 Probe me, God, know my heart; try me, know my thoughts. 24 See if there is a wicked path in me; lead me along an ancient path."

End with Prayer to the Holy Trinity
NIGHT PRAYER: The Examination of Conscience

DAY THREE:
MORNING PRAYER: Acts of Faith, Hope, Charity; Daily Offering

MORNING FACE TO FACE WITH GOD:
Begin with Prayer to the Holy Spirit

Prayer on Psalm 143: A Prayer in Distress

Psalm 143 is a song of lament and is also numbered among the Seven Penitential Psalms which are songs of confession and humility before God. Psalm 143 finds David in crisis. This crisis could have occurred when he was living as a fugitive from King Saul, or when his son Absalom led a rebellion against him and made himself the king of Israel: *"LORD, hear my prayer; in your faithfulness listen to my pleading; answer me in your righteousness. Do not enter into judgment with your servant; before you no one can be just."* David knew he must cry out to God for help or else he would be lost. David appealed to God's faithfulness and righteousness. If God were to deal with him based on His righteousness, it could mean judgment and damnation for him. So, he asked God to deal with him with His mercy. He was appealing to God's righteousness, not his own.

In his tumultuous life, David knew much suffering. David ached and cried out to God out of the intense misery of his soul: *"The enemy has pursued my soul; he has crushed my life to the ground. He has made me dwell in darkness like those long dead. My spirit is faint within me; my heart despairs."* This was misery brought upon David by his adversary.

There were many years he lived as a fugitive from King Saul, having to forsake all because a wicked man sought to kill him without cause. There was also the deep misery when his son Absalom rebelled against him and deposed his father as king. In his profound affliction of soul, God was his refuge and strength. David spoke about his spirit being faint within him and his heart despairing. His words were in the mouth of Jesus, especially during His agony: *"My soul is sorrowful even to death"* (Matthew 26: 38). In this dark season of his soul, David remembered the days of old: *"I remember the days of old; I ponder all your deeds; the works of your hands I recall."* He remembered the joy, simplicity, and goodness of how God met him and blessed him as an anonymous shepherd boy. The prayer of remembrance of our present blessings and in our past lives is an immense pillar of strength in our spiritual lives. David's remembrance of God's gracious deeds in his life led him to the prayer of petition: *"I stretch out my hands toward you, my soul to you like a parched land."* His persecuted soul sought God with an intense thirst and longing.

The second half of the psalm, verses 7 through 12, is an intense prayer of supplication: *"Hasten to answer me, LORD; for my spirit fails me."* His failing spirit could not last long without God's intervention. There is a great sense of urgency: *"Hasten to answer me!"* To feel that God might hide His face from David drove him into despair, and so he pleaded to sense the light of God's countenance: *"Do not hide your face from me, lest I become like those descending to the pit."* David's sense of hopelessness was intense, likened to descending into the grave interminably, if God did not show His face and bless Him! In his state of hopelessness, David needed to hear something of God's great mercy, His *hesed* or *loving kindness* early in the morning, as the afternoon or evening might be too late: *"In the morning let me hear of your mercy, for in you I trust. Show me the path I should walk, for I entrust my life to you."* David confessed that he did not know the way and needed God to show him the way: *"Show me the path I should walk, for I entrust my life to you!"*

David's enemies had persecuted his soul. He prayed not only for God's encouragement and direction, but also for His defense against these enemies: *"Rescue me, LORD, from my foes, for I seek refuge in you."* In his reliance upon God, David knew that God would lead him into the land of uprightness: *"Teach me to do your will, for you are my God. May your kind spirit guide me on ground that is level."* At the request of Jesus, the Father has gifted us with the presence and guidance of the Holy Spirit. As he continued his supplication, David prayed for the revival of his soul: *"For your name's sake, LORD, give me life; in your righteousness lead my soul out of distress. In your mercy put an end to my foes; all those who are oppressing my soul, for I am your servant."* His deliverance would bring glory to God. He could also ask God to destroy his enemies, leaving vengeance to God against those who persecuted his soul. David asked God to deal with him before he asked God to deal with his enemies. He knew that if his own covenant relationship with God were uninspired and undirected, it would pose a greater danger than any enemy.

Reflect and Pray on Psalm 143, using Lectio Divina or the Method of Meditation. Make sure you converse intimately with the Blessed Trinity:

Prayer on Psalm 143: A Prayer in Distress
"1 A psalm of David.
LORD, hear my prayer; in your faithfulness listen to my pleading; answer me in your righteousness. 2 Do not enter into judgment with your servant; before you no one can be just. 3 The enemy has pursued my soul; he has crushed my life to the ground. He has made me dwell in darkness like those long dead. 4 My spirit is faint within me; my heart despairs. 5 I remember the days of old; I ponder all your deeds; the works of your hands I recall. 6 I stretch out my hands toward you, my soul to you like a parched land. 7 Hasten to answer me, LORD; for my spirit fails me. Do not hide your face from me, lest I become like those descending to the pit. 8 In the morning let me hear of your mercy, for in you I trust. Show me the path I should walk, for I entrust my life to you. 9 Rescue me, LORD, from my foes, for I seek refuge in you. 10 Teach me to do your will, for you are my God. May your kind spirit guide me on ground that is level. 11 For your name's sake, LORD, give me life; in your righteousness lead my soul out of distress. 12 In your mercy put an end to my foes; all those who are oppressing my soul, for I am your servant."

End with Prayer to the Holy Trinity
NIGHT PRAYER: The Examination of Conscience

DAY FOUR:
MORNING PRAYER: Acts of Faith, Hope, Charity; Daily Offering

MORNING FACE TO FACE WITH GOD:
Begin with Prayer to the Holy Spirit
Prayer on Psalm 145: The Greatness and Goodness of God

Psalm 145 is the last psalm attributed to David in the collection of psalms, and is the last of the nine psalms using some kind of acrostic pattern, the others being Psalms 9, 10, 25, 34, 37, 111, 112, and 119. Five of these are attributed to David. Psalm 145 is indeed a monumental psalm of praise, a fit summary of all that David had learned about being in covenant with God. The Talmud commends all who repeat it three times a day as having a share in the world to come.

In the first three verses, David teaches us how to praise God: *"I will extol you, my God and king; I will bless your name forever and ever. Every day I will bless you; I will praise your name forever and ever. Great is the LORD and worthy of much praise, whose grandeur is beyond understanding."* David may have been the king of the elect nation of Israel; however, God was the king of kings. David is feverishly ecstatic as he piles praise upon praise, declaring God's greatness and worthiness to be praised! Indeed, David's praise is full-throated and wholehearted!

In verses four to seven, David highlights the importance of passing on the praise of God from one generation to another: *"One generation praises your deeds to the next and proclaims your mighty works. They speak of the splendor of your majestic glory, tell of your wonderful deeds. They speak of the power of your awesome acts and recount your great deeds. They celebrate your abounding goodness and joyfully sing of your justice."* Our covenant God is the God of our history, from one generation to the other, till the end of time. Every time we assemble for Mass, the Church on earth comes together with the Church in heaven, to offer the Father the highest possible praise and thanksgiving through the death and resurrection of Jesus! Through the Eucharist, we have remembered to praise God the Father, through His Son, in the power of the Holy Spirit, from one generation to the next, and will continue to do so till the end of time! Psalm 145 reaches its climax in the Eucharistic celebration. In every verse, David repeated the idea of praising God for what He does and for who He is.

In verses eight and nine, David continues to declare and praise the greatness of God in His abundant mercy: *"The LORD is gracious and merciful, slow to anger and abounding in mercy. The LORD is good to all, compassionate toward all your works."* David uses the description God gave Moses of Himself, to address God: *"The LORD, the LORD, a God gracious and merciful, slow to anger and abounding in love and fidelity"* (Exodus 34: 6). Without question, the Lord is great in His mighty deeds in creation and in the history of Israel. God's greatness, majesty, and splendor point us in the direction of God who is gracious and merciful, slow to anger and abounding in mercy!

Verses ten through thirteen, focus on all creation declaring the praise of God: *"All your works give you thanks, LORD and your faithful bless you. They speak of the glory of your reign and tell of your mighty works, making known to the sons of men your mighty acts, the majestic glory of your rule. Your reign is a reign for all ages, your dominion for all generations. The LORD is trustworthy in all his words, and loving in all his works."* Creation itself praises God according to its nature. Yet, it is human beings, the apex of God's creation, who praise God on their own behalf as His grateful image and likeness, and as the mouthpiece for the rest of the universe! David sensed the responsibility of God's people to tell the world the greatness of what God has done and who the King of humankind is!

In verses fourteen through sixteen, the Psalmist emphasizes the kindness of God to those in need: *"The LORD supports all who are falling and raises up all who are bowed down. The eyes of all look hopefully to you; you give them their food in due season. You open wide your hand and satisfy the desire of every living thing."* God's compassion is especially evident toward those who fall and fail, sinners and those whose backs are bent double. He especially draws near to hold them up. If through their failures, they move to repentance, God will draw near and uphold them.

Verses seventeen through twenty-one, speak of the love and righteousness of the LORD: *"The LORD is just in all his ways,* merciful in all his works. The LORD is just in all his ways, merciful in all his works. The LORD is near to all who call upon him, to all who call upon him in truth. He fulfills the desire of those who fear him; he hears their cry and saves them. The LORD watches over all who love him, but all the wicked he destroys. My mouth will speak the praises of the LORD; all flesh will bless his holy name forever and ever."* God's responsiveness to His praying people demonstrates His commitment to them. He has an unbreakable family bond with them. When they call on Him, He will come to their aid!

David ends the psalm on the same note he began it: *"All flesh will bless his holy name forever and ever."* Psalm 145 are the last words of David in the Bible, his last will and testament. He praises God and invites others to do the same. Indeed, it is a good way of living as disciples of Jesus!

Reflect and Pray on Psalm 145, using Lectio Divina or the Method of Meditation. Make sure you converse intimately with the Blessed Trinity:

Prayer on Psalm 145: The Greatness and Goodness of God
"1 Praise. Of David.
I will extol you, my God and king; I will bless your name forever and ever. 2 Every day I will bless you; I will praise your name forever and ever. 3 Great is the LORD and worthy of much praise, whose grandeur is beyond understanding. 4 One generation praises your deeds to the next and proclaims your mighty works. 5 They speak of the splendor of your majestic glory, tell of your wonderful deeds. 6 They speak of the power of your awesome acts and recount your great deeds. 7 They celebrate your abounding goodness and joyfully sing of your justice. 8 The LORD is gracious and merciful, slow to anger and abounding in mercy. 9 The LORD is good to all, compassionate toward all your works. 10 All your works give you thanks, LORD and your faithful bless you. 11 They speak of the glory of your reign and tell of your mighty works, 12 making known to the sons of men your mighty acts, the majestic glory of your rule. 13 Your reign is a reign for all ages, your

dominion for all generations. The LORD is trustworthy in all his words, and loving in all his works. 14 The LORD supports all who are falling and raises up all who are bowed down. 15 The eyes of all look hopefully to you; you give them their food in due season. 16 You open wide your hand and satisfy the desire of every living thing. 17 The LORD is just in all his ways, merciful in all his works. 18 The LORD is near to all who call upon him, to all who call upon him in truth. 19 He fulfills the desire of those who fear him; he hears their cry and saves them. 20 The LORD watches over all who love him, but all the wicked he destroys. 21 My mouth will speak the praises of the LORD; all flesh will bless his holy name forever and ever."

End with Prayer to the Holy Trinity
NIGHT PRAYER: The Examination of Conscience

DAY FIVE:
MORNING PRAYER: Acts of Faith, Hope, Charity; Daily Offering

MORNING FACE TO FACE WITH GOD:
Begin with Prayer to the Holy Spirit
Prayer on Psalm 147: God's Word Restores Jerusalem

Psalm 147 is the second of the last five psalms of the Psalter known as the Hallelujah psalms, as they begin and end with 'Hallelujah' or 'Praise the Lord!' In Segment I, the Psalmist praises God for His protection and preservation. He offers several reasons as to why it is good and pleasant to give fitting praise to the LORD. The first reason is God's active care for Jerusalem and its restoration after the exile: *"The LORD rebuilds Jerusalem, and gathers the dispersed of Israel, healing the brokenhearted, and binding up their wounds."* This scene is referred to in Nehemiah 12: 27: *"At the dedication of the wall of Jerusalem, the Levites were sought out wherever they lived and were brought to Jerusalem to celebrate a joyful dedication with thanksgiving hymns and the music of cymbals, harps, and lyres."* Probably, Psalm 147 was composed after the return of the exiles from Babylon and upon the rebuilding of the Temple. In restoring Jerusalem and the Temple, God has brought healing to the brokenhearted by binding up their wounds. There were many reasons for Israel to grieve their broken hearts, some reasons of their own making, and others that were foisted upon them by their Babylonian masters!

The next reason for singing the praises of God is because the same God who counts the number of the stars, also cares for the lowly individual. His greatness extends from the vastness of the universe to the poor individual's need: *"He numbers the stars, and gives to all of them their names. Great is our Lord, vast in power, with wisdom beyond measure. The LORD gives aid to the poor, but casts the wicked to the ground."* If God names all the stars, He certainly knows us, and names us. In the lofty aspects of His nobility, God's *'wisdom is beyond measure,'* and in the most compassionate aspects of His majesty, *'The LORD gives aid to the poor.'*

In Segment II, the Psalmist praises God for His work in nature. *"Sing to the LORD with thanksgiving; with the lyre make music to our God, who covers the heavens with clouds, provides rain for the earth, makes grass sprout on the mountains, who gives animals their food and young ravens what they cry for. He takes no delight in the strength of horses, no pleasure in the runner's stride. Rather the LORD takes pleasure in those who fear him, those who put their hope in his mercy."* God's power and loving care come together once again in His work in nature. He brings about rain, makes grass to grow, and gives food to the animals and birds, even ravens! The Jews hated ravens because they were unclean and forbidden for food, besides being greedy and voracious. God takes delight in *"those who put their hope in his mercy."*

In Segment III, the Psalmist highlights four great and compassionate acts of God for His people, each worthy of praise. God gives His people security: *"he has strengthened the bars of your gates;"* The fortifications of Jerusalem have been completed. Their strength gives security to the people gathered in the city. He gives a future to His people: *"Blessed your children within you (Jerusalem);"* He gives peace: *"He brings peace to your borders;"* He gives provision: *"and satisfies you with finest wheat."* Over the land once devastated by war, peace reigns, and the fields that lay desolate now have yielded a rich harvest.

The last six verses of Segment III offer short descriptions of God's presence and work in the natural world. God's work in the natural world begins when God *"sends his command to earth; his word runs swiftly."* The Psalmist considered God's power as it is seen in cold weather: *"Thus he makes the snow like wool, and spreads the frost like ash; He disperses hail like crumbs. Who can withstand his cold?"* Snow, frost, hail, and cold are all expressions of God's power in nature. Another expression of God's power is *"when again he issues his command, it melts them; he raises his winds and the waters flow."*

The same God who orders and directs the natural world through His word has also brought the revelation of His heart and mind through His word to Israel: *"He proclaims his word to Jacob, his statutes and laws to Israel."* He who is the Creator is also the Revealer. Understanding the greatness of God, His care for humanity and all of nature, and the remarkable power and nature of His word, should move us to praise Him. Fittingly, the psalm ends with Hallelujah!

Reflect and Pray on Psalm 147, using Lectio Divina or the Method of Meditation. Make sure you converse intimately with the Blessed Trinity:

Prayer on Psalm 147: God's Word Restores Jerusalem
"1 Hallelujah!

I.

How good to sing praise to our God; how pleasant to give fitting praise. 2 The LORD rebuilds Jerusalem, and gathers the dispersed of Israel, 3 healing the brokenhearted, and binding up their wounds. 4 He numbers the stars, and gives to all of them their names. 5 Great is our Lord, vast in power, with wisdom beyond measure. 6 The LORD gives aid to the poor, but casts the wicked to the ground.

II.

Sing to the LORD with thanksgiving; with the lyre make music to our God, 8 who covers the heavens with clouds, provides rain for the earth, makes grass sprout on the mountains, 9 who gives animals their food and young ravens what they cry for. 10 He takes no delight in the strength of horses, no pleasure in the runner's stride. 11 Rather the LORD takes pleasure in those who fear him, those who put their hope in his mercy.

III.

12 Glorify the LORD, Jerusalem; Zion, offer praise to your God, 13 for he has strengthened the bars of your gates, blessed your children within you. 14 He brings peace to your borders, and satisfies you with finest wheat. 15 He sends his command to earth; his word runs swiftly!

IV.

16 Thus he makes the snow like wool, and spreads the frost like ash; 17 He disperses hail like crumbs. Who can withstand his cold? 18 Yet when again he issues his command, it melts them; he raises his winds and the waters flow. 19 He proclaims his word to Jacob, his statutes and laws to Israel. 20 He has not done this for any other nation; of such laws they know nothing. Hallelujah!"

End with Prayer to the Holy Trinity
NIGHT PRAYER: The Examination of Conscience
DAY SIX:
MORNING PRAYER: Acts of Faith, Hope, Charity; Daily Offering

MORNING FACE TO FACE WITH GOD:
Begin with Prayer to the Holy Spirit
Prayer on Psalm 150: Final Doxology

The Fifth Book ends with Psalm 150, and the entire psalm can be viewed as a doxology, not only for the final book, but also for the entire Book of Psalms. Psalm 150 is an eloquent, passionate cry to all creation to give God the praise due to Him. The command 'Praise' (Hebrew: *Hallelu*) is given *twelve times* in the six verses of this psalm. The number twelve, symbolizes the twelve tribes of Israel, suggesting a complete act of praise from the whole nation. The psalm offers unlimited praise to God who is unlimited in His greatness. This last psalm of the Psalter begins and ends with

'Hallelujah,' as the previous four 'Hallelujah' psalms. God is praised, and His people are exhorted to praise Him.

God's sanctuary in the Temple is the most fitting place to give praise to God: *"Praise God in his holy sanctuary."* In light of the New Covenant, Jesus serves His people in a sanctuary *'in the heavens'*: *"We have such a high priest, who has taken his seat at the right hand of the throne of the Majesty in heaven, a minister of the sanctuary and of the true tabernacle that the Lord, not man, set up"* (Hebrews 8: 1-2). Jesus makes His sanctuary *'among His people'*: *"For we are the temple of the living God; as God said: "I will live with them and move among them, and I will be their God and they shall be my people"* (2Corinthians 6: 16). We have Jesus present in the Blessed Sacrament in our Churches. Jesus makes His sanctuary *'in the individual believer'*: *"Do you not know that you are the temple of God, and that the Spirit of God dwells in you?"* (1Corinthians 3: 16). Ultimately, Jesus will be *'the sanctuary of God'* among His people: *"I saw no temple in the city, for its temple is the Lord God almighty and the Lamb"* (Revelation 21: 22).

The wide expanse of sky is also a fitting place to praise God: *"give praise in the mighty dome of heaven."* Since the firmament stretches from horizon to horizon, it tells us that God should be praised in every place under the sky. While it is right to praise God for the mighty things He does, it is especially right and just to praise Him for who He is, in all the excellence of His greatness: *"Praise him for his great majesty"* This greatness surpasses all else in the entire universe.

The Psalmist summoned an orchestra of God's people who conduct their music in exuberant praise to God: *"Give praise with blasts upon the horn, praise him with harp and lyre. Give praise with tambourines and dance, praise him with strings and pipes. Give praise with crashing cymbals, praise him with sounding cymbals."* The broad list of musical instruments tells us that God wants every class and group of people to praise Him, because these instruments were normally played by different types of people. Psalm 150 tells us that during our liturgy, we need to sing loudly and heartily as God is worthy of our most excellent praise.

Psalm 150 ends with, *"Let everything that has breath give praise to the LORD! Hallelujah!"* It is a remarkably fitting conclusion to this psalm and the entire Book of Psalms. Everything that breathes should give praise to the One who gave it breath. Every breath is the gift of God, and praise is the worthy response we should make for that gift. By the time we reach the hundred and fiftieth psalm, we have lived through just about every human experience in the history of salvation of God's people. We've been through the mighty deeds of God and the rebellious wickedness of humans, through the destruction of the Davidic monarchy and Temple in Jerusalem to the return of God's people and the rebuilding of the Temple, and to understanding that the only right way of living is to acknowledge God as King and Messiah and live under His sovereign rule. Through our wanderings with God's people through the various chapters of their history, we have come to see that their journey could only come to a meaningful end in Jesus, the Son of David who is the Son of God. The psalms have had Jesus as their lodestar from start to finish. The ending of this glorious saga in the establishment of the new and eternal covenant, authored by God through His Son under the inspiration of the Holy Spirit, makes us realize that the Book of Psalms belongs to us, disciples of Jesus, in a special way. What then should be the last line of this story? The last line of the Psalmody tells us: Praise God, *'everyone* in *every way* for *everything, forever!'*

Reflect and Pray on Psalm 150, using Lectio Divina or the Method of Meditation. Make sure you converse intimately with the Blessed Trinity:

Prayer on Psalm 150: Final Doxology

"1 Hallelujah!
Praise God in his holy sanctuary; give praise in the mighty dome of heaven. 2 Give praise for his mighty deeds, praise him for his great majesty. 3 Give praise with blasts upon the horn, praise him with harp and lyre. 4 Give praise with tambourines and dance, praise him with strings and pipes. 5 Give praise with crashing

cymbals, praise him with sounding cymbals. 6 Let everything that has breath give praise to the LORD! Hallelujah!"

End with Prayer to the Holy Trinity
NIGHT PRAYER: Examination of Conscience

DAY SEVEN:
MORNING PRAYER: Acts of Faith, Hope, Charity; Daily Offering

MORNING FACE TO FACE WITH GOD:
Learning Discipleship from the Psalms
Begin with Prayer to the Holy Spirit

- Psalm 138 introduces us to circumstances when it is appropriate to witness boldly to the works and blessings of the LORD! There is a fine blend of humility and reverence before the Lord, and boldness to witness to the Lord's great works: *"I thank you, Lord, with all my heart; in the presence of the angels to you I sing. I bow low toward your holy temple; I praise your name for your mercy and faithfulness."*
- At the end of Psalm 138, David makes a simple and heartfelt plea to the LORD: *"Never forsake the work of your hands!"* God's creating hands brought us into being as His image and likeness; Jesus' nail pierced hands redeemed us on the Cross; Jesus' glorified hands will hold us fast and never let go of us!
- Psalm 139 is a meditative masterpiece on God's omnipresence and omniscience! David reflects on the very personal and intimate relationship that God has with anyone who would choose to be in an intimate relationship with God. It is not just that God knows everything. He knows me! God is everywhere and with me! God created everything with me in mind!
- The Psalmist focuses on the wonder of our creation as God's image and likeness in our mothers' wombs: *"You formed my inmost being; you knit me in my mother's womb. I praise you, because I am wonderfully made; wonderful are your works! My very self you know. My bones are not hidden from you, when I was being made in secret, fashioned in the depths of the earth. ... my days were shaped, before one came to be."*

God's solicitude and concern for life begins at conception.
- David was filled with amazement and adoration at considering how God knew and cared for him. David used a powerful image to illustrate God's ever-present solicitude for us: God's designs on our behalf are more in number than the sands on the seashore and in the deserts! And these designs of God are permeated with enduring mercy, salvation, and transformation leading to re-creation in Jesus, just to name a few of God's thoughts!
- Psalm 143 is numbered among the Seven Penitential Psalms which are songs of confession and humility before God. If God were to deal with David based on His righteousness, it could mean judgment and damnation for him. So, he asked God to deal with him with His mercy.
- In Psalm 145, David highlights the importance of passing on the praise of God from one generation to another. Every time we assemble for Mass, the Church on earth joins with the Church in heaven, to offer the Father the highest possible praise and thanksgiving through the death and resurrection of Jesus! Psalm 145 reaches its climax in the Eucharistic celebration. We praise God for what He does and for who He is, from generation to generation, from now to forever!
- Psalm 147 begins and ends with 'Hallelujah' or 'Praise the Lord!' In restoring Jerusalem and the Temple, God has brought healing to the brokenhearted by binding up their wounds. There were many reasons for Israel to grieve their broken hearts, some reasons of their own making, and others that were foisted upon them by their Babylonian masters!
- The Psalter ends with Psalm 150 that can be viewed as a doxology for the entire Book of Psalms. Psalm 150 is an eloquent, passionate cry to all creation to give God the praise due to Him. The command 'Praise' (Hebrew: *Hallelu*) is given *twelve times* in the six verses of this psalm. The number twelve, symbolizes the twelve tribes of Israel, suggesting a complete act of praise from the whole nation. This last psalm begins and

ends with *'Hallelujah,'* as the previous four 'Hallelujah' psalms. God is praised, and His people are exhorted to praise Him.

- Psalm 150 ends with, *"Let everything that has breath give praise to the LORD! Hallelujah!"* Every breath is the gift of God, and praise is the worthy response we should make for that gift. By the time we reach Psalm 150, we have lived through just about every human experience in the history of salvation of God's people. What then should be the last line of this story? Praise God, *'everyone* in *every way* for *everything, forever!'*

End with Prayer to the Holy Trinity
NIGHT PRAYER: The Examination of Conscience

JOURNAL FOR BOOK FIVE, WEEK THREE: LOOKING TOWARD THE MESSIAH

DAY ONE: Morning Prayer: Psalm 138: Hymn of a Grateful Heart
What is God saying to You?

Nightly Examination of Conscience:
For what are you grateful?

For what are you contrite?

What spiritual discipline, including fasting, do you need to focus on tomorrow?

DAY TWO: Morning Prayer: Psalm 139: The All-Knowing and Ever-Present God
What is God saying to You?

Nightly Examination of Conscience:
For what are you grateful?

For what are you contrite?

What spiritual discipline, including fasting, do you need to focus on tomorrow?

DAY THREE: Morning Prayer: Psalm 143: A Prayer in Distress
What is God saying to You?

Nightly Examination of Conscience:
For what are you grateful?

For what are you contrite?

What spiritual discipline, including fasting, do you need to focus on tomorrow?

DAY FOUR: Morning Prayer: Psalm 145: The Greatness and Goodness of God
What is God saying to You?

Nightly Examination of Conscience:
For what are you grateful?

For what are you contrite?

What spiritual discipline, including fasting, do you need to focus on tomorrow?

DAY FIVE: Morning Prayer: Psalm 147: God's Word Restores Jerusalem
What is God saying to You?

Nightly Examination of Conscience:
For what are you grateful?

For what are you contrite?

What spiritual discipline, including fasting, do you need to focus on tomorrow?

DAY SIX: Morning Prayer: Psalm 150: Final Doxology
What is God saying to You?

Nightly Examination of Conscience:
For what are you grateful?

For what are you contrite?

What spiritual discipline, including fasting, do you need to focus on tomorrow?

DAY SEVEN: Morning Prayer: Learning Discipleship from the Psalms
What is God saying to You?

Nightly Examination of Conscience:
For what are you grateful?

For what are you contrite?

What spiritual discipline, including fasting, do you need to focus on tomorrow?

What prayer would you compose to express what God has said to you this week?

QUICK REFERENCE GUIDE

INTRODUCTION TO THE PSALMS 10
BOOK ONE – PSALMS 1-41: ABIDING TRUST IN DIRE STRAITS
Psalms 1, 2, 3, 4, 5, and 6
WHAT IS AT THE HEART OF BOOK ONE, WEEK ONE? 31
DAY 1   Prayer on Psalm 1: True Happiness in God's Law 34
DAY 2   Psalm 2: A Psalm for a Royal Coronation 35
DAY 3   Psalm 3: Threatened but Trusting 38
DAY 4   Prayer on Psalm 4: Trust in God 41
DAY 5   Psalm 5: Prayer for Divine Help 43
DAY 6   Psalm 6: Prayer in Distress (First Penitential Psalm) 45
DAY 7   Learning Discipleship from the Psalms 48

BOOK ONE – PSALMS 1-41: ABIDING TRUST IN DIRE STRAITS
Psalms 8, 15, 18, 19, 22, and 23
WHAT IS AT THE HEART OF BOOK ONE, WEEK TWO? 54
DAY 1   Prayer on Psalm 8: Divine Majesty and Human Dignity 56
DAY 2   Psalm 15: The Righteous Israelite 58
DAY 3   Prayer on Psalm 18: A King's Thanksgiving for Victory 60
DAY 4   Prayer on Psalm 19: God's Glory in the Heavens and in the Law ... 64
DAY 5   Prayer on Psalm 22: The Prayer of an Innocent Person 66
DAY 6   Prayer on Psalm 23: The Lord, Shepherd and Host 71
DAY 7   Learning Discipleship from the Psalms 75

BOOK ONE – PSALMS 1-41: ABIDING TRUST IN DIRE STRAITS
Psalms 25, 26, 27, 28, 29, and 30
WHAT IS AT THE HEART OF BOOK ONE, WEEK THREE? 82
DAY 1   Prayer on Psalm 25: Confident Prayer for Forgiveness and Guidance ... 85
DAY 2   Prayer on Psalm 26: Prayer of Innocence 88
DAY 3   Prayer on Psalm 27: Trust in God 90
DAY 4   Prayer on Psalm 28: Petition and Thanksgiving 92
DAY 5   Psalm 29: The Lord of Majesty Acclaimed as King of the World . 94
DAY 6   Prayer on Psalm 30: Thanksgiving for Deliverance 97
DAY 7   Learning Discipleship from the Psalms 100

BOOK ONE – PSALMS 1-41: ABIDING TRUST IN DIRE STRAITS
Psalms 32, 33, 36, 38, 39, and 41
WHAT IS AT THE HEART OF BOOK ONE, WEEK FOUR? 106
DAY 1   Prayer on Psalm 32: Remission of Sin 108
DAY 2   Prayer on Psalm 33: Praise of God's Power and Providence 110
DAY 3   Prayer on Psalm 36: Human Wickedness and Divine Providence ... 113
DAY 4   Prayer on Psalm 38: Prayer of an Afflicted Sinner 116
DAY 5   Psalm 39: The Vanity of Life 119
DAY 6   Prayer on Psalm 41: Thanksgiving after Sickness 122
DAY 7   Learning Discipleship from the Psalms 125

BOOK TWO – PSALMS 42-72: CELEBRATION AND PRAISE
Psalms 42, 44, 45, 46, 47, and 48
WHAT IS AT THE HEART OF BOOK TWO, WEEK ONE? 132
DAY 1   Prayer on Psalm 42: Longing for God 135
DAY 2   Prayer on Psalm 44: God's Past Favor and Israel's Present Need 138
DAY 3   Prayer on Psalm 45: Song for a Royal Wedding 141
DAY 4   Prayer on Psalm 46: God, the Protector of Zion 145
DAY 5   Psalm 47: The Ruler of All Nations 147
DAY 6   Prayer on Psalm 49: Confidence in God Rather than in Riches 150
DAY 7   Learning Discipleship from the Psalms 153

BOOK TWO – PSALMS 42-72: CELEBRATION AND PRAISE
Psalms 50, 51, 52, 53, 54, and 56
WHAT IS AT THE HEART OF BOOK TWO, WEEK TWO? 160
DAY 1   Prayer on Psalm 50: The Acceptable Sacrifice 162
DAY 2   Prayer on Psalm 51: The Miserere: Prayer of Repentance 165
DAY 3   Prayer on Psalm 52: The Deceitful Tongue 168
DAY 4   Prayer on Psalm 53: A Lament over Widespread Corruption 172
DAY 5   Prayer on Psalm 54: Confident Prayer in Great Peril 174
DAY 6   Prayer on Psalm 56: Trust in God 176
DAY 7   Learning Discipleship from the Psalms 179

BOOK TWO – PSALMS 42-72: CELEBRATION AND PRAISE
Psalms 57, 61, 62, 63, 65, and 66
WHAT IS AT THE HEART OF BOOK TWO, WEEK THREE? 186
DAY 1   Prayer on Psalm 57: Confident Prayer for Deliverance 188
DAY 2   Prayer on Psalm 61: Prayer of the King in Time of Danger 191
DAY 3   Prayer on Psalm 62: Trust in God Alone 193
DAY 4   Prayer on Psalm 63: Ardent Longing for God 196
DAY 5   Psalm 65: Thanksgiving for God's Blessings 198
DAY 6   Prayer on Psalm 66: Praise of God, Israel's Deliverer 200
DAY 7   Learning Discipleship from the Psalms 203

BOOK TWO – PSALMS 42-72: CELEBRATION AND PRAISE
Psalms 67, 68, 69, 70, 71, and 72
WHAT IS AT THE HEART OF BOOK TWO, WEEK FOUR? 210
DAY 1   Prayer on Psalm 67: Harvest Thanks and Petition 212
DAY 2   Prayer on Psalm 68: The Exodus and Conquest, Pledge of Future Help 214
DAY 3   Prayer on Psalm 69: A Cry of Anguish in Great Distress 221
DAY 4   Prayer on Psalm 70: Prayer for Divine Help 226
DAY 5   Prayer on Psalm 71: Prayer in Time of Old Age 228
DAY 6   Prayer on Psalm 72: A Prayer for the King 231
DAY 7   Begin with Prayer to the Holy Spirit 235

BOOK THREE – PSALMS 73-89: PURIFICATION THROUGH TRIBULATION
Psalms 73, 74, 76, 78, 79, and 80
WHAT IS AT THE HEART OF BOOK THREE, WEEK ONE? 242
DAY 1   Prayer on Psalm 73: The Trial of the Just 246

DAY 2 Prayer on Psalm 74: Prayer at the Destruction of the Temple 249
DAY 3 Prayer on Psalm 76: God defends Zion 252
DAY 4 Prayer on Psalm 78: A New Beginning in Zion and David 255
DAY 5 Prayer on Psalm 79: A Prayer for Jerusalem 257
DAY 6 Prayer on Psalm 80: Prayer to restore God's Vineyard 260
DAY 7 Learning Discipleship from the Psalms 264

BOOK THREE – PSALMS 73-89: PURIFICATION THROUGH TRIBULATION
Psalms 81, 84, 85, 87, 88, and 89
WHAT IS AT THE HEART OF BOOK THREE, WEEK TWO? 271
DAY 1 Prayer on Psalm 81: An Admonition to Fidelity 273
DAY 2 Prayer on Psalm 84: Prayer of a Pilgrim to Jerusalem 276
DAY 3 Prayer on Psalm 85: Prayer for Divine Favor 278
DAY 4 Prayer on Psalm 87: Zion the True Birthplace 281
DAY 5 Prayer on Psalm 88: A Despairing Lament 284
DAY 6 Prayer on Psalm 89: A Lament over God's Promise of Old 287
DAY 7 Learning Discipleship from the Psalms 289

BOOK FOUR- PSALMS 90 TO 106 ISRAEL'S BANISHMENT
Psalms 90, 91, 92, 93, 95, and 98
WHAT IS AT THE HEART OF BOOK FOUR, WEEK ONE? 298
DAY 1 Prayer on Psalm 90: God's Eternity and Human Frailty 300
DAY 2 Prayer on Psalm 91: Security under God's Protection 303
DAY 3 Prayer on Psalm 92: A Hymn of Thanksgiving for God's Family 305
DAY 4 Prayer on Psalm 93: God is a Mighty King 308
DAY 5 Prayer on Psalm 95: A Call to Praise and Obedience 309
DAY 6 Prayer on Psalm 98: The Coming of God 312
DAY 7 Learning Discipleship from the Psalms 315

BOOK FOUR: PSALMS 90 TO 106: ISRAEL'S BANISHMENT
Psalms 99, 100, 101, 103, 104, and 106
WHAT IS AT THE HEART OF BOOK FOUR, WEEK TWO? 322
DAY 1 Prayer on Psalm 99: The Holy King 324
DAY 2 Prayer on Psalm 100: Processional Hymn: A Psalm of Thanksgiving 327
DAY 3 Prayer on Psalm 101: Norm of Life for Rulers 328
DAY 4 Prayer on Psalm 103: Praise of Divine Goodness 331
DAY 5 Prayer on Psalm 104: Praise of God the Creator 335
DAY 6 Prayer on Psalm 106: Israel's Confession of Sin 336
DAY 7 Learning Discipleship from the Psalms 339

BOOK FIVE: PSALMS 107 TO 150: LOOKING TOWARD THE MESSIAH
Psalms 107, 110, 112, 114, 118, and 119
WHAT IS AT THE HEART OF BOOK FIVE, WEEK ONE? 346
DAY 1 Prayer on Psalm 107: God the Savior of Those in Distress 349
DAY 2 Prayer on Psalm 110: God appoints the King both King and Priest 352
DAY 3 Prayer on Psalm 112: The Blessings of the Just 356
DAY 4 Prayer on Psalm 114: The Lord's Wonders at the Exodus 359
DAY 5 Prayer on Psalm 118: Hymn of Thanksgiving 361
DAY 6 Prayer on Psalm 119: A Prayer to God, the Lawgiver 364
DAY 7 Learning Discipleship from the Psalms 369

BOOK FIVE: PSALMS 107 TO 150: LOOKING TOWARD THE MESSIAH
Psalms 120, 122, 127,130, 132, and 136
WHAT IS AT THE HEART OF BOOK FIVE, WEEK TWO? 378
DAY 1   Prayer on Psalm 120: Prayer of a Returned Exile..........................381
DAY 2   Prayer on Psalm 122: A Pilgrim's Prayer for Jerusalem................384
DAY 3   Prayer on Psalm 127: The Need of God's Blessing......................386
DAY 4   Prayer on Psalm 130: Prayer for Pardon and Mercy.....................389
DAY 5   Prayer on Psalm 132: The Covenant between David and God......391
DAY 6   Prayer on Psalm 136: Hymn of Thanksgiving for God's Everlasting Mercy..395
DAY 7   Learning Discipleship from the Psalms 398

BOOK FIVE: PSALMS 107 TO 150: LOOKING TOWARD THE MESSIAH
Psalms 138, 139, 143, 145, 147, and 150
WHAT IS AT THE HEART OF BOOK FIVE, WEEK THREE?................405
DAY 1   Prayer on Psalm 138: Hymn of a Grateful Heart 409
DAY 2   Prayer on Psalm 139: The All-Knowing and Ever-Present God...411
DAY 3   Prayer on Psalm 143: A Prayer in Distress 414
DAY 4   Prayer on Psalm 145: The Greatness and Goodness of God.........417
DAY 5   Prayer on Psalm 147: God's Word Restores Jerusalem.................421
DAY 6   Prayer on Psalm 150: Final Doxology 424
DAY 7   Learning Discipleship from the Psalms 427

Other Titles by Dr. Michael Fonseca, D. Min.:

Lead Me Into the Deep, Lord: A 12-week introductory program that helps you to discover Jesus as your personal savior and Lord, while bringing you into a deeper personal relationship with the Blessed Trinity.

Who Do You Say I Am?: A 12-Week Introductory Program Focused On Prayer And Reflection On Jesus' Question To You About Your Own Discipleship.

Shepherd Me Into Your Kingdom, Lord: In this 14-week program, you will focus on the teachings of Jesus, with the clear understanding that you cannot have Jesus without His teachings, and the biblical understanding of covenant life as Jesus lived and preached it.

Instruct Me in Your Ways, Lord: In this 14 week program, we become familiar with the Pentateuch or the first five books of the Old Testament, so that our understanding of Jesus and the New Testament will be enriched.

Pour Out Your Spirit Upon Us, Lord continues the journey you began with Lead Me into the Deep, Lord. Over 14 weeks, you will be reflecting and praying on The Acts of the Apostles.

Anoint Us in Your Covenant, Abba-Emmanuel: Over 14- weeks you will come to appreciate the importance of the Church in God's Plan of Salvation.

Make Us Your Holy Family, Lord: Over 14-weeks you will come to appreciate the importance of the Church in God's Plan of Salvation. Through the sacraments, God's life and love is celebrated in the midst of His covenant family, because Jesus is Emmanuel.

Mold Me as Your Disciple, Lord: Pray with the Spiritual Exercises of St. Ignatius of Loyola under two formats: a 30-day retreat at our retreat center with daily spiritual direction, or a 6-month retreat, meeting once a week for spiritual direction.

For more information visit
www.godsembrace.org

Made in the USA
Middletown, DE
15 August 2024

58975932R00245